W. G. (Walter Gore) Marshall

Through America

Or, Nine Months in the United States

W. G. (Walter Gore) Marshall

Through America
Or, Nine Months in the United States

ISBN/EAN: 9783337216573

Printed in Europe, USA, Canada, Australia, Japan

Cover: Foto ©Andreas Hilbeck / pixelio.de

More available books at **www.hansebooks.com**

THROUGH AMERICA;

OR,

NINE MONTHS IN THE UNITED STATES.

BY

W. G. MARSHALL, M.A.

ILLUSTRATED FROM PHOTOGRAPHS.

NEW AND CHEAPER EDITION.

London:
SAMPSON LOW, MARSTON, SEARLE, & RIVINGTON,
CROWN BUILDINGS, 188, FLEET STREET.
1882.

PREFACE.

As the ground which is covered in the following pages has been often described before, I feel that some apology is due from me for submitting to the public a book of travel which will take the reader through scenes with the general aspects of which he is, probably, already sufficiently familiar. But America, with its vast natural resources, and with a population at once ingenious and enterprising, is, necessarily, in a continual state of development and change. For the traveller, therefore, who visits, even, the beaten tracks of such a country, there will always be plenty of fresh material to collect, and abundant opportunity for the enunciation of new views of old subjects; and I venture to hope that in the endeavour to present a truthful account of actual experiences of travel in the United States, I may, perhaps, have gathered a few facts which will prove to be something more than mere personal reminiscences, and be interesting and valuable to the public at large.

In the five chapters which are devoted to the Mormons and Salt Lake City, no attempt has been made to give a *complete* picture of Mormon life. What I have endeavoured to do has been to lay before the public some facts in connection with my visits to Utah in 1878 and 1879, which may be of service in exposing what can only be regarded as a monstrous social scandal—a scandal which is, unhappily, strengthened and kept alive mainly by emigration from our shores, and which threatens, unless an effectual check is placed upon it by the Government of the United States, to exercise a very malevolent influence, in the future, upon the great Territories of the far West. I have been induced to write these chapters because I believe there is a common impression amongst English people that Mormonism is dying out. That such, however, is not the case, but that, on the contrary, the power of the Mormon Church is on the increase rather than on the wane, will, I think, be admitted after a perusal of the contents of Chapter XI.

I should state that I have been particularly careful to substantiate the statements I have made respecting the Mormons—their social life, public utterances, etc. And here I will take the opportunity of expressing my thanks to those gentlemen in Utah who, since my return from America, have kindly afforded me information upon certain matters as to which I was somewhat in doubt, and who, besides, have guaranteed the accuracy of certain statements contained in this volume which could not have been placed before the public without having been first properly authenticated.

All the illustrations in this work have been specially drawn and engraved, and, with a few exceptions, have been executed from photographs, the work of engraving having been carried out by Mr. James D. Cooper, of the

Strand. My thanks are due to the following gentlemen for permission to use their views, portraits, etc. :—To Mr. H. Bencke, of New York, for his engraving of the bird's-eye view of New York and vicinity ; to Messrs. Scribner and Co., of New York, for permission to copy two illustrations from the *St. Nicholas Magazine*, namely those which I have placed on pages 29 and 265 ; to Messrs. E. and H. T. Anthony and Co., of New York, for their views illustrative of New York and the Hudson River ; to Mr. Frith, of Reigate (England), for two views which will be found on pages 21 and 50 ; to Mr. C. Davis, of Niagara, for his views of the Niagara Falls and Rapids ; to Mr. C. R. Savage, of Salt Lake City, for his views of Salt Lake City and neighbourhood, as well as for the portrait of Brigham Young, and the portraits of " prominent living Mormons ; " to Mr. G. S. Smith, of Salt Lake City, for his portrait of Joseph Smith, the founder of Mormonism ; to Mr. C. W. Carter, of Salt Lake City, for his view of the Mormon Tabernacle which appears on the title-page— also for the view of the interior of the Tabernacle, given on page 167 ; to Mr. Watkins, of San Francisco, for his views illustrative of the Pacific Railroad (with the exception of those given on pages 134, 144, 241, and 246, for which I have to thank Mr. Savage, of Salt Lake City), and of scenes in California, including all those of San Francisco, the Yosemite Valley, the Giant Trees, etc. ; to the editor of *Frank Leslie's Illustrated Newspaper*, for permission to copy from that journal the cuts which are given on pages 298, 300, 303, and 306 ; and lastly, to Mr. C. Weitfle, of Central City, Colorado, for the two views of Golden and Denver.

In conclusion, I must appeal to my critics for a little consideration, inasmuch as "Through America" is my first literary venture. To one friend—Mr. Francis George Heath—my especial thanks are due, for valuable assistance received; and I cannot send forth this volume without acknowledging the gratitude I owe to him for the several hints and suggestions he has given me, and which have proved of great service in the preparation of this work.

W. G. MARSHALL.

LONDON,
Christmas, 1880.

CONTENTS.

CHAPTER I.

THE EMPIRE CITY.

PAGE

The voyage out — Off Sandy Hook — The Bay of New York — The Empire City—A glance at its history—General plan of the city—The Brooklyn Bridge—Up-town and down-town—The Broadway—Telephoning—Rapid growth of the city—The old City Hall—The " new" County Court House—The Post Office—The private locker system—The *Tribune* building—An aerial newspaper office—Trinity Church—A mammoth store in the Broadway—Mr. Alexander T. Stewart—His Garden City enterprise—American philanthropy—Horace Greeley—The Fifth Avenue—St. Patrick's Cathedral—The water-front of New York—Washington and Fulton Markets—Ferry-boats on the North River—A ferry-boat scene—The elevated railway—Popularity of the enterprise—Dangers ahead—The oil-dripping nuisance—Horse-cars and stages—Family coaches and coupés—Badly-levelled roads—Dirty streets—The white-paint advertisement nuisance—Similarity in the streets—Oysters—An oyster saloon in Sixth Avenue—Oysters by the hundred thousand—The oyster export trade—Cautionary notices about swearing—New York public restaurants—Delmonico's—The Astor House—A typical American restaurant—Rapid bolting of food—A loving darkie—" Are you through?"—Lager-beer saloons—" Family" entrances—A lager-beer saloon on a Sunday—A drive in the Central Park—A ludicrous sight—The Greenwood Cemetery—The City of Brooklyn 1

CHAPTER II.

TO NIAGARA.

Decoration Day in New York—The city *en fête*—Processions and speech-making—Troops of darkies—Starting West—The Hudson River—A procession of canal barges—Bringing grain from Chicago—The Hudson River in the autumn—The scenery about West Point—The Catskill Mountains—American patriotism—The home of Washington Irving—A seminary for young ladies—The diet of American ladies at college—The ice harvest of the Hudson—Brick-making—The white-paint nuisance again—Albany—Its new State Capitol—Utica—A dinner off a cigar—Railway travelling in America—Parlour cars and sleeping cars—Examining tickets—Conductors' checks—Buying and selling—A parlour car pantry—The baggage check system—Its great convenience to the traveller—Niagara 48

CHAPTER III.

AT THE FALLS.

Impressions of Niagara—View from the Clifton House—The American Fall—The giant Canadian—Abuses of Niagara—"Indian variety" stores—Wholesale despoliation of natural scenery—The white-paint nuisance again—Towers for obtaining views—An irrepressible photographer—An awkward situation—The Niagara Falls Museum—The spider and the fly—Putting on oilskins—Walking under the Canadian Fall—Impressions conveyed—The Centre and American Falls—A sensational trip—The Whirlpool Rapids—A visit to an Indian reservation—A Sunday morning service—Setting out for Chicago—London in Canada—Crossing the Detroit River—Chicago 72

CHAPTER IV.

WONDERFUL CHICAGO.

A marvellous city—Its growth of fifty years—A commercial position unrivalled—The greatest livestock mart in the world—The great Union Stock Yards—A wonderful sight—Chicago's livestock trade since 1876—The famous packing-houses—Slaughtering on a mammoth scale—The pork packing process—Chicago as a grain market—Her receipts of 1879—The great grain elevators—The pine lumber trade—Manufacturing establishments of the Queen City—The total value of her trade of 1879—The development of the Great West—The United States seventy years ago—The United States to-day—Agricultural statistics—Exports to the United Kingdom—Railway development—Chicago's Grand Pacific Hotel—The five grand hotels of America—Hotel living—The American at table—Iced water and milk—Apple-pie—A national failing—A disagreeable subject—A disgusting sight—An active people—How Chicago was lifted several feet out of the mud—The new waterworks—A drive in the Lincoln Park—Rivalry of the large cities—Boston's opinion of Chicago—A Chicagoan's opinion of New York—What Boston thinks of Troy—What Troy says of the ladies of New York and Boston—Chicago's opinion of herself—An association of bald men . . 86

CHAPTER V.

WESTWARD TO OMAHA.

To Omaha—Rock Island—The Mississippi River—Crossing Iowa—Council Bluffs—The Missouri River—Its enormous length—Luxury in modern railway travelling—Railway-car meals—A popular newspaper's advertisement—The white-paint nuisance again—A country sadly disfigured—Omaha—A "booming" city

—Gold fever mottoes—A Prusso-Red-Indian—His remarkable history—A wigwam of curiosities—A visit to an Indian encampment—What we found there 104

CHAPTER VI.

OVER PRAIRIE AND MOUNTAIN.

The Pacific Railroad—A mighty enterprise—Rapid progress of the work—Difficulties encountered—The East and the West joined—Starting across the Great Plains—On the rolling prairie—Impressions—Animal life—The "dog" of the prairie—Stations on the line—Elkhorn—The Platte River—Giant rivers of the Plains—The "wickedest town in America"—A lesson in massacre—A breakfast on the prairie—A prairie-dog city—Sighting the Rocky Mountains—The Magic City of the Plains—Passing the eastern overland train—An exchange of greetings—Steeply ascending—The "Summit of the Rocky Mountains"—Nearly left behind—A glorious panorama—The Laramie Plains—The Gem City of the Mountains—A station museum—A double supper—A concert in our sleeping car—Green River—Rocks of the "Rockies"—The Desert House—Evanston—Chinese waiters—Begging Indians—Rapidly descending—Echo Cañon—The Pulpit Rock—An engine's performance— A conductor's diversion — The white-paint nuisance again—Mormon settlements—The Thousand Mile Tree—The Devil's Slide—Ogden Junction—We arrive in "Zion" 119

CHAPTER VII.

MORMONISM.

The origin of Mormonism—Joseph Smith's initiatory vision—His mother's account of the vision—His interviews with an "angel"—Discovery of the golden plates—The origin of the Book of Mormon—The founding of the Church—Principles of the Mormon faith—Originality of the Church—The Book of Mormon—A blasphemous publication—A few samples of its contents—Rubbish and bad grammar—Organization of the Mormon Church—The "First Presidency"—The two priesthoods—The various offices in the Church—"Stakes" and "wards" of Zion—How the people are looked after 147

CHAPTER VIII.

THE ROCKY MOUNTAIN ZION.

The Mormon metropolis—Its luxuriant appearance—A model city—Lovely situation—Clearness of the atmosphere—The Tabernacle—An extraordinary-looking building—Inside and outside—The

Tabernacle organ—Curious subjects of sermons—A horn-blower from the Old Country—An angry spouse objects—The Temple—The Endowment House—Mysteries of the "endowments"—The new Assembly Hall—Brigham's Block—The tithing system—The tithing fund of 1879—The Lion House—The Beehive House—Sign of Mormon stores—The President of the Mormon Church—Holy men of "Zion"—Hypocrisy extraordinary—Revolting picture of Mormon life—A matter for Congress to look into—"The Upper California"—A porter from Didcot Junction—Peculiarity of Mormon houses—Domestic economy—On the road to Fort Douglas—Magnificent prospect over the Salt Lake Valley—The doctrine of polygamy—Its introduction among the Saints—Smith's reason for introducing it—Many-wived Mormons—A bachelor's duty—The spiritual wife system—Sealing — Pleading for polygamy — Remarkable meeting of women in favour of the institution—Utah's delegate to the National Congress 164

CHAPTER IX.

THE ROCKY MOUNTAIN ZION (*continued*).

The Great Salt Lake—Its saline properties—Buoyancy of its water—Mormon Sunday excursions—The River Jordan—Islands in the Salt Lake—Fort Douglas—Ordered off to fight the "Reds"—Wagner and his brewery—Back to the Walker House—A debate on polygamy—Blasphemy extraordinary—An invitation to join a Mormon's family circle—A six-wived Mormon's home—Popular household mottoes—Extraordinary notice in a restaurant—A service in the Tabernacle—Impressions produced by it—A listless congregation—Celebrating the Holy Eucharist—Characteristic sermon—Mormon hymns—The Mormon "Du dah"—Other remarkable hymns 190

CHAPTER X.

PORTER ROCKWELL AND BRIGHAM YOUNG.

Orrin Porter Rockwell—Death of the noted Danite—Origin of the Danite band—"Destroying Angels"—Rockwell's history—A famous assassin—Brigham Young—Joseph Smith's prophecy concerning him—His first interview with Smith—Conversing in "unknown tongues"—Brigham's iron rule—The Church's blind belief in him—Blasphemous utterance of the apostle Heber C. Kimball—Brigham Young's opinion concerning the Deity—Blasphemy extraordinary—The domestic life of the deceased President—A Yankee Mahomet—"Briggy" Young—His wives—A double courtship—John A. Young—His matrimonial proclivities—A specimen "Saint"—Brigham Young's grave—The deceased President's directions respecting the conduct of his funeral 215

CHAPTER XI.

A SERIOUS ASPECT OF MORMONISM.

PAGE

Perversion to Mormonism—The missionary abroad—Missionary work in Great Britain—How British emigrants are imposed upon—European exodus to Utah in 1879—British Mormons in Salt Lake City—The exodus from Great Britain in 1880—Converts from Iceland—A superabundance of clergy—The "trustee-in-trust's" account for 1879—Receipts and disbursements—Christian missionary work in Utah—Result of ten years' labour—Utah's admission to Statedom—Trouble ahead—Defiant Mormons—Treasonable utterances—The Endowment House—A scandalous institution — The Mormon's treasonable oath—Penalty for revealing it—No public record of Mormon marriages—No marriage certificates—International intervention . . 225

CHAPTER XII.

WESTWARD TO SAN FRANCISCO.

Further westward—A run through the Salt Lake Valley to Ogden—A warm spring lake—Mormon husbandry—Successful agriculture—Ogden—An uproarious greeting—Choice of three dinners—Scarcity of berths—Leaving Ogden—Brigham City—"Gentile" Corinne—Promontory Point—The "great railroad wedding"—A word for the poor Indian—The way he is treated—Census of the Indians—A wash and a breakfast at Elko—The American Desert—" All aboard, all aboard!"—A rush for the cars—Battle Mountain—Winnemucca—The "noble red man"—An oasis in the desert—Peaceful reflections—On the rampage again—Junction for Virginia City—The wonderful mines of the Comstock lode—Ascending the Sierra—A twenty-eight mile snow-shed—7017 feet above the sea—Californian mining names—Quartz mining and placer mining—Rounding Cape Horn—A run down into California—Sacramento—I become an object of attraction—A word about English tourists—The State Capitol of California—At the Oakland wharf—On board the ferry—San Francisco 237

CHAPTER XIII.

THE GOLDEN CITY.

The Golden City—Its rapid growth—General plan of the city—Its principal thoroughfare—Monster hotels—Curious street conveyances—The balloon car—The dummy cable car—Bootblacking—Champion boot-blacks—A champion boot-black's challenge—A rush for wealth—Hoodlums—Their vocation and operations—The hoodlum alphabet—Instance of rough handling—A Californian fruit market—A treacherous climate—Wet days and cold days—The great hotel of America—Its form

xii   *Contents.*

                                                              PAGE
and general appearance—Its Grand Central Court—"Barbarism"
with a vengeance—Our suites of apartments—To the Cliff House
—Irrigation in California—The windmill system of irrigation—
Oakland—Marvellous rapidity of growth—The University of California—An anomaly in railway travelling—The white-paint
nuisance again   261

CHAPTER XIV.

A NIGHT IN CHINATOWN.

Preparing for Chinatown—Setting out for the quarters—A walk down
Montgomery-street—An anti-Chinese demonstration—A trouble-
some problem—"The Chinese must go"—We arrive in Chinatown
—Novel street scene—Popular Chinese restaurant—Choice
articles of food—A ceremonious little grocer—Buying shoes—
Very tight fit—A Chinaman's signature—Visit to a joss-house—
Popular Chinese gods—Examining a Chinaboy's head—The
"Royal China" Theatre—A Chinese opera—Music of the past—
An acrobatic performance—"All aboard" for an opium-den—
Double guard—A disreputable locality—Inside an opium-den—
Very close quarters—How to smoke opium—We turn opium-
smokers—The way John Chinaman smokes himself to sleep—
Saving expense—A man of delicate birth—"Old Johnny" counts
up   287

CHAPTER XV.

A TRIP TO THE GEYSERS.

Setting out for the Geysers—A sail up the bay—A barber afloat—
Bird's-eye view of the Golden City—The Bay of San Francisco—
From Donahue to Cloverdale—The road to the Geysers—
Smothered with dust—Dexterous driving—The Geysers Hotel—
Pretty crowded—A rush for beds—Setting out to survey the
premises—A foolish adventure—A remarkable spot—Devil's
conveniences — The "Steamboat Geyser"—The "Witches'
Caldron"—The Geysers mis-named—An early-morning walk
round the cañon—Returning to San Francisco—Splendid ride
over a mountain pass—Luxuriant growth in a Californian forest
—Bark-shedding trees—Fossville—The abode of a veteran
driver—A great man with a Californian reputation—Preparing
for dinner—A gushing matron—A father reproves his son—
Geological curiosity—A forest of stone—The "Pride of the
Forest"—How Charlie Evans became a rich man—Average
weight of the ladies of Calistoga—Back again in the Golden
City   308

CHAPTER XVI.

THE GIANT TREES OF CALAVERAS.

PAGE

Leaving San Francisco—Visions of the Yosemite Valley—How to reach it from the Golden City—Stockton—A night with a mosquito—A Chinese family—On the road to the Giant Trees—A refreshing draught of cold water—An army of small frogs—Dinner in the thick forest—A cosmopolitan mining district—Murphy's—Grand drive through the woods—The Calaveras Mammoth Grove—Passing between the "Two Sentinels"—Fashionable quarters in the wild forest—Wonders of Nature—The "Father" and "Mother of the Forest"—Other fine trees—The Three Graces—A "mother" fifty feet in circumference—A pair of Siamese Twins—The greatest wonder of all—A novel ballroom—"John Bright" and "Richard Cobden," etc.—Monster pitch-pine cones—Lovers again—Other mammoth groves . . 323

CHAPTER XVII.

THE ROAD TO THE YOSEMITE.

On the road to the Yosemite—A "Digger" Indian—No accounting for taste — Columbia gold-diggings — Slightly warm—Dinner at Sonora—The white-paint nuisance again—Chinese Camp—A Polish count—A Jehu madly drives—"Wouldn't you like a wash?"—Driver and passenger take a drive together—Crossing the Tuolumne River—Up Rattlesnake Hill—Under the tender care of Mrs. Priest—We rise at four o' the morning—A Jehu madly drives—A mixture of everything—The village of Big Oak Flat—Colfax Springs—Hodgson's—An ostler's ditty—The charm of a ride in a Californian forest—The Tuolumne Mammoth Grove—Driving through a Giant Tree—Siamese Twins—Almost a collision—Narrow escape—Magnificent view—Our driver's laundry in the Valley—Shakespeare in California—The Yosemite Valley 335

CHAPTER XVIII.

THE YOSEMITE VALLEY.

Our descent into the gorge—A wonderful sight—El Capitan Rock—The Spires and Cathedral Rock—The Bridal Veil Fall—Our first view of this fall—At the bottom of the gorge—The Ribbon Fall—The Three Brothers—Sentinel Rock—The sight *par excellence* of the Valley—The deepest plunge in the world—North and South Domes—At the door of Black's Hotel—Our driver a nuisance—The Yosemite Falls Hotel—Discovery of the Valley—Action of Congress—An hotel largely advertised—Seclusion of the Valley—The word "Yosemite"—How to pronounce it properly—A walk up the Valley—A camp of tourists—The Mirror

Lake—Curious rock formations—Reflections in the lake—Breakfast at the hotel—An agile waiter—An Englishman and a cricketer 346

CHAPTER XIX.

THE YOSEMITE VALLEY (*continued*).

To Glacier Point—The Yosemite Fall—A glorious sight—Mounting the gorge—Union Point—At Glacier Point—The view therefrom—A dangerous leap—A dizzy depth—The great South Dome—Returning to the hotel—A trip up the Merced cañon—The glories of this trip—The Vernal Fall—Its great beauty—View from above the fall—The Cap of Liberty—The Nevada Fall—Peculiar features of this fall—An eagle's nest—Dropping stones into it—A timely rebuke—The "Grand Register"—A few selections from the volume—High charges in the Yosemite—Herr Sinning's curiosity-shop—A house built round the stump of a tree—An ascent of the South Dome—The formation of the Yosemite 366

CHAPTER XX.

AWAY EAST.

Leaving the Yosemite Valley—Eastward to New York—To Chinese Camp—A Jehu madly drives—Copperopolis—To Milton—A bone-shaking ride to catch a train—Back again to Stockton—Left behind—Return to Salt Lake City—791 miles to Ogden—The Fourth of July—Celebrating "the Fourth" at Ogden—On the road to "Zion"—An accident by the way—A serious scrape—Again in the Mormon metropolis—A concert in the Tabernacle—Programme of the concert—Amusements at Lake Point—Brigham Young's Fun Hall—A theatrical performance—Leaving Salt Lake City—Over the Rocky Mountains—A peep into Colorado—A run down to Denver—Cattle in the way—A sample of Coloradan railway-travelling—The chief attractions of Colorado—A glorious country—Denver—Its sudden rise—Its free schools—The American free school system—Denver's situation—Clearness of the atmosphere—Prosperity of the State—Its business record of 1879—The mining, live-stock, and agricultural industries—Invigorating climate—Camping out under canvas—Mining cities of Colorado—The trips to Georgetown and Leadville—A railway 10,139 feet above the sea—The "Great Carbonate Camp"—A mining wonder—The mines of Leadville—Their yield in 1879—A mine 14,200 feet above the sea—Leaving Denver—Eastward to the Missourian capital—The fatal heat of St. Louis—A death-stricken city—A hasty retreat—Back again in New York—Conclusion 389

LIST OF ILLUSTRATIONS.

FULL-PAGE ENGRAVINGS.

The Yosemite Fall, Yosemite Valley, California	*Frontispiece*
New York and Vicinity	To face page 5
The Hudson River	,, 55
Niagara Falls	,, 79
Pulpit Rock, Pacific Railroad	,, 143
Portraits of prominent living Mormons, 1880	,, 160
Salt Lake City, from the Utah Central Railroad	,, 165
Mormon Tabernacle, Salt Lake City	,, 167
Portrait of Brigham Young	,, 219
San Francisco	,, 261
Calaveras Mammoth Grove—"Two Sentinels"	,, 327
,, ,, ,, "Father of the Forest"	,, 328
Yosemite Valley—Three Brothers	,, 358
,, ,, Vernal Fall	,, 373
,, ,, Nevada Fall	,, 375
,, ,, The South Dome	,, 385

SMALLER ENGRAVINGS.

Mormon Tabernacle, Salt Lake City	*Title-page*
New York—The Broadway—View from Houston-street	8
,, "New York Herald" building	12
,, "New York Tribune" building	13
,, A. T. Stewart's Retail Store, Broadway	15
,, North River Water-front	21
,, Elevated Railway	25
,, Elevated Railway—View in Chatham-street	27
,, Under the Elevated Railway	29
,, Trinity Church, Broadway	44
View on the Hudson River—West Point Landing	48
Union-square, New York	50
Hudson River—Day-boat	52
,, Day-boat—Another view	53
,, The Stormking Rock	57
Engine and cars	61
Niagara Falls—View from Victoria Point, Canada side	73
,, American and Centre Falls	74
,, Upper Rapids	80
,, Whirlpool Rapids	83
Chicago—Grand Pacific Hotel	96
,, Tremont House	97

List of Illustrations.

	PAGE
Railway-car laid out for dining	106
A railway-car meal	107
Pacific Railroad—Sherman	134
,, Echo Cañon	140
,, Witches Rocks	141
,, Witches Bottles	142
,, Devil's Slide	144
Portrait of Joseph Smith, the founder of Mormonism	148
Salt Lake City—Interior of the Tabernacle	167
,, Interior of the Tabernacle, showing Organ	168
,, Design of the new Temple	171
,, The Beehive House	176
,, View in Main-street	177
The Black Rock, Great Salt Lake	191
Mormon baptism of Indians	193
"Utah's Best Crop"	214
Mormon Tabernacle, Salt Lake City	236
Pacific Railroad—Ogden	241
,, Elko	246
,, American River Cañon—View from Cape Horn	255
Leaving the Oakland wharf	259
San Francisco—Balloon car	265
,, View in Clay-street, showing the dummy cable car	266
,, Palace Hotel—Exterior view	276
,, Palace Hotel—Grand Central Court	278
,, An all-night supper at the Chinese Theatre	298
,, Performance at the Chinese Theatre	300
,, Interior of an opium-den	303
,, Chinese merchant balancing his accounts	306
Bay of San Francisco—View from Telegraph-hill	310
The Californian Geysers—View of the cañon	314
Calaveras Mammoth Grove—"Mother of the Forest"	329
,, ,, "John Torrey" Group	332
,, ,, "Pioneer's Cabin"	334
Road-tunnel through a Giant Tree	342
Yosemite Valley—Bird's-eye view	346
,, ,, El Capitan	347
,, ,, Cathedral Rocks	348
,, ,, Bridal Veil Fall	350
,, ,, Yosemite Fall	353
,, ,, Mirror Lake	363
,, ,, Yosemite Fall—Another view	368
,, ,, View from Glacier Point	371
,, ,, South Dome	381
Pulpit Rock, Pacific Railroad	393
Golden, Colorado	401
Larimer-street, Denver	405

THROUGH AMERICA;

OR,

NINE MONTHS IN THE UNITED STATES.

CHAPTER I.

THE EMPIRE CITY.

The voyage out—Off Sandy Hook—The Bay of New York—The Empire City—A glance at its history—General plan of the city—The Brooklyn Bridge—Up-town and down-town—The Broadway—Telephoning—Rapid growth of the city—The old City Hall—The "new" County Court House—The Post Office—The private locker system—The *Tribune* building—An aerial newspaper office—Trinity Church—A mammoth store in the Broadway—Mr. Alexander T. Stewart—His Garden City enterprise—American philanthropy—Horace Greeley—The Fifth Avenue—St. Patrick's Cathedral—The water-front of New York—Washington and Fulton Markets—Ferry-boats on the North River—A ferry-boat scene—The elevated railway—Popularity of the enterprise—Dangers ahead—The oil-dripping nuisance—Horse-cars and stages—Family coaches and coupés—Badly-levelled roads—Dirty streets—The white-paint advertisement nuisance—Similarity in the streets—Oysters—An oyster saloon in Sixth Avenue—Oysters by the hundred thousand—The oyster export trade—Cautionary notices about swearing—New York public restaurants—Delmonico's—The Astor House—A typical American restaurant—Rapid bolting of food—A loving darkie—"Are you through?"—Lager-beer saloons—"Family" entrances—A lager-beer saloon on a Sunday—A drive in the Central Park—A ludicrous sight—The Greenwood Cemetery—The City of Brooklyn.

IN May, 1878, I crossed from Liverpool to New York in the Cunard steamship "Scythia," and spent three months in the United States. In June, 1879, I again crossed the Atlantic to New York, and remained six months in the States, returning to England early in December. It is with the record of a

B

few experiences of ordinary travel acquired during these two tours that I shall endeavour, in the following pages, to interest the reader.

It will be superfluous for me to enter into a description of the nine days' journey across the Atlantic. Let me merely observe that should the intending voyager to New York select one of the splendid steamers of the Cunard Company, such as the "Scythia," "Bothnia," or "Gallia," he will find not only every imaginable comfort provided for him on board these floating hotels—chess, draughts, backgammon, cards, smoking-rooms and bath-rooms, an extensive library always available, everything in short to render his comfort complete—provided the weather continues calm; but on board the boats I have mentioned he will meet with a class of passengers among whom, probably, will be found several Americans returning from foreign travel. Thus it was on board the "Scythia" when I crossed with my college friend C——, in May, 1878. Our fellow-passengers we found to be mostly people from the United States—genial, kind-hearted, hospitable Americans, who, finding we were about to visit their country for the first time, courteously extended to us invitations to their homes stationed in various parts of the States, which we innocently accepted at the time, thinking we should have no difficulty in fulfilling them; but that was before we came to realize by actual experience the immense distances that have to be travelled in America in passing from State to State. On the tenth morning, therefore, after leaving Liverpool we sighted Sandy Hook, eighteen miles from New York, and a few hours after we were steaming up the glorious New York Bay, admiring the fine expanse of this beautiful sheet of water. But first, after passing Sandy Hook, we lay in quarantine awhile, about twenty minutes or so, while an officer of health came on board and received a certificate from our ship's doctor that we had brought no infectious diseases with us, while in the meantime we discharged the mailbags into a little tiny wooden, white-painted steamer which came alongside, gaily decked with the Stars and Stripes—great ponderous concerns these mailbags, numbering in all 536. Stopping again a little further on to receive on board two officers of the Customs, who promptly commenced taking (in the saloon) an inventory of our luggage, requesting us to give them our several names, addresses, occupations, the number of articles of baggage we possessed, both large and small; plying each of us with questions as to whether we had anything to "declare," and then making us swear that we were telling them the truth—at eight o'clock we found ourselves approaching our wharf on Jersey City side, separated from New York by the broad North, or Hudson River.[1] Of course we found crowds of people assembled on the landing awaiting our arrival. They were the friends of the voyagers, and as soon as we were alongside a rush was made on board, and the hugging and kissing that went on was truly painful. After being delayed more than an hour by the gentlemen of the Customs, who still were particular to overhaul everything we had, examining our luggage in very earnest, which evidently showed they did not believe what we had previously sworn,— every little and every big thing of mine they opened and searched minutely, making quite a business of it,—we got into an immense antique-looking, springy coach that was in readiness to take us to any part of New York we liked, and were driven on board a ferry-boat, and in ten minutes transported with other coaches and waggons across the river to the metropolis, and taken direct to our hotel, the Brevoort House, which lies in the beautiful Fifth-avenue.

Before proceeding to a notice of some of the prominent features of the chief city of the Western Hemisphere, it may not be uninteresting to take a glance at its history. The site of New York may be said to have been discovered by Europeans in the year 1524, by one Verrazzani, a Florentine. The locality, however, was not further visited by Europeans till 1609, when Henry Hudson, an English mariner in the employ of the Dutch East India Company, having been sent out to search for a north-east passage to India, anchored the "Half Moon" off the southern extremity of Long Island, and then, proceeding twelve miles up the bay, discovered anew, so to speak, the island upon which New York came afterwards to be built. Hudson landed on Sep-

[1] Passengers arriving by the steamers of the Cunard Company are now landed on the New York side of the North River.

tember 4th, accompanied by a mixed crew of English and Hollandese, and found a tribe of "Indians" the sole occupants of what has been described as "an uninviting tract of rocky woodland, swamp, and sandy plain." He seems to have had "a good time" generally with the aborigines, and to have made merry on the occasion of their meeting, for we are told by Heckewelder, the Indian historian, that "mutual salutations and signs of friendship were restored, and after a while, strong drink was offered, which made all gay and happy." A somewhat curious commentary on this event is afforded by the fact that the island, thenceforth, received the name of *Manhattan*, which in the vernacular of one of the Indian tribes signifies, "the place where they all got drunk!" Subsequently colonized by the Dutch,—for in 1625 Manhattan Island was bought from the Indians by Peter Minuits, the first Dutch governor, for the sum of 4*l.* 16*s.*,—the settlement was called New Amsterdam, and in the year 1614 it contained just four dwelling-houses and a little fort. Half a century later, with a population of about 5000, New Amsterdam was surrendered to Great Britain, and its name changed to New York, in honour of the brother of Charles II.—James, Duke of York and Albany, to whom the King handed over the possession of the territory. In 1673 the Dutch again became the possessors of the settlement, and changed its name to New Orange; but in the following year it was restored to the British, re-named New York, and it remained in our hands till we finally evacuated it on November 25th, 1783, at the conclusion of the American War of Independence. The New Yorkers still annually celebrate the occasion of our evacuation with a parade of troops, and other public demonstrations. In 1870, New York had a population of 942,292; in 1875, 1,046,037; now (1880) its population is about 1,200,000. Of this a third, roughly speaking, is German, a third Irish, and a third native. There are more Irish in New York than in any other city in the world, except Dublin.

New York—called the Empire City, for the same reason that New York State is called the Empire or Excelsior State—is spread over an island thirteen and a half miles long, and varying from a few hundred yards to two miles in breadth. Within the city limits are included five miles of the mainland to the

north of the island, though this portion of upper New York has more the appearance of a suburb of the city than part of the busy metropolis, consisting, for the most part, of private residences which have sprung up within the last few years. At its northern end Manhattan Island is separated from the mainland by the Harlem River and Spyten Duyvel Creek,[2] west and east it is bounded by the broader North (Hudson) and East Rivers respectively, the latter an inlet of the sea unit'ng with the former at the southern end of the island, where New York city looks out upon its bay. As Liverpool is separated from Birkenhead by the Mersey, so is New York by the East River from her sister city Brooklyn, both cities facing each other, both built down to the water's edge. Though New York and Brooklyn are now two distinct municipalities, it is not beyond the range of probability that they will, some day or other, be brought under one city government. There was a time when New Yorkers were anxious for the amalgamation, before Brooklyn came to be the great city that it is ; but now, *contra*, the New Yorkers object, while the Brooklynites see more than ever what an advantage it would be to become part and parcel of the prosperous Empire City ; and so the matter stands. An immense bridge which is being thrown over the East River to connect the two cities, although it was begun eleven years ago, is not yet finished. Great efforts are being made to complete the work by the end of May, 1881. This bridge was to have taken only five years to construct, and was estimated to cost 1,600,000*l.* ; but up to February 1, 1880, it had absorbed 2,257,277*l.*, and still a further appropriation of 450,000*l.* has had to be made. Brooklyn contributes a third of the expenses incurred, and New York the rest. There are several buildings now in course of erection in the United States whose progress is just

[2] So named—as Diedrich Knickerbocker (Washington Irving) tells us in his *History of New York*—from a Dutchman, one Anthony van Corlear, trumpeter to Governor Stuyvesant, the "Captain-General and Commander-in-Chief of Amsterdam in New Netherlands, now (1682) called New York" (*vide* the inscription over Governor Stuyvesant's tomb in St. Mark's Church, New York), who swore he would swim over the creek during a gale of wind "in spite of the devil" (*en spyt der duyvel*). He ventured, but lost his life in the attempt. Anthony's Nose, a rocky headland on the Hudson River, is called after the same individual.

as dilatory as that of the Brooklyn Bridge, which were to have been finished years ago and whose cost has already nearly doubled the sums originally intended to be spent upon them, and in each case it is doubtful whether the works will be speedily accomplished. We shall have occasion to notice some of them later on.

The first thing that strikes the British stranger in New York—after indeed he has become painfully aware, in the terrible ride that he took from the ferry to his hotel, that the roads are not quite so evenly levelled here as they are in the Old Country—is the extremely neat way in which the streets are arranged. This will become all the more evident if he acquaints himself with a map of the place, for there he will see at a glance that the greater portion of the city is laid out as regularly as a chess-board, with "avenues" running in parallel straight lines from north to south, lengthwise with the island, and "streets" in like manner from east to west, all numerically indicated,—on the lamp-posts at the corners,—and the Broadway running obliquely from one end of the island to the other, intersecting both avenues and streets. Thus, supposing you are at Eighth-street, and you wish to get to Eightieth-street, all you have to do is to follow along one of the avenues and count the numbers of the seventy-two streets you cross till you come to your destination, walking or taking the street-car in a straight line all the way. The lower, or "down-town," that is the old portion of the city, is laid out somewhat irregularly, whereas the upper or "up-town" portion lies in well-defined, uniform blocks, every block having a frontage of 200 feet, sometimes a little more, and thus is the city laid out for some miles in this unvaried, wearisome fashion. Distances in American cities are generally judged by "blocks." If you ask your way to this or that "store" you will be told to go up or down such-and-such street, and then along so many "blocks" till you come to it. Up-town commences indefinitely somewhere in the neighbourhood of Washington-square, which is two miles above the Battery, a small park at the southern extremity of the island. Above Washington-square, where First, Second, and Third streets commence (for here the city begins to be regularly laid out), the cross streets are numbered east and west, according to the side of Fifth-avenue on which they happen to lie. Thus, West Fifty-sixth street is on the North River side of this avenue, while East Fifty-sixth street lies on the opposite side of the road.

The Broadway is, as everyone knows, the principal street of New York, and a grand one it is. It runs nearly the whole length of the island,—above Fifty-ninth street it is called the Boulevard,—first in a straight line north for two miles to Union-square (or to be more correct, to within four blocks of it), dividing the city into two equal divisions, and then it inclines obliquely westward, cutting across all the streets and avenues up-town, which, as we have just seen, are laid out in this part of the city after the manner of a chess-board. Starting from the Bowling Green,[3] the Broadway, for a couple of miles, is the daily scene of such life and busy turmoil, the roadway so packed with waggons of merchandise and public conveyances, and the pavements likewise thronged with a hurrying, bustling concourse of people, that this street has come to be called (in America) the "busiest street in the world;" but the fact of the matter is that the Broadway is not broad,—at least the part of it below Union-square which is always so crowded,—so that it is not to be wondered that it presents such a busy appearance. In the old or lower part of the city, the streets branching off right and left from the Broadway are the great commercial centres of the metropolis. Glance down any one of these, such as Exchange Place, Liberty, Cedar, or Wall streets,—the latter is the Lombard-street of New York,—and, narrow as each one is, you see what tells you at once of a vast amount of commercial activity, for above, against the sky, you look upon a perfect maze of telephone and telegraph wires crossing and recrossing each other from the tops of the houses. The sky, indeed, is blackened with them, and it is as if you were looking through the meshes of a net.

---

[3] A small park adjoining the Battery, at the southern end of the island, where stood in 1614 the old Dutch settlement, Nieu Amsterdam. An equestrian leaden statue of George III. was set up here in 1770, but the New Yorkers pulled it down on the day that the Declaration of Independence was read in their city, and had it melted into bullets.

And this is the case in every street in this part of New York. The sky is really obscured by the countless threads of wire, and the housetops are made free use of to conduct

THE BROADWAY.
View from Houston-street.

them to their destination. Altogether there are about 5000 miles of telegraph and telephone wires in the Empire City. The telegraph wires are conducted along the streets by means of some 9000 or 10,000 poles. Out of a window of the Western Union Telegraph Company's building in the lower part of the Broadway, from a single shoot, one hundred and thirty-six wires issue forth, and, joined immediately by others, are stretched overhead in the direction of the Battery till they branch off from the street to all parts of the country, one hundred and forty on one side the street and sixty-two on the other.

There were, in February last, 20,000 people in direct telephonic communication in New York, through the exchange offices of the Bell Telephone Company, the Law Telephone Company (licensed by the Bell Company for legal purposes only), and the Gold and Stock Western Union Telephone Company. It would take exactly three minutes for the Bell Company at 923, Broadway (corner of Twenty-first street), to connect, say, John Smith, of 27, Bowling Green, two and a half miles distant, with Richard Doe, of Paterson, New Jersey, seventeen miles distant from the same office; and a like time would be required to connect any two persons in the metropolis or its suburbs similarly provided with telephones. Each subscriber to any one of these companies—the subscription is ten dollars per month—has, of course, a list of all other subscribers to the same company, so that he may know whom he can talk to at any time. At present the furthest places communicated with by telephone in New York are distant thirty miles; but the Bell Company are engaged in setting up lines to Philadelphia, ninety miles distant.[4]

New York has extended itself in a marvellous degree during the last ten or fifteen years. Nineteen thousand eight hundred

[4] Perhaps the longest distance over which the telephone has been successfully operated as yet was accomplished on January 25th of the present year, when a conversation was carried on between the Union Pacific Transfer at Council Bluff, Iowa, and the American Union office at St. Louis, Missouri, a distance of 410 miles. A strong wind, it is said, was blowing at the time, and yet only two or three interruptions of a few seconds occurred. "An ordinary conversation," says the *New York Herald*, "was carried on with the utmost ease, the most noticeable fact being that while the enunciation of the words was perfectly clear, they came invariably with the regular vibration of a musical note. The conversation was varied with singing, of which apparently not a note was lost. A St. Louis singer sent over the wire in clear baritone voice 'Sweet By-and-by,' which Mr. France repeated back. The St. Louis singer then sent 'I'm a Pilgrim and a Stranger,' and this also Mr. France repeated back. The wires over the greater part of the distance were quiet and not in use, but at the St. Louis end there was a heavy induction."

On April 8th, 1880, the New York telephone companies were consolidated into one company, which now has the entire control of all the telephone business of the metropolis, and for thirty-three miles around. The capital of the stock amounts to 300,000*l*.

and eleven buildings were erected from January 1, 1868, to December 21, 1878, at a cost of 56,865,699*l*.,—to which must be added 2605 new buildings erected during the year 1879, at an aggregate cost of 4,513,462*l*.,—and still the city is increasing, and seems likely to increase for many a year to come. A good part of what is now up-town was waste land not half a score years agone. Perhaps as good an illustration as any of the unexpected growth of New York is afforded by the building of the old City Hall, which, facing a park or square of the same name, lies in the busiest quarter of the lower portion of the city. This was begun in 1803, and finished in 1812. It has a frontage of white marble, but the rear is, alas! merely plain brown-stone. It was never imagined that the Empire City would become so big that its citizens would be able to look upon the back of this building without taking a walk into the country. But now there are a good twelve miles of the city at the back of the City Hall. Near this building is the "new" County Court House, which has taken nineteen years in building, having been commenced in 1861, and completed last June. According to the original estimates the building was to have cost only 800,000 dollars; but, owing to the disgraceful peculations of the Tammany ring, headed by the famous "Boss" Tweed, millions of dollars (some say fourteen) have been squandered over the work.

There are some splendid buildings in New York, and some of the finest are in the Broadway. The new Post Office, for instance, down-town, is ornate and imposing, built in the Doric-Renaissance style, and—with the exception of the new Roman Catholic Cathedral now rising in Fifth-avenue—is the finest building on the island. But it has been erected to serve two purposes, for whereas the basement and first floor are devoted to postal business alone, the second and remaining floors are handed over to the United States Law Courts. On the first floor are the money-order and registering offices, and a few private rooms; on the basement the letters are received and sorted, and the mails made up. In the lobby are separate drop-boxes or lockers for the reception of letters and newspapers for the City of New York, for each one of the States and Territories, for Canada and Newfoundland, Mexico, South America, Europe, Asia, Africa, and Oceanica; and besides windows for the sale of postage stamps and stamped envelopes and for the reception of packets too bulky for the drop-boxes, there are 6480 private lockers for the convenience of those citizens of New York who prefer having their letters retained for them in this way, instead of their being brought round by the postman after the arrival of each successive mail, to their private residences or places of business. The owner of such a locker has a private key of his own, so that he can come and open his box whenever he feels disposed, and see if any letters or newspapers have come for him. If a parcel has arrived too large to be dropped in, he will, upon opening his locker, find a notice inside to that effect, and that he can have the packet on his inquiring for it within. This is a system by no means confined to New York: it is in vogue all over the United States. In every large post-office there are similar private lockers. Philadelphia, for instance, has 2840; Taunton in Massachusetts, with a population of 20,000, has 619. Sometimes such a number of communications come at a time for one person alone, or for a particular firm or business house, that a locker is found insufficient to hold the numerous packages that arrive. To meet this emergency a good-sized trunk is provided, and then letters, etc., can be dropped into it *ad lib.* There are eleven "elevators" (lifts) in the building, namely, eight for the transmission of the mails from the basement (and cellar) to the first floor; two for the use of the public ascending to the court rooms aloft; and one for the exclusive use of the clerks employed on the premises. Each elevator cost 6000*l.*, and is worked by hydraulic power.

In the vicinity of the Post Office is the Printing House Square, where—unlike our London square of that name, which accommodates only its one great newspaper establishment—are congregated the offices of the principal journals of the Empire City, such as the *Herald, Times, Tribune, World, Evening Telegram, Evening Express,* etc. The offices of the *Herald* and *Tribune* are located in imposing buildings, the former in an elaborate marble edifice, the latter in—well, this building of the *New York Tribune* is about the most remarkable I ever beheld, for a newspaper office. It towers up above the surrounding buildings like a sort of brick-and-mortar giraffe. Composed of bright-red Philadelphia pressed-brick and granite, it presents a frontage on Printing House Square of ninety feet, rearing its nine stories to a height of 200 feet, at the top of which comes a clock tower of sixty-five feet in height, which is a conspicuous landmark in the lower part of the island. The editorial rooms are

THE "NEW YORK HERALD" BUILDING.

located eight stories up, 170 feet above the street pavement, and the composing-room is still further aloft, occupying the whole of the ninth floor. Other buildings in this neighbourhood may be mentioned, such as the New York Life Insurance Company's building in the Broadway—a splendid edifice of white marble, modelled after the Temple of Erectheus at Athens; the Sub-Treasury in Wall-street,[5]

[5] This street, the great centre of United States finance, has other interesting associations besides those relating to banking and stock-broking. It was here that the installation of George Washington as first President of the United States took place, from the balcony of the old Federal Hall building, which stood on the site now occupied by that

modelled after the Parthenon at Athens; also a beautiful church in the Broadway, facing Wall-street—Trinity Church

THE "NEW YORK TRIBUNE" BUILDING.

(Episcopal), built entirely of brown-stone, with a spire reaching 284 feet in height. In 1705 this church was liberally

of the Sub-Treasury. Though rather late in the day—it is now ninety-one years since this inauguration took place—the New York Chamber of Commerce called a special meeting on February 2nd last, to consider

endowed by Queen Anne, who also presented it with a communion service, which has been preserved. The tower contains a fine set of chimes, and the services are rendered by an excellent choir, though I must say it is one which has been considerably overrated, probably because this is the only church in America where there is any *good* choral singing to be heard. Americans have told me that we have no choir in England to equal it. But it would be easy to point out several that are superior to it in many respects.

It must be admitted that one of the great sights of the Empire City is the mammoth establishment of the late Mr. A. T. Stewart, the draper, in the Broadway, up-town. Built wholly of iron (painted white), it occupies an entire block, covering an area of two and a half acres. The height of this building is 120 feet—from its foundations; but though it stands 100 feet above the street-level, a considerable part of the business is conducted at a depth of twenty feet below, for here is the carpet department and other departments connected with the establishment. The interior is certainly one of the " things to see " in New York. You look upon fifteen acres of flooring almost directly you step inside—so you are told. Tier upon tier, gallery upon gallery does the vast pile soar above you, and if you are fortunate enough to drop in when business is " booming," you will see a sight such as perhaps is not to be found in any other shop of the kind in the world. Then from 2900 to 3000 hands are employed on the premises, and the vast open hall is packed from floor to roof with customers and non-customers, a great many people dropping in simply to stare and look about, without intending to make purchases. There are five elevators for customers, and two for freight. This is the retail establishment of Mr. Stewart's " dry goods' " business; but the wholesale department occupies another block in the shape of a handsome marble structure down-town (also in the Broadway), which, five stories in height, is generally known by the name of " Stewart's marble ' palace.' " This successful merchant established branches of his business in

what steps should be taken for suitably commemorating the auspicious event, when it was decided to erect, subject to the permission of Congress, " an heroic bronze statue " as soon as possible on one of the buttresses of the steps in front of the Sub-Treasury building.

Boston, Philadelphia, and Chicago, as well as in Glasgow, Belfast, Manchester, Nottingham, Bradford, Paris, Berlin, Lyons, and at Chemnitz in Saxony. At the corner of Thirty-fourth street and Fifth-avenue he erected a gorgeous white-marble mansion for himself and wife, which is one of the most superb private residences in the United States. Its equal is only to be found in the palaces of California's millionaires, such as are to be seen in San Francisco and its neighbourhood.

The Americans have been called a benevolent and a gene-

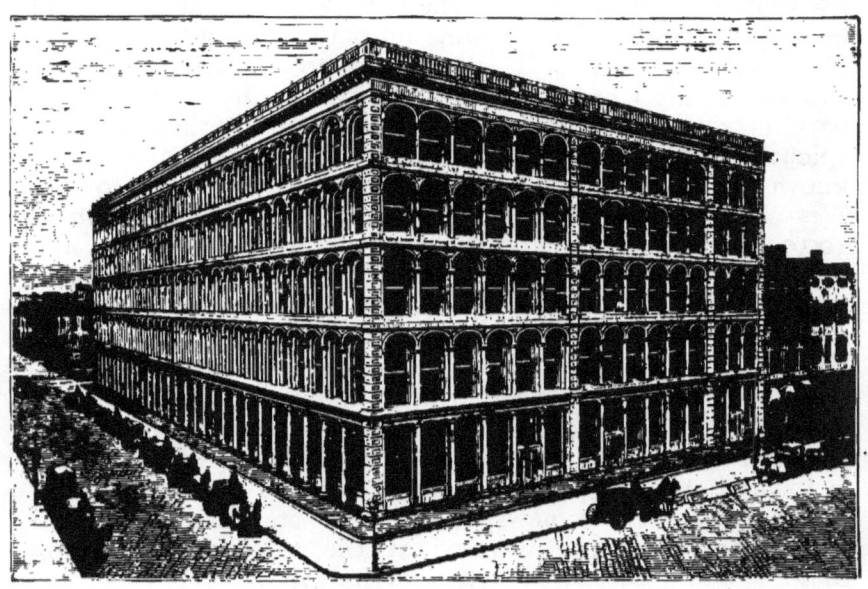

A. T. STEWART'S RETAIL STORE, BROADWAY.

rous people, and no nation in the world has earned a better right to be so esteemed. But surely a grander instance of liberality and large-heartedness on the part of one man cannot be named, than that which characterized the closing years of Mr. Stewart's successful life. What does the reader think of a man founding and setting up a city, furnishing it with a splendid cathedral, with schools, etc.,—a man whose aim and object was to establish a self-supporting community of men of small means, every man being his own landlord, owning the roof he lived under and the soil he tilled? Death overtook him before he could carry out the whole of this enterprise, but he has left behind him those who will continue the good work, which will in time become one of the grandest monuments of American charity and benevolence. The late Mormon president, Brigham Young, did, it is true, the same thing in the case of Salt Lake, planting and building up a city in a barren desert hundreds of miles away from any human habitation, except the wigwam of the wild red man; but then, as we shall see further on, Brigham took care that he should be amply recouped for his pains out of the tithing which every Mormon was (and still is) obliged to contribute for the support of his Church, so that his can hardly be taken as a parallel case. But instances could be multiplied of conspicuous acts of American philanthropy, and one of the best known is that of Horace Greeley, the worthy founder of the *New York Tribune*, who, in the year 1870, took possession of 100,000 acres of good land far away in distant Colorado, and established a colony there by removing 200 poverty-stricken people from Massachusetts, who set to work and reclaimed the land and caused it to bring forth abundantly, and now Greeley (as the settlement was appropriately named) has become a thriving little place, with a population of over 2000, the central depôt of a fine wheat-growing territory, having its churches and schools,—the best free school in the State is located at Greeley,—two banks, and two grist-mills, supporting two weekly newspapers, with its streets planted with shade-trees and watered at the sides by irrigating ditches; and, to crown all,—teetotalers will welcome this piece of intelligence,—the town charter of Greeley enjoins that no house or land can be sold for the purpose of retailing intoxicating drinks. (Vineland, in New Jersey, is, I believe, another such a temperance town.)

But to return to the famous enterprise of the great dry goods' merchant of the Empire City, now deceased. If we turn to the *New York Herald* of January 26 (1880), we shall find an interesting account of what has already been done at Garden City—which is the name given to the enterprise—and what is intended to be done; and this I proceed to quote *in extenso,* as follows:

"You step from the Long Island Railroad cars, about sixteen miles from New York, near the centre of a vast plain, on which are about a hundred houses, and right ahead, as you walk from the handsome railroad station, is a large hotel. At a glance it is seen to be a public-house of the best class. It is supported as a part of the Garden City enterprise, Mr. Stewart having said, 'If I build a city to be rented by men of moderate means, who prefer to hire houses rather than invest in real estate the capital that they need in their business, I must have a good hotel at which these men can find accommodations while they are here looking at the houses that I offer for rent.' Accordingly the hotel is kept up in the style of the best public-houses—of course at a considerable loss as a hotel, for the price of board is only $3 a day. Mr. Stewart reserved for himself a sumptuous room in this phenomenal country-house, and since his death it has been sacredly kept for Mrs. Stewart.

"Precisely what Alexander T. Stewart had in view when he paid the town of Hempstead $450,000 for Hempstead Plains—until about the time of the purchase esteemed a barren waste—no man living pretends to know. He bought 10,000 acres, and in the beginning it was said that he would erect from 20,000 to 30,000 dwellings, each well supplied with water and lighted with gas, and surrounded by an ornamental garden. What he did was, first to make about twenty-seven miles of finished boulevards, 80 feet wide and crossing each other at right angles, and then to plant 50,000 trees. Then he began to erect dwellings, set back in the swards 75 feet from the street lines. It is believed that the merchant-prince actually did contemplate 10,000 houses for clerks and the under-ten of business men, and it is known that he intended that not one shingle should be sold in Garden City. It is conjectured that he desired to bequeath to the world a city that should own itself—a city whose every inhabitant should pay house-rent to the city treasury direct—a city that should ultimately become so wealthy that it might support schools and encourage art, and at length rival the European art centres. There is little doubt, however, that the executors of the great trust will eventually sell homes in Garden City as a means of attracting a class that will be welcomed there.

"Meantime, as a means of making the city self-supporting long before it gets the population that will pay its expenses, Mr. Hinsdale, the manager of the enterprise, is making the rich loam of the once-neglected plains yield considerable crops of oats, corn, and hay. Of oats he raised 14,000 bushels last year; of shelled corn, 45,000 bushels; and of hay he cut 300 tons. He keeps eighty horses and 500 head of Southdown sheep, and in summer employs 450 men and eight steam engines—two of them traction engines. He had not one bag to handle all his grain. It was all trundled in tanks on wheels, and elevated by steam and distributed by gravity. This is only the beginning of Mr. Hinsdale's farming. He has more than 8000 acres of soil at an elevation of 103 feet above the tide, so situated that the ordinary rainfall gives it perfect saturation, and the incline of eight feet to the mile towards the sea affords ample natural drainage, thus depriving it of any malarial qualities. He will speedily put more and more of it under cultivation, employing steam and modern machinery, and probably making it the greatest farm east of the prairies. Farming operations are not, however, to be carried on to the hindrance of the progress of the city. The water and gas pipes are to be extended, and just now Manager Hinsdale is beginning to heat the city with steam. He has already laid two and a half miles of water-pipe, and four and a half miles of gas-pipe. His bank of boilers for heating the city is situated near the water-works, where the men who operate the great engines of the enormous well-room from which the city is supplied with water may be utilized in handling the machinery for sending out steam.

"The water-works are a mile distant from Garden City Hotel, the centre of the city; but in the hotel, yesterday, and in the Cathedral of the Incarnation, near by, it was possible to elevate the temperature to an uncomfortable heat by turning a cock in the pipes that were fed a mile away. In Garden City the possibility of heating cities with steam has already been demonstrated beyond peradventure.

"The ornate gothic cathedral, beneath whose chancel the remains of Alexander and Mrs. Stewart were to have lain,[6] is

[6] Mr. Alexander Stewart died on April 10, 1876, and his body was interred in the churchyard of St. Mark's, in Tenth-street, New York,

nearing completion, and its lofty tower will soon be in readiness for the carillon that has been cast for it. The crypt, for whose exquisitely polished pillars of rare marbles the globe has been ransacked—and which is to cost a round $100,000—needs only the laying of its white marble floor and the placing of the superb sarcophagi. The cast for a statue of Hope, that is to occupy a niche behind the sarcophagi, has been sent to Europe to be worked in marble. St. Paul's Cathedral School, for which ground was broken in April last, has been completed as far as its exterior is concerned. The structure is of Philadelphia brick, made on the premises, and the trimmings are of stone. It is four stories in height, and has towers and other roof ornaments of the renaissance style. It is to be heated with steam. Three hundred pupils as boarders and 300 more as day pupils are to be accommodated. In addition to the ordinary bath-room appliances, the institution has a marble swimming bath, seventy feet in length by thirty in width. The structure is fireproof throughout, every floor being double, and a perfectly fireproof lining being carried between the two floors. Every ceiling is of fireproof material, and so is every partition that is not of brick.

"The foundation of Bishop Littlejohn's mansion, south of the Cathedral, has been completed. With the finishing of this edifice and of St. Paul's Cathedral School, and the Cathedral of the Incarnation, Garden City will be not only the cathedral city of Long Island, and the residence of its bishops, but a university town as well. And to this end Mrs. Stewart has given land and endowments for two church schools, and is considering the endowment and erection of the Theological Seminary of the Diocese of Long Island."

The Broadway is the principal street commercially, but Fifth and Madison avenues are the most fashionable localities, where aristocratic New York reigns supreme. What with its long line of handsome brown-stone churches and its many

there to lie till it could be finally removed to the Garden City cathedral. But on the night of November 6, 1878, his body was stolen by some person or persons unknown, and though a reward of $50,000 was offered for its recovery it has not since been heard of, nor has any clue been obtained as to the perpetrators of the outrage.

elegant and costly private residences, Fifth-avenue is indeed a most beautiful street, one worthy of close inspection. That is a beautiful sight looking up and down Fifth-avenue as you stand in front of the western entrance of the new Roman Catholic Cathedral, between Fiftieth and Fifty-first streets, when for two miles, looking in the direction of the Battery, you have an unbroken view of elegant private residences and a succession of eight brown-stone churches with their spires and towers; on the other side, looking towards Central Park, you have the street continuing in a straight line for some miles, bordered with shade-trees, with the fine towers of St. Thomas's and that of Dr. Hall's Presbyterian Church standing almost in front of you (at the corner of Fifty-third and Fifty-fifth streets) on the opposite side of the road. The new Catholic Cathedral, dedicated to St. Patrick, is undoubtedly the most imposing ecclesiastical edifice in America. It is built of white marble, in the decorated Gothic style of the thirteenth and fourteenth centuries, and was begun in the year 1858, and opened for divine service in May, 1879; but its two western towers are not yet completed. They will attain a height of 136 feet, and be surmounted by octagonal lanterns fifty-four feet high, which will in turn give place to octagonal spires in two stories of 140 feet, so that the culminating height of towers and spires will be 330 feet, thus forming, with a central gable (already completed) between the two towers of 156 feet in height, the west front of the cathedral facing Fifth-avenue. The building is rich in beautiful traceries and emblematical carvings; but no statues as yet adorn the edifice, though a number of tabernacles are ready prepared for them. The first to be erected are those of the Twelve Apostles, which will be placed in the western porch. The interior has noble proportions, and is built entirely of white marble (local). It is cruciform, consisting of choir (apsidal), nave and side aisles, and two transepts, the choir raised six steps above the floor of the nave. There are no chapels—at least what are called the chapels are little recesses under the windows of the side aisles, only fourteen feet high and eighteen feet wide. The total length of the interior is 306 feet; the nave is seventy-seven feet in height. The entire floor was, when I went over the cathedral, covered with pews, 408 in all, seating 2500 people. These, and an organ and choir gallery at the west end of the nave, are made of white ash. The reredos over the high altar is a fine work of art, chaste and beautiful in the extreme. It is fashioned of pure white Poitiers stone, and was carved at St. Brieuc, in France. The altar proper was carved in Italy, and is of white Italian marble. Perhaps one of the finest features about St. Patrick's is its figured stained-glass windows, which are exceptionally beautiful. They were executed in France, the majority of them at Chartres.

THE NORTH RIVER WATER-FRONT.

Turning from the sublime to the ridiculous we come to the water-front of New York. This literally bristles with wooden wharf-houses and piers, which are numbered in order, and are occupied by various railway and steamship companies. But they are a tumble-down, miserable-looking lot, and give one the idea that if a sudden gust of wind were to come it would blow the whole collection to the ground. A great improvement is sadly needed here. Besides better houses and docks, there should at least be a river-wall built. And then the slums in the neighbourhood! It is a locality almost as bad as

Billingsgate; but it is not every Londoner who has to pass through Billingsgate on his way out of town. Yet here, in compact New York, where everything is in a nut-shell, where you feel yourself "at home" in a couple of days when in any other place it would take a week, where you are on an island and cannot leave it by road unless you do so at its northern end, you have almost of necessity to seek the piers of the North or East Rivers if you want to leave the city to go South or West, ferry-boats transporting you over the former river to the great railways which start across-continent from Jersey City on the opposite shore, ferry-boats taking you across the East River to Brooklyn on Long Island, and in order to reach them you must pass through a neighbourhood reeking with every smell in Christendom—you would say so if you found yourself anywhere near the Washington or Fulton Markets on a wet day. These are the two principal markets of the Empire City, but in their present condition they are simply slums, and a disgrace to the place. However, a bill for rebuilding Fulton Market passed the State Senate on the 26th of last May. Washington Market is also to be rebuilt, "at an expenditure not exceeding $200,000."

Now the ferry-boats to which I have just alluded are of immense size. Some of them will hold a thousand people or more. The most capacious ply across the North River, between the metropolis and Jersey City. Once—some years ago now—one of these North River boats crossed over to Jersey City with 1600 on board. The occasion was, undoubtedly, an extraordinary one; yet it only shows how many can be packed on board on an emergency. On to the ferry-boats public and private conveyances are driven—four-in-hands, waggons, market-carts; you go over with a whole cargo of conveyances, which take up their station under cover, in the middle of the boat, while you read your *Herald* or *Evening Telegram* in a spacious "gents' saloon" on one side, if you wish to have a smoke, or in an equally commodious "ladies' saloon" on the other side of the boat, along with ladies *and* gentlemen, if you don't intend to smoke, for, as a matter of fact, the notice "ladies' saloon" is only put up to keep off smokers and chewers. I have crossed over in company with two waggons loaded with pig-iron, two loaded with lager-beer barrels, another laden with great bags of salt, a four-in-hand drag, two private carriages, together with, I should say, about 300 people. But it is a sight to see an East River ferry-boat about five o'clock in an afternoon. Take one on the point of starting from the New York Fulton-street pier to connect with Fulton-street which is continued in the city of Brooklyn, three-quarters of a mile away on the opposite shore. Every inch of the boat is filled, there is not standing-room upon it for ten people more. It is crowded after the manner of an Oxford college barge on the Isis during the racing of College Eights, only more so, for here everyone pushes up unceremoniously against his neighbour till there is scarcely anything of his neighbour left. There are no ladies to prevent a body being literally squeezed into a pancake. All are business men returning to Brooklyn after their day's labours in the Empire City, and for the next two hours every ferry-boat crossing over from the Fulton-street pier will be similarly crowded. On the arrival of one of these boats there is a regular stampede among the passengers to see who can get ashore first. Many jump off before the boat has become stationary, and, like a flock of sheep, those behind them follow suit, and the deck is cleared of several hundred people—yourself among the number, for you are irresistibly pressed forward from the rear and obliged to jump off with the rest—in less time than you would have thought it possible. The boat rapidly cleared in this way, is as quickly filled again, for—having to wait perhaps five or, at the most, six minutes before it has to set out on its return journey—the moment the path is clear for the outgoing passengers to come on board, the gates behind which they have been held in check are suddenly slid open, and a headlong rush is again the consequence, everybody tearing forward as if the boat had already begun to move off, when in reality it wants another three minutes before the departure-bell will ring. "At the present time," says the *New York Herald* of January 11, 1880, "200,000 people are actually carried over and returned each day by the ferries (East River), about half of them during three hours, morning and evening. During such times, 50,000 people and a corresponding mass of vehicles would accumulate at the bridge termini in an hour and a half, if the business of the ferries were for any reason suspended."

And now how to get about New York. There is first the elevated railway. Answering to our "underground" in London, in affording rapid conveyance through the city without interfering with the traffic, it is raised high above the streets instead of being tunnelled under them. The effect of the "elevated"—the "L," as New Yorkers generally call it—is, to my mind, anything but beautiful; but this, perhaps, is only a matter of taste. The tracks are lifted to a height of thirty feet (in some places higher) upon iron pillars, the up line on one side of the street and the down on the other,—in a few of the streets, where there is room enough, there are three tracks built,—and to prevent as far as possible the train from tipping over, the metals are laid on sleepers in a deep furrow or groove cut out of long pieces of timber, which are firmly bolted to the sleepers. Beneath the raised lines is the roadway for horses and carriages, and the lines of rail for the tramway cars, with the pavements beyond. As you sit in a car on the "L" and are being whirled along, you can put your head out of window and salute a friend who is walking on the street pavement below. In some places, where the streets are narrow, the railway is built right over the "sidewalks" (pavements) close up against the walls of the houses. In Pearl-street, for instance, this is especially the case, for just after leaving the Fulton-street station, on your way towards the Bowery, you find you are on a level with the rooms of the third story of the United States Hotel, and able easily to see into them, which is not very pleasant, I should imagine, for the occupants of those rooms.

As might be expected, the elevated railway is immensely patronized. Trains run at frequent intervals on the several lines, from 5.30 in the morning till 12 o'clock at night, and during the crowded hours, namely from 5.30 a.m. to 7.30 a.m., and from 5 p.m. to 7 p.m., they follow each other as fast as can be managed. One company—the Metropolitan, or Sixth Avenue—runs daily 840 trains (420 each way) up and down its line between 5.30 a.m. and 12 p.m.; seventy trains per hour are run during the crowded hours mornings and evenings. The fare during these busy hours is five cents ($2\frac{1}{2}d.$), at other times ten cents. Of course it is needless to observe that there are no classes, as in our passenger trains, but all ride together in a long car, or carriage, the seats ranged lengthwise at the sides, with a passage down the middle and a door at each end, four cars being as many as are run at a time on the "elevated." There is, therefore, the same fare for everybody,—no matter how long or short the distance travelled over,—and the three companies working the elevated railways (the Metropolitan, the Manhattan, and New

THE ELEVATED RAILWAY.

York companies), having carried their lines far into the upper portion of the city, you can, for the sum of five cents, take a ride of some ten or twelve miles, and without changing cars. The trains are run at a good speed, and there is but little delay at the stations; indeed sometimes the train does not pull up at all, and yet people recklessly jump on and off all the same. I have sometimes noticed the conductor obliged to pull people up on to the train, as the halt made is not long enough to enable them to get quietly upon it by themselves. During a trip I once took from Eighth-street to One Hundred and Fifty-fifth street, on the Metropolitan "L," when we stopped at fifteen stations on the way, I noticed that the average length of delay at each station was ten seconds—at three stations we did not even come to a standstill, and yet we took up and put down passengers in each case. There are very few cross tracks, so that the chances of collision are reduced to a minimum; but there are sharp curves here and there, which have to be approached slowly and cautiously, else the train would never get round. In rounding these the engine will give a sudden jerk to one side, so much so that you have a full view of the locomotive ahead of you from out of the side-window of your car—but only for a moment, till you are jerked round into proper position behind it the next. Tickets have to be given up almost as soon as bought, before passengers can enter the train, this arrangement having been adopted since the 22nd of last June, before which date they had to be given up as usual, at the end of the journey. No smoking is allowed in any of the cars, and standing on the platforms at the ends is strictly forbidden. The average height of the "L" above the street-level is thirty feet; but in one place it is fifty-seven feet, namely beyond Central Park, on the west side of the island. From end to end it is a veritable railway in the air, for nowhere does the track descend to the level of the street. As a financial enterprise the elevated railway has turned out a success beyond even the expectations of its promoters. "One hundred and seventy-five thousand passengers are carried over the city lines daily," says a gentleman officially connected with one of the "L" roads, "or 12,000 tons of human flesh, averaging each person at 140 lbs." Thirty million dollars have already been expended on the enterprise,—that is up to the end of 1879, the first "L" line having been opened in May, 1878,—and 5,000,000 more will be required to finish all the city railways that are in contemplation. "L" roads are at present only in operation in New York City, but these lines are rapidly being extended into the suburbs, and Brooklyn already has one in process of erection, and Philadelphia is to have one too, and even

sedate Boston is thinking of providing herself with one, so
that it seems as if the popularity of this mode of locomotion
is on the increase in the large cities: but dangers are looming ahead which bid fair to stem the tide of prosperity which
the promoters of "rapid transit" have been enjoying hitherto,
and to render the enterprise in the future costly rather than

THE ELEVATED RAILWAY.
View in Chatham-street.

lucrative. As a natural consequence of the introduction of
the elevated railway, property lying contiguous to the overhead lines has considerably depreciated in value. The nineteen hours and more of incessant rumbling day and night
from the passing trains; the blocking out of a sufficiency of
light from the rooms of houses, close up to which the lines
are built; the full, close view passengers on the cars can have

into rooms on the second and third floors; the frequent squirtings of oil from the engines, sometimes even finding its way into the private rooms of a dwelling-house, when the windows are left open—all these are objections that have been reasonably urged by unfortunate occupants of houses whose comfort has been so unjustly molested, and the result is, tenants who have found themselves so inconvenienced have chosen rather to remove to other and more eligible quarters, and house-owners have been obliged to lower their rents to get any tenants at all. Only very recently has judgment been delivered by the Supreme Court at Albany, in an action brought by a New Yorker against the Metropolitan Company to recover compensation for damages done to his property in Fifty-third street, by the erection of the "L" railway right in front of his premises, the Court deciding for the plaintiff, and reversing the decision of an inferior Court, where the verdict had been in favour of the railway company; and should the Court of Appeals—whither the defendants will in all probability carry their suit—also decide in favour of the property holder, "rapid transit" companies will begin to see that they have a costly business in store for them, to restrain all the actions for damages that would probably ensue. Far better have carried their lines underground.

With regard to the inconvenience sometimes arising from the bespattering of oil from a passing train, I may here mention a little incident which befell me one day as I was crossing the Sixth-avenue from Twelfth-street, when I halted as soon as I found myself underneath the "L," to look up at a train rushing by overhead of me. It was lucky I had not my mouth open at the time, for as I gazed with my face upturned, I was saluted with a large pat of oil from one of the axle-boxes of a car, which besprinkled my countenance and neck-tie in such a manner that I had to rush into a barber's shop—conveniently close at hand—and be cleansed from the dreadful mess. Oil drippings from passing trains are a source of constant annoyance to foot-passengers crossing the roadway beneath—a nuisance that could be easily remedied by the application of a proper sort of hard grease, such as is used on every English railway.

There are other ways of getting about New York besides

taking the "elevated." Railways for horse-cars are laid along nearly every avenue (all except Fifth and Lexington avenues, I believe), and many of the cross streets : you are said to travel in this way by "car," but by "stage" if you take another form of conveyance, namely a 'bus. But there is no sitting on top of the New York stages as can be done in the case of our London 'buses, for they are small, and only take passengers inside; moreover they are "bobtailed," as are some of the

UNDER THE ELEVATED RAILWAY.

horse-cars. A bobtailed stage or car is one without a conductor or man to collect the fares, there being a box inside with a slit in the top, into which the passenger is trusted to drop the exact amount of the fare. If he wants change out of his money, he can, in a bobtailed horse-car, obtain it from the driver to the amount of two dollars, and no more, and the driver will hand back to the passenger a little sealed packet containing the whole amount returned in the form of small pieces of change, and thus the proper fare, which is generally five cents, can be selected and dropped into the till. In a stage, however, there is no such communication between the passenger and driver, for the former is here left to pay in the exact amount, and if he happens to have no change—well, we will not suppose him so dishonest as to take a ride for nothing. But the fare-box is so placed that the driver can peep down from his seat and see if everyone inside has paid, and if you don't pay immediately you step in, the driver will "rap away" at you till you do—till he sees you have dropped the proper fare into the box, whereupon he will turn a slide and pass the money out of sight, so that there may be no confusion when the next passenger comes to pay in his fare. Stages are painted red, white, and blue, and have bright-coloured pictures (very dauby-looking) illuminating the sides. They traverse the Broadway, and convey up-town New Yorkers to the ferries for Brooklyn. But it is "fashionable" in the Empire City to travel by horse-car, or else take the "elevated."

Of course there are hackney carriages to be obtained, but these are very few and far between. They consist mostly of big family coaches-and-pairs, with room enough inside to comfortably seat six. If you happen to be in one of them by yourself you have abundance of room to pitch about, and the bumping you will receive owing to the unevenness of the roadway will soon cause you to do this whether you like it or no. There is another form of public conveyance called a "coupé," or small brougham, holding only two people. These coupés are invariably well cushioned, and are as comfortable a class of conveyance as one could well desire. The pity is there is not more of them. But driving about in public carriages in New York comes to be absurdly expensive, unless you hire by the hour, when the fare is one dollar. Yet even then there must be an understanding between yourself and the driver before starting, else there may be a "scene." The regulation fare per mile is one dollar; but if you only drive along a couple of blocks you must pay a dollar all the same. I remember once being charged two dollars—that is eight shillings for a drive from the Grand Central Depôt (railway station) to my hotel, the Brevoort House, whereas in London I could have done the distance for eighteen pence.

But the great evil of New York is the unevenness of the roads. In some places they are so bad that you have to walk with the same amount of care you would use in crossing a river on stepping-stones—take Frankfort and North William streets, and others in the vicinity of Printing House Square, as also all the streets leading down to the North River from Broadway or Fifth-avenue. The jolting you get in a stage is terrible, and it is not always convenient to take a car. It is no uncommon thing to see great holes which are allowed to exist in the middle of the street, down into which you bump, though only to be pulled out again with a violent jerk, which would have a serious result if you did not hold on tight. A man returning home late at night the worse for liquor would find these holes rather awkward for him, and in the way, for he would be on his head before he had got very far; and yet if he kept to the pavement he would be just as liable to come down, for on coming to a cross street he would have to descend about a foot, and then have to mount up a foot again so as to regain the pavement on the other side.

It is, however, after a good shower of rain that the New York roads are seen at their worst, let alone their uneven surface. Then some of the most frequented and fashionable thoroughfares are rendered well-nigh impassable for the pedestrian on account of the vast amount of mud that is allowed not only to accumulate,—there being no such thing as a street crossing,—but to remain uncleared away for days upon days together. A man wishing to cross a street in such a state must be careful to tuck up the ends of his trousers ere he ventures to make the experiment, for his boots will, in a step or two, be covered with the slimy mess, and more than this;—he must be prepared to slide about on the slippery surface like a duck trying to waddle to the other side of an ice-pond. And the pavements are just as bad. You could use a pair of skates on them. The thick black mud, so continually trampled upon, here becomes a kind of smooth cake or dough, over which you struggle in vain to walk steady and straight. It would of course be superfluous to draw attention to the disgraceful condition of the New York roads in wet weather, were it not for the fact that no effort, apparently, is made to clean them. (The responsibility for their condition rests with the Bureau or Committee of Street-cleaning, which is appointed by the Board of Police Commissioners.) A street crossing swept *and kept so*, and rendered in a passable condition so that one can cross without fear of getting one's boots well mudded during the passage, is, as far as my experience goes, a thing unknown in the Empire City. It is strange, too, that at least some of the garbage or refuse is not removed from the city sewers, so as to prevent poisonous and obnoxious smells arising, particularly on a warm summer's day, about which there have been so many complaints lately. Such a state of things cannot be conducive to the health of the New Yorkers. And yet the people of the Empire City are highly taxed for the proper cleansing of their streets.

Another of the evils of New York is the conspicuous whitepaint advertisements that disfigure the upper portion of the city. The white and yellow daubing, indeed, that here prevails so extensively, is nothing less than a disgrace to any respectable and well-ordered community. Above Eightieth-street, and on the other side of the Harlem River, where buildings are, as yet, few and far between,—where palatial marble and granite structures give place to wooden and red brick "skin" dwellinghouses with eight-inch party walls,—the huge notices of aperients, liniments, pills, plasters, powders, hair-dyes, etc., completely cover rocks and palings, and the blank walls of houses, although there is a State law which prohibits the disfigurement of natural scenery in this ruthless, shoppy fashion. It is to be hoped that an effort will be made to remove the more objectionable of these advertisements before the forthcoming New York International Exhibition, the great "world's fair" of 1883.[7] Some of them are simply disgusting.

[7] The contemplated international exhibition to be held in New York, in 1883, is in celebration of the one hundredth anniversary of the Treaty of Peace and the recognition of American independence, the evacuation of the British troops from the city of New York, on November 25, 1783, having marked the close of the War of Independence. The Centennial Exhibition, which was held in Philadelphia in 1876, was, it will be remembered, in celebration of the one hundredth anniversary of the Declaration of Independence, that famous Declaration having been first publicly made in that city.

A great number of the streets are built so much alike that it is sometimes difficult to tell the difference between them without the most careful scrutiny and observation. A glance, for instance, up Forty-sixth, Forty-seventh, Forty-eighth, Forty-ninth, Fiftieth, and Fifty-first streets, in the direction of Fifth-avenue, as you pass them in order on the Sixth-avenue "L," or in a horse-car on the same avenue, will fail to reveal any appreciable difference in them, excepting a church spire (that of the Dutch Reformed Church, and a beautiful spire this is) in Forty-eighth street, and a portion of the west front of the new Roman Catholic Cathedral, which just comes into view as you flit past Fifty-first street. Every house has a frontage of Connecticut brown-stone, and a "stoop" or flight of ten steps attached, by ascending which admittance is gained into the front entrance of the building. Most of the private residences in the city are provided with similar "stoops."

In one respect New York excels our English towns, and that is in its shade-trees. Not only in the "avenues," but in the cross streets, also, there are trees growing; and though they are not planted here so numerously as in other American cities, yet they are sufficient to impart to the busy metropolis a delightfully rural appearance. As purifiers of the atmosphere their beneficial influence is indisputable.

If there is one thing more than another for which New York is particularly distinguished, it is for the excellence, the wonderful variety, the illimitable supply, and consequently the cheapness of—its oysters. To one who is partial to a good oyster now and then, this city must be simple bliss. How many saloons there are in the place wholly given up to the cooking of the bivalves in every variety of form, and to the continual supply of them without need of any cooking, and how many of the good people of the Empire City daily and nightly crowd the saloons in the season, and how many oysters on an average each person eats—all this might furnish an interesting subject of inquiry for the lover of statistics. Oysters stewed, oysters steamed, oysters fried, oysters broiled, oysters scalloped, oysters raw, oyster pie, oyster pattie, oyster soup; you can have your oysters prepared in any one of these forms if you step into the first saloon you happen to pass, no matter how unpretentious or humble it may look,—it will not escape your notice for want of sufficient advertisement,—and there you will find piles upon piles of the shell-fish on the counters ready waiting to be opened. Now I advise all who are interested on the subject of oysters to visit the restaurant of Mr. Robert Burns, at No. 783, Sixth-avenue, any time during the season. Mr. Burns, to begin with, is a typical oyster man. He was born (he told me) on an oyster bed, rocked in a cradle of oyster shells, his first play-toy was an oyster, and he has been playing with oysters now for fifty-one years. Very courteous and willing to afford every information within his power on the subject of his shell-fish, Mr. Burns will tell the visitor to his establishment a few facts which may cause him to open his eyes. He will tell him—but perhaps I had better relate my own experiences when I first made the acquaintance of Mr. Burns, and his excellent oysters. This was in the month of November, 1879, at the conclusion of my second visit to the United States, and he had then in stock about fifty thousand: but that was a small matter. In holiday-time, he told me, he has from four to five hundred thousand. Mr. Burns set before me a large plateful of Cow Bays. Now these oysters in particular were of prodigious size; I measured them, shells and all. The shells of the first one I measured were ten and a half inches long, and averaged four and a half inches in width; those of the second I measured were nine inches by six; those of another, nine inches by four. The meat inside each averaged six inches by four. Of course I could do no more than look at them: it would have taken a nigger to have swallowed them. I doubt even if Dr. Tanner after his celebrated fast could have successfully bolted half a dozen of them. I was shown about fifteen thousand of these monsters, all stored away in bins in a cellar under the house. Mr. Burns told me that he sometimes has them much larger. Of the well-known " Blue Points " he had many thousand. Those I tried were in splendid condition, as good as any Whitstable "natives" or Scotch "Pandores"—very much better than those which are sent over to our Liverpool and London markets, and can be bought at ninepence a dozen.

Blue Point is the name given to the upper part of Cow Bay, which is an inlet of Long Island Sound, about fifty miles above New York. A natural oyster bed, it is ten miles in length, and contains two-thirds salt water to one-third fresh. Cow Bay of itself produces more oysters than all the other oyster beds of the country put together. Millions of the bivalves consumed in and around New York are brought from Virginia; but these are not to be compared in flavour with the natural seed oysters of Cow Bay, and other famous beds in the neighbourhood of the Empire City, such as Raritan Bay, the Mill Pond, Rockaway, Flushing and Sheepshead Bays. Again, Virginian "plants," or seed oysters, are sent when they are no larger than one's thumb nail to improve in the New York waters, where they grow fatter and richer. They are sold by the cargo to the large dealers and thrown in—sometimes from fifty to one hundred thousand bushels at a time, according to the extent of the beds. Ninety thousand six hundred and sixty-three barrels of oysters were shipped to England from New York and neighbouring ports in 1879, at a total value of 90,661*l.* In 1878 there were 78,612 barrels shipped; in 1877, 52,124.

I was pleased to see in Mr. Burns' restaurant a notice to the effect that any one of his *employés* found swearing or using bad language on his premises, would be liable to instant dismissal. I have seen similar notices in other shops in New York. One of these, which I found posted conspicuously in a shop in Bleecker-street, though probably it is well-known to most people, will bear re-quoting. It ran as follows:

> TO GENTLEMEN.
>
> It chills my blood to hear the Blest Supreme
> Rudely appealed to, on each trifling theme.
> Maintain your rank, vulgarity despise :
> To swear is neither brave, polite, nor wise.
> You would not swear upon a bed of death ;
> Reflect ! your Maker now may stop your breath.

New York is particularly well provided with public restaurants. Delmonico's, up-town, is indisputably the first in the city. It is the first in America, perhaps the best in the world.

Even Parisian restaurants pale before Delmonico's, and in London we have none that can be compared with it, nor with that of the Brunswick, nor with that of the Brevoort—though this is not a thing for us to take to heart very much, for we are a home-loving people, and do not make it a point of our lives to be continually "dining out" at public restaurants. But Delmonico's is something more than an ordinary public restaurant. Here political (private) meetings are held, committees sit and debate, college societies have their annual social gatherings, and here it is that a distinguished foreigner visiting the United States would be taken and tendered a complimentary banquet,—after he had been first "put through" all the most interesting sights on Manhattan Island,—and here possibly a ball would (as a New Englander would say) be "gotten up" in his honour. Perhaps the distinguished foreigner, bent on a trip to America, is not aware of the reception he is likely to meet with the moment he has set foot in the Empire City? Let me illustrate an instance. Suppose the visitor to New York had, to use a common phrase, a "handle" to his name; or suppose he had made himself celebrated in some honourable profession or pleasurable pursuit, no matter what—anything would do so long as his fame had reached the United States. Suppose, then, he was somebody or other more or less distinguished and famous, and he embarked on a pleasure-trip to New York, he would in the first place be met off Sandy Hook by a *Herald* reporter, and perhaps by three or four more newspaper reporters, and be formally "interviewed" during his progress up the Bay towards the Empire City; his personal appearance and any little peculiarity about his manner would be duly recognized and noted down by these indefatigable gentlemen, and the opinions he happened to express to them he would find duly proclaimed *in extenso* in the columns of their journals the next day—as well as his personal appearance and peculiarity of manner, which would be so minutely described and every little particular so graphically set forth, that when he came to look over the reports in the newspapers the next day he would find a deal of information about himself that he never knew before; he would be dubbed "colonel" forthwith, whether he had a right to that designation or not, and that title would cling to him so long as he remained in the country; perchance a carriage-and-pair would be placed at his disposal, to make use of whenever he liked; he would be "put through" this and that—ciceroned over the elevated railways, trotted round Central Park, taken to inspect the great Brooklyn Bridge, taken over Stewart's immense dry-goods retail establishment in the Broadway, taken to Tiffany's in Union-square and shown the finest and most costly exhibition of jewellery in the United States, taken and shown Jersey City's new mammoth grain elevator, taken and shown the excavations under the channel at Hell Gate, and a host of other things he would have to be "put through" before he could obtain any rest or peace; till at last, after every sort of civility and attention had been shown him, his kind entertainers would, to crown all, "put" him "through" a complimentary dinner at Delmonico's. To quote one or two instances, out of many, to illustrate to what uses these famous rooms are occasionally devoted: on the 1st of March of the present year a grand banquet was given here to M. de Lesseps, in the ball-room, when "over 250 prominent residents met to do honour to the distinguished builder of canals." Here, on Tuesday, the 16th of June last, a "farewell breakfast" was given to Edwin Booth, the actor, prior to his departure the next day for a prolonged trip to Europe, when "150 gentlemen sat down a little after twelve o'clock, and remained until half past five." It was here that "a gentle little Sherman boom"[8] was started one evening in February last, when a private meeting of a few friends of the Secretary of the Treasury was held to promote his nomination as Republican candidate for the presidency of the United States. (This "boom," however, in the graphic language of the *New York Tribune*, had to be "stopped for repairs" shortly afterwards, though not before it had attained the dimensions of "a stalwart Sherman boom.") Here, too, the Citizen's Auxiliary Committee of the Memorial Committee of the Grand Army of the Republic met, on Saturday evening, May 15th, to

---

[8] "English papers are now using the word 'boom.' After a while it will get into the dictionary."—*New York Herald*.

arrange for duly and properly celebrating Decoration Day.[9] Here, once more, the Harvard Club of New York, an association of the alumni (graduates) of the great Massachusetts university, holds its annual dinner; and various other college associations—the "Greek letter" societies, to wit—likewise hold their meetings here annually; and so on. Such, then, is Delmonico's.

But, to descend a scale lower, a typical American restaurant is the one at the Astor House. Nowhere on earth will one see such a rapid bolting of food, or such a deal eaten in a short space of time. The "Astor" is a hotel in the Broadway, down-town, nearly opposite the new Post Office, and is called after one of New York's wealthiest and most beneficent citizens, Mr. John Jacob Astor, now deceased.[10] It is the down-town Fifth-avenue Hotel, where people meet and chat, talk over business and the latest telegrams, the rise and fall of stocks, etc.; but it must not be mentioned in the same breath with the Fifth-avenue, as it is nothing like so "high-toned." It is to the lower part of New York what the Parker House is to Boston, or the Palmer House to Chicago—

[9] What the Fourth of July is as a national holiday in its relation to the War of Independence, so is Decoration Day (May 30th) in its relation to the war of the late rebellion. These are the two great national festivals of the American people. As to the celebration of Decoration Day in New York, *vide* next chapter.

[10] The following is an extract from the will of the late Mr. John Jacob Astor, of New York City : "Desiring to render a public benefit to the city of New York, and to contribute to the advancement of human knowledge and the general good of society, I do, by this codicil, appropriate $400,000 to the establishment of a public library in the city of New York . . . . a library for general use, upon the most ample scale and liberal character . . . . the said library to be accessible at all reasonable times and hours for general use, free of expense, to persons resorting thereto."

Mr. Astor died in 1848. The Astor Library has now a collection of 189,114 volumes. In 1879 there were 2513 books presented to the institution, and 3356 were purchased. During the same year there was an average attendance of 214 readers daily. The endowment fund at present amounts to $1,112,957.

Other public libraries in New York are the Lennox, the Cooper Institute, and the Mercantile Library. The Mercantile Library has (May 12, 1880) 188,167 books, 6439 having been added during the year 1879. Its entire circulation for 1879 was 143,251 volumes, making a daily average of 468 volumes.

a sort of general, everybody's place of meeting, where a noisy, bustling, spitting lot of men congregate together, and make as much clamour as they please. Owing to its supreme location in the very busiest part of the "busiest street in the world," it commands, as may be supposed, a most extensive patronage, so that its public restaurant is always crowded. I went into the Astor House one day to have my luncheon. Ascending a flight of five steps I found myself in a hall filled with men standing about chatting and smoking, the floor *perfectly covered* with emptyings from the mouths of scores of smokers and tobacco chewers, non-tobacco chewers and non-smokers, who had been passing in and out during the course of the morning; and let me here observe,—though I shall have occasion to refer once more, and only once, to this disagreeable subject later on,—that this, the universal habit of spitting everywhere and on all possible occasions, pervading, as it does, all classes of American society, forms one of the most serious drawbacks to one's comfort during a visit to the United States. There is in this hall a telegraph office, a railway-ticket office, a stick and umbrella stand, a newspaper and book stand, a cigar stand, and on each side a flight of stairs leading up to the private rooms of the hotel. A notice-board affixed to the wall, half way up on the right-hand staircase, discloses the fact that several of the rooms upstairs are used as business offices and society rooms—though this is obvious from the street outside, as the names of a good many of them are painted against the windows. Thus we have (on the first and second floors) the offices of the Prudential Insurance Company of America, the rooms of the American Baptist Home Mission Society, the American Railway Improvement Company's offices, also several lawyer's offices; and so forth. Folding doors at the far end of the hall separate this portion of the hotel from the public restaurant. You push open the doors, and—what a scene! What a clatter, what a chatter, what a babel of voices, what a buzz of conversation—what a row! Plates and dishes, knives and forks, human lungs, all are at work doing their utmost to make as much commotion as possible. And what a scene! A long room with a succession of counters nearly encircling it; two large circular counters in the middle; upon them all a splendid array of every esculent delicacy of the season; and a perfect crush of people, all who are not standing up perched on top of high stools round the counters with their legs tucked in under them—just like a lot of lawyers' clerks. Every one so posed is hard at work engaged in devouring, with that rapidity for which our American cousins are famous, his lunch or dinner, composed, in nine cases out of every ten, of a dish of soup followed by a plateful of "rare"—that is, very underdone, almost raw—hot roast beef, accompanied by many kinds of vegetables, including a prodigious amount of celery (of which our cousins are exceedingly fond), all arranged in front on little plates or dishes, after the manner of a Swedish "sexa;" and this would be speedily followed by a large slice of flat apple-pie or pumpkin-pie, the whole washed down with a tumbler of iced water, and this perhaps followed by a cup of hot tea! The counters are loaded, absolutely loaded with huge piles of mammoth beef and ham sandwiches—one of these alone is quite enough to make a meal off—and with all sorts of fruit pies, with towering pyramids of oysters and soft shell crabs—oysters received direct from the oyster bed of John Roe Smith, or some such person; and it is interesting to watch how rapidly the piles of mammoth sandwiches, oysters and soft shell crabs become diminished—how first one hungry city clerk, then another, comes up hastily and gives his order for a dozen or two of Blue Points to be opened immediately "on the half shell," or else asks for some steamed soft shell crabs, or some devilled crabs, etc., all which are obtainable at the shortest possible notice by simply asking for them, as can be seen by the notices pasted about the room to that effect. And to think that these men would dine again the same evening!

I remember once dining at a restaurant in the Broadway where there were coloured waiters to serve me. One of the niggers[11] was very loving, and as I ordered my dinner he kept thrusting his nose into my left cheek; but I put this down at the time to a little deafness on his part. He was very

---

[11] A coloured man objects strongly to being called a nigger. Thus, "A Georgia coloured man tied a white boy up in a stable and made him say 'nigger' 2800 times!"—*Detroit Free Press.*

diligent in his attentions, and every now and then during the repast would come up and bend down over me, and, putting his face close to mine, say, "Are you all right?" This he would follow up with, "Are you through?"—an Americanism equivalent to asking whether I had finished. Bent on having something thoroughly American, I had ordered for my dinner clam "chowder" (soup), to be followed by stewed frogs and lager beer, etc. You acquire a taste for the frogs when you have succeeded in breaking the ice and safely disposing of the first one. In ordering a meal at an American restaurant, it is sometimes convenient to bear in mind that what is enough for one is enough for two. Such a quantity is heaped on to your plate that it is enough for yourself as well as for your friend. Therefore if you dine double, and you both are not very hungry, it is better to order for one only, for the quantity served will be found to be ample for two persons possessed with moderate appetites. Many cents may thus be saved by any two persons who are inclined to be thrifty.

There are 3568 lager-beer saloons in New York, exclusive of other liquor saloons, of which there are over 6000. This light Bavarian beer is the American's staple drink. It is not intoxicating, and generally it is satisfying; but sometimes an uncommon amount is consumed by one man at a sitting, and yet drunkenness is seldom the result. The beer is thoroughly fermented, and is almost invariably free from adulterations and poisonous ingredients of any kind. It is bad whisky, generally, that people get drunk with in the United States. This is taken neat, and tossed off in one gulp like a wineglassful of water. A law in New York prescribes that the liquor saloons shall be closed on Sundays; and so indeed they are, apparently. But a good many of them have their back or "family" entrances, as they are called, the doors of which are left unfastened while the front ones are locked; and I am told on good authority, that there is as much beer and as many whisky and "brandy-smash cocktails" secretly drunk at some of these places on the Sabbath, as on any other day of the week. With the shutters up, or I should rather say with the blinds down, and with the front door closed, and not a sign of any one about, the stranger little dreams what is going on inside a popular lager-beer saloon on a Sunday, any hour of the day. If, however, he wishes to see for himself, let him find out the family entrance, and push open the door, and in a few steps he will be in the presence of perhaps a dozen men—I once counted that number, and it was on a Sunday morning—drinking and smoking away to their heart's content, for they know that Mr. Policeman will not drop in on them, or that if he did it would only be to take a glass quietly with them, for the blinds are well down, the front door is closed, and this is the way the New York liquor saloon keepers manage to evade the law! But though the beer they are drinking is poured down their throats like so much water, no evil result is the consequence,—except perhaps a severe attack of nausea or a splitting headache later on,—and each one is quite capable afterwards of walking straight back to his home. In 1877-78, thirty-two brewers produced in New York 1,228,848 barrels of lager-beer; in 1878-79, 1,342,180 barrels. One brewer alone, in 1878-79, produced 180,152 barrels, which is an amount never before produced in one year by any brewer in the United States.

In the upper part of the city, five miles above the Battery, is the Central Park. This public recreation-ground comprises 863 acres, of which 185 are water. Twenty-two years ago it was little better than a dreary swamp, a fact hard to realize when one sees the wonderful transformation that has since been effected. But now the Central Park is the fashionable promenade and driving-course of the people of the Empire City. Here, at four o'clock of an afternoon, the New Yorkers turn out in their very best style; then is the time to see a bit of the fashionable world. On the day of our first arrival in New York, we of course "did the fashionable" at the appointed time and place. At four o'clock we were slowly driving in the park among an immense crowd of carriages of all shapes and sizes, from a humble little two-wheeled buggy to a "swell" four-in-hand drag; and some of the turn-outs we witnessed were as ludicrous as they could be. There were high, spider-wheeled waggonettes and negro coachmen driving them, who wore white alpaca coats, great striped stuck-out paper collars and tall chimney-pot hats. One turn-out in particular made us nearly choke with laughing—it was that of a nigger driving out his wife and family for an airing in a neat, four-wheeled buggy. I "convulsed" when I caught sight of them, I never saw anything so ridiculous. Darkie was standing up cudgeling his horse with a big stick; his wife, etc., sat and gazed admiringly while he pitched into his beast. But the beast would not budge an inch; so darkie stood and jeered at him, opening his immense mouth till it included half the size of his head. And *such* an animal he drove! You could have counted all its ribs. Not so, however, the other horses in the park. Some of them were splendid creatures, and stepped out at a fine pace. They alone were worth coming into the park to see.

The Americans provide beautiful resting-places for their dead, but there is none more beautiful than the Greenwood Cemetery in Brooklyn. A visit to this famous burial-ground should form one of the first and foremost objects of the stranger on his arrival in New York, were it only for the glorious and comprehensive view to be here obtained of the great metropolis and its surroundings, even supposing he did not care to interest himself in tombstones and graveplots. Occupying a slight elevation immediately overlooking the City of Brooklyn, this cemetery commands, also, an extensive panorama of the splendid Bay of New York and the Long Island Sound, of New York City itself and Jersey City, and of Long Island in the direction of Coney Island and Sandy Hook, all of which can be taken in from the two highest elevations in the cemetery, Battle and Ocean Hills. And Greenwood Cemetery is well named, for it is a lovely park of 600 acres, with hills and dales, lakes and fountains, and numberless quiet retreats from the busy world outside. Perhaps nowhere in the two hemispheres is there a more lovely city of the dead. And yet Mount Auburn near Boston, and Oakwood at Troy, though of less extent, are each of them scarcely less beautiful.[12]

---

[12] There have been 199,747 interments in Greenwood Cemetery since it was formally opened to the public on August 15, 1842, 5132 of them during the year 1879. There were seventy-three cats destroyed in the cemetery in 1879; also 3159 mice, twenty-nine dogs, thirty-three rats, one skunk, two musk-rats, sixty-four snakes, and thirty-three moles.

The road one would take to Greenwood after crossing the East River by the Fulton-street ferry, is not likely, in its present condition, to impress the stranger very favourably with Brooklyn—supposing, that is to say, this is his first visit

TRINITY CHURCH, BROADWAY.
(*See page* 13.)

to the "City of Churches," as Brooklyn is frequently called. The road or street I refer to goes by the name of Hamilton-avenue, and is peopled mostly by Irish. One proceeds along it for about three miles before coming to the cemetery. But the tumble-down appearance of the buildings that here line the public way, the uneven side-walks, and still worse roadway,—fortunately there are tramway cars to take one to the cemetery,—the swarms of dirty little children running about hither and thither without any shoes or stockings on, all this, I say, is not calculated to give one exalted impressions of Brooklyn. And yet Brooklyn is a great city, the third largest in population in the United States,[13] even though it lies so close to New York, the most populous in the Union. But Brooklyn bears the same relation to New York as the shadow does to its substance, for a great many of those who do business in the latter city have their homes in the former. There are but few things for the ordinary tourist to see and do here, great city though Brooklyn is. About the only attractions are the Greenwood Cemetery, the United States Navy Yards, the Prospect Park, and those two notorious divines, Henry Ward Beecher and Dr. T. de Witt Talmage.[14]

[13] According to the estimated census returns of 1880, Brooklyn's population is 566,680.

[14] The terrible railway disaster which happened in Scotland on the night of December 28, 1879, was the theme of a remarkable sermon preached by Dr. Talmage in Brooklyn Tabernacle, on the morning of the Sunday following. The Sunday discourses of this eccentric divine are weekly reported in the New York Monday papers. Perhaps the notice of the sermon in question to which the *New York World* treated its readers, will not be found uninteresting. Prefacing its report with two large and attractive headings,—

TALMAGE IN HIS GLORY.

HE "IMPROVES" THE DISASTER ON THE BRIDGE OF TAY IN MANNER AND FORM FOLLOWING,

the *World* proceeds to say :

" It needed only the advertisement which the careful and business-like managers of Mr. Talmage's Tabernacle inserted in yesterday morning's papers to give to Mr. Talmage yesterday morning an overwhelmingly large audience. It was announced that he would preach on or about the recent railroad disaster in Scotland. Mr. Talmage, true to his advertisement, pitched right into the subject at once. His text was taken from that portion of Holy Writ entitled Nahum, and read : 'The chariots shall rage in the streets. They shall jostle one another in the broad ways. They shall seem like torches. They shall run like lightning.'

" ' If that be not an express train under full headway at night,' said the preacher, ' what is it ? I am inclined to think that the use of steam was one of the lost arts, and that Nahum knew all about it long before Robert

The Prospect Park, indeed,—a large rambling recreation ground of 510 acres,—is too far out of the city to be much resorted to, and hardly repays a visit. It is only within the last few years that there has been any considerable wholesale

Fulton and others were born. When you read this text you hear the clank of the couplings and the ring of the wheels on the iron rails. It may be the sound of a train between Albany and New York, or between Cincinnati and St. Louis; it may be (Mr. Talmage made a dire face) a train between Dundee and Glasgow. For moral improvement this morning I shall call your attention to the terrible disaster of the Tay Bridge last Sunday evening.' Mr. Talmage then told how on the 31st of last July he went down the River Tay on a steamer, which he called by name, and how he was impressed, more than the Hudson or the Rhine had ever impressed him, with its rare beauties. From its birth at Loch Tay to its transformation into the German Ocean the River Tay is, according to Mr. Talmage, a chain of enchantment. He told how, ten or fifteen minutes after leaving the Dundee dock, the steamer passed under the great bridge, and how he remarked to an inquiring Scotchman that there was nothing in America like it, with its eighty-seven spans, its eighty feet of width, and two miles of length. Then from these reminiscences of his pleasant journey down the stream, Mr. Talmage turned at once to his subject. 'When, last Sabbath, the conductor lifted his hand to the engineer of that ill-fated train, what a smooth opening was that great architectural triumph to the horror that followed! Will not some switchman with a red flag run out? Will not the echo of the rocks cry 'Halt'? Will not some friendly voice borne on the wings of the night-wind stop the doomed procession? How dumb and unsympathetic are all the natural surroundings! Not a note of warning as the coaches go swaying to and fro on to destruction! Down through the darkness and the space, down, down! Crash! crash! crash! All dead! Some by fright, some by bruise, some by drowning. Death stopped that train. Death put his foot on the brakes, collected the tickets, seized the royal mail-bags, and horrified the world. The bridge broke. What a text for a sermon!' Mr. Talmage then paused to explain that it was not his intention to draw from the disaster a moral *apropos* of Sabbath-breaking, but to take a broad and Christian view of the catastrophe. 'Learn first,' he continued, 'that God is mightier than science, and that science ought to be reverential. General Hutchings, the supervisor of railroads in Scotland, said that the Tay Bridge was safe beyond all necessity, and yet under a blast from God's nostrils 2000 feet of it gave way. Science says 'I can do anything.' It makes the Creator a superfluity. Yea, it proposes to build a bridge over into the next world. And men start to cross this bridge drawing trains of hope behind them, when behold! midway the Lord blows upon it, and they are lost. Learn in the next place that a bridge which doesn't reach clear across is of no use. The stability of the abutment on the Fife side of the River Tay tempted the train to destruction. We want a complete bridge across the river of death. Thank God, we have one!

business done in Brooklyn. Many of the principal streets are shockingly paved—I mean "cobbled." Let any one take a horse-and-trap and drive the full length of Fulton-street, some seven or eight miles, all in one long straight line except the first mile from the ferry, and the shaking and the bumping he will surely get he will retain a recollection of as long as he lives.

Its abutments are quarried from the Rock of Ages, its timbers are hewn from Calvary, and it is nailed with nails from the Cross!
"'In the third place, learn that all travellers ought to have spiritual insurance. The world goes on wheels. Railroad travelling is every day increasing. Soon the solemn silence of Palestine will be broken by the conductor's shout, "All aboard for Jerusalem," "Ten minutes for refreshments at Damascus," "Change cars for the Dead Sea." How long did the passengers at South Norwalk and Ashtabula and on the River Tay have for preparation? Don't let the future of your soul depend upon a frosty rail or a drunken switchman. Between the top of a bridge and the bottom of a river is a small space in which to prepare for a residence of five hundred thousand million centuries.'
"In the last place Mr. Talmage implored his hearers to learn from the railroad disaster that Death was no respecter of persons. There were on the train, he said, one first-class coach, two second-class coaches, and four for third-class travellers. 'I don't know which went first, but they all went down. How complete the democracy of travel; how complete the democracy of the graveyard! There is no first, second, or third class with Death. He stalks into the house at Gad's Hill and says, "I want that novelist." He enters Windsor Castle and says, "I want that Prince Consort." He walks into the almshouse and says, "Give me that pauper." And in the howling of the winter storm he stood on the Tay Bridge and cried, "Give into my cold bosom those railway passengers!"'
"His sermon finished, Mr. Talmage requested Mr. Morgan to play on the organ the 'Dead March from Saul,' which request Mr. Morgan though evidently taken by surprise, promptly complied with."

VIEW ON THE HUDSON RIVER.
West Point Landing.

CHAPTER II.

TO NIAGARA.

Decoration Day in New York—The city *en fête*—Processions and speech-making—Troops of darkies—Starting West—The Hudson River—A procession of canal barges—Bringing grain from Chicago—The Hudson River in the autumn—The scenery about West Point—The Catskill Mountains—American patriotism—The home of Washington Irving—A seminary for young ladies—The diet of American ladies at college—The ice harvest of the Hudson—Brick-making—The white-paint nuisance again—Albany—Its new State Capitol—Utica—A dinner off a cigar—Railway travelling in America—Parlour cars and sleeping cars—Examining tickets—Conductors' checks—Buying and selling—A parlour car pantry—The baggage check system—Its great convenience to the traveller—Niagara.

THE thirtieth day of May is known as Decoration Day[1] in

---

[1] Called also Memorial Day.

America. It is a national holiday set apart annually for respecting the memories of those soldiers who perished in the late rebellion—a day which is kept sacred all over the United States, when flowers are placed on the graves of the departed and their statues and monuments are publicly and formally decorated. This day is right religiously observed in the Empire City. Speeches are made and processions organized,—the various "posts" of the Grand Army of the Republic are paraded before the mayor; certain civic organizations with their bands accompanied by distinguished citizens in their carriages, and waggons filled with ladies carrying baskets of flowers to decorate the soldiers' graves in the public cemeteries, join the column of the Grand Army and are reviewed by his worship likewise; the whole city, in short, turns out *en masse* to do honour to the illustrious dead.[2] Now it so happened that Decoration Day occurred on the second day after that of our first arrival in the Empire City. On Thursday morning, May 30, 1878, we found New York decked out in gayest attire, flags flying in all directions, stands erected for viewing the processions, everybody rushing about as if everybody was mad; indeed, such evidences were there this day of "a real high old time" in this beautiful Metropolis of the West, that though we had fully made up our minds to make a start in the morning for California, we determined to wait over the day, for it would never have done to have gone away and missed seeing the festivities with which it would be celebrated.

The "exercises" of the day were commenced with a special performance of sacred music upon the chimes of Trinity Church, which, sending forth various hymn-tunes to be found in our "Hymns Ancient and Modern," delighted crowds of listeners assembled in the street below. At the same time the

---

[2] I think there is nothing that brings out more forcibly the keen patriotism of the American people than this their annual observance of the festival of Decoration Day. Not only in New York, but in Boston Philadelphia, Washington, St. Louis, Cincinnati, New Orleans, etc., this day is regularly celebrated, when every cemetery is visited, every soldier's monument is decorated, and not a grave of those who died for their country is omitted to be honoured. In the evening there is generally a memorial "service" held in some suitable spacious building, when the "exercises" take the form of patriotic addresses and songs.

ceremonies of publicly decorating the statues of Abraham Lincoln and Lafayette were taking place in Union-square, when in the presence of an enthusiastic multitude and an array of military a little more floral decoration was formally added to the already profusely-adorned statue of Lincoln, and an oration delivered by Major-General Schulyer Hamilton; after which the statue of the French hero was publicly draped with the tricolor, and his head crowned with laurel, and then another oration was delivered by General M. T. MacMahon.

UNION SQUARE, NEW YORK.

The equestrian statue of General Washington in the same square was next proceeded with, and very profuse and elaborate were the decorations of this the chief monument in the Empire City, mostly consisting of moss, festoons of azaleas, roses, immortelles, rhododendrons, and palm-leaves from Florida. (This monument is decorated every year on Decoration Day by an association of Washington and West Washington Market dealers, formed in 1877 for the purpose.) On one side of the 4-ft.-high pedestal supporting the statue was wrought in flowers the motto, "1777-1878.

THE FATHER OF HIS COUNTRY." On the other side were the words, "THE IMMORTAL WASHINGTON." Near the statue a stand was erected, and here I believe enthusiastic *amatores patriæ* made speeches till they were black in the face: but I did not stay to listen and be fired by their patriotic remarks.

Other statues and monuments were visited and decorated, and then a procession of regiments of soldiers and sailors, battalions of telegraph messengers and members of the Fire Brigade, "disabled comrades" in barouches and a few survivors of the War of 1812, and many decked-out floral waggons containing a number of ladies, paraded the principal streets, and were lustily cheered by a patriotic mob. There were troops of white men and troops of "colored" men, knickerbockered Zouaves and short-trousered coal-black darkies, the latter dressed in the most laughable outfits conceivable. Some of the niggers were fine-looking fellows, handsome and soldierly in their blackness. But the curious way they had of marching—rolling themselves along by putting first one shoulder forward, then the other, while they carried their rifles pointed straight up to the clouds and tried to look fierce, was really fine, and evoked from us much laughter; indeed it was the best pantomime I ever saw. In front of one troop of darkies two gray-haired, or rather gray-woolled old negroes stumped along, carrying between them a large open clothes-basket, containing a cloth, which hid something. I believe there was something good to eat inside, which would be pitched into as soon as the marching was over; but this is only a conjecture of mine. A pouring rain came down in the middle of the marching, and lasted till evening. I got a nigger under my umbrella. He had a nose which connected both his whiskers; it stretched more than half-way across his countenance. He was exceedingly communicative, and kindly afforded me information about himself and his coloured brethren marching by, whom he evidently considered the flower of the army. He grinned and showed his teeth at them; he stamped and kicked and shouted "Golly!" many times when he caught sight of his old comrades and the regiment to which he once belonged. These troops of niggers exhibited a rare and unique collection of noses, the breadth of some of them was really too ridiculous.

Their bands were out of time and tune, and the airs they played were, I should say, with the exception of "Nancy Lee," composed by the two gray-woolled old gentlemen above-mentioned.

I will now ask the reader to accompany me across the continent to San Francisco, on a trip which I took with my friend (already referred to) in the year 1878,—part of which I took again myself in 1879. And first we will set out for Niagara.

DAY-BOAT, HUDSON RIVER.

May 31, 1878.

There are two routes by which the Niagara Falls are generally reached from New York. Either the Erie Railroad is taken direct (445 miles), or one can proceed by boat up the Hudson River or by railway along its eastern bank, for 145 miles, as far as Albany, and from thence take the train for 327 miles *viâ* Buffalo (472 miles in all). It was this latter route that we selected in order to reach the Falls. But the summer navigation season not having yet commenced, we had to content ourselves now with seeing as much as we could of this far-famed river from the crowded window of a Pullman car. Many trips, however, since taken on this river, both in 1878 and 1879, enable me to offer here a few remarks on some of its salient features.

A trip on the Hudson in one of its palatial steamers, among picturesque scenery unrivalled, with a band of music on board, and with the comforts and luxuries of a well-ordered hotel, is one to be remembered. Many persons compare the Hudson with the Rhine, but there are but few points of resem-

DAY-BOAT, HUDSON RIVER.
Another view.

blance between the two rivers. The former is a river on an immense scale. In places it widens to the breadth of some miles. It has large towns on its banks; ships ascend for more than a hundred miles—as far as the city of Hudson, 115 miles from the New York City Hall, though the river steamers ascend to Troy, 151 miles; and during the season many passenger boats ply up and down and continually pass each other in the night, as well as in the day. Scores of canal barges laden with every variety of merchandise, may often be seen lashed together in one long line, tugged by two or more steamers. Once I remember seeing two tugs abreast dragging after them down-stream forty of these barges, which were strung together in eight lots, five in each lot. Following close behind these came a second string of twenty-six, with three steamers tugging them; behind these, again, came a third string of thirty-eight, towed by three steamers likewise. Thus there was a procession of one hundred and four barges in three detachments drawn by eight steam-tugs! These barges are laden with freight, which has come by water all the way from Chicago, nearly fourteen hundred miles inland. (The exact distance of the water route from Chicago to New York is 1379 miles.) They have been loaded at Buffalo on Lake Erie with grain, timber, etc., which have been brought by vessel from Chicago 900 miles across Lakes Michigan, Huron, and Erie, and from Buffalo they have come by the Erie Canal for 350 miles to Albany, whence they have taken the Hudson River to New York. At New York the docks and piers on the East River front of the city, from No. 2 to No. 10 inclusive, are set apart by statute for the accommodation of these boats, except during the months of January and February, and part of March (till March 5), when they are open to all classes of shipping. From 4000 to 6000 barges come to New York annually *viâ* the Erie Canal and Hudson River, the majority of them loaded with wheat, barley, oats, timber, and malt. A canal boat laden with grain may be valued at about 2400*l*. sterling. It holds about as much as can be got into twenty-two railway waggons; that is, about 165,000 feet of lumber, or 7800 bushels of wheat.

It is not now in the late spring, nor is it in summer, that the Hudson River is seen at its best. But in the autumn, when its well-timbered banks are clothed with those rich and glorious tints; when the maples, elms and oaks have put on their autumnal dress, and their leaves have turned to bright crimson and gold; when the whole of this part of the country, in truth, is decked in the gayest and most brilliant colours—*then* is the time to see the Hudson, and a more beautiful and inspiring sight it would be hard indeed to imagine. See this river in October, about the second or third week if possible,

VIEW ON THE HUDSON RIVER.

and the sight you will then witness will not soon fade from the memory.

There is one part of the Hudson which recalls a recollection of the Rhine above Coblenz, and this is at West Point, fifty miles above New York, where the river, contracting into a narrow channel, forces its way through a fine mountainous gorge. Here is centred scenery at once glorious and impressive in the extreme. Between West Point—where is established an important military academy—and Albany, the Catskill Mountains come into sight on the west bank, forming one of the most striking views on this noble river. Distant eight miles away they rise a huge bold barrier, averaging 3000 feet in height, towering abruptly out of the plain which stretches between them and the river. They are covered from top to bottom with one dense forest of timber. The Hudson does not abound in legendary lore; yet here, here among the Catskills has been laid the scene of one of the most popular legends of the day—it is the legend of poor Rip van Winkle, who fell into bad hands and took his nap of twenty years in the Sleepy Hollow of the Catskill Mountains. The spot is still shown were Rip played his game of nine-pins with those strange-looking people, and quaffed the potent nectar. It lies in a deep dark glen, nestled among the wildest mountain scenery, and seems just the proper place for bogies and hobgoblins.

But if the Hudson abounds not in legendary lore; if, too, this river, the (so called) " Rhine of America," cannot boast of

"Chiefless castles breathing stern farewells
From grey but leafy walls, where ruin greenly dwells,"

still it is, from the Americans' point of view, more historically interesting and dear to them than all the legends and "chiefless castles" in the world put together, and only naturally so, for it was here, on the banks of the Hudson, that some of the most important scenes were enacted during the struggle of the American people for independence. Forts Lee, Washington, Clinton, and Montgomery; also West Point (called the " Gibraltar of America "), Jeffrey's Hook, the villages of Tappan and Haverstraw—all these are points on this river as indelibly engraven in the memories of our

Transatlantic friends as any battlegrounds in history in which we as a nation take equal patriotic pride. And the Americans are an intensely patriotic people—of this we may be well assured. Their patriotism is shown by the veneration they pay to the memory of George Washington, by the zealous way they annually celebrate their Decoration Day, and, one might also say, their Independence Day, or Fourth of July ;—for which, indeed, all old sores being now completely healed and forgotten, we ought to give them all the honour and credit that is due.

There are some places on the Hudson which are interesting from another point of view. Thus there is Sing Sing, famous for its convict prison ; also Irvington, noted as being the home of Washington Irving, the "father of American literature." Irving's house, called Sunnyside, stands a short distance from the river, hidden among thick shrubberies, and is covered with ivy grown from a sprig which Sir Walter Scott is said to have presented to Irving when he was at Abbotsford. There is also the city of Poughkeepsie,—the Indian (Mohegan) *Apo-keep-sinck*, the "safe and pleasant harbour,"—seventy-five miles above New York, where is Vassar College, the celebrated seminary for ladies. At this college 300 young women "are educated in the fullest sense of the word." They are taught Greek and Latin extensively, also physics, physiology, mental and moral philosophy, and they have museums of geology, natural history and botany, a laboratory for chemistry, an observatory, a gymnasium, and a riding-school. According to *Scribner's Magazine*, this is what they eat : " Two hundred pounds of beef, mutton, or lamb, or seventy shad for dinner daily, after one hundred and twenty-five pounds of steak for breakfast. They consume two hundred and seventy to three hundred and fifty quarts of milk per day ; from seventy-five to one hundred pounds of butter daily ; one half-barrel of granulated sugar, six pounds of coffee, and three to four pounds of tea for the same time. Canned fruit of all kinds is eaten largely. Twice a week they do away at dinner with one hundred and sixty quarts of ice-cream. Farinaceous food abounds. Two articles, with bread and butter, are always supplied at tea. Twice a day they have some acid. Winter brings buckwheat and rice cakes, and twenty barrels of syrup are used in a year." [3]

One of the most important industries connected with the Hudson River is the annual gathering and storing away of its ice during the winter months, so as to meet the summer

THE STORMKING ROCK, HUDSON RIVER.

requirements of the people of the Empire State. As you sail along the river, you see stationed at various points on each shore enormous (and very unsightly) timber warehouses,

[3] Quoted from "American Pictures," by the Rev. Samuel Manning.

The *Philadelphia Ledger* affords us further interesting information as to what is eaten and drunk by the young ladies at this college. It says: " In the last collegiate year (1879-80), 303 Vassar girls have consumed forty-five tons of fresh meats, two tons and a half of smoked meats, two tons

standing close to the water's edge. These have been erected for the purpose of receiving the ice, which is piled up in them in huge blocks, and kept there till it is wanted. There are from one to two or three of these ice-houses stationed at forty-one points along the river, and some of them are capable of holding from 10,000 to 65,000 tons each. The ice crop of the Hudson was a comparative failure during the winter of 1879-80, and a great number of hands, something like eleven or twelve thousand, were thrown out of employ in consequence. The companies had to go to remote places for their usual supply, such as Lake Champlain, and the Adirondack lake region, and this naturally caused a great increase in the price of the article, at which the consumers were not slow to grumble. Nearly a million tons of ice were procured from Lake Champlain last winter by New York and Hudson River companies, and about 800,000 tons from the Adirondack lake region. There were 67,500 tons harvested in the immediate vicinity of Troy, of which 46,500 tons were sold to the New York dealers. Ice was sold in New York this summer (1880) to small consumers at the rate of 4s. per week for a daily supply of from eighteen to twenty pounds; to large consumers the cost was at the rate of 30s. per ton, perhaps a little under. This was the retail price per ton in New York, the wholesale price being 20s. The Troy dealers charged 3s. per week to families, and 2s. per 100 lbs. to restaurants, marketmen, etc. where a large quantity was required at a time. There were 10,000,000 tons of ice harvested in the United States for summer use during the winter of 1878-79.

Brick-making is another important industry connected with the Hudson River. There were 175 brickyards in operation last spring between the towns of Tarrytown

of poultry, three tons of fish, a ton and a half of salt-fish, and five barrels of mackerel. Also 25,800 clams, 442 gallons of oysters, five barrels of pork, 225 barrels of flour, over two tons of buckwheat, thirty-six bushels of beans, 8409-dozen eggs, 14,740 pounds of butter, 93,602 quarts of milk, 252 barrels of apples, 3823 pounds of grapes, 8005 bananas, 13,846 lemons, 22,611 oranges, 307 cans of potted meats, 154 jars of raspberry jam, 211 gallons of apple sauce, 326 boxes of sardines, 1141 pounds of hickory nuts, 1919 bushels of potatoes, six barrels of onions, 468 gallons of molasses and syrups, etc."

and Troy,—that is within a distance of 123 miles,—these varying in the productive capacity of from 20,000 to 150,000 bricks per day.

The banks of the Hudson are beautifully wooded throughout, and studded with thousands of pretty villas, the suburban retreats of the wealthy merchants of New York, and of other adjacent cities. Here "art and nature"—to quote from an American journal—"so rival each other that one is at a loss which most to praise." But though this may be so, it must not be overlooked that the beauty of this river is sadly marred by a nuisance already referred to, one that blurs all natural scenery in this part of the country—I mean the huge staring white-paint advertisements of pills, plasters, etc., which here figure up as prominently as usual. Who is there who does not call to mind that conspicuous notice relating to "GERMAN LAUNDRY SOAP" planted at the base of the Palisades on the west bank of the river, and which can be plainly read from the opposite shore, though the river must be here more than a mile wide at least? Other enormous notices there are, of a similar nature, in the neighbourhood of West Point. It really makes one feel indignant when one sees the beauties of Nature so dishonoured by such nauseous embellishments from the paint-pot.

Arriving at Albany, the prosperous capital (political) of the State of New York, we put up at the Delevan House, near the station. There is nothing particular here to detain the traveller. A stroll through the city, a visit to the famous Dudley Observatory, a look at the marble walls of the new State Capitol in course of erection,—a building which is causing the unfortunate tax-payers a terrible sum of money,—is sufficient. The Capitol, it may be mentioned, was begun twelve years ago, in 1868. Already it has cost 1,920,136*l.* It will cost a further sum of 700,000*l.* before it is finished. Governor Cornell, in his Message to the State Legislature delivered at Albany on the 6th of last January, held out a hope that the work would be completed before 1883. Originally it was to have cost only 800,000*l.*

After breakfast next morning (June 1st) we took the 9.30 train for Niagara, distant 328 miles from Albany. On the way we obtained views of modern Rome, Verona, Syracuse, Utica, Frankfort, Amsterdam, Waterloo, Geneva, and Rochester. For the first hundred miles we followed the course of the Mohawk River, through pretty, wooded scenery. We saw many turtles on the rocks, both in and beside the river. At Utica, in the middle of the day, we all turned out to dine—except one old gentleman in our car, who preferred remaining behind and contenting himself with dining off his cigar. He had a peaceful chew all to himself while we did full justice to the good things at the station *buffet*.

And now a little about railway travelling in America. Let us take our train to-day from Albany to Niagara—or rather to Buffalo, twenty-two miles from Niagara, for here we leave the main-line, our train dividing, half going with us to "the Falls" and the other half to Chicago, 837 miles from Albany. There is first the engine, whose weight is forty tons. Behind it come the baggage-vans (two in number to-day), which are generally placed next the engine. Behind these is the mail-van, containing all the letters. It has a little letter-box at the side, called a "despatch-box," into which one can slip a newspaper or letter at any time during the journey, and have it duly "mailed." Every mail train carries a despatch-box, and people are frequently running up and posting their letters in this way. Behind the mail-van come four passenger carriages—or "cars," as we must call them in this country. This makes up a fairly long train, for the American car is much longer than the ordinary English carriage, being about sixty feet in length. It is possible to walk through the train from one end to the other, beginning with the first baggage-van behind the engine and so on through the passenger cars till you can walk no further, and here, at the end of the train, you can stand at the doorway of the last car and admire the receding view. There are no platforms at the sides, and there are but two doors to a car, one at each end. I have met with the English form of railway carriage only once in America, and that was on the Old Colony Railroad, which runs between Fall River, Taunton, and Boston.

Now the general effect of our engine is extraordinary.

Massive and clumsy-looking, it has a monster black funnel resembling a wine-strainer, very wide at the top and tapering towards the bottom. It is called a "smoke-stack," not a funnel. In like manner, you seldom hear an engine called an "engine," but a "locomotive." (You "take the cars" to this or that place, not the "train." You "mail" a letter, you never "post" it.) Below, in front, is the large "cow-catcher." Its name suggests its use, and it is

ENGINE AND CARS.

composed of wooden palings. The catcher presents a formidable appearance in the engine's architecture, and is the width of its entire front. Before the funnel is attached a large head-light, or lamp, wherewith to light up the track at night and enable the driver to stop the train quickly if a cow or other animal should be lying in the way, which, as we shall see further on, is sometimes the case. This might happen indeed at any time, for the railways in America are almost invariably unenclosed, being laid over meadow-land and farm-land, and often along the streets of a town, without any protection being placed to prevent the track from being encroached upon. At a street or road-crossing, a notice such as "Mind the locomotive," or "Look out for the cars,' will be put up to warn people; but it is the exception to find a hedgerow or fence planted, or a row of hurdles laid down, to prevent cattle from straying on to the metals. Behind the funnel is a bell, which is rung loudly by the driver when approaching or leaving a station, so as to clear the track. It serves also as a guard's whistle, such a thing being unknown in America. The clamour that is made on nearing an important station, when the bells attached to a number of engines are all clanging away in different keys, is perfectly deafening; but when one is slowly rung, it sounds like a call to prayer.

The cars are not divided into first, second, and third classes. All are equal—at least are supposed to be—out here. If a distinction does exist, it is one of dollars; but not about Boston, however, for there will be found the true aristocracy of the country. One's position in society is not measured according to a superabundance or a deficiency of the "almighty dollar," among the "upper ten" of Boston and neighbourhood. Your neighbour in the railway car will address you with "sir," and you will be careful to address him back likewise. You must be very polite and say "sir" to every man and "ma'am" to every woman, and then you will get on. Even the conductor or guard who comes round so often to take a look at your ticket, you must treat with great civility, for bear in mind he is a gentleman, and expects to be regarded as such. (Some of the best men in the country have been railway conductors in their day.) On no account attempt to "tip" him, as you would do the porter or the guard in the Old Country. *You would never attempt it a second time.* But you can fee your darkie attendant with impunity, and be sure that the poor fellow will pocket what you give him with avidity. Any small trifle will suffice. There is but little "tipping" in the United States, and this is one of the very few instances that could be mentioned.

Pullman cars are generally used on the American railways,

and where they are not called by the name of Pullman they are constructed and fitted in a similar manner. There are two kinds—the drawing-room or "parlor" car, and the palace sleeping-car. The former would answer to our first-class, for a slight extra charge is made for riding in it. With it, as well as with the sleeping-car, we are in a measure acquainted in England; but with the common or ordinary car we are not familiar. As of course with every sort of American railway car, you can promenade the whole length of it. The seats, two in a section, all face one way, namely the engine. But if the section in front of you is unoccupied, you can, if you like, appropriate it with your legs by turning round the back of the seat on its hinges, and lying at full length. (On the Pennsylvania Railroad, however, notices are put up in the car informing you that this is "positively prohibited.") In every car there is a large pitcher of iced water, which affords the cooling beverage by means of a turned tap. The Americans are, in both summer and winter, great iced water drinkers. Indeed they are always drinking iced water.

The arrangements in the sleeping-cars are so excellent that they leave nothing to be desired. In every such car there are separate lavatories for ladies and gentlemen. There are generally twelve sleeping sections, six a side, and every section contains an upper and a lower berth. Such a car is not unfrequently termed a "palace drawing-room *and* sleeping-car," and not inappropriately, for the internal fittings, the gildings, and the paintings, are of the highest order in point of elegance and taste; besides, a transformation is effected, when the berths have been made up, by the car being converted from a dormitory into a sitting-room, and as a sitting-room it is used throughout the day till bed-time, when the berths are again made up. The lower berth of your section is constructed upon the two seats of the section, which are *vis-à-vis*, an extra board being placed in between them. During the day the sheets, mattresses, pillows, etc., which go to make up two comfortable beds, are hidden away in the upper berth overhead, and are so concealed inside the beautifully-gilded case forming the front, that anyone who had never before been inside a sleeping-car would not be aware there was a berth overhead, unless informed of the fact. In the evening the mulatto attendant comes round and makes up the berths, producing the wooden partitions—which enclose and divide you from the sections on both sides of your own—and the curtain belonging to your section, which, when hung up in front, is found to be sufficiently large to conceal entirely both the upper and lower berths. It is advantageous, sometimes, to travel in a sleeping-car with a friend, so that he may share your section with you, for it is not at all pleasant if some rough kind of fellow, whether clean or honest you cannot tell, is put in along with you, especially if he is allotted the upper berth, and has to climb up over yours when he wishes to get into his own. In such a case, if you have not taken the precaution to hide away your valuables, but have innocently left them in the pockets of your clothes, which you have hung upon the pegs above, he would, were he feloniously inclined,—and really you cannot tell who may be put in the section with you,—have an opportunity for a quiet plunder all to himself, and this he probably would not find difficult to avail himself of. But your berth is roomy and wide, so that it is better to take everything in with you, and to make use of the two pegs you will find provided inside; or else you may stow as much as you can into the innermost corners of your berth, where you can be sure all will be safe. Thus protected from the vulgar gaze by the sufficient curtain you can go straight to bed. Or, if you find you have not enough room to accomplish this, you can do what I saw a young mother do to her baby-boy one night. She had not room, I suppose, to undress the little child behind the folds of the curtain, so she took him to the far end of the car, and there put on his night-things behind the scenes, together with her own, and afterwards toddled him up the car—both mother and son clad in white linen tunics—and popped him behind the curtain. This successfully accomplished, the mother herself then disappeared from view.

The two outside pegs at the top of your upper berth are sometimes appropriated by the occupant of the berth under you, who will calmly hang up his things on them if he finds he has not room to do so on his own pegs. The awkwardness of this arrangement is felt when the occupant of the lower berth gets up in the morning before you do, and you happen to be fast asleep overhead, and he has to clamber up on to your bed to unhook his things from the pegs should they chance to have become entangled on them. This once happened in my own case, when I was travelling alone. I was fast asleep at the time, but was suddenly awakened from my slumbers by finding someone on the top of me—a great hulking fellow who had actually crawled up on to my bed to reach down his "pants" from the pegs aloft.

A new conductor comes "on board" the train at each division of the line, and proceeds at once to walk through the cars and examine all the tickets. After he has inspected your ticket, which you purchased at the railway company's office or at your hotel before starting, he will pocket it, and give you in exchange a check, which you are to keep till you have passed over his division into the next one, when the conductor of that division will in his turn give you a check, and receive for it the check of the conductor of the preceding division; and thus it is through the other divisions till you come to your journey's end. If you want to "stop over" at any intermediate station, you can do so by asking the conductor to endorse your ticket, or to give you a "stop-over check," unless the ticket you bought at starting was a "limited" one, as this would not allow you to break the journey, except at specified points. Should you be travelling by a "huckleberry train," or one that stops at every station, the chances are you are liable to have your ticket examined pretty frequently, especially if many people are taken up at the several stations, for the conductor invariably comes round after every single stoppage and diligently looks about—sometimes without success—for all the passengers who have got up on to the various cars, and among such a number as he has to look after he is just as likely as not to become confused and forget, and to repeatedly ask you to show him your check. But you are saved the worry and bother that this frequent examination would entail by simply attending to the wording of your ticket, or rather your check, which will have a notice like "Please keep this check in sight" printed upon it on one side; on the other side all the stations of the divisions and

F

the distances between each. Indeed the strange, not to say familiar action of the conductor upon presenting you with the check will show you what to do with it without need of further explanation, for instead of placing it in your hand, he will suddenly "go for" the band of your hat, and having successfully planted it there he will pass on to the next passenger and present him with his check in the same sort of fashion. Thus the conductor is saved trouble, and the passenger likewise, for every male passenger having his check visibly stuck in his hat, all the conductor has to do is to cast his eye round the car and see if there is a hat unprovided with one, and, if so, to pitch upon the wearer of that hat and ask him for his check. Once, when travelling on the "Shore Line" from New York to Boston, the conductor of one of the divisions of that line presented me with a check, one side of which was printed as follows:

A good deal of buying and selling goes on during a long railway journey. There is always someone walking through the train, who comes round offering to sell you all sorts of delicacies, from a packet of popcorn to—well, the latest English or American novel. To-day, for example, on our journey to Niagara, in the far corner of the car behind ours there was a large box, which was presided over by a boy, and in this box were stored away oranges, bananas, books, newspapers, cigars, etc., and every now and then the boy came round with his books and bananas, and asked us if we wanted to buy. Not only so, but he came and distributed printed slips to everyone, first in one car, then in another, on which was announced some startling novelty that he was about to bring round for the general inspection. One of these sets of slips contained the following information: "GREAT NATURAL CURIOSITY, IVORY THAT GROWS ON TREES. FOR SALE BY THE NEWSAGENTS ON THIS TRAIN, WHO WILL CALL ON YOU FOR THIS CIRCULAR, AND GIVE YOU AN OPPORTUNITY TO EXAMINE THE ARTICLE." "The Article" was then brought round for examination, and specimens dealt out to each person, whether wanted or not, after which they were all collected again, both the slips and the "Natural Curiosity,"—for none of us felt inclined to buy,—and then the same thing was tried on in the next car, and so on. The next wonder brought round for sale, previously announced by the usual distribution of printed slips, was some "Spanish Kisses," price one cent per box. The "kiss" was a poisonous compound of a kind of hardbake, the latest poison from New York, very bad for a cent.

In the parlour car we occupied to-day a nigger presided over a pantry which was at one end of it, and dealt out for consumption fruit, strawberries-and-cream, tea, coffee, milk, lemonade, gin, sherry cobblers, sour-smash cocktails, gin cocktails, mint juleps, and an immense variety of American iced-drinks. He seemed to have a ready and endless supply of everything in this line of trade.

One of the greatest conveniences experienced in travelling on the American railways is the facility with which you can go any distance, no matter how far, with several articles of baggage, and yet not be put to the trouble of looking after them from one end of the journey to the other—no, not even if you have to change trains several times on the way. The companies over whose lines of rail you travel undertake the responsibility of delivering up your luggage to you safely at your journey's end,—you must hand it over into their care, and allow them to transfer it to its destination without let or hindrance on your part,—rendering themselves liable for the loss of or injury to any article to an amount not exceeding one hundred dollars. You are thus saved an infinite amount of bother and trouble, and though you may be a little diffident at first and inclined rather to speculate on the chances as to whether you will ever see your belongings again, still there is no need for any anxiety, for you may rest assured they are in safe hands, and that you will find everything safe and sound when you come to your journey's end. Let me in a few words explain how this is managed.

We will take, for instance, the two almost extreme points of the United States, Boston and San Francisco, the distance between the two places being 3440 miles. You are at the Brunswick Hotel, Boston, and intend starting this evening by the six o'clock train for the Golden City (San Francisco), where you will put up at—suppose we say the Palace Hotel. But it is not your intention to go straight through to San Francisco without stopping and seeing something "by the way." Indeed you intend not only to spend three or four days at Chicago, but to see Omaha as well, and you have also planned for yourself a few days' "hunting" on the Rocky Mountains in the neighbourhood of Laramie—one of the very best sporting centres you could select. Now, having resolved to accomplish all this, you begin to think it would be infinitely more convenient to send on some of your heavier luggage to San Francisco at once, and your gun-case to Laramie, and one of the two portmanteaus you are taking might, you think, be despatched immediately to Omaha, so that you may be saved the trouble of having to look after it at Chicago, which is 490 miles this side of Omaha; besides, you recollect you have to "change cars" four times on the journey, namely at Albany, Chicago, Omaha, and Ogden. Well, then, having arranged all your plans, and intending to start this evening on your travels, the first thing you do is to procure your railway ticket, which you can do at the station (a day or two beforehand if you like), or at a railway ticket office in the city,—the Boston and Albany Railroad, which is the line you intend taking, has its ticket office at No. 232, Washington-street,—having, I say, secured your ticket, you make a start for the railway station, taking with you two large corded boxes, a gun-case, and two small portmanteaus. On reaching the station you take all your luggage to the baggage-room, and tell the baggage-man there that you want two large boxes transported direct to San Francisco, a gun-case to Laramie, a portmanteau (" valise," as the Americans term it) to Omaha—but the other portmanteau you intend taking charge of yourself, as you will have need of this in your "sleeper." First the baggage-man will require you to show him your ticket (a through "unlimited" one to San Francisco), which you must have provided yourself with beforehand, otherwise he will not "check" your luggage for you. This done, he will take the two corded boxes you wish transported direct to your journey's end, and fasten to each a leather strap, to each of which is affixed a small brass plate, which is numbered, and has "Boston" and "San Francisco" plainly stamped on to it; at the same time he will hand over to you two duplicate brass plates (*minus* the straps), having numbers corresponding with those of the checks which have been attached to your boxes. The gun-case, which is to go to Laramie, has a check likewise attached to it, but one with a different number, and with the words "Boston" and "Laramie" impressed on it; a duplicate check for this item of luggage, with corresponding number, etc., will be handed to you; the portmanteau for Omaha is treated in a similar manner, and its duplicate check also handed to you. Thus you find yourself in possession of four small brass plates corresponding with those which have been strapped on to your four articles of luggage: you put them all in your waistcoat pocket and start forth on your journey. When you arrive at Albany (200 miles from Boston), which is the first place where you change cars, you find you have only your one portmanteau to look after, for the railway authorities have charge of the rest of your paraphernalia, and will see them safely transferred into the Chicago train; when you come to Chicago (837 miles further), you find, just before reaching the terminus, that a Chicago baggage-man, who has got on board the train at one of the preceding stations, will come and ask you—as he will ask everyone else in your car, indeed every passenger on the train—if you have any luggage for Chicago, whereupon you show him your portmanteau (the one you took into your sleeping-car), and upon your telling him the hotel you are going to, he will give you a receipt for the portmanteau in the form of a paper ticket, which you keep till you have reached the hotel, where the portmanteau will follow in due course,—if it be not there before you have got there yourself,—and upon handing over the paper ticket to the chief cashier you will receive back your portmanteau. Meanwhile your other articles of luggage have proceeded to their several destinations, namely the other portmanteau to Omaha (490 miles beyond Chicago), the gun-case to Laramie (574 miles further), and the two large corded boxes to San Francisco (1341 miles more). You reach Omaha a few days afterwards and proceed to the baggage-room at the station, and there find your portmanteau, which will be delivered up to you on presentation of the duplicate brass check given you at New York; you reach Laramie in due course, and find the gun-case, and receive it in like manner; and when you come at last to the Golden City, there you will find your two large boxes, and on presenting your checks they are delivered up to you likewise. A more convenient arrangement, even, than this is to proceed direct to your hotel—whether it be at Omaha, San Francisco, or any other place I have mentioned—and have your luggage sent for, thus saving you the trouble of having to bring it yourself from the railway station. This is done by handing your duplicate brass checks to the chief cashier (at your hotel), who will despatch an *employé* with them to the station baggage-room and have your luggage brought up for you. The railway companies will always retain luggage till it is claimed by the presentment of the proper duplicate checks, there being a baggage-room at every station, where all luggage is deposited.

  This excellent system of checking baggage prevails on every railway in the United States. You can transport your paraphernalia in this way from one remote point to another, over a thousand miles or more, over several companies' lines; your luggage is never lost, you are saved an infinite deal of bother and worry, and you are able to travel about the country with the greatest possible comfort.

At eleven o'clock at night we reach the town of Niagara. Hark! the thundering, deadening roar that fills the air as we pull up at the station and alight from the train. Niagara, a living reality at last! Well, we won't go into ecstasies just yet—not till we have feasted our eyes and found that we are really obliged to.

Running the gauntlet of fourteen hotel runners, each one especially anxious to take us under the shelter of his protection, we managed, after considerable difficulty, to "fix" the 'bus of the Clifton House, the hotel lying on the opposite or Canadian bank of the Niagara River, and were quickly driven off to it. In order to reach the hotel, we had to cross the river below the falls by the Clifton Suspension Bridge, which is thrown over the deep wide gulf at the bottom of which the Niagara whirls along in its headlong career. The grandeur of the scene as we looked down on those two stupendous cataracts when crossing the bridge so short a distance below them, seen as they were in the grim darkness of a moonless night amid the hollow, deadening roar of their waters, is indescribable.

CHAPTER III.

AT THE FALLS.

Impressions of Niagara—View from the Clifton House—The American Fall—The giant Canadian—Abuses of Niagara—"Indian variety" stores—Wholesale despoliation of natural scenery—The white-paint nuisance again—Towers for obtaining views—An irrepressible photographer—An awkward situation—The Niagara Falls Museum—The spider and the fly—Putting on oilskins—Walking under the Canadian Fall—Impressions conveyed—The Centre and American Falls—A sensational trip—The Whirlpool Rapids—A visit to an Indian reservation—A Sunday morning service—Setting out for Chicago—London in Canada—Crossing the Detroit River—Chicago.

June 3rd.

WHEN we awoke this morning, lo, what a sight presented itself! The hollow, deadening roar, which like the sound of distant cannonading had been audible throughout the night, prepared us somewhat for a surprise, but never for a sight like the one we now looked upon. In front, in full view from our window lay Niagara,[1] those two broad cataracts, which, tumbling with awful majesty into that fearfully grand abyss, lost in their own white spray long before ever that abyss is reached, form a picture which, as all the world knows, is wonderful, terrible, and unique.

The Niagara Falls are caused by a sudden breach of the Niagara River, which is the outlet of Lakes Superior, Michigan, Huron, and Erie. The river connects Lake Erie with Lake Ontario, the distance between the two lakes being thirty-six miles. At about twenty-two miles from the former and fourteen from the latter, the Niagara, which is here a mile

---

[1] The Indian (Iroquois) "Thunder of Waters."

At the Falls. 73

and a half wide, meets with an island (Goat Island) seventy-five acres in extent, and divides. Descending thence in rapids with a velocity of thirty miles an hour, part of the river is discharged over a precipice 164 feet in height, with a width of 1200 feet, and part—its main volume—is precipitated 158 feet, with a width of 2400 feet. The former of these cataracts is called the "American" Fall, as it lies wholly

THE NIAGARA FALLS.
From Victoria Point, Canada side.

on the United States—the New York side of the river. The latter was until recently called the Horse-shoe; but a landslip having occurred about the middle of the precipice, which has broken the bend of the curve, the name has become inappropriate, and it is now generally known as the Canadian. That part of the river which eventually throws the bulk of its waters over the American Fall, meets also with an island,

and divides. But this third leap which anon ensues—a fine one withal, and called the Centre Fall—sinks altogether into insignificance before its two giant rivals, the American and the Canadian. Indeed, so close is it to the former and so completely is it dwarfed, that it seems from a distance to be part and parcel of the same fall.

From our window, then, we have a full view of Niagara. A few yards from us is the precipice of the deep wide gorge,

THE AMERICAN AND CENTRE FALLS.

which begins with the Canadian or Horse-shoe Fall half a mile away to the right, and stretching past us to the left is soon spanned by the light handsome suspension bridge, over which we were driven last night. Facing us, on the opposite side of the gorge, is the broad sheet of the American Fall, the clear smooth crest of its bright green wave resembling a rich and beautiful skein of silk. The slow, steady descent of this immense wall of water forms a splendid contrast to the headlong rush of the wild rapids above it, the loud continuing thud with which it meets its fate against the hidden rocks beneath, and the clouds of white vapour showered up around, adding life to a picture which surely can only be eclipsed by one other fall in the known world—its great rival, the giant Canadian. Behind the American Fall can be seen the town of Niagara, with the International Hotel towering conspicuously above the other buildings: to the immediate left is the Prospect Park, walled off from the fall by a low parapet of rock, which enables one to approach close enough to look right over the crest of the descending cataract. An iron carriage-bridge, 360 feet in length, connects the town of Niagara—that is the mainland—with an island called Bath Island, which rises in the middle of the rapids; and further to the right another carriage-bridge connects this with Goat Island, which is densely wooded, and is the largest island of the group. It faces the Niagara gorge with a sheer precipice, which extends till it meets the great Canadian Fall in the far distance, and this tremendous cataract connects in the form of a half-circle with the bank we are now upon. Not only the two great cataracts themselves, but the rapids—called the Upper Rapids —which commence more than a mile above them, constitute a very marvellous sight, resembling a moving or agitated *mer de glace*.

It seems presumption on my part to attempt to describe Niagara. I cannot hope to satisfactorily depict its sublimity and awful magnificence. The scene may be laid before one by a faithful description in words, and by means of photographs and drawings; but that "sound of many waters," that continuous roar which can be heard twenty miles away, and *is yet so soft* that a conversation can, without straining the voice, be kept up close beside the cataracts, must needs overwhelm a man and encompass him—must indeed be felt by him before he can realize the majesty of the situation. It is computed that 100,000,000 tons of water pass over the Niagara precipice every hour. "It is the drainage of half a continent pouring over a single wall of rock."

From the Clifton House a road runs along the edge of the gorge to the Canadian Fall, and wonderful and magical is the sight as this stupendous cataract is approached! No word-painting, no spontaneous effusion can convey an idea of the terrible grandeur of this the King of Falls. The immense stretch of that fearful, sweeping wave; the slow measured descent into that hellish, boiling abyss; that roar so loud and thundering, yet so soft, so mellow, so permeating; that glorious iris spanning the flood, glistening amid the snow-white clouds of spray that rise hundreds of feet aloft—all this is but a too inadequate portrayal of this wondrous natural phenomenon. It is a sight to be remembered, that mighty, fearful plunge. It is one that can never be forgotten, nor can its impressions ever be effaced.

Thoughts suggest themselves to you as you stand at the edge of the precipice almost within clutching distance of the swift wave of the Canadian Fall passing over the brink to its destruction. That never-ending flow, that incessant mighty roar, are you not reminded of the continuous flow of Time—Eternity—that day which never dies? A thought such as this, with many others, too, fills you as you stand lost in wonder and awe at the tremendous scene around.

To-day being Sunday, we were in a measure free from the annoyances and importunities of hawkers and guides, who are such pests at this place, harassing the stranger as they do from morning till night. Yet the toll nuisances are equally objectionable. The everlasting half-a-dollar demanded of every person approaching the Falls from this or that quarter, is just as rigidly exacted on a Sunday as on any other day of the week. At some places, where fees are required, the hackman who drives you has a private arrangement with the toll-collectors to receive a percentage for himself, often amounting to half the sums charged. It pays to be a hackman at Niagara.[2]

I have been to many show-places in the world, but the "tout" pest is worse at Niagara than at any of them. I know of no place where one is so continually pestered,

---

[2] A table of the "charges to visitors desirous of enjoying a thorough view and inspection of the Falls and their attractions" was given in the late official report—drawn up by Mr. Mowat (the Attorney-General of Ontario) in December, 1879—respecting the abuses of Niagara, which had become so serious as to lead to a suggestion for the formation of an international park around the Falls. The report in question was submitted to the

At the Falls.

where hackmen so incessantly worry you when you want to be at peace, where you are so dogged over every inch of the ground you tread, where guides and photographers, shop-mongers and toll-gatherers—all combine to get as much as they can out of you, besetting you as if you were the only human being besides themselves who ever came near the place. It is the same in the little town of Niagara as it is close to the Falls. You are just as much set upon when you are walking through the streets. Here every other shop is an "Indian variety" store, and every one possesses an attractive-looking young woman ready to pounce upon you, and ask you to buy something or other, and if you begin to hesitate, she will invite you, by way of further inducement to purchase, to step inside her store for one moment and take a look at all the pretty things. But if you are wise you will not be caught in this way. New York prices, which are proverbially high, are low compared with those you must expect, and will find, at Niagara. Indeed, a great many of these so-called "Indian" curiosities are no more Indian than the clothes you are wearing. They are made in New York, and are palmed off on you as Indian.

But worse, far worse than these annoyances is the wholesale, ruthless destruction of the natural beauty of the gorge. Trees, aye, forests have been cut down to make room for unsightly factories, for hotels, museums, drinking saloons and what not. White-paint notices, too, of the usual

Secretary of State at Ottawa, and the table accompanying it, which was published in the *New York Herald* of April 13, 1880, was as follows:

	For a Party of Four Persons.	Of which the cabmen get
The Museum	$2 00	$1 00
Table Rock	4 00	2 00
Burning Spring	2 00	1 00
Prospect Park	2 00	1 00
Upper Bridge	1 50	0 50
Shadow of Rock	4 00	2 00
Goat Island	2 00	Nil.
Cave of Winds	4 00	2 00
Add for hack	3 50	Nil.
Totals	$25 00	$9 50

kind are even here permitted to thrive. On the Canadian side, "RISING SUN STOVE POLISH—BEST IN THE WORLD," meets the eye wherever it turns; and the American or United States side simply revels in "FRASER'S AXLE GREASE," "HERRICK'S PILLS AND PLASTERS," "CRUMBS OF COMFORT FOR WIVES—SOLD BY ALL," "LIGHTNING OIL, SURE CURE FOR PAINS," "BARTLETT'S BLACKING WILL SHINE 'EM UP," etc. Towers are erected at the best points for obtaining views, and a notice-board nailed against a tree will remind you that "THE GRANDEUR AND AWFUL SUBLIMITY OF THE FALLS NOWHERE CAN YOU SEE BUT FROM "—such-and-such tower or point of elevation. And when you have selected your tower, you can, if you feel so disposed, go up and have a view by paying the sum of half-a-dollar, which will enable you as well to gaze at, admire, and buy many stuffed birds and animals, fossils and minerals, Egyptian mummies and half-breed Indian (Tuscarora) beadwork, which you will find collected together and attractively arranged for your inspection at the bottom of the building. A bottle of Niagara-water must really be obtained by the visitor before he leaves the neighbourhood, otherwise it cannot be said that he has "done" the Falls properly.[3]

There are rare opportunities for having your photograph taken, opportunities that should not be missed if you wish to have a background to your portrait which will create a sensation. As you proceed towards the Horse-shoe by the cliff road—and here I allude to a little incident that occurred when I paid a second visit to Niagara—you pass a shanty on your right, outside which is announced, "PICTURES OF PARTIES TAKEN HERE WITH THE FALLS IN THE BACKGROUND." You smile, and think whether it is worth trying. While so engaged, a man comes up and accosts you. He takes off his hat to you, and politely asks if you want your likeness taken

[3] Thanks to the exertions of the late Governor-General of Canada (the Earl of Dufferin) there is a likelihood of Niagara being protected by law from the above-mentioned abuses, through the joint action of the Dominion and the New York State Legislatures. It is proposed to form an international park round the cataracts, so as to restore Niagara as far as possible to its ancient pristine beauty, and, by rescuing it from the hands of the petty land-jobbers, toll-gatherers, hucksters, and sharpers, preserve it as a glorious public resort free and open to rich and poor alike.

THE NIAGARA FALLS. View from Prospect Point, American Side.

to-day, saying, " Now, du jist wait a minute and stand where y' are. Y'll make quite an ilegant pictur', and I'll catch ye right 'andsome." Meanwhile four ladies are approaching from the hotel. You see them, and your courage shrinks, for you do not want to make an exhibition of yourself in their presence; so you decline, and pass on. Photographer, however, not to be outdone, suggests to the ladies that he would be pleased to take the whole lot, "the gentleman and all." A happy thought! a bright idea! But how is this proposal received by the ladies? One bestows on the photographer a withering scowl, which causes him to look ashamed of himself. A second deigns even to reply, telling him to mind his own business. All four of them quicken speed, and hasten in the direction of the Horse-shoe, and you yourself slowly follow with a slight feeling of guilt—or rather, you feel as if you would just like that photographer to taste the tip of your boot.

But the great thing to do on the Canadian side is to put on oilskins, and walk under the Horse-shoe. Close to this Fall is a large curiosity shop, or general museum, called the " Niagara Falls Museum," where waterproof suits are let out to those who desire to go behind the descending mass of water; where, too, you can ascend to an observatory at the top of the building, and (to quote from the museum prospectus) see "one of the most magnificent panoramic views on the face of the earth;" where also is "the finest collection on the continent of America, consisting of upwards of 100,000 specimens, such as birds, animals, minerals, insects, Egyptian antiquities, a whale fifty feet long, and the finest Egyptian mummy in the world;" where also is attached " the beautiful Pleasure Garden, with its fish-pond and fountain, Indian wigwams and summer-houses, living animals, comprising buffaloes, bears, wolves, eagles, etc.," and where (the prospectus adds) " thousands of visitors every year testify to its richness, variety, and beauty, and to the fact that this is *the* place, above all others, for spending a while delightfully, with pleasant memories.—Admittance to the Museum, Observatory, Gardens, and living Animals, only 50 cents." (Before reaching this Museum you see a notice-board informing you that there is on view, in some gardens bordering on the road, "a live buffalo from the Rock*e*y Mountains.") There is generally someone outside waiting to pounce upon passers-by, and induce them to step in and inspect the curiosities, or to dress up in oilskins, and thus "do" the Fall. In my own case a nigger caught me looking at some pretty things in the window, and, spider-like, was down on me in a moment. Beckoning me by putting up his finger, he asked me to "come an' see a vu." As I was in need of photographs at the time, I stepped in to look over, as I thought, a selection

THE UPPER RAPIDS.

of views. Great was my surprise when he handed me some waterproof oilskin leggings, waterproof vest, waterproof head-cape, adding, as he gave them to me, "There y' are, colonel." Then he intimated again that I should follow him : I did so, darkie taking the oilskins along with him. We reached a chamber, a sort of dressing-room, in a far corner of the building, and appropriated chairs opposite one another. My darkie then told me to slip on my suit, first of all showing how it was done by putting on his own. Enveloped from head to foot in overalls, with hoods coming over our heads, leaving visible just the nose, mouth, and eyes, and with oil-skin coat and continuations reaching down to the feet, which were encased in bags, we, my darkie and I, looked like two beautiful beings about to take a trip together in a diving-bell. Darkie seemed pleased, and cried, "Yah, yah!" Waddling out of the house, we had to cross the road to a tower on the opposite side, containing a staircase leading down to the rocks below. A man stopped me as I waddled as swiftly as I could across the turnpike—it was another irrepressible photographer, who wished to take me in my garb, "with the Falls in the background," before I descended, informing me that my Lord This and my Lord That had honoured him with sittings, and wouldn't I do the same "jist as I was"? I told him to wait till I came up again and then I would think about it. Arrived at the bottom of the tower—!— the booming, terrible roar, the fearful, stupefying grandeur of the scene! No expression or collection of epithets can convey a particle of an idea of the sight or the sound—it would be folly to attempt a description. My guide exclaimed, "Look, colonel, look at it! *H*ain't it mighty, *h*ain't it glorious!" "'Tis immense," said I, "'tis really too terrible.—Lead on."

We now crept carefully along the path which lay at the bottom of the precipice on our right, with the boiling caldron of water sharp away on our left, into which we should inevitably have slipped if once we had missed our footing, and fallen. A few steps, and we were under the Fall. As I write I feel the utter hopelessness of attempting any form of language which could give expression to my feelings, or by the aid of which I can convey even a rough idea of the wondrous sight that we now looked upon—that great long vista beneath the arched descending sheet—that measured fall, seeming

"As if God pour'd it from His hollow hand,"—

the thing is too fearful to contemplate, too sublime to grasp. My guide burst into exclamations of wonder and delight, all got up for my special edification, and, grinning broadly, said, "*H*ain't it a vu, colonel ; *h*ain't that scenery for you!" I differed from him, however, and told him that it was undoubtedly an unique and wonderful sight, but that I thought the view he spoke of rather too limited and confined.

From Goat Island, on the opposite side of the gorge, a stairway leads down to the rocks at the foot of the Centre and American Falls. Under the escort, once more, of a guide, and enveloped in a waterproof suit, you can pass behind the entire wave of the Centre Fall till you find yourself confronting the tremendous sweep of the American, the full volume of which pours down, as it were, upon you from the clouds above. The utmost caution must here be exercised in treading from rock to rock, for, encompassed as you are by a veritable whirlwind of driving spray, with gallons of water thundering continuously on to your head, with your eyes perfectly blinded so that you cannot see how or where to step, with merely the guide's hand for a support to prevent you from slipping and being carried away by the fatal current, you find it as much as you can possibly do to keep your balance while endeavouring to secure a firm foothold as you step on to and between rocks covered with two-feet-deep rushing water. But so transported are you with rapture and amazement that you pay little heed to the danger of the moment, though danger there need be none if you only do what the guide tells you. Come what may, you will never forget the thrilling sensations of this trip. It is worth all the trouble, all the risk involved in its accomplishment.—It is also worth the expense, for the charge is but a dollar for guide, dress and all. This is the cheapest dollar's worth in America.

At the top of the stairs you will find another photographer ready waiting to take you in your waterproof suit, dripping wet though you are, before you doff it in the dressing-room. He will throw in part of the Horse-shoe as a background to your portrait.

Besides the Falls themselves, and their immediate surroundings, there is one great sight which the visitor to Niagara must be sure and not overlook. This is the Whirlpool Rapids, about two miles below the Falls. After leaping the precipice the Niagara plunges on down a narrow ravine, which it has hollowed out for itself from the hard limestone rock, for seven miles till it reaches the flat country at Queenstown, the width of this ravine—which Sir Charles Lyell tells us has taken 30,000 years to become excavated, the cataract of the Niagara receding at the rate of one foot

THE WHIRLPOOL RAPIDS.

per year—varying from 300 to 400 yards, and averaging 200 to 300 feet in depth; but so great is the force with which such an immense mass of water is projected over the precipice that for more than a mile it forms an underwater current at the bottom of the river bed, the surface-stream for this distance presenting a comparatively smooth and placid appearance, yet bearing evidence, by its eddying flow, of the swift rush of the torrent beneath. But at the narrowest part of the gorge this under-current rises to the surface, and here occur the famous rapids, where the stream, compressed into the smallest limits, bounds along at a furious rate, seething, raging, roaring, throwing up its waters high into the air, displaying a magnificent series of leaping mountains of white foam, presenting a sight that is simply terrific. By means of an elevator you can descend the cliff (260 feet) to the water's edge. You can also be photographed here if you like, "with the Rapids in the background."

Seven miles from Niagara Falls is the Tuscarora-Indian reservation, where 300 of this tribe live on a territory comprising about 1000 acres. This is among the oldest of the reserved localities assigned to the various Indian tribes, having been established so far back as the year 1780. There are two churches on the reservation, a Baptist and a Presbyterian, and the services in each are performed by ministers supplied by the American Board of Home Missions. One Sunday morning (August 24, 1879), I drove out to the reservation, and attended a service in the Baptist church. The congregation mustered 167, namely 125 men and 42 squaws, the two sexes sitting apart, and, it need scarcely be said, clad in ordinary civilized attire. The men wore black coats and trousers, and were provided with tall beaver hats; the women were brightly dressed, scarlet and green being the predominating colours. I cannot say that I was particularly struck with the cleanly appearance of the tribe, nor indeed with the religious devotion displayed by the members of the congregation who sat around me. All looked as if they had never known what it was to be well washed with soap and water, all sat perfectly still during the service as if they were having their photographs taken, though the majority of them seemed to be fast asleep, and those who were not asleep sat listlessly bolt upright with their eyes half closed. The only one who seemed to take the least interest in what was going on was a squaw, who, sitting near me, bent forward in prayer and paid attention to the sermon, and lustily sang during the hymns like a religious woman that she was. The service was performed in the language of the tribe. The musical portion was rendered by a choir of seven voices, two girls and five men, who sang—and sang very fairly, too—from a gallery, to the accompaniment of a harmonium.

Taking leave of Niagara for a while, we proceeded (June 3rd) on our overland trip.

A run of 120 miles through the province of Ontario brought us, *viâ* Paris, and by Great Western Railway, to London-on-Thames,—in the county of Middlesex,—a prosperous city of 25,000 inhabitants, the capital of its county, and the centre of a famous agricultural district. Here we delayed a few hours ; and a slight acquaintance with the capital now, which afterwards became closer on the occasion of a stay with some friends, enabled me to become familiar with Westminster, Victoria, London and Blackfriars Bridges, Hyde Park, Piccadilly, Kensington, Oxford-street, Regent-street, the Crystal Palace, and Sydenham, etc. The country around is so thickly wooded that London has acquired the name of the Forest City.

Resuming our journey at 6 p.m., we took a through sleeping-car to Chicago, distant from London 394 miles. Passing through, among other places, Glencoe and Chatham, in four hours we came to Windsor. We here had our baggage overhauled before re-entering the States from Canada. This was accomplished while we crossed over the Detroit River, which forms the connecting link between Lakes Huron and Erie, the whole train, barring the engine, being run on to a ferry-boat, split into three divisions and taken over to the other side, while our baggage was examined—very slightly examined during the passage across. Entering Michigan State at Detroit, we arrived there at 10 p.m. We stopped twenty minutes to rush out and get supper, and then, turning in again, soon retired to bed, to wake up in the morning at Chicago.

CHAPTER IV.

WONDERFUL CHICAGO.

A marvellous city—Its growth of fifty years—A commercial position unrivalled—The greatest livestock mart in the world—The great Union Stock Yards—A wonderful sight—Chicago's livestock trade since 1876—The famous packing-houses—Slaughtering on a mammoth scale—The pork packing process—Chicago as a grain market—Her receipts of 1879—The great grain elevators—The pine lumber trade—Manufacturing establishments of the Queen City—The total value of her trade of 1879—The development of the Great West—The United States seventy years ago—The United States to-day—Agricultural statistics—Exports to the United Kingdom—Railway development—Chicago's Grand Pacific Hotel—The five grand hotels of America—Hotel living—The American at table—Iced water and milk—Apple-pie—A national failing—A disagreeable subject—A disgusting sight—An active people—How Chicago was lifted several feet out of the mud—The new waterworks—A drive in the Lincoln Park—Rivalry of the large cities—Boston's opinion of Chicago—A Chicagoan's opinion of New York—What Boston thinks of Troy—What Troy says of the ladies of New York and Boston—Chicago's opinion of herself—An association of bald men.

CHICAGO,[1] a city with a population of nearly half a million, when fifty years ago there were not to be found twenty buildings—not a hundred people in the place! Then, in 1830, a solitary Indian trading-post; now the Metropolis of the North West!

[1] Popularly called the Prairie City, or the Prairie Metropolis; also the Garden City, the Phœnix City, the Lake City, and the Queen City of the Lakes. The name, perhaps, is derived from an Indian word meaning "wild onion," though some persons have interpreted it to mean a certain strong-smelling animal (? a skunk), while others, again, say that it is the Indian name for thunder, or the voice of the Great Manitou. The Chicagoans, however, to be on the safe side, split the difference and say that the word at any rate means something "strong."

The marvellous rapidity of the growth of Chicago is perhaps without a parallel in the history of modern times. Within half a century has this great city sprung into existence; from the smallest of beginnings it has become one of the most populous cities in the Union.[2] Not a mere collection of "skin" buildings, indeed, sparsely scattered over a large extent of country. But with its streets closely and solidly laid out; with their long lines of iron, stone and brick business blocks of four and five stories high; with an appearance of massiveness and stability pervading the whole place, Chicago more resembles a European than an American city, indeed I do not believe there is a city in America that can be compared with it. And when we think of the disastrous fire of 1871, and look at the Chicago of to-day; when we realize the fact that the best portion of the city, three-and-a-half square miles in extent, was consumed,—17,450 buildings in all, the damages estimated at 40,000,000*l.* sterling,—and then call to mind the magnificence and solidity with which the new city has risen out of the ashes of the old wooden one, we cannot but admire the marvellous activity, the enterprising spirit of determination displayed by the inhabitants in restoring their city so thoroughly and in so masterly a manner as they have done. Three years later than the great fire—in 1874—another terrible fire broke out, when 800,000*l.* worth of property was destroyed, including 800 buildings (covering sixty acres) which had escaped the previous conflagration. But now the building law of Chicago forbids the erection of any frame building, or of any wooden roofs or wooden cornices, within the city limits. It also directs how commercial buildings, factories, hotels, theatre-houses, etc., should be constructed, how they are to be protected from becoming overheated, and prescribes that every wall shall be of a certain thickness. Possibly the building law of Chicago is permitted to be evaded as commonly as is that of New York; but there is this to be said of the Queen City,—that

[2] In 1830 the population of Chicago was 80; in 1835, 1006; in 1840, 4479; in 1845, 12,088; in 1850, 29,960; in 1855, 83,509; in 1860, 109,206; in 1865, 187,446; in 1870, 298,977; in 1875, 450,000; now (1880) its population is a little over 500,000.

of the houses which have been erected since the great fires of 1871 and 1874, there are none that look as if they were about to topple over. There are no "skin" buildings in modern Chicago.

It is to its supreme position as a commercial centre that Chicago owes its prosperity. Lying at the south-west corner of Lake Michigan, at the head of the navigation of the great inland lakes—a seaport several hundred miles from the sea, yet in direct water communication with the Atlantic;[3] with

[3] The distance by water from Chicago to the open sea viâ the great lakes and Montreal, is 2050 miles ; to New York, 1397 miles. During the season of lake navigation of 1879—from May 1 to November 30— Chicago had more than twice as many arrivals and clearances of vessels as New York had during the same period. The following table will show how Chicago figures as a shipping port when compared with New York and four other leading ports, during the period just mentioned :

	Arrivals.		Clearance.	
	No.	Tonnage.	No.	Tonnage
New York	4386	4,826,473	5551	5,044,316
Boston	2287	1,259,209	2619	1,440,907
Baltimore	2080	1,552,278	2413	1,747,793
Philadelphia	1902	1,269,652	1890	1,266,962
Portland	607	419,516	527	319,822
Chicago	11,859	3,887,095	12,014	3,870,360

Vessels of considerable tonnage, and carrying 80,000 bushels of grain, ply on the upper lakes, but only those of from 500 to 600 tons burden can at present pass between Chicago and Montreal. With the enlargement, however, of the Welland Canal (connecting Lake Erie with Lake Ontario) and of the six St. Lawrence River canals, a work which is already in progress, vessels of 2000 tons carrying 60,000 bushels of grain and drawing 13½ feet of water, will be able to pass direct from Chicago to Montreal and Quebec, and therefore, of course, to Liverpool if necessary. The facilities for navigation are not nearly so great by the Erie Canal to New York. The depth of this canal is but seven feet, and boats only of 250 tons, carrying 7000 bushels of grain, can pass through its locks. There are seventy miles of canal navigation by way of the existing Montreal route, with fifty-four locks, and 365 miles by the Erie Canal route, with seventy-two locks.

The opening of the Erie Canal for this year's navigation season took place on Tuesday, April 20th. This was not a day too soon, for between three and four million bushels of grain had already accumulated at Buffalo, awaiting shipment to New York by the canal boats.

some of the most fertile and productive lands in the whole country stretching for hundreds of miles to the south and west of it; with a perfect network of railways opening out these immense tracts, all converging at this point; the natural depôt for the unloading and re-shipping of endless cargoes of grain and other produce, as well as of "lumber," shingles, coal, iron, salt, etc., that come pouring into the place daily by water and by rail; the primary market in America, if not in the world, for the receipt of livestock, of hogs and oxen to be slaughtered and boxed, of cattle, sheep and hogs to be shipped alive to different parts of the country, and to other countries as well; the central market, in short, of a grand agricultural, food-producing country, Chicago has a position which is simply unrivalled; and when we think of the illimitable resources of the vast extent of country to the westward, of the lands to be peopled, of the soil to be cultivated and rendered productive, of the mining and other industries which will in time be developed, it seems that Chicago is destined sooner or later to take its stand as one of the very foremost cities on the face of the globe.

As a livestock market Chicago is pre-eminently famous. The Union Stock Yards, lying on the outskirts of the city, have capacity for holding 147,000 head, namely 100,000 hogs, 25,000 cattle, 22,000 sheep; and there are stalls besides for 500 horses. The sight when I visited this market of such an immense number of animals herded together in the pens, the miles of water-troughs and feed-troughs,[4] the bustle and confusion caused by the hundreds of drovers who were looking after their stock which had lately come in by the trains from distant parts of the State, and from places beyond, and who mingled their shouts with the lowing of the oxen and the bleating of the sheep, of which there were thousands, was one to be ever remembered. The following tables of the receipts at these yards, and of the shipments therefrom, during the

---

[4] "There are in the yards 32 miles of under drainage, 8 miles of streets and alleys, 3½ miles of water-troughs in the various pens, 10 miles of feed-troughs, 2300 gates, 1500 open stock-pens for cattle, and 800 covered pens for sheep."—*Seven Days in Chicago.*

last four years, will show the enormous development of the livestock trade of this place:

Receipts.

Years.	Cattle	Hogs.	Sheep.	Total.
1876	1,096,745	4,190,006	364,095	5,659,005
1877	1,033,151	4,025,970	310,240	5,369,361
1878	1,083,068	6,339,654	310,420	7,733,142
1879	1,215,672	6,448,933	325,119	7,989,724

Shipments.

Years.	Cattle.	Hogs.	Sheep.	Total.
1876	797,724	1,131,635	195,925	2,125,284
1877	699,083	952,912	152,908	1,504,913
1878	699,108	1,266,906	156,727	2,122,741
1879	715,125	1,684,338	157,159	2,556,622

Adjoining the Union Yards are the great pork and beef packing-houses, which are thirty in number, where the slaughtering of hogs and oxen is prosecuted on a mammoth scale—where as many as 80,000 can be "handled" during the course of a single day. The number of hogs packed here in 1872 amounted to, in round numbers, 1,900,000, and 1,781,900 during the year 1875. I was once taken over the slaughter-house of the Anglo-American Packing Company,— it was in September, 1879,—and I watched how Mr. Porker was put through his facings. Two thousand hogs had just come in to be slaughtered—that was the number to be dressed on the day of my visit; but I was told by one of the superintendents that sometimes as many as from 7000 to 8000 are packed by this company daily.[5] There is one house where

[5] In 1879 the Anglo-American Company "erected a building which will hold some 50,000 packages, and 10,000,000 to 15,000,000 pounds of meat. If necessary," says the *Chicago Tribune* of January 1, 1880, "our

20,000 animals can be slaughtered and dressed in one day. The process the pig has to go through is as brief as it can be made. First he is driven into a pen in one of the slaughter-houses, in company with many of his fellow-victims, all doomed like himself to be turned into bacon and sausage-meat within the course of the next fifteen or twenty minutes; a chain with ring attached is fastened round one of his hind legs; a hook attached to another chain is let down from a wheel in a sliding frame overhead, and passed into the ring; the hog is then jerked into mid-air kicking and squealing—but the executioner now stepping forward suddenly silences him for ever by cutting his throat with a sharp knife, and his body, passed on to the end of the frame, is seized hold of by a boy, unhooked and let drop into a large vat of boiling water, where it remains immersed for three or four minutes, other pigs meanwhile closely following behind and being dropped into the vat, one after another, at the rate of one every twenty-five or thirty seconds; caught up out of the vat, the body is placed on a long scraper or gridiron, having a surface of steel blades, which, all set in motion by machinery, tear off the animal's skin,—far quicker than hand-labour could effect the same operation, for in less than a quarter of a minute every bit of it is scraped off, not a vestige of the hide is left,—a man catching hold of one leg while the body is being wriggled and tossed about on top of these moving blades like an india-rubber ball; swung up aloft once more, the body is cut open and disemboweled, the heart, liver, lungs, stomach and intestines being carefully distinguished and put aside, while the head is chopped off, and the brain, tongue, eyes and ears are removed and put aside (to be potted) likewise; and lastly, what there is by this time remaining of our luckless porker is passed into the hanging-room, where it is left dangling by its heels to cool till it is ready to be cut up, salted, and packed. Each animal takes about fifteen minutes to go through the whole operation, from the time that he is first swung up into the air till he is dangling skinless, headless, "intestineless" in the hanging-room waiting

packers and operators could now find room for 300,000 barrels of pork, 400,000 tierces of lard and hams, and 90,000,000 pounds of meat; or 140,000 tons of stuff, the product of nearly 1,250,000 hogs."

to get cooled so that he may be properly seasoned and boxed. One hog after another is despatched in this way as fast as can be managed. More than 4,000,000 head of pork were packed in Chicago in six years, from 1872 to 1877 inclusive. There were 4,805,000 hogs slaughtered here in 1879.

As an important grain market the Queen City is scarcely less famous. In 1872 she was the recipient of 88,426,842 bushels of breadstuffs (flour, wheat, barley, Indian corn, rye, and oats), of which 83,364,324 bushels were shipped. Even this is far exceeded by the receipts of 1879, which reached the amazing total of 137,624,833 bushels, including 62,164,238 bushels of Indian corn alone : and yet this, again, is only 3,538,238 bushels in excess of the receipts of 1878. The shipments in 1879 amounted to 129,851,553 bushels. For receiving the grain and transferring it to the railway waggons when it is brought in by ship, immense towers or "elevators" (of corrugated zinc), twenty in number, have been set up along the shore of Lake Michigan, and they have a storage capacity of 16,000,000 bushels. Some of them are eighty feet high or more. They unload at the rate of about 7000 bushels an hour each.

As a market for one more important article of commerce, Chicago stands unrivalled, and that is for "lumber," or timber for industrial purposes, such as is used in the construction of houses, for flooring, mouldings, doors, sashes, blinds, etc. The total quantity of pine lumber received at this port in 1879 by water and rail—as I find by the annual report of the Chicago Lumbermen's Association—reached 1,467,720,091 feet, an increase of 287,735,381 feet, or about twenty-five per cent. over the receipts of any previous year in the history of the trade. This added to what remained over in the city yards from the year 1878, namely 410,773,000 feet, brings the aggregate supply for 1879 to 1,878,493,091 feet. The average increase in the receipts of lumber at this market has been at the rate of about 50,000,000 feet per year.

One might continue giving facts and figures like these to show the enormous interests which this wonderful city has at stake, but I think enough has been said already, indeed it would occupy more space in this work than can be spared to detail one half, even, of the annual amount of business transacted at this place. Besides occupying so important a position as a market centre, Chicago's growth and increasing prosperity as a manufacturing centre within the fifty years of its existence, is a fact almost equally marvellous. The manufacturing establishments of the Queen City have acquired a world-wide reputation, and their name is legion. There are iron foundries and brass foundries, marble works, brick yards (in 1879 Chicago turned out 40,000,000 bricks), silver-smelting works, silver-plating works, reaping-machine manufactories, sewing-machine manufactories, cotton mills and flour mills, tanneries and breweries and distilleries by the dozen. Each and all of these have done a " rushing " business during the past year; other industries, too numerous to mention, have been prosperous likewise. The total value of Chicago's manufactures during the year 1879 amounted to 236,500,000 dollars: the total value of her entire trade of 1879 amounted to 764,000,000 dollars, a net gain of seventeen-and-a-half per cent. over her entire trade of 1878. Surely with this, and with such facts as we have above indicated, it may truly be said that this city, so young, so flourishing, possessing such vast interests, such grand resources, the great emporium of a new world springing up, as it were, into life, has a future before it such as no other city in the world can anticipate.

And the prosperity of Chicago may, in a measure, be said to foreshadow the future prosperity and development of the lands of the Great West. America is even still in its infancy. Not one half of the country has yet been peopled and taken possession of, and even at the present rate of emigration to the New World,[6] it will take an immense

---

[6] Emigration to the United States has proceeded on a gigantic scale during the past year. From January 1 to May 31 the total number of arrivals at Castle Garden, New York, was 135,336, which is the largest number of arrivals at that port in any five consecutive months in the annals of the Emigration Department. During one month alone (May) 55,083 immigrants were landed, which, in so short a period, is a total altogether unprecedented. Employment is soon found for the vast numbers that come pouring into the country. Emigrant trains are ready to convey them at once to the lands of the far West, such as to Colorado, where they may help to construct the railways in that

number of years, far beyond the life of any one now living, before those great lone lands have become opened out and developed, as in all probability they some day will be. But it cannot be denied that the peopling of America is proceeding at a great rate. The population of the United States to-day is more than six times the number that it was seventy years since. According to the *New York Times* of August 18, 1879: "Seventy years ago the Union included seven States and five Territories, with an area of 708,000 square miles, and a population of 7,000,000; to-day it includes thirty-eight States and nine Territories, with an area of 3,600,000 square miles, and a population of probably 45,000,000." Wisconsin is a good case in point, as illustrating the rapid development of the great Western States. Forty years ago it had nothing but a single military post; now it possesses a population of 1,315,000 inhabitants. And then look at the well-nigh illimitable resources of the vast area that is included under the term the United States of America! To give only a very few statistics—for this is a subject that is infinite: 420,122,400 bushels were the total product of wheat in 1878, a net gain of 55,928,254 bushels over the yield of the previous year—72,404,961 bushels were exported during the fiscal year ending June 30, 1878 (40,431,624 bushels during the previous year), and of this, 54,664,732 bushels went to Great Britain and Ireland; in 1878, 1,388,218,750 bushels of Indian corn alone were raised, a gain of 45,660,750 bushels over the yield of 1877—48,030,358 bushels were exported during the fiscal year just mentioned, 65,915,851 bushels of which found their way to our shores. The total value of the crops in 1878 was 1,480,570,866 dollars; the value in 1879 amounted to 1,904,480,000 dollars, which is the highest total reached in the history of the country. There were 12,062,236 hogs packed in the United States during the packing season of 1877–78, and

rapidly-developing State; and similarly with other States and Territories. On Wednesday, May 5th last, application was made at Castle Garden for 1000 immigrants to be despatched direct to Colorado, to assist in the extension of the Denver and Rio Grande Railway from Denver to El Paso in Texas. Similar applications are constantly being received at Castle Garden, for hands to aid in constructing new railways "out West."

14,480,703 in 1878-79: 54,046,771 pounds of fresh beef were exported from the country during the year ending June 30, 1878 (a large amount being brought from Chicago to eastern ports by means of refrigerator cars), at a value of 5,009,856 dollars. There were 112,986,300 horses, sheep, hogs, mules, milch-cows and other cattle in the United States in January, 1878, and 118,776,200 in the same month in 1879. Two thousand five hundred and seventy horses, 15,038 sheep, 7867 hogs, 57 mules, and 24,982 head of other cattle were exported to the United Kingdom in 1878, or five times as many farm animals as were shipped to our shores during the year before.[7] And the railway development in the United States is a fact which is also worthy of notice. In 1830 there were twenty-two miles of railway in operation; in 1835, 1098; in 1840, 2818; in 1845, 4633; in 1850, 9021; in 1855, 18,374; in 1860, 30,635; in 1865, 35,085; in 1870, 52,914; in 1875, 74,374; in 1878, 81,955; and, judging by the immense strides that have been taken since 1878 in the construction of new lines and in the extension of old ones, it is not improbable that when this year's census is completed the United States will be found to have close upon 100,000 miles of railway. (The United Kingdom of Great Britain and Ireland has, of all the countries of the world, the nearest approach to this, having a total of 17,696 miles.)

And so we might go on and on. With a country like this, having such wonderful resources at its command, Europe need never fear death from starvation—or at any rate not for some time to come, till America has become well stocked with inhabitants and the home consumption of its produce is far greater than it is at present. It has been estimated that there are 200,000,000 acres of corn-land in the United States capable of cultivation, which, with the average yield per acre of the past ten years, would render an annual yield of over 5,250,000,000 bushels.[8] America appears destined indeed to be the future granary of the world—granary, storehouse, farmyard and kitchen garden, all combined.

[7] The statistics given here are taken from the official reports of the Commissioner of Agriculture.
[8] Robert P. Porter in "Our Goodly Heritage," *International Review*, June, 1880.

The hotel at which we located ourselves (June 4th, 1878) was the Grand Pacific, a monster, six stories in height, built of stone and brick (65,000 square feet of stone, and 7,000,000 bricks), with a south and east frontage of 750 feet. It is magnificently furnished throughout. Inside, right within the building, are several shops, or "stores," for this is a characteristic of all the large American hotels. The entrance hall, called the Grand Exchange, is 100 feet by 60; and here crowds of men may be seen standing and sitting about all day long, smoking and reading the leading journals of the

THE GRAND PACIFIC HOTEL.

United States and Canada, as well as the *Times*, *Standard*, and other London papers. On the first floor is the grand parlour, which is 100 feet by 24; also the ladies' ordinary and the grand dining-hall, with a promenade from the parlour to the dining-hall of 130 feet by 30. The dining-hall itself is 130 feet by 60. Its floor is laid with red and black marbles; its ceiling is beautifully frescoed; it is lighted at night by seven bronze chandeliers, and innumerable gas-jets along the walls; and twenty-three windows look out upon the streets of La Salle and Quincy below. The kitchen department occupies the largest space in the house. It is 140 feet by 60, and is on the first floor, on a level with the grand dining-hall. Other hotels there are in Chicago, notably the Palmer House and the Tremont House, which are built on a similar scale of magnificence to the Grand Pacific. Indeed the Palmer House is said, in Chicago, to be the most splendidly furnished hotel in America, surpassing not only the Grand Pacific in that city, but the Palace Hotel and Baldwin's at San Francisco, and the Windsor Hotel at Montreal, these five hotels having the reputation of being the very grandest in the

THE TREMONT HOUSE.

country. For my part I would certainly yield the palm to the Windsor. On the roof of the Palmer House a large conservatory has been set up, Mr. Potter Palmer's idea being to grow tropical plants in it wherewith to adorn his hotel, the corridors, dinner-tables, etc.

Hotel-living in America is either on what is called the "American plan," or it is on the "European." At an hotel on the former plan there is always a fixed price for board, everything—meals, charge for rooms and attendance, the use of gas (gas and electric bells are invariably found in your rooms)—being included in the one general charge of the so-much per day. At an hotel on the European plan there is no such fixed price of board, for here one's expenditure is regulated according as one sees fit. In the best hotels on the American plan, living is from four to five dollars per day. Sometimes there will be two prices to select from, and in making your choice between the two you will be guided by your desire as to what part of the house you would prefer to go to. If you chose to board at the lesser amount you would be put somewhere in the neighbourhood of the top of the building, and perhaps be given only a single apartment, instead of a suite of several, which you would get if you chose to board at the higher rate; but as there is an "elevator" in every first-class hotel, which you would be sure to make use of whether you occupied a humble little attic at the top of the house or whether you lived like a prince in a magnificent suite of rooms on the first floor, it really does not much matter which of the two you choose— but the case would be different if you had to climb up a number of stairs. Hotel-living is much cheaper in America than it is in England. At some of the large hotels you can even board at the rate of twenty-eight dollars per week, with meals, etc. included. Or you can also have a bedroom on one of the higher floors, and take your meals away from the hotel altogether, or *à la carte* at the public restaurant in the hotel, though this, it is obvious, is a more expensive mode of living than the arrangements already mentioned. There are stated hours for meals (at an hotel on the American plan), breakfast generally being obtainable from 6.30 to 11, early dinner from 1 to 3, another dinner from 4.30 to 6, tea from 6 to 9, supper from 9 to 12. This is the arrangement at the Grand Pacific. Americans seldom take any stimulants at meals. Wine on the table is a rarity rather than otherwise. Water, invariably iced, may be set down as the most popular beverage. Milk is also very popular; also tea, the latter being drunk during dinner. It is iced and served in tumblers when the weather is very warm. I have often been filled with wonder and admiration upon seeing the amount of milk an American will drink at one meal, without apparently getting bilious. And the immense amount of food a man will sometimes consume, and so quickly, that he surely cannot allow himself time while he is eating for a fit and healthy digestion, has also often surprised me, especially if I happen to be sitting opposite him, or next to him, so that I can see him, and we both began the meal at the same time, and I find that after I have only got "through" with my second course my neighbour has finished his dinner altogether and is quietly walking away! It is a wonder to me there are not more accidents like the one which overtook poor Charlie Pierce one day, at Erie, Pennsylvania, who "met his death (says the *New York Herald*) by swallowing a huge piece of beef, which stuck in his throat and killed him in less than three minutes!"

Our Transatlantic cousins are very fond of apple-pie. It is consumed to a large extent all over the country. Not raised apple-pie; but flat, and with a paste that is invariably very coarse and indigestible. You have a triangular-shaped slice put on your plate, and (in some parts of America) if you do not want to be singular you will eat it with a bit of cheese, Yorkshire fashion. As an American lady once graphically put it :

"Apple-pie without cheese
Is like a kiss without a squeeze."

And now I propose, once more and finally, to allude to a very disagreeable subject. There is often experienced the greatest possible discomfort in some of the very best hotels in America, by reason of the continual spitting that prevails, sometimes even in rooms which are not set apart for the tobacco smoker and chewer, who have, naturally enough, occasion to expectorate more frequently than the absolute abstainer from the familiar "weed." Perhaps I may be allowed, by way of illustration, to enter here a note which I made during a stay in Boston, in one of the principal hotels of that city, on the 1st of November, 1879. Entering the central hall of this hotel, I found a room on my right, about 20 feet square, with marble floor, etc. (no carpet). I did not venture inside, for that was well-nigh impossible, as the crush was so great; indeed I saw quite enough to deter me from making the attempt, for the floor presented a disgusting exhibition to one unaccustomed to the spectacle, being simply covered with expectorated matter, although there were spittoons in the room lying about the marble floor; but these on the present occasion seemed to be studiously avoided. Withdrawing, I sought a room on the opposite side of the hall, of about the same size, containing a long writing-desk for the use of the hotel guests; but in this room smoking was not permitted. True the order against smoking was respected by the twenty or thirty men assembled; nevertheless the floor of this room also was absolutely covered with saliva, nor was there a single spittoon visible for those who were in the habit of expectorating to make use of. And this disgusting habit of spitting prevails everywhere. It pervades the railway-cars (the non-smoking ordinary cars, I refer to more especially, not so much the Pullmans), it pervades the street tramway-cars, it pervades the hotels; and though in this latter case there are some notable exceptions, particularly those hotels which are frequented by Europeans and the more refined among the Americans, it may indeed almost be said that the nauseous habit of expectorating in places which are not set apart for the lover of smoking and chewing, is universal. I should be very sorry to take any lady of my acquaintance to some of the hotels I could mention.

In some respects Chicago is *un*like a European city. Its streets are all laid out at right angles in "blocks," in true American fashion,—Chicago is the most right-angle city in the United States,—many of them running in long straight lines for some eight or ten miles, crossing the Chicago River (which flows through the city) by means of tunnels and drawbridges. Telegraph wires are conducted along the principal streets as if they were railways, and countless threads of telephone wires are stretched over the housetops above them. Everybody communicates by telephone in Chicago. Shops, hotels, private houses, factories—all are connected. The man who has not got a telephone is very much behind the age in Chicago, as indeed is the case, more or less, throughout America.[9] The facilities for getting about

---

[9] Telephones are now being employed in some of the mines in Colorado.

Chicago are pretty much the same as they were in New York before the introduction of the "elevated," the tramway-car being the only means of locomotion, unless you adopt the big family coach-and-pair, or take to your legs; and people *do* rush about Chicago as if they were mad. I never saw such racing. Men and women stride along as if they were hurrying to the railway station to try and catch a train. Whether at meals or engaged in their several avocations and employments, the Americans are an active people, there is no denying.

One of the most remarkable events that have happened in the history of Chicago's existence is the raising of a portion of the city from its original level, not by building houses afresh, but by forcing up from their foundations those already built, and placing them beyond reach of inundations from Lake Michigan. The original site of the city was on a level with the lake, where the land was low and swampy, and the water was continually getting into the buildings and flooding the basements; so what did the Chicagoans do? They placed jack-screws under the walls of their houses and raised each building to a height of fourteen feet, not suddenly, or in violent jerks, with the possibility of upsetting the whole fabric during the operation, but gently and imperceptibly—

A medical friend of mine living in a New England town can talk to thirty of his patients from his bedroom by means of the telephone. He has his "transmitter" fastened by the side of his bed, and every now and then he is summoned something after the following style:
"Doctor, doctor!"
"Holloa there!"
"Doctor, I want to see you!"
"All right—coming." And the medical man hops out of bed, hurriedly dresses himself, and is off to his patient in a twinkling.

On Sunday, April 18, 1880, the sermons preached in Plymouth Church, Brooklyn, N.Y., were for the first time heard by telephone by certain members of the congregation in their own rooms at their homes stationed in six different cities and towns in the neighbourhood, namely in Brooklyn, New York, Jersey City, Newark, Orange, and Elizabeth, all within a radius of twenty miles of Plymouth Church. Every sound was heard with distinctness, even the music of the choir and the organ accompaniment—even, too, the thumping of the preacher on his Bible, at which it is said there was "a whiz and a whir that was anything but solemn."

so imperceptibly, indeed, that it is said that the inmates at the time had no idea of what was taking place, but things went on just the same as if nothing unusual was happening!

Under the escort of an English friend whom we met unexpectedly at our hotel,—who had been in Chicago a fortnight, and was therefore well posted up in what was to be seen, and what might be left unseen,—we employed the greater part of the day in driving about the city and visiting the principal objects of interest. We went over the new water-works and visited two of the immense grain elevators, and we were at the Union Stock Yards at eleven o'clock, and stayed there an hour. The new water-works on the shore of Lake Michigan are well worth inspecting. In order to obtain the purest water possible, the people of Chicago have had a shaft sunk under the works, and have thrown out a tunnel from it under the lake for a distance of two miles, and at the end of this tunnel, at the bottom of the lake, have (by sinking a huge timber-iron coffer-dam) constructed another shaft, through which the water finds its way and hence is conducted to the shore. Pumped up by four engines at an average rate of 75,000,000 gallons a day, it is distributed through pipes to every dwelling in the city. There are forty artesian wells for supplying Chicago with fresh water, besides what is obtained from the lake.

In the afternoon we drove up the fashionable Dearborn-avenue, and into the Lincoln Park, and returned along the shore of the Michigan Lake. We happened to be in the park at the fashionable hour of five, and saw many of the *élite* driving about in their buggies. There was every description of this the national vehicle. We noticed several ladies racing each other. They drove splendid trotters, and it was a sight indeed to watch these beautiful creatures step out at a sixteen-mile-an-hour pace, proudly arching their necks as they whisked along guided by the fair ones who drove them.

It is amusing sometimes to take note of the friendly rivalry that exists between these rapidly-growing cities, and of the opinions they entertain of each other. The *Boston Herald*, for instance, expresses itself as follows concerning the great North-Western metropolis: "Chicago is a large city, a smart city, and a city with a fair degree of confidence in itself, but its total valuation, which is 123,000,000 dollars for all of Cook County, is equalled by some wards in Boston. In fact, Boston could buy all Chicago with its loose change and have enough money left over to take every man, woman and child to the circus. We do not say this in a boastful spirit, for Boston people care little about material things; but simply to make our own people content with what little dross has stuck to them while studying theology, philosophy, and ethics."

A Chicago man once took a trip East. When he returned he was asked what he thought of New York. "Wal," he replied, "I guess it's too far away from Chicago to do any partic'lar amount of business!"

"Troy," says the *Boston Post*, "has never produced a sweet singer, a philosopher, or a great infidel; but she can trot out enough prize-fighters to keep the nation supplied."

"New York women," says the *Troy Times*, "whistle in the horse cars. Boston women snore in bed, and call it culchaw."

Said a Chicagoan to a friend of mine, when I visited the Queen City in the autumn of last year: "New York has the money, Boston the brains, but *we* start the big ideas, and carry them out with eastern money!" [10]

A New York paper informs its readers that Chicago has started a society for the purpose of discovering a cure for baldness. It is called the Bald Men's Society. If a man can show on the top of his head a bare spot not less than four square inches in extent, he is eligible for membership of that society. The president cannot even show a hair—he is perfectly bald, and for that reason he was elected.

[10] "A citizen of Chicago said to me: 'Our city is the biggest thing on the planet. We've had the biggest fire. We lifted the city five (?) feet out of the mud. We made a river run up hill; it wouldn't go where we wanted it, so we turned it end and end about. And it's the only city on earth every inch of which is covered three inches deep in mortgages!'"— Rev. Samuel Manning in *American Pictures*.

CHAPTER V.

WESTWARD TO OMAHA.

To Omaha—Rock Island—The Mississippi River—Crossing Iowa—Council Bluffs—The Missouri River—Its enormous length—Luxury in modern railway travelling—Railway-car meals—A popular newspaper's advertisement—The white-paint nuisance again—A country sadly disfigured—Omaha—A "booming" city—Gold fever mottoes—A Prusso-Red-Indian—His remarkable history—A wigwam of curiosities—A visit to an Indian encampment—What we found there.

FROM Chicago to Omaha in Nebraska is a distance of 494 miles, by the Rock Island and Pacific Railroad. Leaving at ten o'clock next morning (June 5) we continued to pass through a rich agricultural country, but did not meet with anything of consequence till, 182 miles from Chicago, we came to the town of Rock Island, where we obtained our first view of the great Mississippi River.[1] A mile wide at this point it flows the colour of chicken-broth. An immense number of turtle clung to floating logs of wood, basking in the sun as they were carried down-stream. This river rises in Minnesota State, to the north-west of Lake Superior, in lat. 49°, long. 76° 47'. We crossed it 1500 miles from its source. It flows south from Rock Island for 1410 miles before reaching the Gulf of Mexico. More than a thousand steam-boats navigate this mighty river and its tributaries. "Put it in which way you would, Europe could not hold the Mississippi."[2]

Rock Island, situated on the Illinois side of the river, is a manufacturing town of some 8000 inhabitants, and is so called

---

[1] The *Miche Sepe* of the Indians, the "Father of Waters."
[2] Sir Charles Dilke.

from an island in the Mississippi, of three miles in length, lying a little below the town at the mouth of the Rock River. Crossing the former river by a fine iron bridge we entered Iowa State at Davenport, a beautifully-situated city extending for three miles along the river bank. Iowa has an area of 50,914 square miles. A vast prairie of rich land, it is uninteresting, perhaps, to the ordinary observer; yet it is one of the most fruitful States in the Union, a veritable farmer's paradise, where the soil is fertile enough to bear exuberant crops of every variety of grain,[3] where the grass is of the richest, where the climate, too, is the most invigorating; and for 300 miles after crossing the Mississippi we passed through a country studded with the homesteads of a thrifty people, who have "dug wealth from the soil"—it is by taking a ride such as this, a ride through the rich farm-lands of Iowa so soon after leaving Chicago, that one is able to form some idea of the wondrous resources of that prosperous city.

Three hundred and eight miles from Davenport we came to the city of Council Bluffs. It is separated from Omaha by the Missouri, or the "Mud River," twin sister of the Mississippi, just as dirty, and containing about the same number of turtle floating about on its surface. Another fine iron bridge is thrown over the river to Omaha. It is a mile in length with its approaches, and its total cost was 600,000*l*. Before this bridge was forthcoming, passengers bound West had to be conveyed over the river in boats, to the cars of the Union Pacific Railroad on the other side. The intervening land between Council Bluffs and the Missouri, a distance of three miles, is what is known as "bottom land," or grassy swamps which are at times entirely covered by the river, which is in the habit of constantly shifting about and changing its bed. Council Bluffs is so named from a meeting held on the bluffs in the vicinity, in the year 1804, between the Indians and the explorers Messrs. Lewis and Clark; but the place was not settled till 1847, when the Mormons, persecuted and driven forth

---

[3] In October, 1879, there was wheat standing in Iowa eighteen inches high, which had been sown the month before to be gathered the following summer.

from Illinois for their preachings and extravagant assumptions, established here a "frontier city," under the name of Kanesville, preparatory to setting out over the Great Plains for the far West in quest of a land where, as they thought, they would be free for the future from the murderous attacks of their enemies. It was here that Brigham Young was elected, on December 24, 1847, "President of the Church of Jesus

RAILWAY-CAR LAID OUT FOR DINING.

Christ throughout the whole world," after the assassination of "Prophet" Joseph Smith, the reputed founder of Mormonism, in Carthage gaol, Illinois. In 1853 its name was changed to Council Bluffs. At present it is a city with a population of 15,000, and forms the "transfer grounds" of many railroads. Everyone has to get out here and "transfer" into the cars of the Pacific Railroad, and everyone's baggage has to be shifted here likewise. The Pacific train is made up on the Iowa side of the Missouri River, the transfer grounds being two miles west of the Council Bluffs station.

Who can comprehend the enormous length of the Missouri? The Mississipi is under 3000 miles from source to mouth, but the Missouri flows for 3096 miles from its rise among the Rocky Mountains in Montana Territory to its point of junction with the Mississippi, and including the 1410 miles to the Gulf of Mexico below the confluence of the two rivers, its total length would be 4506 miles! The Missouri can be ascended by steamboat for 2540 miles above its junction with

A RAILWAY-CAR MEAL.

the Mississippi. But it is such enormous branches as the Missouri; such, too, as the Ohio, the Arkansas, and the Red River, that make the Mississippi the great "Father of Waters" that it is. It drains an area of 1,226,600 square miles with its branches, and 1500 of these are navigable.

I think we to-day experienced the highest pitch of luxury to which railway travelling can be brought. All our meals were cooked and served in a dining-car devoted to the purpose. At one end of this car was the kitchen, and from it were brought to light many dishes and dainties, wines, and a variety of "cocktails"—whatever, in short, you chose to order from an elegantly printed *menu,* at the back of which was a coloured illustration of the way in which these spreads are conducted. The car is, for the time being, turned into a little dining-room, with six small tables a side ; and you can either walk into it from your car and dine there publicly with your friends, or you can have your dinner brought to you in your "sleeper" and served privately in your section, a temporary table being soon set up by your coloured attendant, whereon you can have the meal. The cooking to-day was all that could be desired. Each meal cost seventy-five cents, and swallow-tailed darkies were in attendance as usual. A bottle of "fine French wine" was, if desired, served at each meal, at an additional charge of fifteen cents. (The less said about the wine the better.) Guests were requested to exercise a little patience, as the dishes were cooked after the order had been given. On other lines, such as the Pennsylvania, Pittsburgh and Fort Wayne, and the "Panhandle" route between St. Louis and New York, the meals provided are far more *recherchés* than those served on this railway. Still a specimen of a railway-car dinner may be given by quoting our to-day's bill of fare, which, with the request "Put this in your pocket," led off with the following list of good things:

Soup.
Tomato.

Fish.
Boiled White Fish.

Boiled.
Sugar-cured Ham, Champagne Sauce.
Corned Beef and Cabbage.   Leg of Mutton, Caper Sauce.
Beef Tongue.

Roast.
Ribs of Beef.   Mutton.   Spring Lamb, Mint Sauce.
Veal, Stuffed.

Cold Dishes.
Boiled Tongue.   Ham.   Pressed Corned Beef.

Entrées.
Stewed Beef, with Vegetables.   Chicken Pot Pie.
Baked Corn and Beans.   Maccaroni, with Cheese.

Vegetables.
Mashed Potatoes.   Beets.   Stewed Tomatoes.
Turnips. New Cabbage. Spinach. Sweet Corn. Lima Beans.
Green Peas.   Asparagus.   Cucumbers.

Relishes.

Horse-radish. Mixed Pickles. Chow Chow. Queen Olives.
French Mustard. Worcestershire Sauce.
Tomato Catsup.

Dessert.

Pie-Plant Pie. Apple Pie. Peach Pie. Custard Pie. Cake Cheese.
Iced Tea. Coffee. Iced Milk. Ice Cream.
Float Pudding. Fruit. Strawberries.

The breakfast and supper bill of fare was as follows:

Boiled and Fried.

Veal Cutlet, Plain or Breaded.
Beef Steak, Plain, with Mushrooms, with Tomato Sauce.
Chicken. Mutton Chops, Plain or Breaded. Breakfast Bacon.
Codfish Balls. Calves' Liver, with Salt Pork.
Sugar-cured Ham.

Fish.

Lake Whitefish. Salt Mackerel.

Stewed.

Chicken. Kidneys.

Cold.

Beef. Ham. Tongue. Sardines.
Corned Beef. Pork and Beans.

Eggs.

Boiled. Fried. Scrambled.
Omelets, Plain, with Ham, with Herbs, with Cheese,
with Tomatoes.

Vegetables.

Baked Potatoes. New Potatoes. Fried Potatoes.
Cucumbers. Radishes.

Bread.

Vienna Bread. Hot Rolls. Hot Corn Bread.
Plain Toast. Buttered Toast. Milk Toast. Oatmeal Porridge.
Golden and Mapel Syrups.
Peaches. Pears. Currant Jelly. Apple Butter.
English Breakfast Tea. Black and Green Tea.
Iced Tea. Coffee and Chocolate. Iced Milk.

Before night the newsboy came round, and offered for sale the *Detroit Free Press*, one of the smartest and most humorous papers in the United States. He first presented everybody with a printed advertisement relating to the newspaper in question. He did this in every car, and then came and offered us bananas and peppermint drops. On the following page will be found the advertisement relating to the *Press*.

Read! Read! Read! Read! Read! Read!

HIP, HIP, HURRAH!
THE DETROIT FREE PRESS IS FOR SALE ON THIS TRAIN BY THE NEWS AGENT.
    It makes the poor rich, sick well, and alters your appearance so that when you meet the girl you proposed to (and was refused), she will jump for you. In short, it is a certain cure for all the ills of human nature.
    The difference between gossip and truth is, that no one ever stops to question your veracity when you are indulging in the first, but he wants you on oath when you are speaking solemn facts.—DETROIT FREE PRESS.

Try it, Buy it, a Nickel does the Job.
LADIES AND GENTLEMEN, ONE AND ALL, READ THIS TALE.
    Life is full of uncertainties. We are here to-day, there to-morrow, and may be running for office next week. All things considered, you will be perfectly justified in asking the conductor if the train is on time; if he can change a $20 bill; if the road-bed is in good order; if it is a cold day, if he isn't tired of railroading, and any other question you may happen to think of. By the way; ask the train-boy if he has THE DETROIT FREE PRESS. Buy it, and you will be happy for ever.
    Railroads were discovered in 1828; conductors were invented a year later; the first train-boy was domesticated in 1850; brakemen were imported from Australia in 1841; but it was many years before they could shut a car door with the report of a cannon. Further particulars can be had from THE DETROIT FREE PRESS. For sale on the spot; price, 5 cts.
    READ IT ONCE. And be convinced that it is edited by a second George Washington.

Be Happy While Life Lasts, and Take Things Easy.
    There is no excuse for any vigorous language because you can't turn the seat in front of you, or because the window won't go up. Take it calmly, appear not to care, and wink to the boy to bring you THE DETROIT FREE PRESS. All will then go well.

Important Notice to the Travelling Public.
    It is the intention of the stockholders of this road to put on coaches with bay windows next year. In the mean time the passenger who doesn't get a fair view of the girl waving the dish-cloth at the train, should ask the conductor to refund his money, but don't fail to buy a DETROIT FREE PRESS from the train agent.
    Important Information to Owners of Cattle.—A succession of short sharp whistles from the locomotive means that there is an old cow on the track ahead, and that if she doesn't make a bee-line for the fence, the engineer won't be responsible whether she makes a barrel of beef or only a nail-keg full of hoofs and horns. After the collision is over, ask the boy for THE DETROIT FREE PRESS. It's better than quail.

Certainly, with Pleasure.
    If you are anxious about it, we'll explain, that one whistle from the locomotive means take your feet off the other seat; two signify that there is a bridal party in the car; three whistles warn you to put your satchel on the floor and divide up your seat; and four sharp toots indicate that if you bet on three-card monte you'll reach home strapped. N.B.—When the boy comes along with THE DETROIT FREE PRESS, have your nickel ready, and be generous and tell all your friends what a prize the paper is.

Confidential.
    In reply to various letters just received from a few of our distant relatives, Aunt Vic., Uncles Dismeli, Bismarck, Ben. Butler, Bounding BB. and others, we desire to say that in the future THE DETROIT FREE PRESS can be found for sale all the world over. Price, 5 cents. AIN'T YOU GLAD? Get your nickel ready; here comes the train agent with it.
    Why is the news agent on this train a philanthropist? Because he picks up your nickels and gives you the finest paper published—THE DETROIT FREE PRESS.

(Facsimile of the *Detroit Free Press* advertisement.)

America is daubed from one end of the country to the other with huge white-paint notices of favourite articles of manufacture, with an endless array of advertisements puffing off the medicines of pretentious quacks, with announcements of mixtures without number to meet the requirements of suffering humanity, with every information, indeed, relating to the newest and the best and most attractive and cheapest articles of merchandise, both liquid and solid, which may be the most likely to arrest the attention of the traveller as he journeys along. I have drawn attention to this nuisance more than once already, for it is one of the first things that strike the stranger as soon as he has landed in the New World : he cannot step a mile into the open country, whether into the fields or along the high roads, without meeting with the disfigurement. At first it seems to him a simple nuisance, an eyesore, an ugly blotch spread over a fair country ; but at length he becomes quite accustomed to the sight, and is able to look upon it with complacency and expect " Bitters," " Gargling Oil," " Horse Powders," etc., at every turn of the path. If a house has a blank wall to it, that blank wall is certain to be appropriated and daubed with a great staring white-paint notice with a background of black paint, sometimes with the letters two feet or more long and the strokes of the letters a couple of inches broad. If you have the toothache and want to get rid of it, if you are afflicted with a pain in the stomach and would have it removed, if you are in low spirits and want a " pick-me-up," if you are anxious to know the best chewing tobacco, the best stove-polish, the best tooth-paste, hair dye, or blacking for your boots, whatever be your ailment or whatever your need, whether it is a draught to be taken internally or an application to be used externally, you have simply to look on the blank walls, rocks and palings you come to as you flit by them in the railway train, and depend upon it you will not be long before you have found just the sort of remedy you are in quest of, and, once found, it will not be so easy to get rid of—the "painting" will haunt you to your journey's end. I have room here to mention only a very few instances out of the many thousand I refer to. To take, for example, our route from New York up to this point. On leaving the Empire

City, you see continually displayed in large white characters on both sides of the railway along the shore of the Hudson River, for 150 miles to Albany, the following information and advice: "USE CARBOLINE FOR THE HAIR;" "TARRANT'S SELTZER APERIENT CURES DIARRHŒA;" "GARGLING OIL;" "TWIN BROTHERS YEAST;" "SAPOLIO;" "DIXON'S ICE CREAM," etc. You cannot look on the beauties of this river from the train without being reminded that there are hair-dyes, pills, and horse-powders—"HARVEY'S HORSE-POWDER" being about the most fashionable—claiming your immediate attention. After leaving Albany, "VINEGAR BITTERS" begins to be prominently brought forward, and one is continually recommended to "SMOKE VANITY FAIR" and to "CHEW WOOD TAG NAVY." Even at Niagara, as you gaze in awe on the sublimity of the scene, on those hundred million tons of water pouring every hour over those two great precipices, your thoughts which have wandered heavenward are suddenly recalled to earth when you turn round and find that the "RISING SUN STOVE POLISH" is the "BEST IN THE WORLD!" As you approach Chicago, you find that "BIXBY'S IS THE BEST BLACKING;" that "FOR FLAVORING PUDDINGS AND CAKE" you should "USE ONLY THE TRIPLE REVOLUTION EXTRACTS;" and you are a hundred times requested to "USE GILLET'S CREAM YEAST" and to "EAT GUNTHER'S CANDY AND BE HAPPY." (In one place I found "Rising Sun Stove Polish" painted up in letters some five or six feet high. You see the polish on your right soon after passing out of the Chicago station, on the Rock Island and Pacific Railroad.) Out of an infinite number of similar notices that disfigure Chicago, I would just mention one or two more, but before doing so let me observe that the nuisance culminates at Chicago, for here is the paradise of whitepaintism. In the distant future, when one thinks of this place, it will be impossible to disassociate it in one's memory from its splendid exhibition of medical and chemical notices. "USE DR. KING'S NEW DISCOVERY FOR CONSUMPTION, COLDS AND COUGHS;" "ASK FOR BADEAU'S PURE BLOOD MAKER;" "CHEW OLD FORT DEARBORN PLUG TOBACCO;" "CLEAN YOUR TEETH WITH ZOZODONT;" "WIZARD OIL

GOOD FOR NEURALGIA;" "USE GAIL'S AND AX'S SCOTCH SNUFF"—these may be taken as specimens of the rest. And so it is all the way on to Omaha. Notices of a similar nature, several feet high many of them, meet the eye of the traveller as he journeys through Iowa. We shall have occasion to refer to a few more before we come to our journey's end, but shall only do so where reference is necessary, else there would be no end to what might be written on the subject. "Gargling Oil," the most popular notice in America, is invariably painted up in yellow lettering—probably the colour of the mixture.

No one who has not travelled in the United States has the least idea how sadly the country is disfigured by the daubing I have referred to. I am sure every sensible person will agree with me in the opinions I have expressed, and heartily join with me in condemning the nuisance. The *Boston Herald* spoke freely, yet to the point, when it said that the Americans are "a people who has brought to the highest development the arts and graces of publicity."

Arriving at Omaha (June 6th) after twenty-four hours' journey from Chicago, we repair to the Grand Central Hotel,[4] an imposing five-story red brick building, but rather a "come down" after the magnificence of the Chicagoan Grand Pacific. We have now come 1480 miles from New York, and, barring a slight *détour* from the main track to Salt Lake City, we commence to-morrow a run of 1916 miles to the capital of the Pacific coast. For several days the palace car will be our home.

Omaha lies on the border of that vast stretch of prairie which extends between the Missouri River and the Rocky Mountains. It is named after a tribe of Indians now extinct, or nearly so, and its population is over 30,000, having increased 15,500 during a space of ten years (1865–75). It has seen the light of but twenty-four summers. Things are "booming" in Omaha, and things will continue to "boom" so long as the great trans-continental railway remains a fact. Its position is a happy one. It is half-way house for

[4] This hotel was burnt to the ground in the autumn of 1878.

those pioneers who seek the Golden Land, the rich meads and yellow cornfields of California. But before California became connected with the East by the iron road there was another class of pioneers, who, excited by the Coloradan gold fever, mad with anxiety to throw in their lot with the discoverers of the hidden treasure, struck a more southerly course from Omaha in the direction of Pike's Peak, that great mountain across the prairie which was then to them the goal of every earthly ambition. To them it was "Pike's Peak or bust,"—they must either reach the mountain or "bust" in the attempt; and this elegant motto they painted conspicuously on the sheets of their waggons, in order that the gold excitement already kindled might not be allowed to flag. When, however, a break-down occurred, a very different motto would be painted on the waggon-sheet, revealing the deplorable condition of the party, and this was, "Busted, by thunder!"

A "tub" followed by a hearty breakfast, and we strolled out to see the sights of Omaha. These are *nil* to one in quest of the wonderful. Yet even here there is a good deal to learn, and certainly something to supply food for reflection in the existence of a city which, born so lately, has been run up so suddenly, teeming with life and vigour, with its shops connected by the telephone, and its streets metalled with railways, even though there may be nothing in it that would be considered particularly worth seeing. Still, Omaha is a thriving manufacturing city, and besides iron foundries, distilleries, breweries, flax, starch and flour mills, etc., it contains, perhaps, the largest smelting works in the United States. With seventeen hotels and about twenty churches or chapels, Omaha, besides, supports three daily and two weekly newspapers, and one tri-weekly; but it is for its flourishing educational establishments that this city is chiefly famous. It has 86,195*l.* invested in free school property, and some of its public schools have attained to very high merit. The building of the High School, the cost of which amounted to 56,000*l.*, is a beautiful structure, and crowning a hill overlooking the city, with its spire of 185 feet, is the first object the eye rests upon as Omaha is approached.

We were wandering along Farnham-street, the principal

thoroughfare, when we came to a shop which announced itself as "The Indian Wigwam" of "Julius Meyer, Box-ka-re-sha-hash-ta-ka, Indian Interpreter, Indian Trader and Dealer in Indian Curiosities." A handsome-looking man dressed in a well cut, black frock coat, the lightest-coloured trousers, with a tall "beaver" covering a head of curly jet-black hair, was standing at the entrance, smoking. Presuming him to be the "dealer and Indian interpreter" aforesaid, we saluted and entered. He was indeed the veritable Box-ka-re-sha-hash-ta-ka; and the following is his history, and a remarkable one it is. A Prussian by birth, he came out to America several years ago to visit his two brothers at Omaha. One day Herr Meyer and six or seven white neighbours went buffalo-hunting with a company of friendly Pawnee Indians who were encamped in the vicinity, and, as chance would have it, they fell in with a party of the bloody Sioux, sworn foes to all Pawnees and pale-faces, and an engagement took place. The result of the meeting was that the Pawnees were taken prisoners and were walked off to be scalped at leisure, but the pale-faces, except the Prussian, were all scalped on the spot. The Prussian was allowed to retain the top of his head because of his youth, for he was then scarcely old enough for an Indian to consider his scalp of sufficient value to dangle from his girdle, or to tie on to a bit of stick to brandish in the scalp-dance. However, he was carried away by the Sioux to their retreat, and given a squaw to live with, a wigwam to live in, a war-dress, some war-paint, and all the savage equipments of a Red Indian life. He accompanied the Indians on their wanderings and war-paths, and became, in truth, a semi-savage. But, more than all, he "got on" with Ta-kong-ka-you-ta, or Sitting Bull, the dreaded Sioux chief, and acquired the honour of smoking the *calumet*, or pipe of peace, with him. He received, too, the name of Box-ka-re-sha-hash-ta-ka, or "The Curly-haired White Chief with One Tongue" (*i.e.* one who never lies), by which little word he became known among the Sioux tribe, but generally among the Indians as simply the White Chief. His father offered large rewards for his redemption, but it was of no avail. In time he learnt the language of the tribe, and the languages of other tribes; and considering the Indians have no written dialects, but each word has to be committed to memory according to the way it is pronounced, this must have been no slight difficulty for him to have overcome. At length he received his freedom, and was made Indian interpreter to Congress and (Indian) agent of the Interior Department, and he now receives an annual stipend of 600*l.* He goes periodically among the various tribes and learns the state of feeling among them, and, where able, settles their grievances and disputes. Having returned only a few weeks since from a visit to his old tribe, he had brought back with him Sitting Bull's favourite tomahawk and buffalo robe, also the tomahawk of Spotted Tail, another famous Sioux chief; and what with many other interesting relics of Indian warfare obtained during his visit among the tribes, his "wigwam" of wild-Indian curiosities was well worth spending the greater part of the morning in, and this we did. White Chief was unwilling to part with Sitting Bull's paraphernalia for any reasonable sum of money, preferring the rather to keep them himself, or at any rate till he could find a customer who would give him the fancy price he asked for them. But other curiosities almost if not quite as interesting were to be had, and before we quitted the premises we had bargained for several of the valuables.

In the evening Box-ka-re-sha-hash-ta-ka came and dined with us at the hotel, and when we had waxed merry on bad claret he proposed taking us the next morning to a camp of the Wenabago Indians, which lay a few miles out of the city.

"Indians?" we exclaimed. "Won't they scalp us?"

"You shall see," was the reply.

So we arranged to go early in the morning, and left it with our friend to get the horses.

The next morning (June 7th), at seven o'clock, after an early breakfast with White Chief, we got on our horses, and a canter of five miles over a plain brought us to a forest on the shore of the Missouri; and here we began looking about for the Indians. Curly-Haired White Chief, who rode in his tall "chimney-pot," frock coat, and yellow corduroys, taught us on the way certain familiar Wenabago-Indian terms, which he said we might find useful if we felt at all conversational, and wished to have a talk with any members of the tribe. Some of these expressions were, *Ho-coo-la*, meaning, how d'ye do; *How-oo*, my friend; *Nu*, good-bye, etc. After riding backwards and forwards several times shouting or rather yelling *A-ha-hee?* (where are you?), White Chief was answered by a faint yell in the distance, and we advanced in the direction of the sound. In a minute or two we came upon the camp. On a bare spot cleared away in the thick brushwood were pitched four low tents or wigwams, each constructed simply of patches of canvas sewn together and stretched in one large sheet over bent strips of bamboo-cane. A hole at the bottom of each was just large enough for one person at a time to crawl through. The ground around was scarcely fit for a human being to tread upon. Three men—"bucks," as the male Indians are called in contradistinction to the "squaws"—were standing outside the tents smoking, but unpainted and dressed in civilised costume. Inside one of the "lodges" were three squaws, the filthiest-looking creatures I ever set eyes upon. They were squatting *à la Turque*, with legs doubled in and knees doubled out, and the costumes they wore were appropriate to the extreme heat of the weather. Ugly and bloated in appearance, their skin was a dark copper brown, and their long black hair fell stiff and straight —like a horse's mane—over the bare shoulders. One of them was studiously occupied in examining among the hairs of a dog that lay beside her; another was engaged in needlework, in making a pair of moccasins which would afterwards be sold in Omaha; the other one did nothing but grin. The stench inside was simply unbearable. That we might examine the creatures, they crawled to the entrance and looked at us; and one old girl, whose name was Ho-an-ni-ka, was presuming enough to ask me to give her a kiss!—but I declined the honour with thanks. One of the tents seemed to be used as the sleeping-quarters of the whole crew: the ground was not earthen, as inside the others, but bestrewn with hay. This family, at least the grown-up portion of it, consisted of seventeen souls, four bucks and thirteen squaws. The preponderance of ladies was owing to one gentleman having gone in strongly for polygamy, for he kept a collection of eight wives. We made his aquaintance. He had no eyebrows, for he had amused himself by pulling all the hairs out.

Two of his wives were at home to-day, squatting with Ho-an-ni-ka in the tent above-mentioned. They wore ear-rings, and upon my expressing a desire to examine them their husband made them take them off and sell them to me, as he said he wanted money very badly. (They proved simply to be half-dimes, or American five-cent silver pieces, strung on to strips of leather.) The poor things did not seem to relish the idea of parting with their valuables; but they were obliged to submit, else they would have had the squaw-whip about them. And considering that the amount I gave for them far exceeded their market value, they—or rather he—certainly got the best of the bargain. But the money given in exchange was of course pocketed by their lord and master, who would spend it on himself when he next visited Omaha.

"And are these your Indians?" we inquired of White Chief, as we were riding back to the hotel.

"They are our tame ones," he replied; "but their glory has departed. You will see plenty more of them before you reach San Francisco."

CHAPTER VI.

OVER PRAIRIE AND MOUNTAIN.

The Pacific Railroad—A mighty enterprise—Rapid progress of the work—Difficulties encountered—The East and the West joined—Starting across the Great Plains—On the rolling prairie—Impressions—Animal life—The "dog" of the prairie—Stations on the line—Elkhorn—The Platte River—Giant rivers of the Plains—The "wickedest town in America"—A lesson in massacre—A breakfast on the prairie—A prairie-dog city—Sighting the Rocky Mountains—The Magic City of the Plains—Passing the eastern overland train—An exchange of greetings—Steeply ascending—The "Summit of the Rocky Mountains"—Nearly left behind—A glorious panorama—The Laramie Plains—The Gem City of the Mountains—A station museum—A double supper—A concert in our sleeping car—Green River—Rocks of the "Rockies"—The Desert House—Evanston—Chinese waiters—Begging Indians—Rapidly descending—Echo Cañon—The Pulpit Rock—An engine's performance—A conductor's diversion—The white-paint nuisance again—Mormon settlements—The Thousand Mile Tree—The Devil's Slide—Ogden Junction—We arrive in "Zion."

FROM Omaha stretches that great line of railway which, replacing the old emigrant road, connects eastern North America with the shores of the Pacific. Wildly impossible as the idea at first seemed of linking the two cities of Omaha and San Francisco, yet in time—in a marvellously short time—this was effected, and the Pacific railroad now stands as one of the most wonderful achievements of the present day.

It was no doubt chiefly owing to the great gold discoveries in California, and the consequent flow of emigrants into the far West, that the Pacific Railroad came to be devised; but it was also devised to bring the States into closer affinity and union—"to keep our country together," as one patriotic gentleman observed in Congress about the time of this great railway movement. It was the beginning of the month of July, 1862, that the charter by which the Pacific Railroad was initiated was granted by the United States' Government. According to the provisions of that charter the line was bound to be completed by July 1, 1876 —just fourteen years from the passing of the Act. Three years and four months elapsed before the work was commenced in Nebraska, for it was not till November 5, 1865, that the ceremony of "breaking ground" was celebrated at a spot near Omaha City.

But to the Californians must be given the honour of being the most ardent promoters of the enterprise. So early as 1861 a company, called the Central Pacific Company, was started at Sacramento, 140 miles north-east of San Francisco, —the Western Pacific Railroad already uniting these two cities,—and the great work was begun by breaking ground near Sacramento on February 22, 1863, scarcely eight months from the granting of the charter. Thus the Californians got a considerable start of their eastern brethren, anticipating them by the space of two years and eight months.

The work being at length commenced in earnest, in Nebraska as well as in California; both companies in a friendly spirit of rivalry vying with each other as to which could accomplish the greatest distance in the shortest space of time; the rapidity with which the works were advanced dispelling the fears of the desponding, and far exceeding the expectations of the most sanguine—this great railway, the completion of which had been limited to fourteen years, was actually laid, ready and open for traffic—a vast stretch of 1916 miles—on May 10, 1869, six years ten months and ten days from the passing of the Act, the full time occupied in the work itself from its very commencement in California, on February 22, 1863, being just six years, two months, and eighteen days! Thus what seemed little better than a dream in February, 1863, was an accomplished fact in May, 1869.

Every effort was made and inducement held out to the competing parties to hasten the completion of the enterprise. Lands were promised to the men of both companies—little short of 20,000,000 acres are said to have been so assured.

Large additional sums of money, too, were promised. But so strong was the opinion of the workmen on the line that the enterprise would fall through—so stupendous and impossible a scheme did it seem to them—that they even refused to work till their wages had been paid them before their labour. The rush came at the end; the voluntary struggle against time between the two rival companies was redoubled and persevered in, as the distance between them became less and less. The history of the final efforts of rivalry is most interesting, and it is as follows: "Day after day the average rate of building rose from one to two, three and five miles. . . . The Union Pacific men laid one day *six* miles; soon after the Central followed suit by laying *seven*. The Union Pacific retaliated by laying seven and a half; to this the Central sent the announcement that they could lay ten miles in one day; to this, Mr. Durant, the vice-president, sent back a wager of $10,000 that it could not be done. The pride and spirit of the Central Pacific Company had now been challenged, and they prepared for the enormous contest, one of extraordinary magnitude and rapidity. The 29th of April, 1869, was selected for the decision of the contest, as there remained but fourteen miles of track to bring a meeting of the Roads at Promontory Point.

"Work began; the ground had already been graded and the ties placed in position, and at the signal the cars loaded with rails moved forward. Four men, two on each side, seize with their nippers the ends of the rails, lift from the car and carry them to their places; the car moves steadily over the rails as fast as they are laid. Immediately after follows a band of men, who attach the plate and put the spikes in position; next a force of Chinamen, who drive down the spikes solid to their homes, and last another gang of Chinamen, with shovels, picks, &c., who ballast the track. The rapidity of all these motions, which required the most active of exercise and alert movements, was at the rate of 144 feet of track to every minute. By 1.30 p.m. the layers had placed *eight miles of track in six hours*. Resuming work again, after the noon rest, the track-laying progressed, and at 7 p.m. exactly the Central men finished their task of ten miles, with 200 feet over. Mr. James Campbell, the superintendent of the division, then seizing a locomotive, ran it over the ten miles of new track in forty minutes, and the Union men were satisfied."[1]

The difficulties in the way of progress must have been singularly formidable, and must at first have seemed insurmountable. Two great mountain ranges, the Rocky Mountains, and the Sierra Nevada, had to be surveyed, and the best and easiest points ascertained for conducting the line over them. Immense stretches of timberless plains of prairie-land and barren alkaline deserts had to be crossed, where fuel was not to be obtained, water was scarce, and exposure to the sweeping blasts sharp and certain. There is no doubt that at the outset of the enterprise the western company met with the greater difficulties of the two, for the Sierra Nevada, over whose heights the railway had at once to be threaded, lay immediately before them. We read that "the first 100 miles was a total ascent of 7000 feet. . . . At the height of 5000 feet the snow-line was reached, and forty miles of snow galleries had to be erected at an additional expense of $20,000 to $30,000 per mile, and for a mile or more, in many places, these must be made so strong, that avalanches might pass over them, and yet preserve the safety of the track. Even after passing the Sierras the railroad descended into a vast plain, dry, and deserted, where there was not a sign of civilized life, nor any fuel. For over 600 miles at a stretch no water could be found for either man or machinery. . . . Every bar of iron and every tool had first to be brought and started on a sea voyage round Cape Horn some four or six months before it was needed."[2] However, all obstacles at length overcome, the union of the two lines took place at Promontory Point, Utah Territory, 1084 miles from Omaha and 832 miles from San Francisco (or 692 from Sacramento), and the East and the West became linked by the iron road. New York and San Francisco were joined, the distance between the two cities by the most direct lines of rail being 3230 miles. It now takes just a week to cross the North American Continent. The distance could be accomplished in less time, of course, for the average rate of

[1] Williams' *Pacific Tourist*.
[2] *Ibid.*

speed on the Pacific Railroad does not exceed eighteen to twenty miles an hour.

To America in general, San Francisco in particular, the advantages accruing from the construction of the Pacific Railroad are incalculable. This is obvious to any person who gives the subject a moment's consideration. Massachusetts and California are brought into immediate connexion. The future of the Golden City—as San Francisco has been termed—at once becomes one of the most promising of all the cities in the Union; its position as a shipping port the most commanding. Great Britain, too, is benefited. A new route is opened for her trade with China. The products of California are brought within her easy access.

Proceeding on our journey to-day (June 7th) we took sleeping berths to Ogden, the junction for Salt Lake City.

We are now on the rolling prairie. For over 500 miles after leaving Omaha the Pacific Railroad is thrown in an almost continuous straight line across the Great Plains. Everything is strange and new—all seems changed. We turn our faces westward, and feel as if we are leaving life and civilization behind us. We look around and see nothing but a boundless sea of grass, a verdant undulating ocean stretching to the far distant horizon in one vast perpetual sweep. An overpowering sense of vastness is conveyed to us as we speed over these immense plains. An indescribable feeling of solitude, a mighty loneliness which no words can well represent, is engendered by the contemplation of such an immensity of open space. And to think that we are crossing but a very tiny portion of this tremendous sweep of plain! "Into the Plains and Plateau you could put all India twice."[3] It is scarcely possible to comprehend the idea of so enormous an extent of sameness, such an uniformity of feature over so vast a portion of the country: yet thus it is. But that lonesome feeling which is engendered does not produce, as might be expected, a depression of the spirits—far from it. There is a kind of charm in one's first ride over the prairie which drives away melancholy. Though surrounded by what seems to be an interminable monotony, there is life all around if

[3] Sir Charles Dilke.

you only choose to look for it. For the first 200 miles you find the Plains in the vicinity of the railway dotted with the settlements of a frugal people, who have turned the land to the best account, and found it wonderfully fertile and productive. Groves of cottonwood-trees are frequently seen in the "valley" of the Platte, and are said to thrive amazingly, growing some eight feet or more a year. After the Platte Valley is passed cultivation is left behind, and the rest of the prairie crossed by the Pacific Railroad is devoted to the raising and grazing of stock. Seen now at the beginning of summer the Plains present an appearance of exquisite freshness and bloom. The tall prairie grass is of the greenest, and bright-coloured flowers springing from a smooth stoneless surface deck the ground in gayest profusion. But what a change will have been wrought in another two months! The green grass will then have become brown and dried up, the beautiful flowers will have disappeared, ugliness will reign supreme, and scarcely a more unpromising and cheerless sight will be found on the face of the earth. Then indeed if you take a trip across the Plains you will wonder how sheep and cattle can find food enough to keep themselves alive. The thick brown bunches of buffalo grass which you see springing up on all sides, look the very reverse of nourishing; yet it is only the colour of the grass which has changed. The hot sun has dried and cured it like hay, and has given it a sweet savoury taste particularly agreeable to cattle. Any farmer out West will tell you that this grass, so seemingly destitute of every nutritive quality, is equal if not superior to some of the best fresh grasses in the country.

Very little animal life is seen in crossing the prairie by the railway. Buffalos are not seen now. Time was when they covered the plains of Nebraska, and the story goes that they used to be shot down from the cars as the train proceeded, and their carcasses left by the side of the line to rot in the scorching sun. But this noble beast is no longer seen from the window of the Pullman car. Both the buffalo and the Indian have retired before the advance of the white man—far, far away over the boundless sweep of the vast open plains. Antelopes may occasionally be seen from the train, but only in a few solitary herds, for they, like the buffalo, have been scared away to seek "fresh fields and pastures new." But away from the railway antelopes are found in abundance, and an immense variety of other " big game " besides ; indeed many of the stations on the Pacific Railroad, throughout its whole length to California, are splendid starting-places for the sportsman. From Sidney, Cheyenne, Hazard, Laramie, Fort Saunders, Green River, Wells, Elko, Winnemucca, or Wadsworth, the hunter is within easy reach of some of the finest hunting regions in the New World.

But the chief curiosity of the Plains is the comical little prairie marmot (*Cynomys ludovicianus*), called a "dog" by the Americans, and as such he is generally known. He is very like a rat when seen from a distance, but he is as amusing and interesting in his movements and habits as a juvenile monkey. In length about fourteen inches from snout to tip of the tail, his colour is a greyish-red, and he stands on all fours at a height about equal to the length of his tail, which is a couple of inches long, and is tipped at the end with black. The male is slightly larger than the female, and is more brisk in his movements. Both male and female have long whiskers, small holes for ears, large claws on the feet, and a huge protruding pair of teeth, which are awkward customers if once they get hold of you, but which are never brought into requisition unless provocation has first been offered to their owner.

The prairie-dog is a very sociable and hospitable animal. He lives underground in a "town" or "village" (as his home is called) with many of his own kind, and receives as his guests company, I must say, rather of a mixed and questionable character, for in his dwelling are to be found burrowing owls, tortoises, prickly frogs, and rattlesnakes—a family living not so happily and harmoniously together, or so adapted to each other's peculiarities, as some have alleged, for it is said that the snake and the owl so far abuse the hospitality of their host as to make a quiet meal off him, when hunger dictates. The Indians call him "Wish-ton-Wish," not a very musically-sounding name, certainly, but one, nevertheless, which is supposed to represent their idea of the sound the little creature makes. The Americans call him "dog," from the resemblance of his cry (so they say) to the yelp or bark of a small fretful puppy. Another cry he has, which he utters when he is frightened, and that is a most remarkable sound: it would be a puzzle to find its equivalent. It is a kind of squeak—a stuffed, gagged, and yet a loud and somewhat shrill sort of squeak, unlike the noise of any other animal, as far as I am aware. It somewhat resembles the pronounced "chuck" of an over-fed hen, or again it puts one in mind of the cackling of a guinea-fowl; but, as I have said, it would be difficult to find its equivalent. Though their numbers are becoming less and less every year along the route of the Pacific Railroad, the noise of the train gradually scaring them away, hundreds of the little creatures may still be seen close to the line, but seldom or never more than one at a time,—that is one to every "town,"—for the sound of the approaching train will depopulate the district for the time being, and the solitary dog that is seen keeping guard outside, sitting bolt upright on his hind legs on the top of the earth-mound of his excavated home, is the old and experienced sentinel instinctively deputed by the rest of the community to look after their interests, and to tell them, by means of a loud squeak, that the danger they feared is past and that they may safely come up again. A prairie-dog's natural position, except when he is eating or is on the *qui-vive*, is on all fours; but he takes his food, which principally consists of the roots and stalks of grass, squatting on his hind legs and holding it in his fore paws, monkey fashion. Always remaining near his hole and never wandering far from its vicinity, with a pair of sagacious, clever-looking eyes watching you he will munch away what he is grasping till it has all disappeared, and then, with a squeak of satisfaction accompanied by a quick jerk of the tail and a backward toss of the head—very much like a cock throwing up its head at the commencement of a good long crow, only with rather more briskness—he will suddenly tumble out of sight into his hole hard by, and leave you wondering as to what has really become of him. Very tenacious is Wish-ton-Wish of his precious little life. His fat, plump little body added to his circumspect habits render him difficult to be secured, either dead or alive. It requires a good-sized bullet, and one carefully aimed for the brain, to bring him down, and even then it is ten to one if you get him, for he is sure to be near his hole, and will manage to wriggle himself into it; and then supposing he does get into his hole, and dies there, and you put in your hand to pull him out, all I can say is, Beware of the rattlesnake! The prairie-dog can be tamed so as to become a great pet, as I am able to testify. I brought back to England several live specimens in 1878; and with a large heap of sand to burrow in and plenty of fresh grass to eat every morning, they are, I fancy, as happy and contented with me in close confinement as if they were at liberty on their own native prairie.

There are 230 stations between Omaha and San Francisco; distance, 1916 miles. Most of the settlements which are passed have sprung up since the construction of the railway. Roughness and lawlessness have hitherto characterized the inhabitants of these places, and though time and civilization have wrought here and there a change for the better, their condition, it must be owned, is still rather barbarous. A man's life goes for a very little out West. If you hear people talk of "a man for breakfast," it means that someone has been shot during the night.

The train stops at every one of these little stations. (There is but one train a day starting from Omaha for San Francisco, and *vice versâ*.) Meals are supplied on the way at eating stations set up by the two railway companies. You are obliged to step out and take your meals at these places, unless you happen to have laid in a stock of provisions for consumption *en route*, for there is no food to be obtained at the intermediate stations. Nor are there any dining-cars as yet on the Pacific Railroad.

Twenty-nine miles from Omaha we reach the first little place of importance—Elkhorn, situated on a river of the same name. About 300 miles in length the Elkhorn abounds with a great variety of fish, and in the fall of the year its banks are covered with flocks of geese, ducks, and wild turkeys. It is a paradise for the angler, and has been so since the spring of 1873, when, as the story goes, a car-load of spawn *en route* for California was accidentally upset at this point and turned into the water. Ever since then fish have been plentiful.

Soon after leaving Elkhorn we come within sight of the Platte River, the great drainer and fertilizer of this region, and for 345 miles, as far as Julesburg, we follow along its northern bank. The Platte is one of the giant rivers of the Plains. Only can an idea be formed of this immense stretch of level country by glancing at the enormous length of the rivers that water it. "The Arkansas, which is borne and dies within the limits of the Plains, is 2000 miles in length, and is navigable for 800 miles." The Missouri, as we have already seen, flows 3096 miles before meeting with the Mississippi. Then there is the Yellowstone,—one of the great northern tributaries of the Missouri,—which takes its rise in the northeast of Wyoming, and flows 1300 miles before its junction with the Missouri. From the source of the Yellowstone to the point where the waters of the Mississippi empty themselves into the Gulf of Mexico, is one continuous stream of 5800 miles.

The Platte is not very navigable. At the best of times it is no more than a couple of feet deep. Its channel is constantly shifting, and often the river spreads out to a mile in width. Sometimes there is no river visible at all. The stream in places dries up entirely in the late summer, and with a bed of soft quicksand it resembles at that season a bog more than anything, and is quite as difficult and treacherous to cross, except at the proper fording-places.

It was now time to look about us. It had been smooth water so far. As yet we had had no occasion to use our revolvers. But we had now come to Julesburg, popularly known in its earlier days (since 1867) as the "wickedest town in America," near which place the Pacific train, a few days since, had been attacked and robbed, and $25,000 stolen. A similar robbery on the train had been committed a few days previous to this event. Unfortunately I am unable to make this description of our route at this point more interesting by giving an account of some thrilling adventure with a band of thieves, for the truth is, that we passed through this critical period without a scratch, without even a ground for suspicion that there was anything wrong. To prevent mischief, however, or rather escape after mischief, the doors of all the cars of our train were locked long before we reached the "wickedest town," and kept locked until long after we had left it. The way the desperadoes go to work is as follows.—Half a dozen of them, say, will get into the train as ordinary passengers, having duly paid their fares. In the middle of a long run, one of them, at a given signal, will leave his companions and walk through the train to the engine driver and stoker, and, placing a couple of six-shooters at their throats, command them to pull up. This is a signal for another of the confederates to get up and suddenly plant himself against the door of his car with a couple more six-shooters, and, pointing them at all present, cry, "Hands up!" If your hands don't go up you go down, that's all. Then another fellow calmly goes round and makes a collection. You dare not shoot at the fellow who is pointing at you, for you would be immediately "polished off" by two of his confederates in the same car. The bravest man in these cases is as helpless as the most cowardly, for a six-shooter takes all the courage and fight out of him. These robberies, however, are of very rare occurrence, indeed travelling on the Pacific Railroad may be said to be almost as safe as it is on any of our English railways.

June 8th.

Thirty-seven miles beyond Julesburg we come to Sidney, an eating station, and therefore a place of importance. We stop half an hour to hurry out and get breakfast. Arriving at 8 a.m., having been roused from our slumbers twenty minutes beforehand by our coloured attendant, we quickly bundle out of the train and rush into the breakfast-room, to make sure of getting ourselves seats. We have, as I have observed, thirty minutes allowed for breakfast; but on these occasions one generally contrives to despatch one's meal in five.

Tearing into the station-house past a man standing at the doorway, who was vigorously proclaiming, on a loud-sounding copper-tin gong, that the feast was ready prepared and spread within, we found ourselves in a room furnished with many neatly-arrayed tables. We had plenty of the gentler sex to wait on us. There was plenty of time to eat and plenty of room to spare. There were given us eight little dishes apiece, containing hot beefsteak, two slices of cold roast antelope, a bit of cold chicken, ham and poached eggs, a couple of boiled potatoes, two sticks of sweet corn, stewed tomatoes, and four thin buckwheat "hot cakes" laid one on the top of the other, to be eaten with golden syrup the last thing of all. We were all served alike: everyone was given the same as his neighbour. Knives and forks were lamentably scarce, as usual. One knife and fork each to last through the whole meal is the order of the day out here. Cold tea in tumblers, with a quantity of sugar added, seemed to constitute the popular beverage—if it was not cold milk: but there was hot tea and coffee for those who preferred. It was a typical American feast, all ate as if for their very lives. We, my friend and I, *began* slowly and properly; but we soon found that the eagerness of our neighbours to be "through" with their meal provoked a similar eagerness on our part, and the result was that we were all "through" together a quarter of an hour before it was time to start. For this and for every meal (except two) along the route of the Pacific Railroad from Omaha to San Francisco, the charge is one dollar.

There is a gradual although an almost imperceptible ascent in the journey across the plains of Nebraska from the Missouri River. The Great Plains are not level, but sloping. Omaha itself, to begin with, is 966 feet above the sea, and Julesburg, 376 miles from Omaha, has an elevation of 3500 feet, the rise along the whole distance being gradual, though at the same time nearly imperceptible. Sidney stands 570 feet higher than Julesburg. The railway continues to ascend after leaving Sidney, and in the next nineteen miles we rise 297 feet. Close to Potter, a station we now reach, is a famous prairie-dog city, a rather more extensive community than the ordinary town or village, where Wish-ton-Wish is to be found at home in his honeycombed domain with many thousands of his companions, in a territory comprising several hundred acres.

About sixty miles further, between the stations Hillsdale and Archer, we sight the Rocky Mountains. Everyone is now astir. We crowd to the windows and steps of our car, and strain our eyes across the prairie in the direction of the range. There is a sort of romance attached to the bare mention of these mountains. We know that they form one of the great mountain chains of the world; but there seems to be a touch almost of mystery—something vast and incomprehensible about them that we cannot grasp. And it is no wonder when we remember that they extend in an almost unbroken line throughout the entire length of North and South America, from the Arctic region to the south of Patagonia, a distance of 8200 miles! The Andes in South America are but a continuation of the "Rockies" in Colorado. Mount Acongagua in Chili, with a height of 23,910 feet, and Mount Hooker in British North America, with a height of 16,730 feet, may be said to form the culminating points of one and the same range, in South and North America respectively.

It is a long blue line of mountains that we see, distant far away in Colorado to the south, and there is Long's Peak, snow-capped, towering above all to a height of 14,270 feet. No need of field-glasses in this part of the world. If the day were clearer we should see Pike's Peak, said to be 140 miles distant, "as the crow flies." But though it is glorious weather to-day, the sky a deep, cloudless blue,—and the sun scorching hot,—Pike's Peak and Long's do not come into view together. The Black Hills now appear to the north, and soon we are approaching Cheyenne (pronounced Shienne), the "Magic City of the Plains," and the blue distant lines far away to the north and south become more and more distinct.

Approaching the Magic City by a couple of snow-sheds, which are rendered necessary owing to the violence of the storms in winter, we reach it at 1.40 p.m., and stop half an hour to get dinner in the station-house. We have now reached an elevation of 6041 feet, and are distant 516 miles from Omaha. We have also quitted the State of Nebraska, and entered the Territory of Wyoming.

Cheyenne can boast of being the largest town between Omaha and Salt Lake City. It is the capital of Wyoming, and has seen a fluctuating population, which can now (1880), at all events, be estimated to be about 4000. Gold was discovered in the Black Hills a few years ago, and then up sprang the city almost magically; hence the popular name by which it is designated. Like many of these "magic" cities it has had its day of lawlessness and vice. But the construction of the Pacific Railroad has brought within the last few years a certain amount of civilization and enlightenment to this once barbarous community, and churches and schools have taken the place of drinking taverns and gambling dens. Not that the present condition of the Magic City is irreproachable or blameless. It can scarcely yet be recommended as a haven for a peaceable and law-abiding citizen who is endowed with a liberal supply of this world's goods, to come and end his days in. There can sometimes be obtained a man for breakfast here, as well as at Julesburg.

From Cheyenne a line branches south for 106 miles to Denver, the capital of Colorado. Another line branches off to the same destination from Hazard, or Colorado Junction, the next station we come to after Cheyenne. The former is the Denver Pacific Railroad, the latter the Colorado Central. Both form a junction at Denver with the Kansas Pacific, which connects the Coloradan capital with St. Louis in Missouri and the East, running parallel with the Union Pacific across the Plains about 200 miles south. Connexions are also made at Denver with various other lines, which lead to some of the most important mining "camps" in the State.

A few miles beyond Hazard we pull up on a side track at a shanty named Otto, to allow the eastern overland train to pass us. The two trains pull up close by the side of each other, and greetings are exchanged between the respective conductors and baggage-masters. Our newspaper man hands over to the newspaper man of the eastward-bound train a bundle of the latest issues of the principal Chicago and Omaha papers, and in return we are presented with the latest issues of the principal San Francisco and Salt Lake journals. One is as anxious to get hold of a paper out here, to ascertain the latest news, as one is at the end of that long week at sea, upon the anxiously looked-for arrival at New York, or Queenstown Harbour, when you make a dash for the first paper available, to see what has been happening in the world you have been out of for so long a time, and on these occasions you do not mind paying double the proper price of the first paper that comes to hand. And so it is on a railway journey like the present. Anything to break the monotony of the long ride over the Plains. At length, the conductors and baggage-masters having engaged in ten minutes' conversation, someone cries "All aboard, all aboard" —we jump up on to the cars, the engine bells commence ringing and once more we proceed. The eastern overland train is passed every twenty-four hours between Omaha and San Francisco.

We now rise rapidly and perceptibly, and in four miles, between Otto and Granite Cañon, we ascend 574 feet. Six miles more, a further ascent of 482 feet, and we have reached an altitude of 7780 feet. Snow galleries are now frequent, and the line is cut through heavy masses of red granite. Ravines open out beneath, and you feel you are ascending the Rocky Mountains. Low stunted firs sparsely clothe the heights around, and you begin to associate the "Rockies" with bears, elks, and wild cats. Big game, in truth, abound in the vicinity, and the mountain streams literally swarm with trout.

A further ascent of 464 feet in seven miles, and we reach Sherman, the highest elevation which the Pacific Railroad attains. It has an altitude of 8242 feet. We are 2192 feet higher than the Rigi near Lucerne, 3836 feet higher than Ben Nevis in Scotland, as high, indeed, as some of the loftiest passes in Switzerland—and this in a railway train! If the eye could see so far we should have an uninterrupted view back to Omaha, a distance of 550 miles. As it is we have (a little beyond Sherman station, for there is no view from the station premises) a noble panorama southward of the "Rockies" in Colorado, of a fine snow-capped belt of dark-blue heights containing some of the highest elevations of these North American Andes.

Just before reaching Sherman, we pass a notice board on our right which informs us that this is the "Summit of the Rocky Mountains!"

We pull up at the station, and the train is to wait ten minutes. It is rather cold up here to-day, so I turn into a little inn—the Sherman House—near the track, expecting to find a fire; but instead of this I find some cider—real, good, excellent cider, to which I in company with others commence helping myself. While thus engaged, the engine bell is rung and the conductor shouts "All aboard," the signals that it is time to be moving away. Now it happened that I was engaged at this moment in a lively debate on polygamy with the man at the bar, who was himself half a Mormon, and, it seemed to me, thought somewhat favourably of the institution. But it all of a sudden flashed upon me that I was being left behind. So, tossing the man a dollar greenback, with a bottle of cider in one hand and a cup to drink out of in

SHERMAN.

the other, I dashed out of the building, and there was the train steaming away quite fifty yards ahead of me! I think I never put on the pace with greater alacrity than I did to catch that train. I raced as for my very existence, and fortunately succeeded in reaching the hindmost car, for the engine had not yet got up sufficient steam so as to proceed very fast.

Descending gradually for about three miles, suddenly, without any warning, we emerge from a deep cutting in the red granite cliff on to the Dale Creek Bridge—a wooden trestle-work structure 650 feet long, thrown 127 feet across the creek or ravine which so unexpectedly opens out beneath. We go over it at a snail's pace, and so fragile and thin does the bridge appear to be that it seems almost a wonder it is able to support the heavy weight of the train. When you reach the middle and look down below, you experience a kind of "creeping" sensation, which causes you to very much wish you were safely arrived on the opposite bank.

We now quicken pace. Then we shut off steam, apply the brakes, and descend rapidly into the Laramie Plains. What a glorious panorama is now before us! What intensity of colour! How clear is the atmosphere, how blue the mountains, how diversified the landscape! All around and about us the colour of rock and soil is a crimson red, and dark green fir-trees starting up here and there afford an agreeable contrast to the general aspect of the picture. The Medicine Bow Mountains shut in the view to the west, rising dark and blue into the region of perpetual snow. The Black Hills we have just crossed are seen looming in the far north, and then spreading out before us, in one grand sweep of a hundred miles or more, are the Laramie Plains, a very paradise for sheep, for the grass is of the richest—160,000 to 170,000 head of stock revel here in one of the finest grazing-lands in North America.

Descending through a series of snow-sheds into the plains, many curiously-formed rocks of red sandstone, called the Red Buttes, are seen on the right, about ten miles before we come to the settlement of Laramie. They present a most peculiar and fantastic appearance. Some of them are 100 feet in height.

Soon we reach Laramie, called the "Gem City of the Mountains," for reasons which need not here be enumerated, and we turn out into the station-house and have supper. On the platform is a collection of fossils and minerals, heads of animals shot in the vicinity, and other interesting curiosities. Collections such as this are to be found at all the eating-stations on this part of the overland route. Elk, deer, and cinnamon bears abound on the mountains in the neighbourhood of Laramie, and hunters bring their heads and place them in these museums for sale. Moss-agates, variegated opals, amethysts, and mountain rubies, are not to be picked up every day cheaply; but here were heaped together these precious stones, and others, in great variety, collected like the animals' heads from the adjacent mountains, and certainly the prices asked for the several specimens could not be called excessive.

At Laramie we are 7123 feet above the sea-level, having descended 1119 feet from Sherman in twenty-four miles. We resume our journey after supper and proceed for fifty miles to Rock Creek, where we have another supper. Time allowed for second supper, half an hour. Resuming our journey once more, night overtakes us, and we—go to bed, the reader will say. No, not just yet; for we have an eight-stop little organ in our sleeping car, the "Palmyra," and this evening we bring out its tone, and our companions in the car contribute a few songs. The instrument has two manuals,—but will only sound in one,—and the upper part is devoted to pillow-cases and blankets. So for two hours we amuse ourselves with singing and playing, our conductor—who was a bit of a musician in his way—coming and helping us and treating us to a few songs. I believe if we had only had room enough we should have got up a little dance; but, as it was, this was entirely out of the question. In this way we spent a very pleasant evening.

June 9th.

When we rose this morning (at seven) we found ourselves near Green River station, 846 miles from Omaha, and at an altitude of about 6000 feet. During the night we passed over that high table-land or dividing ridge of the Rocky Mountains which constitutes the continental watershed, from which the waters of this portion of North America flow eastward into the Atlantic and westward into the Pacific. At Creston, the highest altitude we attained,—we halted there at 1.45 a.m.,—we were 7030 feet above the sea.

The settlement of Green River is so called from a stream of the same name in the vicinity, and the stream is so named from the greenish hue of its water. Not that the actual water is green, but, flowing through a slaty, clayish soil of that colour, it has the appearance, until examined, of being the same colour also. At Green River the peculiar scenery of the Rocky Mountains commences—not scenery in the character of grand and beautiful views, for it is a woe-begone, desolate region we are passing through; not a tree is visible, nor, I believe, have we passed one for the last 300 miles. But the bluffs in the neighbourhood of the river, and solitary rocks starting up here and there, assume every variety of fantastic shape, and, further on, as Ogden is approached, the railway is laid through a remarkable gorge, called Echo Cañon, where Nature is strange and weird in the extreme. The variety of colour in many of these rocks, and the regularity with which the layers of each are arranged, is most extraordinary. Red and grayish-buff are the predominating colours; but there are also yellow and green layers—layers of arenaceous clay alternating with layers of calcareous sandstone, and here and there a layer of white sand, so that such a variety of formation appearing in so many colours, when found in a single rock, presents it immediately as an object requiring more than a passing glance. The sight that we witnessed early this morning of a valley enclosed by such rocks, lit up by the light of the morning sun, bathed in an inexpressible glow rendering their colours all the more brilliant and glorious, is one not likely ever to be forgotten.

There is evidence enough to show that the whole of this region was once covered with water, for upon the face of many of these "buttes" are to be seen clear and beautiful impressions of fish, and not only one or two here and there, but sometimes hundreds together on one and the same rock. Thus during a prolonged course of corrosion caused by the action of climate and damp, or water, affecting the soil around, have these rocks come to assume such remarkable shapes, the soil composed of a softer and less durable substance having sunk by degrees, leaving these evidences of the former level of the valley. In 1870 an exploring party sent out under the auspices of Yale College, New Haven (Conn.), discovered near Green River many specimens of fossil grasshoppers, beetles, dragon-flies, and other insects; also, near Antelope, not far from Cheyenne, a petrified three-toed horse, a rhinoceros, besides turtles, birds, and other fossil specimens in the same locality. There is no finer field for the geologist and fossilist than this section of the Rocky Mountains; and the mineralogist, too, will find ample scope for the further development of his particular branch of natural science.

The names which have been given to some of the rocks that are passed between Green River and Ogden, according to their more or less curious formation, will help to convey some idea of their general form and appearance. Thus we have (at Green River) a Giant's Club, a Giant's Thumb, and a Giant's Teapot, and further on we pass a Pulpit Rock, a Sentinel Rock, a Castle Rock, and within perceptible distance of some Twin Sisters, Egyptian Tombs, Church Buttes, Monument Rocks, and a few Witches' Bottles. I cannot take these in detail, for a rush past them in the train, though it be only at an eighteen-mile-an-hour pace, does not allow one to do more than gain a very superficial impression of their characteristic features. But suffice it to say that the proportions of a number of them are truly gigantic, and that while some are seemingly detached from the cliffs behind, others stand up out of the earth by themselves without prop or support, looking indeed as if Nature had placed them in their positions in order to puzzle everybody.

We breakfasted at Green River, and a very good breakfast it was, too, considering the distance some of the things must have been brought. Besides the usual supply, we had a quantity of fruit, which had probably been brought all the way from Salt Lake City or California, for none can be got to grow up in this desert region.

The station inn, the only hotel in the place, is called the Desert House. A more appropriate name could not have been chosen. The following notice I found framed and hung about the breakfast-room:

THE
DESERT HOUSE.

This hotel has been built and arranged for the special comfort and convenience of summer boarders. On arrival, each guest will be asked how he likes the situation; and if he says the hotel ought to have been placed up upon the knoll or further down towards the village, the location of the house will be immediately changed. Corner front rooms, up only one flight, for every guest.

Baths, gas, water-closets, hot and cold water, laundry, telegraph, restaurant, fire alarm, bar-room, billiard-table, daily papers, coupé, sewing machine, grand piano, a clergyman, and all other modern conveniences in every room. Meals every minute, if desired, and consequently no second table. English, French, and German dictionaries furnished every guest, to make up such a bill-of-fare as he may desire, without regard to the bill-affair afterwards at the office. Waiters of any nationality and colour desired. Every waiter furnished with a libretto, button-hole bouquet, full-dress suits, ball-tablets, and his hair parted in the middle. Every guest will have the best seat in the dining-hall, and the best waiter in the house.

Any guest not getting his breakfast red-hot, or experiencing a delay of sixteen seconds after giving his order for dinner, will please mention the fact at the office, and the cooks and waiters will be blown from the mouth of the cannon in front of the hotel at once. Children will be welcomed with delight, and are requested to bring hoop-sticks and hawkeys to bang the carved rosewood furniture especially provided for that purpose, and peg-tops to spin on the velvet carpets; they will be allowed to bang on the piano at all hours, yell in the halls, slide down the bannisters, fall down stairs, carry away dessert enough for a small family in their pockets at dinner, and make themselves as disagreeable as the fondest mother can desire.

Washing allowed in rooms, and ladies giving an order to "put me on a flat-iron" will be put on one at any hour of the day or night. A discreet waiter, who belongs to the Masons, Odd Fellows, Knights of Pythias, and who was never known to even tell the time of day, has been employed to carry milk punches and hot toddies to ladies' rooms in the evening.

Every lady will be considered the belle of the house, and row-boys will answer the bell promptly. Should any row-boy fail to appear at a guest's door with a pitcher of ice-water, more towels, a gin-cocktail, and pen, ink, and paper, before the guest's hand has left the bell-knob, he will be branded "Front" on his forehead, and be imprisoned for life.

The office clerk has been carefully selected to please everybody, and can lead in prayer, play draw-poker, match worsted at the village store, shake for the drinks at any hour, day or night, play billiards, is a good waltzer and can dance the German, can make a fourth at euchre, amuse children, repeat the Beecher trial from memory, is a good judge of horses, as a railway and steamboat reference is far superior to Appleton's or anybody else's guide, will flirt with any young lady and not mind being cut dead when "pa comes down." Don't mind being damned any more than a Connecticut river. Can room forty people in the best room in the house when the hotel is full, attend to the annunciator, and answer questions in Hebrew, Greek, Choctaw, Irish, or any other polite language at the same moment, without turning a hair.

Dogs allowed in any room in the house, including the w(h)ine room. Gentlemen can drink, smoke, swear, chew, gamble, tell shady stories, stare at the new arrivals, and indulge in any other innocent amusements common to watering-places, in any part of the hotel. The proprietor will always be happy to hear that some other hotel is the best house in the country. Special attention given to parties who can give information as to how these things are done in "Yewrup."

The proprietor will take it as a personal affront if any guest on leaving should fail to dispute the bill, tell him he is a swindler, the house a barn, the table wretched, the wines vile, and that he, the guest, "was never so imposed upon in his life, will never stop there again, and means to warn his friends."

G. W. KITCHEN.

Continuing our journey through a waste, monotonous region, in 111 miles we come to Evanston, half-way house between Omaha and San Francisco. From Omaha the distance is 957 miles, from San Francisco, 959 miles. During the preceding 111 miles we ascended a little over 700 feet. At Green River our elevation was 6140 feet; here it is 6870 feet.

At Evanston we had dinner, and a novelty in the form of Chinamen to serve us. There were several, and they one and all wore an amazing lot of hair, the black flowing locks of some twisted and allowed to trail down the back and legs

ECHO CAÑON.

in one grand, magnificent pigtail. One fellow's hair reached down to his ankles; others had theirs curled up round the back of the head, like a young lady's used to be—alas, that plain and simple style!—before chignons became the fashion. These Celestials are extraordinarily like one another in their countenances. Men or women, it's all the same—they're all alike. For all the world it is hard to tell John Chinaman when you see him whether he is a man or a woman.

There were also, at Evanston, several Indians (Shoshones) squatting on the platform, begging. They had dogs as usual—ill-fed, half-starved curs; and I noticed that one animal was sharing his dinner with his master, both Indian and hound tugging away together at a piece of meat. Filthy and dirty-looking in the extreme, their faces were thickly besmeared

THE WITCHES ROCKS.

with red and blue paint, and their clothing, as with those at Omaha, was suitable to the oppressive heat of the weather. The paint was so thickly laid on that it had become like a hard cake, and cracked by the heat of the sun.

From Evanston, or rather from Wahsatch, nine miles further, the line rapidly descends, and in the succeeding nine miles, between the stations Wahsatch and Castle Rock, we descend 580 feet. We are now approaching the well-known Echo Cañon, where we expect to revel in scenery remarkable and strange. We pass Castle Rock station, and find the rocks around us worn into many queer shapes, and the cliffs on our right assuming larger and loftier proportions as we descend beneath them from a higher level. The old emigrant road is beside us—that old, beaten track so often traversed before the iron road was laid across the prairie and mountain, and which is still used by those who cannot afford the luxury of the railway train. We have been running close beside it for some distance, and have passed many oxen-drawn, canvas-covered waggons loaded with whole families on their way to seek new homes in the still far-off West. Now the road crosses the line, and there is a cartful of emigrants drawn up at the side, waiting till we have passed so that they may cross in safety.

THE WITCHES BOTTLES.

As we pass them they give us a cheer, and we of course cheer them back, and wave our pocket-handkerchiefs.

But the increasing grandeur of the scene, which every mile becomes more and more impressive, requires all our attention now. Standing on the steps of the last car we have a fine view of Echo Cañon as we descend into it gradually, and slowly, with plenty of time to look about us and take in every point of interest that is passed. The characteristic feature of this gorge is that while on the right or northern side of the line, during the descent towards Ogden, the cliffs, of dark red sandstone, are bold and massive, abrupt and bare, castellated and turreted, of all shapes and sizes, almost overhanging the

THE PULPIT ROCK.   *Page* 143.

rails in some places, on the left side the hills are perfectly smooth and rounded, and thinly clothed with grass. A curious formation close to the railway in this cañon is the Pulpit Rock—a gigantic "three-decker," about seventy feet in height, towering straight up above you as you pass only a few yards from it. There is a tale told by some clever people that Brigham Young preached from this "pulpit" to his Mormon band of pioneers, as he led them over the mountains to Salt Lake City, the newly-revealed "Zion." But the story is a mere invention, for he did nothing of the kind. Even if it were true, I do not see how he could have mounted on to the rock—unless he happened to have been provided with an exceptionally long ladder.

We pull up in the middle of the pass to allow a performance of our engine, for this is "Echo" Cañon, and some wonderful resounding effects are here supposed to be produced. The engine performed while we listened. It gave three long jerks, then stopped awhile, then jerked again; but the result of all this could scarcely be deemed a success. The echo was clear and defined, but not of long duration. I should have mentioned above that we pulled up at Wahsatch station, just before descending into the gorge, to allow the eastern overland train to pass us. As it was a little behind time our conductor amused himself by taking shots at one of the telegraph posts with his revolver; and about half a dozen of us followed suit and fired at the same.

The sublimity of Echo Cañon is considerably reduced in the estimation of the lover of the picturesque and beautiful by the conspicuous white-paint advertisements which are seen daubed up against the red sandstone precipices just in the most striking part of the whole gorge, and in other parts of it as well. The most frequent are "SOZODONT;" "GARGLING OIL;" "PLANTATION BITTERS;" and "SALT LAKE HOUSE, SALT LAKE CITY, $1.50 to $2.00 pr. day."

Just before entering the gorge, the Territory of Wyoming is quitted for that of Utah. We are now among the Mormons, we have reached the "Promised Land." All the settlements we pass between this and Ogden are inhabited by the "People of the Lord." We come to the village of Echo City—city indeed, with a population of only 300! It is a Mormon settlement, lying just outside the cañon. We ascertain from a man standing and loafing about at the station, watching the train, that a bishop is located here, but that he has just gone "a missionizing" in California—to preach polygamy to the Gentiles there. We are shown Mormon dwellings close to the station, and we gaze at them. But our curiosity is unrewarded.

THE DEVIL'S SLIDE.

Emerging from the cañon, we have a grand view on our left of the snowy Wahsatch Mountains, on the other side of which lies Salt Lake City. The view of the range from this point is singularly beautiful and impressive.

Traversing for eight miles an open, well-cultivated valley, we come to another cañon, called the Weber. As we enter it we pass on our left a tall solitary pine-tree bearing on its lower branch a sign-board, upon which can be discerned the notice, "1000 M. Tree." This is the "Thousand Mile Tree," and marks the exact distance we have travelled since leaving Omaha. A little beyond this tree we come to a remarkable formation in the mountain side, consisting of two parallel ledges of granite, fourteen feet apart, projecting some sixty feet or more from a smooth surface, and running down the cliff for a height of 800 feet. It has been aptly called the "Devil's Slide." Several other instances of the same peculiar formation, only not so perfect and entire as in this particular case, may be seen while passing through this gorge.

We emerge from the cañon and enter a fertile valley of ten miles in length, hemmed in by lofty heights, which assume loftier proportions as we approach the opposite end. Then, with the Weber River flowing beside us, we come to the Devil's Gate Cañon, the third and last gorge which is penetrated by the Union Pacific Railway. It is only five miles in length, but the twists and turns of the line become so frequent and sudden that we can only proceed at a four-mile-an-hour pace. The rugged cliffs on both sides, averaging 900 feet, sometimes almost hang over the railway and meet—almost, so to speak, shake hands across; and they would do so were it not for the river at the bottom, which dashes along taking up for itself all the room, so that the railway has to be cut out of the side of the mountain, or else must force its way by means of a tunnel. Just as we are leaving the cañon we pass a deep gap in the mountain on our right, from which the gorge receives its name.

The Rocky Mountains now crossed, we emerge from them into the Great Salt Lake Valley, which is 120 miles in length, and from thirty to forty miles in breadth. Passing through green fertile lands, in ten miles we reach Ogden, the junction for Salt Lake City and the terminus of the Union division of the Pacific Railroad. The distance from Omaha is 1033 miles, and from San Francisco, 883 miles. Passengers bound West now change into the "silver palace" cars of the Central Pacific, which are waiting to take them as soon as they have had their supper; passengers bound for the Mormon metropolis proceed by the cars of the Utah Central. Forty-five minutes after our reaching Ogden find us covering the thirty-seven miles between that place and Salt Lake City, and, at 8.45 p.m., we find ourselves in Utah's capital, called "Zion" by all good Mormons—the "Centre of the Kingdom of God upon earth," the "Dwelling-place of the Prophet," the "City of Refuge for the down-trodden Saints;" and placing our baggage in a hotel 'bus and ourselves in a street-car drawn by a quartette of mules, we are taken off direct to the Walker House.

CHAPTER VII.

MORMONISM.

The origin of Mormonism—Joseph Smith's initiatory vision—His mother's account of the vision—His interviews with an "angel"—Discovery of the golden plates—The origin of the Book of Mormon—the founding of the Church—Principles of the Mormon faith—Originality of the Church—The Book of Mormon—A blasphemous publication—A few samples of its contents—Rubbish and bad grammar—Organization of the Mormon Church—The "First Presidency"—The two priesthoods—The various offices in the Church—"Stakes" and "wards" of Zion—How the people are looked after.

BEFORE proceeding further, it may be useful to give a slight sketch of Mormonism in general, one that, though it must be brief, may be found of service by enabling the general reader to understand the principles that govern the religious life of the "Saints" of the Rocky Mountains. I would fain pass on and omit dwelling here upon a religion that must be pronounced to be so empty and false, so demoralizing in its tendencies, a religion whose teachings are fraught with such sad and shocking blasphemies; but when—as will be shown in a later chapter—so large a number of persons continue to pour every year into Utah from Great Britain, Scandinavia, and other parts of Europe; when, too, it is remembered that the greater proportion of Mormons in western North America are people from the British Islands alone, it will, I think, serve a useful purpose if publicity be given to their doctrines,—which are, I believe, little known or understood,—in order that it may be seen to what kind of religion, and to what a state of moral and social degradation, too many of our uneducated emigrants are being introduced; for, though Brigham Young is dead,

148   *Through America.*

Mormonism is, at this moment, in as thriving and flourishing a condition as ever.

First, then, as to the origin of Mormonism. "The Church of Jesus Christ of Latter-day Saints"—this is the full title—

JOSEPH SMITH, FOUNDER OF MORMONISM

was founded, as is well known, by one Joseph Smith, who in the year 1820, when he was fifteen years of age, is said to have had a remarkable vision while praying to God one day in the woods near his home at Manchester, Ontario (now Wayne) County, in New York State, upon which occasion "a vision of the heavens opened unto him, two glorious persons descended towards him, and one, pointing to the other, said, 'This is my beloved son; hear him!'"[1] The lad appears to have been quite overcome for the moment; but, on collecting his thoughts, and remembering that the object of his prayer was to know which of all the religious societies on the earth was the one he should join,— for Joseph was a boy of strong religious principles; and his mother and sister having just turned Presbyterians, and having himself half a mind to become a Methodist, he was as yet undecided what to do,—he made bold to inquire, and the following was the reply which, in curious phraseology, he tells us he received, as it is given in the *Biographical Sketches of Joseph Smith the Prophet and his Progenitors for many generations*, by Lucy Smith, his mother: "I was answered that I must join none of them, for that they were all wrong, and the personage who addressed me said that all their creeds were an abomination in his sight; that those professors were all corrupt, they draw near me with their lips, but their hearts are far from me. . . . . He again forbade that I should join with any of them. When I came to myself again I found myself lying on my back looking up to heaven." But this was not all. Three years later, on the night of the 21st of September, 1823, after Joseph had "retired to bed for the night, and had betaken himself to prayer and supplication to Almighty God," an "angel," Moroni by name, appeared unto him three times, and told him how that there were "hid up" in a stone box under a hill near his home at Manchester, some golden plates containing a record written in hieroglyphics, "in a language called the Reformed Egyptian, not then known on the earth," giving a history of the ancient inhabitants of America, and that two stones in silver bows, anciently called the Urim and Thummim, were to be found fastened to a breastplate, together with the record, in the same stone box. (The "angel" seems to have appeared unto him again on the following day, and told him to relate this vision to his father.) Joseph accordingly went to the hill as directed, found the plates, and was on the point of carrying

---

[1] Mormon *Catechism for Children*, by John Jacques.

them away when the angel again appeared and told him that he must leave them, for that the time had not yet arrived for taking them, and would not be for four years longer. But Joseph was allowed to come once a year and have a talk with the angel, yet the possession of the plates was denied him awhile, for reasons which have not been explained. At the end of the four years, therefore, the plates, etc., were presented to Joseph; but still he was only allowed to keep them a little while, "till the angel should call for them," during which time he was to translate them by means of the Urim and Thummim; and this he did. Before, however, he returned them, "the Lord, by a heavenly messenger, showed the plates to three witnesses," and "Joseph Smith, by commandment, showed the plates to eight witnesses,"[2] whose testimonies were considered essential to prove that Joseph had practised no deception in the matter. This translation from the "Reformed Egyptian" constitutes what is known as the Book of Mormon, so called, we are told, from a prophet of that name who flourished in America about the fourth century of this era.[3] But Joseph, although evidently "called," had not yet been fully "ordained of God." He had still to receive—to use his own expression—the "gift of the Holy Ghost." This was necessary before he could set about organizing a church. So on May 15, 1829, he retired as

---

[2] Mormon *Catechism for Children*.

[3] "Joseph Smith, when questioned on the subject, gave the following as the proper derivation of the word (Mormon):

"'I may safely say that the word Mormon stands independent of the learning and wisdom of this generation. Before I give a definition, however let me say that the Bible, in its widest sense, means good; for the Saviour says, according to the Gospel of St. John: I am the good shepherd; and it will not be beyond the use of terms to say that good is amongst the most important in use, and though known by various names in different languages, still its meaning is the same, and is ever in opposition to bad. We say from the Saxon, *good;* the Dane, *god;* the Goth, *goda;* the German, *gut;* the Dutch, *goed;* the Latin, *bonus;* the Greek, *kalos;* the Hebrew, *tob;* and the Egyptian, *mon.* Hence with the addition of more, or the Egyptian, *mor,* we have the word Mormon, which means literally, more good.'

"Notwithstanding all this pedantic parade of learning on the part of the Prophet, uninspired scholars have expressed an opinion that the word was derived from the Greek μορμών, a spectre or hideous shape."—*Rocky Mountain Saints*, by T. B. H. Stenhouse.

usual into the woods to pray, taking with him Oliver Cowdery his scribe, one of the "three witnesses" above alluded to. As they prayed—they took care to select a spot where there was some water (a pond) conveniently close at hand—they were suddenly confronted by St. John the Baptist (!), who "descended from heaven in a bright light," laid his hands on them and ordained them, and commanded them to baptize and ordain each other in his presence. The two men then entered the water together and baptized each other by immersion, "Joseph Smith baptizing Oliver Cowdery, and he baptizing Joseph," and then "Joseph re-ordaining Oliver, and he re-ordaining Joseph." It is said that as they came out of the water they "experienced great and glorious blessings," and "stood up and prophesied." After this—though not until April 6, 1830, more than a year after the ordination of Joseph and Oliver—the Mormon Church was organized in earnest at Fayette, in Seneca County, New York, at the house of one Peter Whitmer, when six persons were present, including the Prophet and his scribe. They all "entered into covenant to serve the Lord," received the "gift of the Holy Ghost," and thus was the "Church of Christ" (*sic*) fairly launched upon a disbelieving and a persecuting world.

This, then, briefly, is the origin of Mormonism. But unfortunately for the veracity of Joseph Smith, and for that of three of his witnesses,"[4] this unknown "Reformed Egyptian" has

[4] It is the testimony of the three witnesses who protested as to the plates, which must be discredited, not that of the eight witnesses who merely testified that Smith had shown them certain plates. It may be noted that the "three witnesses," a few years after, formally renounced their testimony, declaring it to be false, for which they were "disfellowshipped" from the Church and "turned over to the buffetings of the devil." The following are the two testimonies referred to, as appended to the Book of Mormon:

"*The Testimony of Three Witnesses.*

" Be it known unto all nations, kindreds, tongues, and people unto whom this work shall come, that we, through the grace of God the Father, and our Lord Jesus Christ, have seen the plates which contain this record, which is a record of the people of Nephi, and also of the Lamanites, their brethren, and also of the people of Jared, who came from the tower of which hath been spoken; and we also know that they have been translated by the gift and power of God, for his voice hath declared it unto us; wherefore we know of a surety that the work is true. And we also testify

been proved by Professor Anthon, of New York City, to whom the plates were submitted before they were returned to the angel, to be a jumble of "Greek, Hebrew, and all sorts of letters, more or less distorted either through unskilfulness or design, and intermingled with sundry delineations of half-moons, stars, and other natural objects, the whole ending in a rude representation of the Mexican Zodiac!"[5]

And now comes the question, what is Mormonism? Of what elements of faith is the religion composed? These we shall find if we turn to the code of prominent doctrines with

that we have seen the engravings which are upon the plates; and they have been shown unto us by the power of God, and not of man. And we declare with words of soberness, that an angel of God came down from heaven, and he brought and laid before our eyes, that we beheld and saw the plates, and the engravings thereon; and we know that it is by the grace of God the Father, and our Lord Jesus Christ, that we beheld and bear record that these things are true; and it is marvellous in our eyes, nevertheless the voice of the Lord commanded us that we should bear record of it; wherefore, to be obedient unto the commandments of God, we bear testimony of these things. And we know that if we are faithful in Christ, we shall rid our garments of the blood of all men, and be found spotless before the judgement-seat of Christ, and shall dwell with him eternally in the heavens. And the honour be to the Father, and to the Son, and to the Holy Ghost, which is one God, Amen.

" OLIVER COWDERY,
" DAVID WHITMER,
" MARTIN HARRIS.

"*The Testimony of Eight Witnesses.*

" Be it known unto all nations, kindreds, tongues, and people unto whom this work shall come, that Joseph Smith, Jun., the translator of this work, hath shown unto us the plates of which hath been spoken, which have the appearance of gold; and as many of the leaves as the said Smith has translated we did handle with our hands; and we also saw the engravings thereon, all which has the appearance of ancient work, and of curious workmanship. And this we bear record with words of soberness, that the said Smith has shown unto us, for we have seen and hefted, and know of a surety that the said Smith has got the plates of which we have spoken. And we give our names unto the world, to witness unto the world that which we have seen; and we lie not, God bearing witness of it.

" CHRISTIAN WHITMER,   " HIRAM PAGE,
" JACOB WHITMER,   " JOSEPH SMITH, SEN.,
" PETER WHITMER, JUN.,   " HIRUM SMITH,
" JOHN WHITMER,   " SAMUEL H. SMITH."

[5] *Rocky Mountain Saints.*

which Joseph Smith furnished the Church in the year 1842. A Mormon's creed, therefore, is as follows: Belief in the Three Persons of the Godhead; man's punishment for sin; Christ's atonement, and the consequent redemption of mankind; the four ordinances of the Gospel by which mankind may be saved, namely (1) Faith in the Lord Jesus Christ, (2) Repentance, (3) Baptism by immersion for the remission of sins, (4) Laying on of hands for the gift of the Holy Ghost; the divine calling of a man by prophecy, and the laying on of hands by those in authority to do so; the *régime* of the primitive church, in its having apostles, prophets, teachers, evangelists, etc.; the gift of tongues, prophecy, revelation, visions, healing, interpretation of tongues; that the Bible and the Book of Mormon are the Word of God, the former "so far as it is translated correctly;" the literal gathering of Israel and the restoration of the Ten Tribes; the selection of North America for the location of Zion, according to the prophecies of Isaiah[6] and Zechariah;[7] the personal reign of Christ upon earth, and that the earth will be renewed, and will receive its "paradisic glory;" and lastly, "We believe," says Mr. Smith, "in being honest, true, chaste, benevolent, virtuous, and in doing good to *all* men; indeed, we may say that we follow the admonition of Paul, 'We believe all things, we hope all things;' we have endured many things, and we hope to be able to endure all things. If there is anything virtuous, lovely, of good report, or praiseworthy, we seek after these things." To the above may be added: Belief in unrestricted polygamy; a heaven where there will be perpetual eating and drinking, to last on for ever and ever; that man was existing in the form of a spirit before he came into the world; that all good Mormons will be "resurrected" into gods, and that their existence in the next world will be the

[6] Isaiah xxix. 4.—"And thou shalt be brought down, and shalt speak out of the ground, and thy speech shall be low out of the dust, and thy voice shall be, as of one that hath a familiar spirit, out of the ground, and thy speech shall whisper out of the dust." Mormons claim that this was a prophetic allusion to Joseph Smith's discovery of the golden plates.

[7] Zech. ii. 4.—"Run, speak to this young man, saying, Jerusalem shall be inhabited as towns without walls for the multitude of men and cattle therein." The young man here referred to is supposed by Mormons to be no less important a personage than Joseph Smith himself.

same as in this, the only difference being that their bodies will consist of flesh without blood, spirit supplying the deficiency caused by the removal of the latter constituent; that Joseph Smith will be the first one "resurrected," and that then he will proceed immediately to "resurrect" in order all Latter-day Saints who have kept the faith, gentlemen first, *then* the ladies (!); and that last of all he will "resurrect" the Gentiles, the best first, and the worst—that is, those who have been hostile to Mormonism—coming last.

An authority already quoted[5] gives the following information respecting the originality of the "Church of Christ." I give *verbatim* the questions and answers therein contained on the subject:

"Q. What are those who believe and obey the truth called?

"A. Saints.

"Q. What are they called as an organized body of people?

"A. The Church of Jesus Christ of Latter-day Saints.

"Q. Are there more Churches of Christ on the earth than one?

"A. No. There can be but one, and though that one may have many branches, they must all be united, and be subject to one head.

"Q. Is it right that any branch of the Church of Christ should call itself the Church of England, or the Wesleyan Methodist Church, or the New Connexion Methodist Church, or the Reformed Methodist Church, or the General Baptist Church, or the Particular Baptist Church?

"A. No. God highly disapproves of such names being applied to his Church or any portion thereof.

"Q. Are these societies which use such names branches of the Church of Christ?

"A. No. They have been founded in the wisdom of this world, by men who have not received authority from God.

"Q. Why are such names given to societies of men who profess to belong to the Church of Christ?

"A. Because the founders of those societies, not being in-

[5] Mormon *Catechism for Children*.

structed of the Lord, have not shown His will in the matter; consequently such societies have been founded according to the taste of the founders, or of the people, after the names of the founders, or after some peculiar doctrines or circumstances connected with the societies.

"Q. Are such societies united, and subject to one head?

"A. No. They are divided, and they contend one with another. Indeed, some have separated themselves from others, for instance—the Reformed Methodist Church, and the New Connexion Methodist Church, separated themselves from the Wesleyan Methodist Church; the Wesleyan Methodist Church separated itself from the Church of England, and the Church of England separated itself from the Roman Catholic Church.

"Q. Why is this called the Church of Jesus Christ of *Latter-day* Saints?

"A. To distinguish it from the Church that existed in former days, as these are the latter days in which we live.

"Q. How can the Church of Christ be known from other religious societies?

"A. By various characteristics, among which may be named: Its Priesthood and organization; its being led by a prophet having direct revelation from God; its enjoying the gifts and blessings of the Holy Ghost, and promising the same to all believers; its purity and consistency of doctrine: its unity and oneness of spirit; its gathering its members from among the wicked; its building of temples dedicated to the Lord instead of building churches and chapels dedicated to men and women; its being persecuted and evil-spoken of by every other society and by every other people under heaven; and lastly, men may know the Church of Christ by obeying its doctrines, and obtaining a testimony for themselves by revelation from God."[9]

[9] In the same work there occur also the following remarkable passages:

"Q. Are bread and wine used in the Sacrament?

"A. No. Water is occasionally used, when wine made by the Church cannot be obtained.

"Q. When wine is not to be had, is the use of water equally acceptable in the sight of God?

"A. Yes. It was through a revelation from him that water was first

We will now examine, very briefly, the contents of the book of Mormon—that translation from the "Reformed Egyptian" by means of the Urim and Thummim vouchsafed to Joseph Smith by the holy angel. This publication is, in a word, a

used in the Sacrament. *Doctrine and Covenants* 1. 1, 2; new edition, xxvii. 2—5.

Repeat the passage.

'For, behold, I say unto you, that it mattereth not what ye shall eat, or what ye shall drink, when ye partake of the Sacrament, if it so be that ye do it with an eye single to my glory; remembering unto the Father my body which was laid down for you, and my blood which was shed for the remission of your sins; wherefore a commandment I give unto you, that you should not purchase wine, neither strong drink, of your enemies; wherefore, ye shall partake of none, except it is made new among you; yea, in this my Father's kingdom which shall be built upon the earth. Behold, this is wisdom in me.'"

. . . .

"Q. Who are the proper subjects of baptism?

"A. Those persons who have come to years of accountability. *Doctrine and Covenants* ii. 20; xliii.; new edition xx. 71; xviii. 42.

Repeat the passage.

'No one can be received into the Church of Christ unless he has arrived unto the years of accountability before God, and is capable of repentance.

'For all men must repent and be baptized, and not only men, but women, and children who have arrived to the years of accountability.'

"Q. Do not many persons teach that little children will not be saved, unless they are baptized?

"A. Yes. But such doctrine is very wicked, and an abomination in the sight of God. *Book of Mormon*, Moroni, viii. 2, 3.

Repeat the passage.

'Wherefore, my beloved son, I know that it is a solemn mockery before God, that ye should baptize little children. . . . Wherefore, if little children could not be saved without baptism, these must have gone to an endless hell. Behold, I say unto you, that he that supposeth that little children need baptism, is in the gall of bitterness, and in the bonds of iniquity, for he hath neither faith, hope, nor charity, wherefore, should he be cut off while in the thought, he must go down to hell. For awful is the wickedness to suppose that God saveth one child because of baptism, and the other must perish because he hath no baptism. Woe be unto him that shall pervert the ways of the Lord after this manner, for they shall perish, except they repent. Behold, I speak with boldness, having authority from God. . . . Little children cannot repent: wherefore it is awful wickedness to deny the pure mercies of God unto them, for they are all alive in him because of his mercy. And he that saith that little children need baptism, denieth the mercies of Christ, and setteth at nought the atonement of him and the power of his redemption. Woe

history of the "ancient inhabitants of America." It is a complete and very original description of the lives and actions of the remote ancestors of the present race of human beings, commencing about the time of the confusion of tongues at Babel in or about the year 2247, B.C., and coming down to the year 400, A.D.,—from the migration from Babylon to America of a certain Jared and his family, who increased and multiplied and covered the vast continent,—which is called in the book of Mormon an "isle of the sea (!),"—down to the final extermination of all Jared's descendants through their innate love of slaughtering one another, for they did nothing but fight, fight, fight till there was none of them left! (It seems that Jared and his family escaped the confusion of tongues, and were not confounded like the rest of the people at Babel.) There is an account given in the work of perhaps the most disastrous battle on record, one in which we are told that 2,000,000 men were slain! Two hundred and thirty thousand had been killed in a previous engagement! Talk of our battle of Hastings, our Crecy, Poitiers, Waterloo, and other famous battles of modern times, why, they are a mere bagatelle compared with some of these (fictitious) civil engagements of the primitive Americans.

But there is a sad as well as a humorous side to an examination of this extraordinary publication. To anyone with the least particle of νοῦς, the Book of Mormon—deemed, be it remembered, by the followers of Joseph Smith to be the Word of God—will appear, before many pages of it have been turned over, to be nothing but a sham from beginning to end: moreover, the consummate audacity, the cool barefaced way in which the most sacred Name of Names is brought into its pages and made use of to serve the ends of the compilers of the wildly impossible stories that are to be found in the volume, stamps blasphemy on the very face of the production. Even the poor feeble style of composition, with statements in some

unto such, for they are in danger of death, hell, and an endless torment. I speak it boldly, God hath commanded me.'

"Q. At what age are children considered accountable, and old enough to be baptized?

"A. The children of the Saints are considered old enough at eight years to be baptized."

places vague and unmeaning, in others ill-formed and badly put together, is, in itself, quite sufficient to give rise to doubt as to the divine origin of the work. And when we do come to examine its contents, what do we find? We find that the phraseology of the Bible is imitated in every page, every paragraph throughout the volume. We find passages collected from different parts of Holy Scripture—mostly from the four Gospels and the Acts of the Apostles—and strung together indiscriminately, without any thought or regard being paid to the occasion or circumstance to which each has reference. We find some of the sublimest passages in Isaiah quoted wholesale and placed side by side with subject-matter so loathsome and disgusting as to be totally unfit for publication. And, worse than all, we find our Lord's own words to His disciples freely introduced, here word for word as He uttered them, there interpolated with supplementary matter purely imaginary, which is not only altogether foreign to the text of the New Testament, but is, in many cases, quite out of harmony with the spirit and "style" —if such a term may be used—in which Holy Scripture is written.

Blasphemy, rubbish and bad grammar are the leading characteristics of the Book of Mormon. The grammar is simply atrocious. It is a remarkable thing, that among the immense number of revelations vouchsafed to Prophet Joe Smith—there are 133 recorded in his Book of Doctrine and Covenants—there was not one imparting to him the art of writing with correctness. As illustrating the illiterate style of composition pervading the work, the following passages, taken at random, may be quoted:

"Now behold, it came to pass that I, Jacob, having ministered much unto my people, in word, (and I cannot write but a little of my words, because of the difficulty of engraving our words upon plates,) and we know that the things which we write upon plates must remain; but whatsoever things we write upon any thing save it be upon plates, must perish and vanish away; but we can write a few words upon plates, which will give our children, and also our beloved brethren, a small degree of knowledge concerning us, or concerning their fathers." (Page 120, edition 1877.)

"But we have been led to a better land, for the Lord has made the sea our path, and we are upon an island of the sea." [10] But great are the promises of the Lord unto they who are upon the isles of the sea; wherefore as it says isles, there must needs be more than this, and they are inhabited also by our brethren." (Page 78.)

"And now it came to pass that when Jesus had said these words, he said unto them again, after he had expounded all the scriptures unto them which they had received, he said unto them, behold, other scriptures I would that ye should write, that ye have not." (Page 481.)

"Now whether there shall be one time, or a second time, or a third time, that men shall come forth from the dead, it mattereth not; for God knoweth all these things; and it sufficeth me to know that this is the case." (Page 318.)

"And he said go, and tell this people, hear ye indeed, but they understood not; and see ye indeed, but they perceived not." (Page 337.)

"And I saw wars and rumours of wars among them; and in wars and rumours of wars, I saw many generations pass away." (Page 24.)

"Let your communication be yea, yea; nay, nay; for whatsoever cometh of more than this are evil." (Page 460.)

"And there were some who died with fevers, which at some seasons of the year was very frequent in the land." (Page 337.)

The following remarkable passages in the Book of Mormon may also be cited:

"And when Moroni had said these words, he went forth among the people, waving the rent of his garment in the air, that all might see the writing which he had wrote upon the rent." (Page 335.)

"The Lord God hath opened my ear, and I was not rebellious, neither turned away back. I gave my back to the smiter, and my cheek to them that plucked off my hair. I did not hide my face from fear and spitting, for the Lord God will help me; therefore shall I not be confounded. . . . .

---

[10] North America, as already noted, is the "island" here referred to.

Who is my adversary? let him come near me, and I will smite him with the strength of my mouth; for the Lord God will help me. And all they who shall condemn me, behold, all they shall wax old as a garment, and the moth shall eat them up." (Page 69.)

"And it came to pass that they all sware unto him, by the God of Heaven, and also by the Heavens, and also by the earth, and by their heads, that whoso should vary from the assistance which Akish desired, should lose his head; and whoso should divulge whatsoever thing Akish made known unto them, the same should lose his life. And it came to pass that thus they did agree with Akish." (Page 553.)

"Now the joy of Ammon was so great, even that he was full; yea, he was swallowed up in the joy of his God, even to the exhausting of his strength, and he fell again to the earth. Now was not this exceeding joy? Behold this is joy which none receiveth save it be the truly penitent and humble seeker of happiness." (Page 285.)

"There were no robbers, nor murderers, neither were there Lamanites, nor any manner of ites." (Page 493.)

Concerning the organization of the Mormon Church the following may be said. It is governed by a president and a council or "Quorum" of twelve apostles,—the president of the Church ranking as one of the twelve apostles,—and these constitute the Mormon hierarchy. Their word is infallible, their behests incontrovertible, their power supreme. Originally —when the Church was first started—it was governed by a "First Presidency," or a "Quorum of Three," who considered themselves the representatives upon earth of the Three Persons of the Blessed Trinity! These, in the first place, consisted of "Prophet" Joseph Smith and his two counsellors, namely Hyrum Smith his brother, and Willard Richards, the "Keeper of the Rolls;" but after the two Smiths were assassinated in 1844, the First Presidency lapsed, and the twelve apostles—or rather, a "Quorum of Twelve"—ruled the Church for three years, till Brigham Young restored the First Presidency by procuring his own election to the prophetship and re-appointing two counsellors. Brigham died in 1877; and his death, again, dissolved the First Presidency,

PROMINENT LIVING MORMONS, 1880.

which has not since been revived.[11] The various offices in the Church are contained under two priesthoods, the Melchisedec or higher priesthood and the Aaronic (Levitical) or lesser priesthood. The former of these includes the offices of apostle, seventy, patriarch or evangelist, high priest, and elder; the latter includes the offices of bishop, priest, teacher, and deacon. Taking these in order, an apostle has to organize and preside over the Church. A seventy, or a Quorum of seventy or seventies,—any number may form a Quorum in this case,—has to travel about the world and promote the general welfare of the Church, by preaching the Gospel to the "heathen" and inducing as many as possible to gather to "Zion." A patriarch or evangelist's duty is to bless—bless the Saints and tell them of the joys that are in store for them (in the next world) if they will pay in their tithing regularly, and say their prayers morning and evening on behalf of the Holy Priesthoods. The duty of a high priest is to preside at collective meetings, and to travel about (like the seventy) and aid in converting the heathen. An elder preaches, baptizes, administers the Sacrament, blesses little children, ordains other elders and the officers of the lesser priesthood, presides at meetings in the absence of the high priest—indeed he can perform an official duty in almost any capacity, provided that no higher authority is present to officiate. A bishop's duty is, in Mormon phraseology, to "administer all temporal things." He is "a judge in Israel," a magistrate among the inhabitants of "Zion." A priest baptizes, administers the Sacrament, and visits the Saints

[11] Information has reached me at the last moment from Salt Lake City, that at the late semi-annual Conference of the Latter-day Saints, held on October 6th and four following days, the Quorum of the First Presidency was re-established, two counsellors being appointed to John Taylor, the President of the Church. The Mormon Church, therefore, is now governed by a president and two counsellors, and a council of twelve apostles. The two counsellors who have just been appointed are George Q. Cannon, as "First Counsellor in the First Presidency," and Joseph F. Smith, as "Second Counsellor in the First Presidency." The names of the twelve apostles are as follows: John Taylor (president), Wilford Woodruff, Orson Pratt, Charles C. Rich, Lorenzo Snow, Erastus Snow, Franklin D. Richards, Brigham Young, Albert Carrington, Moses Thatcher, Francis Marion Lyman, and John Henry Smith.

in their homes, occasionally praying with them. A teacher likewise attends to the spiritual and temporal wants of the Saints, by visiting them, etc.; and he has, besides, according to the Book of Doctrine and Covenants, to "see that there is no iniquity in the Church."—But I fear he sadly neglects his duty in this respect. Lastly, a deacon assists the teacher, visiting the fatherless and widows, and offering them what aid he can in their prayers, besides performing several menial offices, such as keeping order at public assemblies, seeing that the meeting-halls are properly ventilated, etc.

The people are parcelled out into large districts, or "stakes," and these are sub-divided into smaller districts, or "wards." A president and two counsellors exercise control over each stake, their duty being to attend to the spiritual wants of those who have been entrusted to their care: a bishop and two counsellors preside over each ward, their duty being to look after the temporal wants of their *protégés*—to look after their secular affairs, and report their condition to the presidents and counsellors of their respective wards. Again, there are the teachers and deacons, who are under the bishops and counsellors, each having his own little district to attend to, and these must in their turn report to the bishops upon the position and state of affairs of the people over whom they have been appointed, and they are expected to go round at least once a month and visit every family. Thus we see that the οἱ πολλοί of "Christ's Church" are pretty well indeed looked after, and that their spiritual and temporal necessities are liberally taken into account—especially the latter. The Territory of Utah is divided into twenty stakes, and these are split up into 230 wards. The Salt Lake stake is divided into twenty-one wards. Conferences of the Church are held in Salt Lake City twice every year, in April and October. Of these, the spring meeting is the most important, for then the "trustee-in-trust" presents his annual budget; missionaries are selected to go forth and preach "the Word" to the "heathen" in Europe; and the well-being of "the elect," both spiritual and material, is thoroughly and satisfactorily investigated.

Thus much for Mormonism in general. We have now given a brief account of its origin, and of some of its principal characteristics, with which it is essential that the reader should be acquainted before he is introduced to the Saints in their mountain home. With the history of the Church from the day that it was founded on the 6th of April, 1830, ten years after Joseph Smith's first vision, and (according to the calculation of Orson Pratt, one of the twelve apostles) exactly 1800 years to a day from the resurrection of Christ (!), it is not within the scope of this work to deal, however slightly. Yet I may remark, that the history of the persecutions of this people and of their barbarous and sanguinary retaliations upon their oppressors, is quite enough to gratify the appetite of the most ardent lover of sensational romance; and the story of the wanderings of that band of devotees across the great American plains and Rocky Mountains, going they scarcely knew whither, under the leadership of their late president, Brigham Young, till they sighted the beautiful valley where they have founded and built up a "city of refuge" for themselves, forms indeed a very remarkable and interesting page in the history of the great Transatlantic continent. However much we may cry down Mormonism and heap shame upon the Saints,—which we are bound to do when we turn to and examine their domestic life,—or pity them for their ignorant and superstitious belief, there is still one fact that cannot be ignored, and that is, that their frugal habits and patience in the endurance of many privations have enabled them to reclaim a region that once was barren, and to transform a desert into a garden. There can also be no doubt that they have mainly contributed to the development of the great hidden wealth of the Territory.

CHAPTER VIII.

THE ROCKY MOUNTAIN ZION.

The Mormon metropolis—Its luxuriant appearance—A model city—Lovely situation—Clearness of the atmosphere—The Tabernacle—An extraordinary-looking building—Inside and outside—The Tabernacle organ—Curious subjects of sermons—A horn-blower from the Old Country—An angry spouse objects—The Temple—The Endowment House—Mysteries of the "endowments"—The new Assembly Hall—Brigham's Block—The tithing system—The tithing fund of 1879—The Lion House—The Beehive House—Sign of Mormon stores—The President of the Mormon Church—Holy men of "Zion"—Hypocrisy extraordinary—Revolting picture of Mormon life—A matter for Congress to look into—"The Upper California"—A porter from Didcot Junction—Peculiarity of Mormon houses—Domestic economy—On the road to Fort Douglas—Magnificent prospect over the Salt Lake Valley—The doctrine of polygamy—Its introduction among the Saints—Smith's reason for introducing it—Many-wived Mormons—A bachelor's duty—The spiritual-wife system—Sealing—Pleading for polygamy—Remarkable meeting of women in favour of the institution—Utah's delegate to the National Congress.

June 10*th*.

THIS morning we got up early, had breakfast sharp, and began to arrange our day's programme. In this we were aided by an English gentleman who had been located in "Zion" for more than a twelvemonth, who courteously came and offered us his services for the day, proposing to conduct us over the city, explain everything, and introduce us to the best of the Saints—an offer which we only too readily accepted. So we started forth to see "Zion's glories."

Stepping out of the hotel we found ourselves in the chief thoroughfare, called Main-street, and began making our way through a busy throng of people towards the Tabernacle, the Mormon House of God, which lay at the farther end. To

SALT LAKE CITY, FROM THE UTAH CENTRAL RAILROAD.

one who expects to find in the principal street of the Rocky Mountain "Zion" a narrow highway composed of two rows of tumble-down wooden shanties, separated by a rough, half-made road, as no doubt is the impression of some, the sight of the Main-street would be an agreeable surprise. True the majority of the houses are built of wood, and those that are not of wood are built of "adobe," or sun-dried bricks; and true, again, that the great width of the roadway (128 feet between the two pavements, each of which is 28 feet wide) completely dwarfs the height of the buildings, making them look small and insignificant—albeit there are three buildings at least in this street that would not disgrace the State-street of Chicago or the Broadway of New York. But, with luxuriant shade-trees separating the pavements from the road; with streams of pure water, fresh from the mountains, flowing down at the sides; with the road laid with a tramway and continually traversed by mule-drawn cars, this street is but a specimen of others in the Mormon metropolis, for they most of them have similar features. Irrigating streams—as I have implied—run through every street, and not only at the two sides but down the middle of some of them as well; tramways are laid from one end of the city to the other, connecting the "depôt" (railway station) with the hotels and chief places of interest; shade-trees, such as the cottonwood, locust, Lombardy poplar, and box elder, border the sidewalks; trim landscape gardens full of fruit-trees (peach, apricot, pear, and plum), and gay with beautiful flowers, abound; and every garden-lot can have a limited supply of water turned into it whenever the occupier feels disposed, by having it conveyed into his premises from the pure mountain stream which flows down the paved gutter of the street in front of him. A garden is this Salt Lake City, a very oasis in a desert, a luxuriant plantation in a once-waste wilderness; and when, considering the extraordinary circumstances under which it sprang into being, we regard the freshness of everything, the fertility of everything, the wonderful growth of trees and plants which spring up above the alkaline soil that underlies the fair surface, and which, in many instances, where the roots have sprouted deep enough, has changed the colour of the leaves from bright green to yellow, we cannot but come to the conclusion that this "City of the Saints" is one of the sights of the great American continent. Thirty-three years ago there was not a tree growing where the city now stands—there was not even a log-hut to be found for hundreds of miles around. Brigham Young in the year 1847 sighted the valley of the Great Salt Lake. First he consecrated it to the "Kingdom of God." Then he marked out "Zion,"[1] founded it, built it up, divided it into wards, planted it, irrigated it by diverting the streams from the neighbouring mountains, and the result is that we have a city of a little over thirty years' growth built, as it were, by one man, for Brigham's word was law, and everything had to be done according to the peculiar taste of the Prophet as "divine" architect. But the situation of the Mormon metropolis is most lovely. It lies twelve miles to the south-east of an immense salt lake,—whose greatest length is eighty miles, and breadth forty-five miles,—nestled at the base of a grand range of mountains, which rise immediately above the city. Mountain ranges close in the entire valley around, mountain isles rise out of the Great Salt Lake—all around is mountainous, the sublimity of the situation is supreme. The air, too, is so clear, that the glorious purple mountains by which the valley appears to be enclosed, seem to be scarcely half a dozen miles away, when in reality they are more like twenty. Just begin to step out to them before you have your breakfast one morning, and you will seem to be no nearer them when you have walked half way than when you first started.

But we are on our way to the Tabernacle, and must digress no longer. Turning off to the left after walking three "blocks" up Main-street, we come within view of the building. This is one of the most extraordinary-looking structures it has been my lot to look upon. Let me endeavour in some way to describe it. Regarded from a distance, it may be said to resemble a great pie-dish turned upside down, and resting on pegs; or, again, it is not unlike the back of an enormous turtle. It consists of an arched roof of an immense single, unbroken span, 250 feet long and 150 feet wide, reaching to a height of seventy-seven feet above the ground, and resting on

[1] Salt Lake City is laid out in 260 ten-acre blocks, each block split up into lots of an acre and a quarter.

VIEW OF THE MORMON TABERNACLE, SALT LAKE CITY.
Showing walls of the new Temple in course of erection.

Page 166.

the top of forty-nine massive pillars of cut sandstone ranging from fourteen to twenty feet in height. The roof is composed of interlaced pieces of timber, which have been cut the size of small slates, and it is daubed over with white paint. Its shape is an oblong with the corners rounded off. There are doors between nearly every column all round the building, to be used for exit in case of panic, and there are windows above the doors, directly under the "cover" or roof. Upon entering you find an open, free and unobstructed building.

INTERIOR OF THE TABERNACLE.

At one end is a rostrum (for the President, the twelve apostles, the bishops, the preacher, the choir, the conductor of the choir, and the band), and behind it, at the back of all, a large organ, with an elaborately carved case and a frontage of gilded pipes. A gallery runs round three sides, supported by seventy-two thin columns of wood painted to resemble marble, each column being about sixteen inches in diameter, composed of two-inch plank, hollow in the centre and gradually tapering towards the top; and these are the only props inside that can be seen. Low benches cover the entire floor, and a passage runs down the middle. The floor is level to about the centre of the building, when a grade commences (of about four feet), to enable those sitting in the back benches to see and hear the more comfortably. Six or eight rows are allotted to the "Gentiles" who may happen to attend the services. They are by far the best seats, commencing about the seventh row. No corners are visible, and one cannot fail to be struck with the impression that the main object

INTERIOR OF THE TABERNACLE.
Showing Organ.

in the mind of its ingenious architect was to effect such an arrangement, that no person in the building could be prevented from seeing the preacher. That such is the case I myself proved, for I was unable to place myself where I could not obtain an unobstructed view of the rostrum, and of anyone who might happen to be upon it. The ceiling is plain. It is whitewashed, and two small square apertures in the roof admit a little more light than what is afforded by the windows which are hidden right away beneath the gallery. Paper festoons made in imitation of flowers, and suspended aloft, considerably relieve the bare effect produced by this plain whitewashed ceiling, besides giving the building a festal appearance—these having been put up on the 24th of July, 1877, the thirtieth anniversary of the Mormon arrival in the valley. Prior to this anniversary there were certain familiar inscriptions hung about the building, such as " Brigham our leader and friend," " Joseph Smith the Prophet of the Lord," " Utah's best crop—children," " Lamanites the battle-axes of the Lord," etc. ; but these were all taken down on July 24, 1877. The organ was built by an English Mormon, a Mr. Ridges, and contains 2000 pipes. Mormons tell you that it is the largest organ in America. I believe, however, that the one in the Music Hall at Boston, and that in the Plymouth Church, Brooklyn, also the one in the Cincinnati Music Hall, are each of them much larger. The Saints also tell you that their Tabernacle is constructed to seat 13,000 persons—at a push. But allowing eighteen inches for each person, it just holds 6280.

The Mormon Tabernacle possesses remarkable acoustic powers. A common pin let drop at one end of the building,—or an ordinary whisper,—can be heard distinctly at the other end, a distance of 250 feet. Not only so, but a pin dropped twenty-five feet from the wall at one end, or even fifty feet from the same place, can also be heard by one standing at a distance of thirty feet from the wall at the opposite end of the building. I proved this to be so in each one of these cases.

The services in the Tabernacle are generally well attended. Divine (?) service is held in it only once a week, on Sundays at 2 p.m. Other services, such as they are, are held in the twenty-one wards into which the city is ecclesiastically divided. No one knows who the preacher will be till he stands up on the daïs just before commencing his sermon. The sermons are practical enough, it cannot be denied, and must sometimes be rather entertaining. An authority thus writes : " In the Great Tabernacle one will hear sermons or advice on the culture of sorghum ; upon infant baptism ; upon the best manure for cabbages ; upon the perseverance of the saints; upon the wickedness of skimming milk before its sale; upon the best method of cleaning water-ditches; upon bed-bug poison; upon the price of real estate; upon teething in children; upon the martyrs and persecutions of the Church; terrible denunciations of Gentiles and the enemies of the Mormons; upon olive-oil as a cure for measles; upon the ordination of the priesthood; upon the character of Melchisedec; upon worms in dried peaches; upon the crime of fœticide; upon chignons; upon twenty-five-yard dresses; upon plural marriages, etc."[2]

Our guide over the building was the Tabernacle porter, an English Mormon, who had been dwelling in "Zion" as one of the faithful for fifteen years. He used to blow the French horn in our Drury Lane and Crystal Palace orchestras. He still continues to blow his trumpet in the Tabernacle orchestral band, and occasionally does a little organ-playing. He is the husband of but one wife—a "Lancashire lass." Not very long ago he wished to take unto himself another wife, but his present one would not let him. She gave him such a drubbing for his impudence that he was laid up after it for six weeks!

Close beside the Tabernacle are the walls of the new Temple in course of erection. They are built of granite procured from quarries near at hand, and are nine feet nine inches thick. *When* completed, the building will, it is said, have cost 6,400,000*l*. (!) : but it was begun twenty-seven years ago,—the corner-stone was laid on April 6, 1853,—and the walls are as yet only thirty feet high. According to design of the building, the walls will be from eighty-six to ninety-nine feet in height, and the middle of its three great eastern towers will attain a height of 225 feet. Feeling curious on the subject, I asked the porter, who was with us, what would become of the Tabernacle when the Temple was completed? He said that it would remain to be used as it was now used, "for the purposes of divine worship." "Then you intend holding your religious services in two buildings?" I replied. "Not exactly," said the porter. "Our Temple will be devoted to the celebration of those mystic ceremonies which are the necessary accompaniments of our religion." I asked him to explain; but the man declined.

[2] *The Pacific Tourist.*

At the north-west corner of this block—which is generally known as the "Temple Block"—is the Endowment House. This is not much of a building to look at, but in it all the

DESIGN OF THE MORMON TEMPLE.

baptisms as well as all monogamous and polygamous marriages are celebrated. It is enclosed within a stone wall some ten or twelve feet high. There is a good deal of mystery attached to the performance of certain rites in this building. No one, I believe, outside Mormonism is aware of the actual nature of the "endowments" which a person receives in order that he or she may fully and entirely be taken into the bosom of the Church. From what I have been able to gather, re-baptism is necessary in order to receive them, this being immediately followed by the rite of confirmation, the latter ordinance conferring (*sic*) upon the person the gift of the Holy Ghost; and then a drama is acted, founded, it would seem, upon Milton's *Paradise Lost*, in which the leaders of the Church sustain the principal characters, and the man or woman who is to receive the "endowments" sustains also a principal part, and comes out of it all with a new name, an "endowment name," which is secretly given and is to be secretly kept, and by which he or she is to be "resurrected" at the last day. It can scarcely be said that much light is thrown on this subject by Mr. Stenhouse, who, in his valuable work before quoted,—Mr. Stenhouse was himself a Mormon elder and missionary for twenty-five years,—says, in referring to the Endowment House, "Within its portals are performed all the rites and ceremonies that hold Mormonism together." But in another portion of his work he says, "In due time every man is to receive the priesthood of Aaron and Melchisedec, and thereby becomes entitled to commune with the heavens; and when all have accepted the 'Celestial Law'—that is, polygamy—and have passed through the ordinances of the 'endowments,' they are presumed to be fairly started for 'honour, glory, and eternal lives with the gods above.'" No doubt the "mystic ceremonies" which, according to the porter, will be performed in the Temple, will be similar to those which are at present performed in the Endowment House, for the former is built only to supersede the latter, which is to be a far more glorious edifice, for "thither the angels will come, and there 'the Lord' will find rest upon the earth."

There is a winter tabernacle, or "assembly hall," in course of erection beside the Temple and large Tabernacle. This building was sufficiently far advanced to allow of the last annual spring conference of the Mormons taking place under its roof, on April 6, 1880. The large Tabernacle is not used in cold weather, as there is no way of heating it, Mormons say; so this new tabernacle has been devised, although it is a smaller building, seating about 4000 persons. The ceiling is being adorned with frescoes illustrating the history of the Mormon Church, this work having been commenced in the middle of last February.[3] A large organ has already been set up in the building, upon which the sum of 990*l*. 9*s*. 8*d*. ($4952.38) was expended. This building was the late Prophet's final idea, and the plans he drew up for its construction are being faithfully carried out by a Mr. Obid Taylor. It is built of granite, and the interior will, in some respects, resemble that of the present tabernacle. The block containing this and the other buildings above mentioned is enclosed by a strong plastered wall of about ten feet high, and no "Gentile" can enter the premises without rendering himself liable to be pounced upon by the porter or keeper of the large Tabernacle, who will ask him his business, or at least keep very close to him as long as he remains inside. And if he gets too inquisitive in asking questions about the mysteries of the Endowment House or the purposes to which the Temple is to be turned, the porter is just as likely as not to inform him that his room is far better than his company.

[3] The *Salt Lake Daily Herald* (a Mormon journal) of Sunday, February 29, 1880, gives the following account of the frescoes which adorn the new Assembly Hall : "On the west ceiling," it says, "is a large bee-hive, the emblem of Deseret, and on either side are the two temples built by the Latter-day Saints before they were driven to this country. The one on the north side of the bee-hive is a painting of the temple at Kirtland, the one on the south side is a representation of the temple at Nauvoo. On the north ceiling are paintings of Peter, James and John in the act of conferring the Melchisedec priesthood on the Prophet Joseph Smith, who is kneeling. To the east is a representation of the Salt Lake Temple, as it will be when completed ; and further on the Logan Temple. Over the first of these temples is a large-size portrait of the Savior ; and above the latter, one of Elijah. At the east end of the ceiling is a large view representing the Hill of Cumorah, with the Angel Moroni pointing out to Joseph—of whom there is an excellent painting—the spot where the tablets of the Book of Mormon were hidden. This view is supposed to be a fac-simile of the position of the stone under which the plates were discovered. On the south side are paintings of the Manti and St. George Temples, with a portrait of Elias over the former, and one of Moses— who holds in his hand a scroll containing the Ten Commandments in Hebraic characters—over the latter. West of the St. George Temple is a representation of John the Baptist conferring the Aaronic priesthood on the Prophet Joseph and Oliver Cowdery. . . ."

We next crossed over to the other side of Main-street, to "Brigham's Block" opposite. Here Prophet Brigham had his private residence, and the private residences of his principal wives, besides a few other establishments chiefly devoted to the transaction of that public and official business which keeps the Church alive. Thus there is the tithing house, the tithing office, the late Prophet's private office, and his two family mansions, the Lion House and the Beehive House; also a printing-office, the office of the *Deseret News* (the leading Mormon organ), and a telegraph office. Here, too, is the immigration house, which is used as a receptacle for new arrivals in "Zion." Here, into one room, are thrown whole families, husbands and wives, men, women, and children, all together, there to live like pigs till homes have been found for them. Should this room be overcrowded at any time and there are some unfortunates who cannot get in, these must make shift as best they can in the yard outside, and make their beds in the open air. But each family has to pay twenty-five cents for the privilege of doing so.

The tithing house is where "Zion's" Saints come and pay in their tithes. A tenth of a Mormon's income must be given to the support of his Church. If he has no money he must give in kind—anything will do so long as the Church gets it. Now the tithing fund is controlled wholly by the priesthood, who use it as they think fit, *and make no report*. In 1879 it amounted to the enormous sum of 9166*l*. 12*s*., and the total receipts of the Church for the year exceeded 219,000*l*. There is a tithing house in every Mormon town, which is presided over by the local bishop; but the tithing house in Brigham's Block is the head and chief of all, for into it are paid all the receipts from the other towns. Brigham Young was absolute comptroller and sole disburser of all the money that was paid into the Church during his sovereignty over it. He was the "'trustee in trust' (as he called himself) of the Church of Jesus Christ of Latter-day Saints." What he did with all the money, it is not for us to inquire. But it is a well-known fact that he was immensely rich, even with his enormous family; and it is also a fact, though one not so well-known, that he collected millions of dollars in this way, chiefly from Mormons in England, solely for the purpose of carrying out the work of the building of the Temple. That edifice, however, as we have seen, has not yet risen more than thirty feet above its foundations, although it was begun twenty-seven years ago.

The Lion House is an unpretending little building, and was used as a shelter for several of Brigham Young's consorts. There were living in this house a dozen wives of this remarkably-married man, at his decease; but more have been crowded into it at one time, for there is provision made for twenty ladies. Upstairs, at the top of the building, went the children of the several mothers; downstairs were the ladies' apartments. If one wife had a larger family than usual, extra accommodation was provided for her, and she was allotted more rooms accordingly. There is, besides, a large dining-hall, a kitchen, a laundry, a cellar, and some general or weaving rooms. There are still a few widows left in the house to mourn over their lamented Brigham.

The Beehive House was Brigham Young's private residence, though in strictness it should be said that this and the Lion House formed together his home or family mansion. In 1879 I found twelve widows in all residing in the two houses. The two buildings are only separated from each other by the adjunct buildings of the tithing office and the late Prophet's private office, as they stand all in a row, in one continuous block. The Beehive House and the Lion House are connected together inside, for a passage leads from the former through the two intermediate buildings into the latter. In his private office Brigham used to receive visitors who called upon him during their stay in the metropolis. It was also used by him for the transaction of his official business. A stout high wall used to stand in front of this row of buildings; but after the Prophet's decease his wives—those in the Beehive—agreed to have it pulled down, and to have railings put up instead, so that they might in future see a little more of the outside world since their lord and master had been taken from them, which is but natural. The wall was standing when I was in "Zion" in 1878, but the railings had taken the place of it when I was there in 1879. Part of the wall, however, is still remaining, namely the private gateway to the block, which is called the Eagle Gate, there being a large wooden spread-eagle over the entrance standing on a wooden beehive. There is also the imitation of a hive (in yellow plaster) at the top of the Beehive house, the principal family residence—as we have seen—of the deceased Prophet.

Coming out of Brigham's Block, there was pointed out to us an apostle giving one of his wives a turn in a buggy. This good man had eight consorts, all told. He happened to pull up, with the one he was now driving, at the door of a linen-draper's store, which we, very fortunately, were just

THE BEEHIVE HOUSE.

then on the point of entering. He gallantly tendered the lady his hand, and made belief to aid her in her descent; but she, rejecting the proffered assistance, alighted quickly from the vehicle with a graceful, pretty bound. The two then went into the shop to make purchases, and we closely followed them, and, standing behind them as they sat at the counter perched on the top of two high stools, took notes of their conversation and proceedings as they examined, and I think also purchased, a quantity of linen.

In the upper part of Main-street is an imposing brick and iron building, 318 feet long and fifty-four feet wide, with a skylight covering its entire length, and the letters " Z. C. M. I." standing out conspicuously on the roof—or more properly the skylight. This is the chief "co-op" (co-operative) store in

VIEW IN MAIN-STREET.

Salt Lake City, a strictly Mormon mercantile establishment, having, besides the letters on the skylight, a sign over the entrance, which describes more fully the purpose to which the building is devoted. The sign consists of the representation of an eye surrounded by a halo, the eye and the halo surrounded by the words, "HOLINESS TO THE LORD," and under all the inscription, "ZION'S CO-OPERATIVE MERCANTILE INSTITUTION." This is the well-known sign of a Mormon store, and though its adoption, now that Brigham Young is dead, is becoming less frequent, it is still to be found over several of the shops in Salt Lake City. In 1868 Brigham conceived the idea of a co-operative association to crush the trade of the anti-Mormons in the city. To use his own expressive language, he wished to " freeze the ungodly Gentiles out of Zion." He also directed the Mormon shop-keepers to place over their doors the sign I have described, and required the Saints to deal only with those that had this sign, and in no way to deal with " ungodly Gentiles," on pain of incurring his wrath, which would indeed have entailed consequences the most dreadful. But circumstances arose which frustrated all these benevolent intentions.

Into this co-operative store we stepped, and found it perfectly crowded with the Saints of " Zion," some buying, others selling. While we were there, Mr. John Taylor, the President of the Mormon Church, entered, and he was immediately pointed out to us. To give him his full, recognized title, he is Prophet, Seer, Revelator, and, by " divine " appointment, " God's Vice-regent upon the earth and the Religious Dictator to the whole world." He is also known as the " Champion of Right," just as Brigham Young was sometimes called the " Lion of the Lord." Such an important personage as this should receive a minute description, and here it shall be attempted. Aged apparently about seventy, he is a tall thin man with thick-set features; is grey-headed; has short, stubby white whiskers shaved far back on his countenance; wears no moustache, yet retains the semblance of a beard in a thick crop of white hair kept well away under the chin, and connected with the whiskers; has deep penetrating eyes; very protruding eyebrows; quite a large mouth; and, on the whole, has a very determined look about him. Added to his other accomplishments, he is the Poet Laureate of Zion. (We shall presently give a specimen of his poetry.) He is not a very great polygamist for a man in such an exalted position, for he is the husband of but six wives. We were promised an introduction to President Taylor, for he is always glad to welcome illustrious strangers in " Zion ;" but unfortunately this did not take place, as he stayed upstairs all the while conversing with the brethren and making purchases. However, we looked forward to being more fortunate on a future occasion. One of Brigham Young's grandsons was pointed out to us, lolling against the counter at the far end of the shop. This man had married his aunt! Another man was shown us who had married a couple of sisters! Other holy men of "Zion" were pointed out to us, and the number of their wives given. To some we were introduced, but in conversation avoided the "ugly" subject, which had it once been introduced would only have brought on argument and heated debate. So we contented ourselves by referring instead to the hot weather and the beauties of "Zion."

Little need be said of the present head of the Mormon Church. The story of his hairbreadth escape from assassination at the hands of the infuriated mob which murdered Joseph Smith and his (Smith's) brother Hyrum in Carthage gaol,—so exasperated were the people of Illinois at the gross presumptions of the Church,—forms indeed a wonderful and a thrilling narrative; but it is sufficient for my purpose here simply to make this bare allusion to the incident. Yet there is one act of President Taylor's life that may as well be mentioned: it is really too glaring and hypocritical to be passed over. It was in the year 1850 that Elder John Taylor was engaged on a mission at Boulogne-sur-mer, in France. Success attended his missionary efforts, and many "heathen" were converted and received into the fold.—But he preached and he proselytized with a lie in his right hand. It had been charged against the Church that its Saints were practising polygamy. So grave an imputation as this required an immediate explanation; so what did Elder Taylor do? He represented to his hearers that such a state of moral degradation could not possibly be; that the reports which had reached their ears were "too outrageous to admit of belief;" that the Book of Doctrine and Covenants had expressly denounced polygamy as a principle of the faith; and that according to his views of chastity and marriage, and according to the views of his brother missionaries who were at Boulogne with him, the practice of such a degrading doctrine would be decidedly wrong. Yet all this time, while he stoutly repudiated polygamy as an established ordinance of the Church, he had five wives living at Salt Lake City, one of his brother missionaries with him at Boulogne had two wives also living there, and another friend of his, also with him at Boulogne, had left behind him at Salt Lake two wives, namely, a mother and her daughter!! If an incredulous reader should be inclined to call in question this last statement, I have only to remark that its corroboration is to be found in works of authority, which anyone interested in Mormonism can obtain, and see that what I have stated is only the simple truth. Indeed I myself received testimony of its correctness from the lips of several when I revisited Salt Lake City in 1879, and the instance is one out of more I could quote of the horrible and disgusting state of things that the doctrine of polygamy has engendered. From a pile of letters before me as I write, which I have received since last January from resident gentlemen in the Mormon Metropolis, whose veracity I consider unquestionable, and whose names, were I to give them, would be accepted as a sufficient guarantee of the truth of what they tell me, I have evidence of a state of immorality existing among certain Mormon families in Utah, the knowledge of which would sicken and disgust even those who might on any grounds entertain the least sympathy for the followers of Brigham Young. "So far as I know," writes one of my correspondents, "no one has ever been molested by the church authorities for maintaining such infamous practices." But, it may be asked, why does not the Government of the United States interfere and wipe out this plague-spot from the national escutcheon? Why is such iniquity tolerated, why are people allowed to exist in a manner which debases humanity, lowering themselves to the level of brute beasts? Such a state of social corruption would never be tolerated in England, either by law or by public opinion. It will redound to the eternal discredit of American civilization if the evil be not speedily suppressed.

But to return to "Zion's" chief Saint, the Mormon President, who, as we have already said, is somewhat of a poet. There is a hymn called "The Upper California," which he wrote during the journeying of the Saints under the guidance of their leader Brigham Young across the Great Plains in search of the "promised land," which had already been revealed as being located somewhere indefinitely in the far West. Apostle

Taylor—he was one of the twelve apostles then—conceived the idea that its location would be in the northern part of California; and this he endeavoured to impress upon the Saints by composing the hymn which I will now quote, and which was sung by the people over and over again during the course of their wanderings:

"THE UPPER CALIFORNIA."

The Upper California—Oh, that's the land for me!
It lies between the mountains and the great Pacific sea;
    The Saints can be supported there,
    And taste the sweets of liberty
In Upper California—Oh, that's the land for me!

We'll go and lift our standard, we'll go there and be free:
We'll go to California and have our jubilee;
    A land that blooms with endless spring,
    A land of life and liberty,
With flocks and herds abounding—Oh, that's the land for me!

We'll burst off all our fetters and break the Gentile yoke,
For long it has beset us, but now it shall be broke:
    No more shall Jacob bow his neck;
    Henceforth he shall be great and free
In Upper California—Oh, that's the land for me!

We'll reign, we'll rule and triumph, and God shall be our King;
The plains, the hills and valleys shall with hosannas ring;
    Our towers and temples there shall rise
    Along the great Pacific sea,
In Upper California—Oh, that's the land for me!

We'll ask our cousin Lemuel to join us heart and hand,
And spread abroad our curtains throughout fair Zion's land:
    Till this is done, we'll pitch our tents
    Along the great Pacific sea,
In Upper California—Oh, that's the land for me!

Then join with me, my brethren, and let us hasten there;
We'll lift our glorious standard and raise our house of prayer;
    We'll call on all the nations round
    To join our standard and be free
In Upper California—Oh, that's the land for me!

But Apostle Taylor should not really have been quite so positive. The "Upper California" might have been the land for him, but it was not the one for Brigham Young. Upon Brigham sighting the valley of the Great Salt Lake, he was so entranced with the lovely prospect spread out before him,

—such a suitable location did the valley appear to offer for founding a rocky mountain "Zion,"—that the bright idea occurred to him to seek council from "the Lord" as to what he had better do. He did so then and there, and was successful in obtaining a revelation which fixed "Zion's" location in the valley before him. So the "Upper California" became a myth after all.

We now took a carriage-and-pair to Fort Douglas, a Government military post lying three miles out of the city. It is situated 750 feet above the valley, on the slopes of the neighbouring mountains. We stopped on the way at an unpretending little restaurant (or lager-beer saloon), to get some refreshment. The keeper of the place was, thirty-two years ago, a porter at the Didcot Junction station of our Great Western Railway, who in course of time had thought fit to change his religion and become a Mormon. Upon our explaining whence we came, he held out his hand for a good squeeze, and commenced "treating" us very kindly. He had one wife only. He told us he would like to be at Didcot Junction now, see our luggage right for Oxford—and take our fees.

As we passed out of the region of shops we could not help noticing how strangely the houses were built. Few were higher than one story. All were detached, and standing in little gardens. But the peculiarity about them was that they were built in groups of threes and fours, and occasionally a house would be seen having three, or perhaps four entrances facing the street. The meaning of this was thus explained to us.—Each group was a Mormon home, one family mansion, so to speak. In one little building the gentleman himself resided, and into the other little buildings he stowed away his wives. One house for each wife. Sometimes, for the sake of economy, he would crowd several into one house. In this case the wife was given a separate set of rooms, a separate entrance from the street, a separate knocker—and perhaps a separate latch-key.

The view we obtained over the valley as we ascended to the fort was magnificent. At our feet lay the verdant City of the Saints, its numerous gardens and green shady avenues giving it a delightfully fresh and luxuriant appearance; while away beyond stretched the Great Salt Lake, fifteen miles from where we stood, with lofty mountains rising from its midst, its motionless waters spreading far away among still loftier heights. The white-crested range of the Wahsatch Mountains rose behind the city to the east, attaining a culminating height of 11,200 feet above the sea-level (or 7000 feet above the valley); and then a glorious amphitheatre of broken heights almost encircled the valley, fir-trees dotted over their slopes and springing from their summits of snow, gaps in the nearer ranges disclosing beautiful peaks far away beyond in the dim distance. There was Mount Nebo, for instance, a blue peak visible eighty-five miles away to the south, rising to a height of 13,200 feet above the sea. On the other side of the Wahsatch range to our right were the Little Cottonwood Cañon—just twenty-six miles from us —and the Emma Hill, the locality of the celebrated Emma Mine, close to which are other well-known silver mines, such as the Flagstaff, Savage, Magnet, North Star, Monitor, Prince of Wales, and Wellington mines.

As even the briefest glance at the social life of the Latter-day Saints would be incomplete without a special reference to that institution which is universally associated with Mormonism as one of its distinguishing characteristics, it may not be out of place to add a few words to what has already been said incidentally on the subject.

I believe it is not generally known that polygamy—or, as it is called in Mormon revelation, the "Patriarchal Order of Matrimony"—did not originally form part of a Mormon's creed. Many people seem to be under the impression that Mormonism began with its practice; but such was not the case. Polygamy was not introduced into the religion until twenty-three or twenty-four years after Joseph Smith's first vision, for it was not till the year 1843 that he received a somewhat lengthy revelation respecting the "divine" ordinance, and this may be set down as the date of its formal introduction among the Saints. Here then is a grave inconsistency in the religion of this people. In the Book of Mormon plurality of wives is strictly forbidden, for in that extraordinary publication there occurs the following passage: "Wherefore, my brethren, hear me, and hearken unto the word of the Lord; for there shall not any man among you have save it be one wife, and concubines he shall have none, for I the Lord God delighteth in the chastity of woman." And again, the following curious passage: "Behold the Lamanites your brethren, whom ye hate, because of their filthiness and the cursings which have come upon their skins, are more righteous than you; for they have not forgotten the commandment of the Lord, which was given unto our fathers, that they should have, save it were one wife."

There is evidence enough to show that Joseph Smith introduced the doctrine of polygamy simply to protect himself against certain charges made at the time respecting his own private character. And it should be noted, that eight years before he gave out the revelation on this "partiarchal marriage," he published a book[3] containing all the revelations he had received up to that time, in which he explicitly stated that the Saints were "monogamic and pure;" but he also took care to insert into it the following passage, which, it will be noticed, admits in its first sentence of a conveniently equivocal interpretation: "We declare that we believe that one man should have one wife,[4] and one woman but one husband, except in case of death, when either is at liberty to marry again." Eight years later, as I said, was the revelation made known, but then only to a chosen few, for it was kept secret and was not publicly proclaimed to the Church at large till nine years afterwards, namely in 1852. Then was the bad seed sown, and the ground, alas! was fully prepared to receive it, for within three years after publicity had been given to the revelation, and countenance had been given to the practice of what is nothing more nor less than a barbarous, sensual and debasing doctrine, both apostles and saints were living "in open and undisguised polygamy."

It will be as well to make a note of the ingenious reason which the remarkable Joseph Smith gave for his introduction into the Church of this celestial doctrine of "spiritual" mar-

---

[3] *Book of Doctrine and Covenants*, published in Liverpool (1849, first edition).

[4] This sentiment of Joseph Smith will be found aptly illustrated in the course of a conversation which I had with a Mormon elder on the subject of polygamy, and which will be given in the following chapter.

riage. In a sermon he once delivered he is said to have thus expressed himself: "People of polygamous nations will be converted to the Church, and will desire to gather with the Saints in Zion, and what will they do with their wives? We must have polygamy among us as an established institution, and then they can bring their wives with them."

Now Polygamy among the Mormons involves a good deal more than what we understand by the term. Its consequences *in the next world* are truly infinite. A Mormon talks of "building up" or "adding to the glory of his 'kingdom,' for time and for all eternity." By which is meant that the more wives he has now the better it will be for him hereafter, for that when he dies he will become a god, and all his wives goddesses; and as the marital relation in the next world will be the same as in this, that there he will beget millions upon millions of spirits; but what is to become in the end of all the spirits so begotten, we are not clearly informed. A man may, in this way, if he collects a sufficient number of wives before he dies, constitute himself and family into quite a respectable little world, in truth, "for time and for all eternity." This is indeed laying up treasure in heaven with a vengeance! It is the doctrine of "Celestial Marriage;" and the text in Holy Scripture upon which this doctrine is based is, we are told, Mark x. 29, 30.

It should not be inferred from the above that a man who is a Mormon must be a polygamist. Mormonism does not necessarily involve polygamy; and yet it must be acknowledged that monogamy among the Saints is decidedly the less popular system of the two. A man does not rank very high in the estimation of the Church if he intends to build up his "spiritual" kingdom with the help of only one consort.

All Mormons in Utah are polygamists, theoretically. About one-third of the Mormon men in Salt Lake City are living with from two to ten wives each!"[5]

Considerable disgrace attaches to a Mormon if he lives a bachelor life. It is a duty he owes to the Church, and one that becomes him as a true Saint, to get married as soon as

---

[5] Extract from a private letter received from Salt Lake City in March, 1880.

he can. He should have three wives at least, and then he will command respect.

There is certainly every facility afforded the Mormon for entering the marriage state. Thus, a man can either have a woman "sealed" to him as his consort for this world only, or he can have her sealed to him both for this world as well as for the world to come. Again, a man may have a woman sealed to him for this world only, while another man may have the same woman sealed to him for the world to come—she is A's wife while she is on earth, but she becomes B's as soon as she has reached heaven. Or, again, a woman—a spinster, for instance—who has taken a particular fancy to any deceased Saint, and who wishes to become his consort in the world to come, can be sealed to him *by proxy* by becoming the wife of some living Saint. She has first to be sealed on earth before she can obtain the necessary introduction into heaven.

Now this term "sealing" is liable to be misconstrued. When a woman is said to be sealed to a man it does not necessarily imply that she is married to him. It may mean marriage, or it may simply amount to an "arrangement" to marry, to be consummated in the next world, made either directly between the two parties, or by proxy by another party in place of one of the two interested parties who is dead, as for instance—as we have seen above—where a woman wishes to become (in the Mormon heaven) the wife of a deceased Saint, *scil.* Joseph Smith or Brigham Young ; or again, where, even, she prefers being the consort of one of the patriarchs of the Old Testament, *scil.* Abraham, Isaac, Moses, Job, etc., for the Mormon spiritual-wife doctrine even ventures to go the length of this ! Thus Brigham Young is said to have had 185 "spiritual" wives ; that is to say, he entered into a holy compact with that number of women during his life-time that they should become his wives (or the wives of somebody else) in heaven. We now see how the Mormon "builds up" his extensive spiritual kingdom.

It may astonish the reader to know that there are hundreds —nay, thousands of women in Utah who are staunch advocates of polygamy, who even go so far as to give expression to their approval of the system by holding mass-meetings in public, whose battle-cry is "Polygamy or Death," and who look upon the "divine" institution as "the greatest of all earthly blessings!" Whether these devoted creatures are under the power of the priesthood, or are moved by religious fanaticism, or whether they uphold the degradation of their sex because they seriously think it right for woman to be so degraded, it would be hard to say; but I cannot believe that their submission to such moral debasement is spontaneous on their part, and voluntary. The opportunities I have had of judging for myself by conversing with Mormon women, have not been many; but the conclusion I have come to is that they are not happy under the system, and would wish themselves well out of it. And yet it seems strange that there should be found so many as 2000 women in the neighbourhood of Salt Lake City, who could lower themselves to such a degree as to assemble together and stoutly plead for the unnatural institution. Yet such was the case one day in the autumn of 1878, when the theatre-house in the Rocky Mountain "Zion" was packed to overflowing with indignant wives, mothers and daughters who came to make a vigorous protest against a crusade which had been undertaken against "patriarchal matrimony" by the Gentile women in the Territory. I have to thank the Principal of the Salt Lake Collegiate Institute, Mr. J. M. Coyner, for placing in my possession an account of this meeting, namely a portion of a letter which he wrote to the *Boston Educational Journal*, dated January 28, 1879. It occurs among a series of letters contributed by this gentleman to the same publication, and which have since been collected and published in pamphlet form under the title "Letters on Mormonism." The following is Mr. Coyner's account of the meeting: "The history," he says, "of Mormonism from its beginning shows that the women have been more devoted than the men, and to-day there is more true devotion to Mormonism, from principle's sake, among the women than among the men. I was therefore not surprised to find the theatre packed from pit to dome with some 2000 women, the most of whom, as shown by the up-lifted hand when a vote was taken, were devoted Mormons. It was the most remarkable meeting I ever attended. There were the aged mothers of seventy, who among storm and privation had emigrated among the first to this desert wilderness. There was the grown-up matron, whose life marks the growth of the Mormon power in the Territory. There were also many buxom lassies, some brought up in the Territory, others the latest importations from the Old World, many of whom had lately become the third, fourth or tenth wife of an aged elder. There was no excitement, no enthusiasm, but seemingly that fixed determination that causes one to do, suffer, and if need be, die for what he considers right. The meeting was regularly organized. The president, who was dressed in silk material entirely made in this Territory, spoke readily and fluently for more than half an hour. Among other things she said: 'Polygamy is as essential to woman's happiness as her salvation.' Mormon theology teaches that all those who are faithful Mormons, living up to the privileges of their religion in this world, and having many wives and numerous children, will be kings in the celestial world, and their wives queens, while those who are not married at all are compelled to be the slaves of those kings. Just think of the Apostle Paul being the servant of Brigham Young throughout the ages of eternity! Those who have but one wife, if they are faithful to the priesthood, and pay tithing, will have a home in the celestial world, but will not occupy any place of honour. Hence if any ambitious woman wishes a place of honour in the celestial world, she must be a polygamous wife. Another, who remarked she was seventy years old, said: 'I thank God that I am a polygamous wife, and that my husband is a polygamist;' and she had a 'feeling of great pity for those who did not enjoy this good blessing.' One old lady said: 'I would not abandon it (meaning polygamy) to exchange with Queen Victoria and all her dependencies.' The secretary of the meeting said: 'The women of this country want to crush us, but it will be diamond cut diamond.' And thus for nearly three hours one speaker after another defended polygamy, all believing it to be an inspired doctrine given by God to aid in redeeming a sinful world from a condition of sin and pollution, to one of holiness and purity. The following resolution, amongst others was unanimously adopted by the meeting: '*Resolved*, That we solemnly avow our belief in the doctrine of the patriarchal order of marriage, a doctrine which was revealed to and practised by God's people in past ages, and is now re-established on earth by divine command of Him who is the same yesterday, to-day, and for ever—a doctrine which, if lived up to and carried out under the direction of the precepts pertaining to it, and of the higher principles of our nature, would conduce to the long life, strength and glory of the people practising it ; and we therefore endorse it as one of the most important principles of our holy religion, and claim the right of its practice.'

"It can be seen from these extracts that the leading Mormon women of Utah are in earnest in their plea for polygamy. They recognize the fact that their leaders have so interwoven this doctrine into their system of religious belief, that if it be removed their system must fall. Hence their cry of religious persecution if anything be said or done against polygamy."[6]

There is one fact I wish to impress upon all who may happen to read these lines, and it is this. The delegate of the Territory of Utah to the National Congress at Washington is a man who is in the possession of four wives. The name of this person is Mr. George Q. Cannon, an apostle of the Mormon Church, and therefore, it will naturally be expected, one who would strenuously advance, as far as he dared, the interests of his polygamous brethren.[7] How can we expect Mormonism to do aught but flourish when such a scandal as this is permitted ? As Brigham Young's nineteenth wife has written,—yet none the less truly because she happens to come so late in the catalogue,—Mr. Cannon "helps to make the laws which send George Smith of Massachusetts to State Prison for three years for the crime of having two wives. Only let George Smith remove himself and wives to Utah, and then he would be able to enjoy the confidence of the Government and the protection of its laws as fully as the apostolic George Q. C."

[6] A meeting of women similar to the one just mentioned was held at Provo City, Utah, on December 7, 1878.

[7] Mr. Cannon had five wives living towards the close of 1878, but during the winter of 1878-79 one of them died.

CHAPTER IX.

THE ROCKY MOUNTAIN ZION (*continued*).

The Great Salt Lake—Its saline properties—Buoyancy of its water—Mormon Sunday excursions—The River Jordan—Islands in the Salt Lake—Fort Douglas—Ordered off to fight the "Reds"—Wagner and his brewery—Back to the Walker House—A debate on polygamy—Blasphemy extraordinary—An invitation to join a Mormon's family circle—A six-wived Mormon's home—Popular household mottoes—Extraordinary notice in a restaurant—A service in the Tabernacle—Impressions produced by it—A listless congregation—Celebrating the Holy Eucharist—Characteristic sermon—Mormon hymns—The Mormon "Du dah"—Other remarkable hymns.

LOOKING down from our elevated position, on our way to Fort Douglas, the Mormon metropolis and the glistening waters of the Great Salt Lake beyond are the two prominent objects that especially arrest our attention. We have a fine bird's-eye view of the first-named of these. Its buildings, its beautiful gardens, its shady streets, its white cover-shaped Tabernacle the most conspicuous object of all, the single line of railway running from the city across the desert, till it seems at length to join with the lake—all is clearly seen from our standpoint. The Great Salt Lake is of considerable density, the solid matters held in suspension being in the proportion of 22·422 of solid contents in every 100 parts of the lake water, the specific gravity of which (1·170) is said, curiously enough, to correspond with that of the Dead Sea. Such at least is the opinion of one authority; but another considers the water of the Dead Sea to be slightly denser than that of the Great Salt Lake, and to contain 24·580 of solid contents in every 100 parts of the general volume of its water. However, the density of the water of each considerably exceeds that of the ocean. Four barrels of the water of the Great Salt Lake will leave after evaporation nearly a barrel of salt. The lake was discovered in the year 1820, and no outlet from it has yet been ascertained. Four or five large streams empty themselves into it, and the fact of its still retaining its saline properties seems to point to the conclusion that there exists some secret bed of saline deposit over which

THE BLACK ROCK, GREAT SALT LAKE.

its waters flow, and that thus they continue salt; for, though the lake may be but the residue of an immense sea which once covered the whole of this region, yet by its continuing so salt with the amount of fresh water poured into it daily, the idea of the existence of some such deposit from which it receives its supply seems to be only too probable. For the past fifteen years (until last year) the lake has been gradually rising; but in 1879 it receded some two or three feet—a most unusual occurrence, owing to the exceptionally warm summer. There are no fish in the lake, but myriads of small flies cover its surface. The buoyancy of the water is so great that it is not at all an easy matter to drown in it. There is no such thing as "treading water"—one must float. I had several baths in this lake in September, 1879. I found when I attempted to swim that my feet were buoyed upon the water, and that it was as much as I could do to make any progress. My shoulders, too, were well above the water when I thrust out my legs from me and assumed a sitting posture. The Mormons are great bathers, and have erected fifty or sixty "boxes" or dressing-sheds on the shore, at a place called Lake Point, where are kept many fanciful and becoming water costumes. It is necessary to wash in fresh water after bathing in the lake, because of the thick deposit of salt which adheres to the skin after emerging from it; so tubs of fresh water for the second bath are accordingly provided. A steamer, called the "General Garfield," plies up and down the lake on Wednesday and Sunday afternoons, calling at the most interesting places, and affording "Zion's" Saints a choice on the Sabbath between going to church in the Tabernacle and a luxurious sail in a two-decker to the strains of a band of music. These excursions are often made from Lake Point already mentioned, which is reached from Salt Lake City by train; and after a little cruise in the steamer the Saints will return and disembark, and regale themselves by eating and drinking, and perhaps with a "hop," for the "People of the Lord" are ardent lovers of dancing, and they commence and end their balls—with prayer! We were told that, on one occasion, during one of the Sunday excursions, a slight breeze sprang up, causing "General Garfield" to sway just a little from side to side. The up and down motion was too much for the Saints, for they all fell on their knees and immediately began praying.

Flowing into the Great Salt Lake is the River Jordan, where the Mormons used to receive their baptisms, but which are now performed in private in the Endowment House. The river forms the western boundary of the Rocky Mountain "Zion," and connects the Salt Lake with Lake Utah, a considerable body of fresh water lying forty miles to the south. There

The Rocky Mountain Zion. 193

are seven islands in the Salt Lake, all of them mountainous, and some containing, it is said, rich and rare minerals. The largest of them—Antelope or Church Island—is sixteen miles long and six miles broad, and its mountain peaks rise to a height of 3000 feet above the lake, or 7300 feet above the level of the sea. The next in size is Stansbury Island, which

MORMON BAPTISM OF INDIANS.

is twelve miles long. It has a circumference of thirty miles, and its mountains likewise rise to a height of 3000 feet above the lake. These two islands contain springs of fresh water. There is also Fremont or Castle Island, fifteen miles in circumference, and rising 1000 feet above the lake; also Carrington, Gunnison, Hat, and Dolphin Isles. The entire length of the Salt Lake is, as we have seen, eighty-five miles,

O

and its breadth, forty-five miles. Compared with the Dead Sea, the Great Salt Lake is longer by forty-three miles, and broader by thirty-five miles.

When we reached the fort, we found an order had just come for a detachment of fifteen men to leave it within two hours to go and fight the "redskins." There had been, during the preceding fortnight, a general uprising among the Indian tribes, which was assuming every day larger and more serious proportions. We had found the papers of the "magic cities" we passed on the Pacific Railroad full of details respecting the incursions and encroachments of the Indians upon the settlers from their allotted reservations. Armed with Winchester rifles, the Indians know well enough how to handle them, being dead shots at short ranges, though they are not so unerring with the rifle at long ranges as they are with the bow and arrow. The detachment of fifteen was ordered off to Kelton (a small settlement on the Central Pacific Railroad, which we should pass on our way to San Francisco), to protect the settlers there from the Bannack Indians, who had been scouring the neighbourhood—scalping the "palefaces" and making off with the cattle. We made the acquaintance of the officer in charge of this detachment in the city before commencing our ascent to the fort, and he was then anxiously expecting a telegram, which would decide his movements one way or the other. He had therefore received the telegram by the time we reached the fort. Notwithstanding the hurry and bustle of the moment, the rush of the men to get their kit together and the anxiety to see the very last of their comrades, whom they had been so suddenly called upon to leave behind, we were treated most kindly to the inevitable "lager"—we drank success to the expedition and confusion to all redskins.

We visited some of the officers' quarters, and then drove on further for a mile or two, to the commencement of the pass in the mountains where Brigham Young first sighted the Salt Lake Valley, and which is called the Emigration Cañon. The mountain-slopes here are extensively covered with forests, and contain a variety of big game. A brewery has been set up near the entrance to the cañon, and we alighted there and made friends with its owner, Mr. Wagner, with whom I arranged to put up my horse the next morning, as I intended coming up early with my gun in order to secure a few specimens of the beautiful-plumaged birds of the region. Wagner was successful in enlivening us with sensational accounts of his adventures with certain ferocious animals, such as bears, wild cats, and other dangerous creatures. One adventure, in particular, which he told us he once had (in California) with a "thunderation grizzly," quite made our hair stand on end, so graphically was it related!

Returning to the hotel, we came upon an elder of the Melchisedec priesthood, and I "wrestled" with him. In other words, we had a warm debate on polygamy, which he was the first to commence—a fact somewhat strange, for a Mormon Saint is very seldom found willing to converse on the subject of his religion with an "ungodly Gentile." However I was especially privileged, I suppose, and as the religious ideas the man had got hold of completely startled me at the time, I think they may as well be made public. The man in question had four wives and thirty-six children, and one of his sons was a bishop of the Church. He chewed tobacco all the while he conversed with me, and profusely expectorated on the floor around. After informing me that he considered me as good as a heathen, that I was but chaff that would one day be burned "with fire unquenchable," we closed our interview with the following discussion on polygamy:

"Can you tell me," he began, "where the Bible says a man may not have more than one wife?"

I waited a moment before answering, and began to consider, lest I should commit myself. I thought of all the texts I could remember on the subject, but soon replied, "In one of St. Paul's Epistles, the apostle says, A bishop should be the husband of one wife."

The Mormon quickly retorted, "Not good enough, not good enough; that doesn't prevent him from having two, three, or a dozen wives if he likes!"

I confess I felt the force of his remark. But I was not to be beaten yet, so I continued: "But can *you* tell me where in the Bible polygamy is enjoined?"

"Solomon had many wives, I reckon."

"So he had, I know, a very great many, and so had others whom no doubt you could quote from the Old Testament. But I intend adhering to the New Testament, so can you give me an instance from that portion of Holy Writ?"

"Well then," said the Mormon, "Jesus Christ Himself was a polygamist! He was married to Martha and Mary, Lazarus's sisters; Mary Magdalene was His wife; and when He turned the water into wine at Cana, in Galilee, He was present at the celebration of one of His own marriages!!"

The reader will readily imagine that it was not easy to reason with, or to patiently listen to, a man so utterly ignorant and depraved as this. Brigham Young had preached the same blasphemy from the Tabernacle rostrum, and here was one of his followers preaching the very same to me! It is not surprising that the Mormons commence one of their hymns with the line,

"The God that others worship is not the God for me."

I will, before going further, quote the hymn from which this line is taken. It is No. 297 of the collection of the Mormon "Sacred Hymns and Spiritual Songs" (16th edition), and runs as follows:

"The God that others worship is not the God for me;
He has no parts nor body, and cannot hear nor see;
But I've a God that reigns above—
A God of revelation—Oh, that's the God for me!
    Oh, that's the God for me!
    Oh, that's the God for me!

"A Church without a Prophet is not the Church for me;
It has no head to lead it; in it I would not be;
But I've a Church not made by man,
Cut from the mountain without hand;
A Church with gifts and blessings—Oh, that's the Church for me!
    Oh, that's, etc.

"A Church without Apostles is not the Church for me;
'Tis like a ship dismasted, afloat upon the sea;
But I've a Church that's always led
With the Twelve Stars around her head;
A Church without foundation—Oh, that's the Church for me!
    Oh, that's, etc.

"The Hope that Gentiles cherish is not the Hope for me;
It has no faith nor knowledge; far from it I would be;
But I've a hope that will not fail;
It reaches far within the vail;
Which Hope is like an anchor—Oh, that's the Hope for me!
   Oh, that's, etc.

"The Heaven of Sectarians is not the Heaven for me;
So doubtful its location, neither on land nor sea;
But I've a Heaven upon the earth,
The land and home that gave me birth—
A Heaven of light and knowledge—Oh, that's the Heaven for me!
   Oh, that's, etc.

"A Church without a gathering is not the Church for me;
The Saviour would not own it, wherever it might be;
But I've a Church that is called out
From false tradition, fear and doubt—
A gathering dispensation—Oh, that's the Church for me!
   Oh, that's, etc."

But returning to the Mormon, he took leave of me thus:

"Ta ta," he cried. "Ta, ta, friend, ta, ta. I must be off now and strike the next train home, else I shall be late for dinner. Come and see me out at ———. I'll fix you for a week, or as long as you like, and you shall see how happily we all live together."

So, shaking hands, we parted company. He jumped into a passing car which was being drawn towards the station by a quartette of mules, and was taken home to dinner. I should much have liked to have accepted his kind invitation, and to have made the acquaintance of his several wives; but time was pressing. I am inclined to question, however, the domestic felicity that he spoke of, for from what I have read on the subject, and have heard from the lips of the women themselves, Mormon wives have, as a rule, rather a miserable time of it.[1]

Upon my return to England in 1878 I published a description of my interview with this Mormon in the columns of an English newspaper. When I revisited Salt Lake City in 1879 I was rather surprised to find that the Mormons there had been made acquainted with what I had written, and were, in consequence, considerably incensed. Acting on the advice of a friend I changed my name during my stay in the metropolis, and thus fortunately escaped recognition. Under my assumed name I paid a visit to the Mormon's home (described below)—but with a loaded six-shooter in my breast-pocket, so as to be prepared for all emergencies.

On another occasion—in 1879—I did avail myself of the Mormon's kind invitation, and he then introduced me to two of his wives, for at the time that I paid my visit all his consorts were not visible. He was, I ascertained, a Scotchman and a farmer, and his wives were scattered in little houses over his estate. Each wife had a house to herself, and in this she lived together with her children. From what I could gather, the Mormon's home for the time being was at the residence of his second wife. The houses I went into were, in every respect, clean and comfortable; but it should be mentioned that this Mormon was a well-to-do man, and could easily maintain a very large family.

"Are not your wives jealous of each other?" I asked, when I came to take my departure, at the conclusion of this visit.

He answered me evasively.—" I wouldn't give a cent for a woman who isn't jealous; 'tis their nature. You know that that lady which Abraham took didn't get along with him quite so happily as she might have done, for she left him, and the Lord had to send His angel and tell her to go back to him." Then he added, "I'll swear to you on a stack of bibles that we've no misery here. We live as happy as the day is long. You've seen me and you've handled me. You've been into my houses and seen for yourself, so now you can judge."

There was one thing, certainly, that I did happen to see, and that was a scroll of perforated cardboard nailed on to the wall in one of his rooms, having the following motto painted (in blue) upon it:

"What is home without a baby?"

This is something after the style of a motto of similar design which I noticed in another Mormon's house I visited, and that was:

"What is home without a mother-in-law?"

Here, too, I may perhaps be allowed to quote a characteristic notice I found posted up in a restaurant in Salt Lake City, namely in that of Messrs. O— and P— (Gentiles), in Second South-street. This remarkable specimen of Western vulgarity ran as follows :

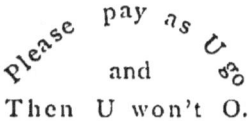
Please pay as U go
and
Then U won't O.

To Trust is to Bust
To Bust is Hell
No Trust no Bust
No Hell.

I also found the following notice in another room in the same restaurant :

In God We Trust
All Others Cash.

During my visit to Salt Lake City in 1879, I happened to be present at a Mormon service in the Tabernacle. At two o'clock on the afternoon of Sunday, August 31st, I found myself seated in the third row of the "Gentile" seats, with the service about to commence, the building well filled with Saints—men, women, and children, there being plenty of the last-named present, indeed the immense number of babies-in-arms brought to church struck me at the time as something remarkable. Upon the rostrum in front of the organ were seated the Mormon hierarchy in full force, and on either side were ranged the choir, about a hundred voices in all, fifty men on one side and fifty women on the other. Conspicuous behind the organist stood, with *bâton* in hand, Mr. George Careless, the conductor. On the floor of the building, below the rostrum, stood a long table, which, covered with a white linen cloth, supported twelve silver pewter-shaped vessels ; also eight piles of bread, the bread cut into large slices, and each pile containing about as much as a quartern loaf. This, it will be easily surmised, was the Table of the Lord's Supper. The Holy Sacrament is celebrated in the Tabernacle regularly every Sunday. Behind the Table sat six officers of the Church, namely three elders and three bishops—coarse, common-looking men, whose duty consisted in breaking and blessing the bread before it was taken round by the "teachers" to the congregation assembled. Upon the table, also, were two large vessels, containing water, which would be poured into the pewters, and be brought round—after it had been blessed—by the teachers to the congregation likewise. Water is generally used in the Mormon celebration of the Lord's Supper. This was explained to me by the Tabernacle porter at the conclusion of this service, for when I asked him whether wine had been used in the service I had just attended, he replied, "No, indeed. We prefer pure water to impure wine!"—an answer for which I was rather unprepared.

The service was opened by one Elder A. Cannon getting up from his seat and giving out a hymn. Then the great organ pealed forth, disclosing the melody of the composition, which was cheerful and animated. But, inspiriting as the tune certainly was, I could not help being strangely impressed, not with feelings of devoutness engendered by the solemnity of the occasion, but in another way altogether, for to me—and it could hardly be called sentiment on my part—the deep, sacred tones that proceeded from the glorious instrument seemed incongruous and out of place in such a service as this, a service performed by men who were such open blasphemers and evil-livers; and when I tried to imagine myself actually "in church" and about to listen to, and perhaps join in, prayer and praise to the Almighty, I could not, do what I would, reconcile my feelings and make myself believe that it was a House of God, and not a music-hall, that I was in. There, upon the rostrum, was the very man who had told me, a year before, that he considered our Saviour a polygamist! There, too, sat a member of the hierarchy who had acquired such a reputation for cursing and blaspheming, that the designation by which he was commonly known was, "the cursing apostle!" Were these the kind of men fitted to be the religious instructors of the people?

During the singing of the hymn I noticed that nobody stood up, except the choir and conductor. Very few members of the congregation seemed to be provided with hymn-books. The hymn was sung (and played) *forte* throughout. At its conclusion, Elder Johnson offered an extempore prayer, which was as follows:

"O our divine Father, in the name of Jesus Christ we approach thee at this time to ask that thy spirit rest upon us while we are assembled here to worship thee and call upon thy name and sound thy praise, and commemorate the death and sufferings of Him who died so that thy will might be done. Bless us and give us power to bear like Him who suffered for us and died for our sins. Look in mercy upon us, and upon all others, and may they be converted to the truth and receive blessing at thy hand. May the faithful realize that thou art with them, and that, according to thy promise, where two or three are gathered together, thou wilt be in their midst, and there to bless them. O our Father, we have come before thee with desire to be blessed, and to have thy blessing rest upon thy servants throughout the world. Pour out thy spirit on all who are instructed to teach the people, and influence them with words of wisdom, strength, and power to call upon all the nations of the earth to come unto that way which thou hast pointed out for them to turn into, that they may receive the gift of the Holy Ghost. Bless, our heavenly Father, all who are in authority. Pour out thy spirit upon the President, and upon the bishops who are presiding over the several wards, and all others who are in authority, in order that light and intelligence may beam upon them, and upon the people generally. Prepare them for whatever may come to pass. May all the nations and peoples of the earth be filled with the light of the Holy Ghost, and obey thy Word, and be brought into a perfect knowledge of Him who suffered for their sins. And may the Holy Father have mercy on us all, we ask in the name of Jesus Christ."—The congregation responded, "Amen."

Those who were present seemed to pay but little attention during the offering of this prayer. I did not see any of the congregation bending forward, or assuming that reverential demeanour by which one might infer that their feelings were in accord with what was being said. All sat listless and unconcerned, and not a few seemed to be fast asleep. At the conclusion of the prayer just mentioned, another hymn was sung; and while this was taking place, the three elders and the three bishops who were seated at the Table, "broke" the bread preparatory to the celebration of the Holy Communion. The irreverent way in which they proceeded to work induced, in my mind, a feeling of absolute disgust. Slice after slice was hastily seized and torn into pieces—the men seemed to pay no more respect to the solemnity of the sacred rite they were performing than if they were shelling peas or peeling potatoes. The hymn concluded, one of the three bishops already referred to—Bishop Shaats—offered the following consecration prayer, holding up his hands as he did so:

"O God, the Eternal, we ask thee in the name of Jesus Christ to bless and sanctify this bread unto the souls of all those who shall partake thereof. And may they always bear witness unto thee that thou art God, the eternal Father, and keep thy commandments as they have been given unto them, and be filled with thy Holy Spirit."—The congregation again responded, "Amen."

The same utter indifference characterized the demeanour of the congregation during the consecration of the sacred elements. No one seemed the least interested in what was taking place. The Sacrament was brought round to the people in their seats by twelve teachers of the Eighth ward of the Salt Lake stake, the custom in this stake being for the teachers of the various wards to distribute the bread in the Tabernacle every Sunday in turn. This Sunday, therefore, it was the Eighth ward's turn to distribute; the Sunday following it would be the Ninth ward's turn; and so on. While the Sacrament was being administered, there was complete silence, which lasted for ten minutes. I could not help being struck with the careless and—I may say—irreverent manner of the several recipients of the consecrated elements, for no signs of devotion and thankfulness were displayed: people received the bread and ate it with no more concern than if they were sitting and eating at their own family breakfast-tables. There was not enough bread to go round; but no more was consecrated, so that many of those present were not even given the chance of communicating.

I will now pass to the sermon, which was delivered by Elder Cummings. I am indebted to the editor of the *Daily*

Tribune, the chief "Gentile" organ in Salt Lake City, for his kindness in furnishing me with a *verbatim* report of the sermon —as well as of the prayers which I have previously quoted— taken by a representative of the journal in question, who was present at the service. Elder Cummings took for his text verses 6 and 7 of the xivth chapter of the Revelation: "And I saw another angel fly in the midst of heaven, having the everlasting gospel to preach unto them that dwell on the earth, and to every nation, and kindred, and tongue, and people, saying with a loud voice, Fear God, and give glory to him, for the hour of his judgment is come: and worship him that made heaven, and earth, and the sea, and the fountains of waters." I would particularly request the reader to note a statement which he will find given below relating to Joseph Smith, the founder of Mormonism, and which will throw new and important light on the question of the presumed "divinity" of that extraordinary individual! Omitting the earlier part of the sermon, Mr. Cummings concluded as follows:

"We must be excused for criticizing the religions of the world of the present time. We are set down, I presume every one is aware, as a class of ignorant, illiterate fanatics, and that we are influenced by the impulse of the moment; that our passions are exercised and wrought upon in order to accomplish what is termed Mormonism. Now if you will take the trouble to examine every organization and all the doctrines taught now, outside of what is taught here, you cannot find among any sect a single iota of the doctrine of Jesus Christ. Where is the organization that Jesus left upon the earth? Do we find it in the Catholic church? Verily not. The organization of the Catholic church is just as different as the light of the mid-day sun is different from midnight darkness. Do we find any apostles for evangelization? Any pastors? Any teachers?—What do we find? A Pope and Cardinals. We find a heterogeneous organization that was never instituted. Consequently, it lacks that which Jesus established when he was here in the flesh. Well, now, let us come down to the old lady's daughter, the Episcopalian church. Do we find there anything similar to the organization that Jesus established when he was here? We find there that the Queen of England is Head of the church, with bishops. Indeed we find a curious organization, but nothing that represents anything that was instituted by our Saviour. And so we come down through the other denominations that have sprung from the Catholic church, and have descended from her down to the last one that has made its appearance on the face of the earth, and where do you find an organization like that that was instituted by the Saviour when he was upon earth? Where do you find among them all the practice of what Jesus Christ taught should be performed—the preaching of faith and repentance; baptism according to the ordinance; the laying on of hands and the giving of the Holy Ghost; the doing of that which Peter, James and John did when they received their commission? Then, if they are not doing this, not one of them is the Church of Christ. Now, to turn to the Latter-day Saints, when we come to examine their organization we find in the Church apostles, prophets, and so on; we find they are qualified to perform that which was instituted by the Saviour when he was upon the earth; we find that they preach the doctrine of faith, of repentance, and baptism for the remission of sins, and the laying on of hands for the giving of the Holy Ghost. We find they do not omit one single iota of what was preached by the Saviour when he was upon the earth. Among the priesthood there is just the same authority that existed in the Church after her organization when the Saviour was in the flesh. Well, now, some one may say, Where do you get the authority for this new dispensation? Where do you get the authority that God is going to speak from heaven again to the people upon the earth? I answer, In the text I have read: 'And I saw another angel fly in the midst of heaven. . . . .' If the Latter-day Saints have not the gospel, no one else has got it. If the gospel had remained as it was instituted by the Saviour, there would be no necessity for sending an angel in the last days. But the Church has apostatized. There is no similarity between the sects called Christians and the gospel of the Church established by Jesus when he was upon earth. *We claim that this angel that John saw, ninety-six years after the commencement of the Christian era, was Joseph Smith (!);* that unto him was committed the keys of the gospel of the dispensation of the fulfilment of time; and that he was the instrumentality used to give it to the children of men. He conversed with God, and Jesus himself. He organized the Church just precisely the same as that which existed when Jesus was upon the earth, with all the ordinances instituted at that time. The Almighty gave him the authority to proclaim that everlasting gospel to every man and woman, and all the ordinances connected with it, until at last they shall enter into the kingdom of heaven. . . . .

" Now, with all the abuse the Latter-day Saints get, and the ridicule heaped upon them, there are no more lies told about them than were told about Jesus, and Peter, James, and John. They, too, had to suffer here in the flesh. But when the Master comes down from the heavens to marshal his host, those who were doing this will see their mistake. The people of the ancient time wanted the believers to do just precisely what the papers want us to do now. They spoke of the priesthood as ignorant, and heaped calumny upon them. They might make the desert to blossom as the rose, but that made no difference. All we want here is to pursue our religion. We stand to-day in the same relation that the first apostles did to the heathen world around them when they were on earth ; but all this will be met and overcome. The doings and sayings of sects and denominations, and of the Papal power with all its deformity and wickedness,—and that was never more corrupt than it is at the present time,—all this will be met and overcome. The Latter-day Saints present you the gospel in its purity just precisely as it was when Jesus was upon the earth. The priesthood is just the same ; nothing has been changed. The Church is organized just precisely as it originally was ; the fundamental principles are exactly the same. . . . .

" Our enemies persecute us ; but God will help us and destroy them. They persecute and prosecute our apostles for doing only that which was done of old and is authorized of God. And when these people die they expect to go right to heaven and sit with Abraham, Isaac, and Jacob, who did the very same things thousands of years ago ! The charge against us is that we are polygamists. This is the consistency of this generation, and of the world at the present time. Yes, under the power of God we are polygamous, and will remain so until and after our enemies are destroyed. We have received the dispensation to do this, and we are endeavouring to do it. It is only this that we are trying to do. We care nothing about monogamy. It is our business to preach the gospel, and it is our duty to practise the principles of it. We are as immovable as these mountains around us. We know our duty, we understand our calling. We have thousands who can stand up and tell you the same things that I have; tell you that angels have come to earth; that they know it is true; who will testify to the full organization of the priesthood of the Latter-day Saints. And now I may say to our enemies: you might just as well save your breath to cool your porridge, as to expect to persuade the Latter-day Saints to forsake their religion and turn unto your ways. No, no! God the Father helping. We understand the gospel, and we are going to preach it; of the things that are yet to come, and of the coming of the Son of Man. There will be trial, trouble and tribulation, earthquakes, storms and disaster, until the wicked have passed away and the Kingdom of the Son of Man upon earth has been fully established; until the coming of the Kingdom of God in all its beauty. And then there will be peace and quiet, and no more persecution on account of polygamy. Then there will be peace and quiet. The good work is in the hands of God our preserver, in the hands of God our Father and helper. Amen."

Perhaps it will not be out of place to quote here a few popular Mormon Hymns. The reader will, in this way, be able to comprehend, more fully, the sentiments that pervade the mind of a true, zealous, Latter-day Saint. And first I will take the hymn known as the Mormon "Du dah." Unfortunately I am only able to give three verses of this remarkable composition. They are to be found on pages 370-1 of Mr. Stenhouse's work already mentioned. This hymn was sung in the Tabernacle in Salt Lake City during "divine" (*sic*) service, after the discomfiture of the Federal troops which had been sent out against the Mormons in the year 1857, when the Saints succeeded in burning three of the supply trains, including seventy-three waggons, containing the provisions, clothing, etc. of the troops, and in driving off 1300 head of oxen from the rear of the army. This success, so gallantly achieved by the "warriors of Zion," provoked the wildest enthusiasm among the Saints; and the following pæan was sung in honour of the event in the Tabernacle one Sunday, *after the celebration of the Sacrament of the Lord's Supper!* The hymn had been composed previous to the overthrow of the Government army in 1857; but it so happened that the last of the three verses which I will now give, fitted in almost exactly with the circumstances of the time:

> Old Sam has sent, I understand,
>   Du dah! Du dah!
> A Missouri ass to rule our land,
>   Du dah! Du dah day!
> But if he comes, we'll have some fun,
>   Du dah! Du dah!
> To see him and his juries run,
>   Du dah! Du dah day!
>   *Chorus.*—Then let us be on hand,
>   By Brigham Young to stand,
>   And if our enemies do appear
>   We'll sweep them off the land.
>
> Old Squaw-killer Harney is on the way,
>   Du dah! Du dah!
> The Mormon people for to slay,
>   Du dah! Du dah day!
> Now if he comes, the truth I'll tell,
>   Du dah! Du dah!
> Our boys will drive him down to hell,
>   Du dah! Du dah day!
>   Then let us be on hand, etc.
>
> There's seven hundred wagons on the way,
>   Du dah! Du dah!
> And their cattle are numerous, so they say,
>   Du dah! Du dah day!
> Now, to let them perish would be a sin,
>   Du dah! Du dah!
> *So we'll take all they've got for bringing them in,*
>   Du dah! Du dah day!
>   Then let us be on hand, etc.

The Mormons have composed a hymn after the style of our "Cheer, boys, cheer," as the following quotation will show. It is No. 307 of the collection of *Sacred Hymns and*

Spiritual Songs. The reader should notice particularly the "roaring of the Lion," in verse 4. It refers, no doubt, to the voice of Brigham Young, who was often called the "Lion of the Lord."—

> Cheer, saints, cheer ! we're bound for peaceful Zion !
>   Cheer, saints, cheer ! for that free and happy land !
> Cheer, saints, cheer ! we'll Israel's God rely on ;
>   We will be led by the power of His hand.
>
> Long, long in Bab'lon we have lived in sorrow,
>   But God in His mercy hath opened up our way ;
> " Hope points before and shows the bright to-morrow ;"
>   Let us forget the darkness of to-day.
>
> See, see the judgments o'er the earth extending,
>   Pestilence and earthquakes, famine, fire, and sword ;
> Soon shall the rulers of this world come bending,
>   Shorn of their glory, for thus saith the Lord.
>
> Come, come away unto the hill of Zion ;
>   Come, come away to the temple of the Lord ;
> Come ye and hear the roaring of the Lion,
>   Where Ephraim's children tremble at the Word.
>
> Away, far away to the everlasting mountains,
>   Away, far away to the valley in the West ;
> Away, far away to yonder gushing fountains,
>   Where all the faithful in the latter days are blest.
>
> Sing, sing aloud, the song of adoration ;
>   Yea, sing aloud for the goodness of our King ;
> Ye who are blest to see this great salvation,
>   Lift up your voices, and make the mountains ring.

The following verses have been composed to the well-known tune, "So early in the Morning :"

There is a people in the West, the world call Mormonites in jest,
The only people who can say, we have the truth, and own its sway.
Away in Utah's valleys, away in Utah's valleys,
Away in Utah's valleys, the chambers of the Lord.

The world in darkness long has lain, since Jesus and the Saints were slain,
Until these glorious latter days, when Joseph did the standard raise,
And brought the book of Mormon, etc.,
And brought, etc., to cheer our souls with light.

The truth in many lands is known, in power the Lord rolls forth the
    stone,
Which from the mountains has gone forth, and will in time fill all the
    earth.
Go forth from Utah's valleys, etc.,
Go forth, etc., the chambers of the Lord.

And all ye Saints, where'er you be, from bondage try to be set free,
Escape unto fair Zion's land, and thus fulfil the Lord's command,
And help to build up Zion, etc.,
And help, etc., before the Lord appear.

    The verses given below are sung to the tune of the "King of the Cannibal Islands:"

> Come, Mormons, all attention pay,
> While I attempt to sing my say;
> I've chosen for my text to-day,
> Come forward and pay up your tithing.
> These may not be the very words,
> Which ancient Holy Writ records;
> But Malachi, I think, affords
> A verse with which the sense accords.
> It seems that he had cause to scold
> The Saints, or Israelites of old;
> In fact, they needed to be told—
> Come forward and pay up your tithing.
>   *Chorus.*—Then, if to prosper you desire,
>   And wish to keep out of the fire—
>   Nay, if you to be Saints aspire,
>   Come forward and pay up your tithing.

> Just as it was in olden times
> With ancient Saints, in other climes,
> The call is now, bring out your dimes,
> Come forward and pay up your tithing.
> Our prophet says, "When elders preach,
> The law of tithing they should teach,
> Pay up themselves, and then beseech
> All those that come within their reach."
> This makes me now appeal to you,
> To follow counsel; right pursue;
> And whilst all evil you eschew,
> Come forward and pay up your tithing.
>   Then, if to prosper, etc.

> Now male and female, rich and poor,
> Who wish to keep your standing sure;
> That you salvation may secure,
> Come forward and pay up your tithing.

A tenth, that is, and nothing less,
Of all you do or may possess :
In flocks and herds, and their increase,
In pigs and poultry, ducks and geese ;
A tenth, indeed, of all your toil,
Likewise the products of the soil ;
And if you've any wine or oil,
Come forward and pay up your tithing !
    Then, if to prosper, etc.

The following "hymn" goes to the tune of the "D pointed Milkman :"

I'm a merry-hearted Mormon, by the truth I'm set free,
And I wish all the world were as happy as me ;
I've started for salvation, and hope I shall win,
So with this explanation my song I'll begin.

On board the good ship Zion we all have set sail,
Our captain we rely on, who never can fail,
And the officers and the ship's crew, whene'er it doth storm,
Will bring us safe through—so then feel no alarm.

Sometimes when a calm doth come over the deep,
Our nets we spread out, and the fish they will leap,
And into the great net the fish they will throng,
So we pull them on board and bring them along.

We get garfish and blackfish, and minnows and whales,
And sharks in abundance, and good fish ne'er fails ;
There are flying-fish and star-fish and suckers and trout,
And all sorts of fish from the net we take out.

We've cat-fish and dog-fish and lobsters and crabs,
And cuttle-fish and devil-fish and thorn-backs and dabs ;
Many scorpions and pollywogs and crocodiles grim,
With shoals of big sea-hogs fill the net to the brim.

And now I say to you fish who in the net have been caught,
I hope you are the true fish that can never be bought ;
Else old Satan will buy you and you'll slip through the sieve,
And go to destruction as sure as you live.

The Savior's true parable I now bring to view,
Who also declared, " The saved would be few ;"
For straight is the entrance and narrow the way ;
Now, mind you're not late on the great trying day.

The tune of "Tramp, Tramp" is adapted for the following composition:

In our lovely Deseret,[2]
  Where the Saints of God have met,
There's a multitude
  Of children all around;
They are generous and brave,
  They have precious souls to save,
They must listen, and
  Obey the Gospel sound.

That the children may live long
  And be beautiful and strong,
Tea and coffee and
  Tobacco they despise;
Drink no liquor, and they eat
  But very little meat,
They are seeking to be
  Great and good and wise.

They should be instructed young,
  How to watch and guard the tongue,
And their tempers train,
  And evil passions bind.

---

[2] "Deseret" is the name usually given by the Mormons to the Territory of Utah, although they also apply the term so as to include the whole of the Rocky Mountain region colonized by them, as well as other States and Territories in the West which they hope will be peopled by them some day. In 1859 a convention of Mormons was held in Salt Lake City, when a constitution was framed, establishing "a free and independent government by the name of the State of Deseret, including all the territory of the United States within the following lines, namely, within a line commencing at the 33rd degree of north latitude, where it crosses the 108th degree of longitude west of Greenwich; thence continuing south and west to the boundary of Mexico; thence west to and down the main channel of the Gila river, and the northern boundary of Lower California to the Pacific Ocean; thence along the coast north-westerly to about the 108th degree of west longitude," etc. The word, which signifies a honey bee, takes its origin from the Book of Mormon, where we are told that Jared and his family, previous to setting out (from Palestine) on their 344 days' journey "across many waters,"—a voyage which eventually landed them on the shores of America,—"did prepare a vessel, in which they did carry with them the fish of the waters; and they did also carry with them Deseret, which, by interpretation, is a honey bee; and thus they did carry with them swarms of bees, and all manner of that which was upon the face of the land, seeds of every kind."

They should always be polite,
  And treat everybody right,
And in every place
  Be affable and kind.

They must not forget to pray
  Night and morning every day,
For the Lord to keep
  Them safe from every ill,
And assist them to do right,
  That with all their mind and might,
They may love Him, and may
  Learn to do His will.
Chorus.—Hark! hark! hark! 'tis children's music,
  Children's voices, O! how sweet!
When in innocence and love
  Like the angels up above,
They with happy hearts
  And cheerful faces meet.

To the tune of the "Bonny Breast Knots" the subjoined "hymn" is sung:

What peace and joy pervade the soul,
And sweet sensations through me roll,
And love and peace my heart console,
  Since first I met the Mormons.
    Chorus.—Hey, the merry, O, the busy,
      Hey, the sturdy Mormons;
      I never knew what joy was,
        Till I became a Mormon.

They sing the folly of the wise,
Sectarian precepts they despise;
A heaven far above the skies,
  Is never sought by Mormons.
    Hey, the merry, etc.

To Sabbath meetings they repair,
Both old and young assemble there;
The words of inspiration share,
  No less can suit the Mormons.
    Hey, the merry, etc.

At night the Mormons do convene
To chat awhile, and sing a hymn;
And one, perchance, repeat a rhyme
  He made about the Mormons.
    Hey, the merry, etc.

> The Mormon fathers love to see
> Their Mormon families all agree ;
> The prattling infant on his knee
>   Cries, " Daddy, I'm a Mormon !"
>   Hey, the merry, etc.
>
> As youth in Israel once decried
> To wed with those that heaven denied,
> So youth among us now have cried,
>   " We'll marry none but Mormons."
>   Hey, the merry, etc.
>
> So, while we tread our foeman's ground
> We'll make the trump of freedom sound,
> And scatter blessings all around,
>   Like free and happy Mormons.
>   Hey, the merry, etc.

The late Mormon President has been the theme of a good many complimentary poems. The following remarkable effusion may be taken as a specimen :

> O, Brigham, the friend of the brow-beaten Saints,
> I think of the cause of so many restraints
> You've long labored under, which still do remain,
> It troubles my spirit, and causes me pain.
>
> 'Tis strange, that the man whose designs are so pure,
> Should be hated and hunted, and made to endure
> The scoffs and the taunts, with the venom and ire,
> Which the spirit of evil in some doth inspire.
>
> While rogues o'er the earth with impunity range,
> And the plans of Jehovah delight to derange,
> You are cramp'd and coop'd up and deprived of free air,
> And the sunlight of heaven, your spirits to cheer.
>
> But, who can imprison a soul such as thine
> By walls, or in dungeons ?—in darkness 'twill shine !
> And be free and as pure as the sweet mountain air,
> Which the hate of the wicked can never impair.
>
> Then, cheer up, dear Brigham, the time is at hand,
> When those who oppress you shan't cumber the land ;
> By the power of the Father, they'll soon be laid low,
> And His kingdom in glory forever shall grow.

Of the above compositions, one, namely " Cheer, saints, cheer," is taken from the afore-mentioned *Sacred Hymns and Spiritual Songs* (16th edition, 1877); the remainder are to be found in the *Mountain Warbler*, a collection of songs, etc. "for the use of Choirs, Sabbath Schools, and Families." In the former publication occur three of our well-known hymns commencing with the lines, "Glory to Thee, my God, this night" (Ken), "O God, our help in ages past" (Watts), and "From Greenland's icy mountains" (Heber). These are quoted *in extenso*,—with four extra stanzas added to the first-named; and there are, besides, in the same collection, adaptations from such beautiful hymns as "Behold the Lamb of God," "Guide me, O Thou great Redeemer," "Who are these like stars appearing," etc.

"UTAH'S BEST CROP."
From a photograph by C. R. Savage, Salt Lake City.

CHAPTER X.

PORTER ROCKWELL AND BRIGHAM YOUNG.

Orrin Porter Rockwell—Death of the noted Danite—Origin of the Danite Band—" Destroying Angels "—Rockwell's history—A famous assassin—Brigham Young—Joseph Smith's prophecy concerning him —His first interview with Smith—Conversing in "unknown tongues"— Brigham's iron rule—The Church's blind belief in him—Blasphemous utterance of the apostle Heber C. Kimball — Brigham Young's opinion concerning the Deity—Blasphemy extraordinary—The domestic life of the deceased President—A Yankee Mahomet—" Briggy" Young—His wives—A double courtship—John A. Young—His matrimonial proclivities—A specimen " Saint "—Brigham Young's grave— The deceased President's directions respecting the conduct of his funeral.

WRITING in 1869, Sir Charles Dilke, in his work *Greater Britain*, says : " Since 1840, there has been no name of greater terror in the West than (Porter) Rockwell's." On the morning of June 11, 1878, we were surprised, upon taking up that day's issue of the *Salt Lake Daily Tribune*, to find that a man answering to this name had died in Salt Lake City the previous evening. We found also, in the columns of the journal in question, full details respecting this man's extraordinary life and actions. It was, indeed, the famous Porter Rockwell who was dead. It may therefore be interesting to offer a few remarks concerning him.

About the year 1838, when the Mormons were in Missouri, which was then their " Land of Promise,"—and remained so until they were driven out of the State and obliged perforce to seek another " Canaan,"—there was a " death society " formed among them for the purpose of putting quietly out of the way all obnoxious persons who, by their actions or otherwise, hindered the progress and development of "Christ's Church." The members of this society were, as a body, called at different times by different names. Originally they were known as the "Daughters of Zion," being so designated from the text in Holy Scripture that they took for their motto, namely Micah iv. 13. But this title was thought to be hardly suitable, for many of these "Daughters" were bearded, and to have bearded daughters as the instruments for effectually removing the object of Prophet Joe Smith's wrath, was looked upon as slightly out of place. So they were called the "Avenging" or "Destroying Angels;" sometimes also the "Flying Angels," or "Destructives." But perhaps they are better known as the "Sons of Dan," or the "Danites," so named from another text in Holy Scripture—Genesis xlix. 17—which they found applicable to their case.

The chief of this Danite Band was a man of the name of Orrin Porter Rockwell. "Port" Rockwell, as he was familiarly called, was the archangel of all the "Destroying Angels;" he was (to quote Mormon phraseology) the "Chief Avenger of the Lord"—the most destructive angel of the Band. He was called, too, the "Brother of Gideon;" or again, the "Big Fan of the thresher that should throughly purge the floor." A life devoted to the most heinous crimes had rendered the name of this man famous throughout the continent of civilized North America. Wholesale murders were "managed" by him: he died guilty of having assassinated more than a hundred victims with his own hand. His butcheries were performed, in the first instance, at the instigation of or through a significant hint let drop by "Prophet" Joseph Smith, that such and such persons were obnoxious and "in the way," and similar "hints" were subsequently given to the assassin by "Prophet" Brigham Young. "Port" Rockwell was the chief confidant, the trusty and well-tried friend of Joseph Smith. But though he enjoyed high favour at the court of Brigham Young, he was not, perhaps, the most trusted avenger of this last-named personage (though at the same time it is true that he was his chief instrument), for another, one of the name of William Hickman, was the favoured confidant of the late President—till he, indeed, turned "State's evidence" and startled the world with a full confession of his crimes, which are said to have nearly equalled in number those of his friend and brother-angel, Rockwell. "Port" and "Bill" went hand-in-hand together. They were the prime instruments for "glorifying the name of Israel's God."

Now Porter Rockwell was no ordinary man. He played an important part in the history of his country, and therefore it will be as well, I think, to turn to the *Salt Lake Tribune*, and see what that authority has to say concerning him. First we are informed of his death, which took place at the Colorado stables in First East-street, Salt Lake City, and was helped on by his getting drunk the night before at the theatre. No inquest was held over the remains of the deceased, nor was there any *post mortem* examination made, but the body was removed to the office of "Holy Joe," the sexton or undertaker, where it was visited by many of the leading Saints in the Territory. As illustrating the remarkable career of this notorious Mormon, the following extracts from the paper referred to may perhaps be found interesting:

"Porter Rockwell was under indictment in the First Judicial District for participation in the Aikin murder, and was to be tried at the next September term of Judge Emerson's court. There was strong evidence against Rockwell, but it is extremely doubtful whether a jury could have been impanelled that would convict him on the proof of the crime charged. Although Porter held many secrets of the Mormon priesthood, it is quite probable that the Church, by allowing John D. Lee to be executed, learned a lesson which convinced the guilty living ones of Mormondom that it would be far safer to stand by Rockwell in his trial, than to bear the odium of the exposures he could and would have made had they sacrificed him as they did Lee. Hence many a Mormon will rejoice at the demise of this great criminal.

"The deceased Danite chief was an extremely ignorant, illiterate man, being unable to write his own name, and was as superstitious as a savage. He was a firm believer in ghosts, witches, evil spirits, and spooks, as well as in the revelations of Joseph Smith and the divinity of the utterances of the Mormon high priests and prophets. It was Rockwell who shot Governor Boggs in the early troubles of the Mormon Church in Missouri, for which service to the cause Smith declared him the Samson of the Church, and promised him, in the name of the Lord, that if he would never allow his hair and whiskers to be cut, the bullet of his enemies should be turned aside, and wicked, designing men should never prevail against him. Rockwell, therefore, always wore his hair long, and a full beard, both of which, however, were thin, as well as gray. He wore his hair in two braids, tied up with two small ribbons across the back of the head on a line with his ears. It is estimated that he participated in at least a hundred murders for the Church, none of which he ever divulged. He used to own the Dunyan ranch, at the point of the mountain, south of the city; and a short distance from that point on the road to Camp Floyd, there is a deep well, where there was, in early days, a stage station. This place he firmly believed to be haunted by evil spirits, who delighted in bringing trouble upon him or his horses every time he passed. He used to tell that on one occasion, when he was passing this well with a band of wild mustangs, some thirty of his animals fell down in the road sick. He directed the man to split the tail of each sick horse, put some of the blood of each on a wisp of straw, and set the straw on fire. This rite broke the spell of the witches. The horses immediately recovered, and he went on his way rejoicing. .... Rockwell had a decided objection to sleeping in the dark. During the few months he stopped at the Colorado stables, he never permitted the lamp to be turned out. Not unfrequently, too, he would insist on sleeping with the hostler, as if afraid of shadows.

"When Joseph Smith first organized the 'hosts of Israel,' Rockwell was made the chief of the Danite Band, which branch of the aforesaid 'hosts' was charged with the work of secretly assassinating the enemies of Smith and the Church. This organization had its signs, the principal one of which was placing the palm against the cheek in such a manner that the right ear protruded between the index and the middle fingers. With this, Porter Rockwell and his band could do their bloody work in a crowd without danger of colliding with each other. After the death of Smith, Rockwell transferred his allegiance to Brigham Young, whom he served as devotedly as he did the original prophet, doing the priesthood's work of assassina-

BRIGHAM YOUNG.

From a Photograph taken in 1876.

Page 219.

tion, when ordered, as cheerfully as other elders of the Church went on proselyting missions when called by the Mormon authorities. To murder for the Church was his calling: it was his religion. It is but justice to him, however, to say that he never was a polygamist, though he had been married three times, and was the father of three families of boys and girls. .... In stature Rockwell was small, but heavy and compactly built. His eyes were little blue peepers, his features small, and his florid face always wore an expression of mingled disgust and contempt, as if something were constantly offending his olfactory nerves. He usually dressed in Brigham's homespun, and he wore a faded felt hat turned up at both sides."

There is no name with which Mormonism has been more identified than with that of Brigham Young. This remarkable personage, to whose zeal and master-spirit the Mormon Church owes, it may be said, its present development and state of activity, was born on June 1, 1801, at Whittingham, in Windham County, Vermont. His parents were, in religion, Methodists, and he was the fourth of a family of five sons and six daughters. He followed the trades of carpenter, painter, and glazier, and became a Mormon in 1832, and at once came out as an ardent supporter of "Prophet" Joseph Smith. Brigham became a staunch upholder of the tenets of the "new religion;" and such promising signs of an arbitrary temper, of determination and tenacity of will must he have given to his chief, Joe Smith, that he (Smith) is said to have prophesied that one day, "Brother Brigham should rule the Church." Some persons, however, have affirmed that Smith, on one occasion, prophesied that "Brother Brigham" would eventually "lead the Church into hell," so that it is as well to be careful how we accept the predictions of the "inspired" founder of the Mormon Church.

When Brigham Young first encountered Joseph Smith, which happened in the month of November, 1833, both of them, we are told, became "inspired," and began speaking in "unknown tongues." They both set to and gabbled away to each other in languages that no one had ever before heard of, and which neither of them could understand! This is the first recorded instance when the power of the "gift of tongues" was made manifest.

It was three years after the assassination, in 1844, of Joseph Smith, when disorganization had followed that tragical event, and schism and apostasy from the "true fold" were rife among the Saints in "Zion," that Brigham Young was elected to the presidency as the only man who had sufficient tact and ability for despotic government to prevent the Church from falling to pieces; and the power that he assumed at the commencement of his rule he retained up to the day of his death, on Wednesday, August 29, 1877. He ruled the Church with a rod of iron—no mandate of his could possibly be disobeyed with impunity. It is remarkable what an amount of faith an ignorant and fanatical people seem to have placed in his utterances, how implicitly they believed all that he told them, especially if he qualified his remarks with the prefatory words, "Thus saith the Lord." They carried their belief in him to such a length that they even looked upon his word as the Word of God! Apostle Heber C. Kimball, for instance, once expressed himself after the following fashion: "I have often said that the word of our leader and Prophet is the Word of God to this people. We cannot see God, we cannot hold conversation with him; but He has given us a man that we can talk to, and thereby know His will, just as well as if God himself were present with us. I am no more afraid to risk my salvation in the hands of this man than I am to trust myself in the hands of the Almighty. He will lead me right if I do as he says in every particular and circumstance."[1]

Brigham Young entertained an extraordinary opinion concerning the Deity. He once announced that Adam was God. An idea publicly proclaimed to the Church implied something more than a mere private opinion, which he, or anyone else, was at liberty to hold, if he chose. But a statement made by the Mormon "Prophet" meant simply a doctrine which all were bound to believe, because Brigham's word was supposed to be infallible, and speaking to the Saints as a prophet he was, of course, "inspired." So, in the Tabernacle

---

[1] *Deseret News*, October 1, 1866.

in Salt Lake City, on April 9, 1852, he made the following remarkable declaration: "Now hear it, O inhabitants of the earth, Jew and Gentile, Saint and sinner! When our father Adam came into the Garden of Eden, he came into it with a celestial body, and brought Eve, one of his wives, with him. He helped to make and organize this world. He is Michael the Archangel, the Ancient of Days, about whom holy men have written and spoken. He is our Father and our God, and the only God with whom we have to do. Every man upon the earth, professing Christians or non-professing, must hear it, sooner or later." *Apropos* of this sentiment may be mentioned the extraordinary blasphemy uttered by a prominent member of the present Mormon hierarchy, who once declared that "God is the most egotistical of all existing beings!!"[2]

We have already taken a brief glance at the domestic life of Brigham Young; but a little more, perhaps, may be added to what has already been said on the subject. This Yankee Mahomet first took unto him a wife in the year 1824, that is, when he was twenty-three years of age. The name of the lady I do not know; she is now deceased, like her husband. Eventually her original importance became seriously diminished, for, as far as one can gather, Brigham Young had altogether the number of nineteen wives: but as to the number of his children, I really cannot venture upon any positive statement. Mary Ann Angell is the name of his surviving "legal" widow, and to her he was married in the year 1834. He was certainly very assiduous and diligent in building up a most extensive "spiritual kingdom," and for the pains he must have taken in doing so we ought to give him all the credit we can.

Mary Ann Angell had five children, who were named (in order) Joseph A.; Brigham; Alice; Luna; and John W. His second son, Brigham "Junior," as he is called,—or "Briggy," as he is more familiarly known among Saints and Gentiles,—was a great favourite with his father, and resembled him in many respects. It was the late "Prophet's" wish that "Briggy" should succeed him in the presidency; but that wish was not fulfilled. "Briggy" is the husband of three wives.

[2] According to Mormon doctrine, God is not a spirit, but a material being.

Katie Spencer, Jane Carrington, and Lizzie Fenton are their names. Both father and son courted Lizzie, the double courtship lasting for several months, till, in the long-run, age had to give way to youth, and Lizzie became " Briggy's " bride. Brigham Young had six of his daughters married to three of the Saints, two to each, namely, Alice and Emily to Hiram Clauson; Luna and Fanny to George Thatcher; and Mary and Caroline to Mark Croxall.

The matrimonial proclivities of John A. Young, the last of Mary Ann Angell's five children above-mentioned, are, perhaps, worth noting. The following account of him, in brief, I have received from a reliable authority in Salt Lake City. In his early youth he loved a Miss Spencer, who "jilted" him; whereupon he married a Miss Lucy Confield, out of spite. A year subsequently he married a Miss Clara Jones, thus demonstrating his faith in the doctrine of polygamy. He happened to be in Philadelphia a year or so later, where he met a Miss " Libby " Confield, the cousin of his first wife Lucy. This woman he also married; but the condition on which the nuptials were celebrated was that he should dismiss his two former wives, which he did, though he did not divorce them until some years afterwards. A few weeks after his father's death, in 1877, " John A." startled the community by marrying his father's step-daughter, Luella Cobb. About twelve months later he married a German woman, and with these last two wives he removed to the Territory of Arizona—" where he now is," my correspondent concludes, in a letter dated March 19, 1880. I have received confirmation of the correctness of these incidents in Mr. Young's career from another correspondent residing in Salt Lake City.

It will of course be supposed that Brigham Young has been honoured with a splendid tombstone erected to his memory; or perhaps with a mausoleum, at which all the world may marvel, a fitting sepulchre for so distinguished a Saint: but no. The mortal remains of the " Prophet of the Lord " are laid in one of his own private gardens—in a plot of ground which is little better than a rough, neglected brickyard, where a plain stone slab, with no inscription upon it, marks the place where the remains are deposited; nor are there any railings around to fence off "ungodly Gentiles" who might at any time walk over the deceased "Prophet," and desecrate the spot with their unhallowed tread. In the same yard—for the cemetery is worthy of no better name—are the graves of some of the late President's wives and relations, which are well-nigh indistinguishable, for they lie hidden amongst a mass of rubbish with which the ground is thickly bestrewn.

The deceased President entered minutely and characteristically into particulars as to the conduct of his funeral. I will here give *verbatim* the document which he prepared:

"I, Brigham Young, wish my funeral services to be conducted after the following manner:

"When I breathe my last I wish my friends to put my body in as clean and wholesome state as can conveniently be done, and preserve the same for one, two, three or four days, or as long as my body can be preserved in a good condition. I want my coffin made of plump $1\frac{1}{4}$-inch redwood boards, not scrimped in length, but two inches longer than I would measure, and from two to three inches wider than is commonly made for a person of my breadth and size, and deep enough to place me on a little cotton bed with a good suitable pillow for size and quality; my body dressed in my Temple clothing and laid nicely into my coffin, and the coffin to have the appearance that if I wanted to turn a little to the right or to the left I should have plenty of room to do so; the lid can be made crowning.

"At my interment I wish all my family present, that can be conveniently, and the male members wear no crape on their hats or their coats; the females to buy no black bonnets, nor black dresses, nor black veils; but if they have them they are at liberty to wear them. The services may be permitted, as singing and a prayer offered, and if any of my friends wish to say a few words, and really desire, do so; and when they have closed their service, take my remains on a bier and repair to the little burying-ground which I have reserved on my lot east of the White House on the hill, and in the southeast corner of this lot have a vault built of mason work, large enough to receive my coffin, and that may be placed in a box, if they choose, made of the same materials as the coffin— redwood, then place flat rocks over the vault, sufficiently large to cover it, that the earth may be placed over it—nice, fine, dry earth, to cover it until the walls of the little cemetery are reared, which will leave me in the southeast corner. This vault ought to be roofed over with some kind of a temporary roof. There let my earthly house or tabernacle rest in peace and have a good sleep until the morning of the first resurrection; no crying, nor mourning, with anyone that I have done my work faithfully and in good faith.

"I wish this to be read at the funeral, providing that if I should die anywhere in the mountains, I desire the above directions respecting my place of burial to be observed; but if I should live to go back with the Church to Jackson County, I wish to be buried there.

"BRIGHAM YOUNG,
"President of the Church of Jesus Christ of Latter-day Saints.
"Sunday, November 9th, 1873.
"Salt Lake City, Utah Ter."

These directions were carried out to the letter, and publicly read, by the apostle George Q. Cannon, on the day of the funeral.

CHAPTER XI.

A SERIOUS ASPECT OF MORMONISM.

Perversion to Mormonism—The missionary abroad—Missionary work in Great Britain—How British emigrants are imposed upon—European exodus to Utah in 1879—British Mormons in Salt Lake City—The exodus from Great Britain in 1880—Converts from Iceland—A superabundance of clergy—The "trustee-in-trust's" account for 1879—Receipts and disbursements—Christian missionary work in Utah—Result of ten years' labour—Utah's admission to Statedom—Trouble ahead—Defiant Mormons—Treasonable utterances—The Endowment House—A scandalous institution—The Mormon's treasonable oath—Penalty for revealing it — No public record of Mormon marriages — No marriage certificates—International intervention.

A FEW facts relating to the growth and influence of the Mormon religion will probably be of interest to English readers. Mormonism has now become so firmly established in the United States, that it is important, at the present time, when so many of our poor and ignorant countrymen are yearly decoyed to Salt Lake City, to direct attention to some of the evils, beyond those which have already been mentioned, to which Mormon emigrants to Utah are exposed. But with regard to these evils, the reader will have seen, from what has been said in the four preceding chapters, that it is impossible for me to place before him the whole truth of the practices and professions of the Latter-day Saints. There is perhaps no religious organization—not at least in any country calling itself Christian—where vulgarity so predominates; where doctrines so hideous and revolting are held up for acceptance and belief; where men's minds, manners, and language are so deplorably deficient in cultivation and refinement; where profanity so abounds, and where—let it be added—the marriage relationship is so shamefully abused and its sacred digntiy so notoriously degraded. It is therefore not to be wondered that one should recoil with disgust when brought face to face with a society of people so professedly religious, yet amongst whom such social corruption prevails, and the doctrines of whose religious belief are really too shocking to admit of calm examination.

It is a mistake for people to suppose, as many do suppose, that Mormonism is not increasing. On the contrary, Mormonism was never so prosperous—in a quiet way—as it is at the present moment. Recruits from Great Britain and other European countries continue to pour into Utah by hundreds every two or three months—not, as might be supposed, from various quarters of the United States and Canada, for but a very few number of converts to the religion are obtained in the New World; but it is in England, Wales, Scotland, Denmark, Sweden, and Norway—among the poor and uneducated masses of these countries—in remote districts where the truth of this pernicious "faith" is unknown—that the Mormons win their greatest triumphs; and it may be as well to note the fact that their chief recruiting-ground is Wales. What the Mormon missionaries impress on the people is not so much the peculiar doctrines of their Church as the opportunities offered for bettering their condition. They tell them that Utah is "a land flowing with milk and honey;" that it is a garden ready made, and blossoming like the rose; that there they will find a panacea for every ill, and be as happy as the day is long; that in "Zion" liberty—both civil and religious—abounds, poverty is unknown, truth and virtue flourish, and that there they will find a holy and a loving priesthood ready to minister to their spiritual necessities—far more than they have ever been ministered unto before; that by becoming Mormons they will have all the sins they have hitherto committed forgiven them,[1] and be able to begin life anew, pure and spotless, and with every probability of remaining so—in the Church's esti-

---

[1] A popular Mormon song, set to the tune of "The Low-backed Car," commences as follows:
  When first I joined the Mormons,
   My soul was filled with light;

mation—provided they pay in their tithing and say their prayers morning and evening regularly. They tell the ignorant masses all this, they hold up before their eyes a picture of future happiness and prosperity, and a religion founded, they say, upon direct revelation from God: but what they do *not* tell them is the truth, and that is that Utah, far from being a garden, is in the first place a desert—a barren, alkaline desert, whose soil has to be properly irrigated and prepared, and all the poisonous ingredients washed out—and this oftentimes at considerable expense—before anything can be got to grow. The new convert is *not* told that, far from civil and religious liberty abounding, liberty of action and freedom of thought are denied the poor deluded Mormon emigrant to Utah, his actions and religious convictions being controlled by a dictatorial and fanatical priesthood, who will not allow him to move so much as his little finger in opposition to its behests,[2] or to put forward his opinions in repugnance to doctrines, however profane, which they tell him are "inspired," or have been acquired also by direct revelation from God. He is *not* told that poverty and destitution are the rule rather than otherwise in Utah, for, however needy may be the Mormon's condition in life, he must still contribute his tithing annually,—the bishop of his district will see that he is not

> My sins were gone, and that alone
> Convinced me I was right.
> When from the pure baptismal stream
> I rose, my guilt was fled,
> The Spirit, then, by chosen men
> Was sealed upon my head.

[2] "In the most tyrannical way," says the Rev. R. G. McNicce, pastor of the Presbyterian Church in Salt Lake City, "this priesthood directs all the affairs of the people, telling them what store they must trade at, what newspaper they must read, what school they must patronize, and how much every man must contribute in order that the priesthood may continue to wax fat. This overbearing tyranny was well illustrated when one of the apostles, on one occasion, while speaking in one of the ward meeting-houses about the solemn duty of obeying the priesthood, happened to look through the window and see a load of wood passing by. 'Now I want you,' said he, 'to obey the priesthood so implicitly, and to have so much confidence in everything they tell you, that if any of the twelve apostles should tell you that load of wood is a load of hay, you would all say: Amen, that's a load of hay.'"

negligent in his duty in this respect,—and be prepared, even, to surrender his all for the Church's benefit should it be required of him to do so. Lastly, the convert is *not* told that instead of truth and virtue abounding in "Zion," in the one case the sacred truths of the Gospel of Christ are perverted and misrepresented, or are put aside altogether, and the heresies of the Book of Mormon and of the Book of Doctrine and Covenants are brought forward and thrust in their place ; while in the other case it is a fact, and one which cannot be gainsaid, as I can prove from my inquiries on the subject made during my visit to Utah in 1879,—that, despite the pretensions of the Latter-day Saints that their polygamous system has brought about a better state of morals, and that they are a more chaste and virtuous people than other communities on earth, virtue is no better cherished among them than it is among any monogamous community all the world over.

If we turn to the latest official census report of the Latter-day Saints, namely that produced at the annual spring conference held in Salt Lake City on the 6th of last April,[3] and two following days, we shall obtain a few interesting statistics. From this we learn that there are 111,820 Mormons in Utah (out of an entire population of about 144,000), 1895 in Arizona, 600 in Colorado, 5257 in Great Britain, 5205 in Scandinavia, and 798 in Germany; total, 125,575. Last year, 1500 were baptized into the Church, and there were upwards of 600 excommunications and removals. The number of births amounted (in 1879) to 2461, or 1230 males and 1231 females. In the same year, 880 British were added to the Church by baptism. European emigration to Utah in 1879 was distributed amongst nationalities as follows : British, 812 ; Scandinavia, 515 ; Swiss, 90 ; German, 34 ; Dutch, 5 ; Irish, 2 ; French, 1 ;—total, 1459.

In the report from which these particulars are taken, no mention is made of the Territories of Idaho and Wyoming, which are fast being peopled with Mormons, Idaho in particular. It would be safe to say that there are not less than 150,000 Mormons in the Rocky Mountain region. In New Mexico, also, colonies of the Saints have been established, as well as in Tennessee, Georgia, and other States in the South.

[3] This day was one of special importance to the Mormons, as it was the semi-centennial anniversary of the founding of their church.

There are about sixty missionaries propagating the doctrines of Mormonism in the Southern States. In Europe there are 400 missionaries, eighty of these having been sent out from Salt Lake City in 1878. Of the population of Utah, former British subjects and their children may be estimated at about one-third. At the spring conference of 1879, it was reported that there were then 19,938 Mormons in Salt Lake City (4071 families), and a little over 5000 non-Mormons or "Gentiles." From a list compiled for me in September, 1879, of British Mormons holding office in the several "organized stakes of Zion," I find that there were then forty-two (at least) British-born presidents, counsellors and bishops in eleven of these stakes, namely in the Salt Lake, Sanpete, Sevier, St. George, Tooele, Utah, Weber, Morgan, Davis, Cache, and Box Elder stakes. In the Salt Lake stake alone, both the two counsellors and thirteen out of the twenty-one bishops holding office in that stake were British-born. Nine of these bishops were Scotchmen. I am told on reliable authority that one-half the Mormon population in Salt Lake City are British-born.

About 1800 Mormons have embarked from Liverpool and Glasgow for Utah during the current year. The exact number it is difficult to ascertain on this side of the Atlantic; but the number stated may be taken as the very lowest estimate. All outgoing Mormons are taken to New York (from Liverpool) by the steamers of the Guion Company, this company having conveyed the Saints for the last eighteen or twenty years. Among the batch of converts that left Liverpool on May 1st last were fifteen natives of Iceland.

As is probably well known, Liverpool is the headquarters of the Latter-day Saints in Great Britain. At the Mormon book-store located at 42, Islington (Liverpool), is published the *Latter-day Saints Millennial Star*, a monthly publication containing the chief items of news from Salt Lake City; the reports of conferences held from time to time in Great Britain and elsewhere; directions to intending emigrants, etc. Elder Albert Carrington is the present leader of the British mission.

There were 109,218 Mormons in Utah in the spring of 1878. Of this number, 33,661 were children under eight years of age. Only those over that age are considered members of the Church, so that the number of Church members in the Territory was 75,557. Of this latter number, 23,002 were office-holders, or two out of every six! This naturally takes in every specially bright and intelligent man in the community, besides serving as a bribe in the case of any who might be disposed to be independent.

Returning to the annual report already referred to, the tithing receipts in 1879 reached 91,666*l.* 12*s.* To the Temple (Salt Lake City) fund, 1247*l.* 15*s.* was contributed, and 28,806*l.* 3*s.* 6*d.* was expended on the work of that building! President Taylor and the bishops received 6775*l.* 9*s.* 3*d.*, and, in addition to this, Taylor "took" 4466*l.* as his salary as "trustee-in-trust" (? chancellor of the exchequer). There was 5689*l.* 1*s.* 11*d.* spent on the work of the new Assembly Hall or winter tabernacle in Salt Lake City, and—as we have seen above—990*l.* 9*s.* 8*d.* (in addition) on the organ with which that building has been furnished : 44,701*l.* 1*s.* 2*d.*, besides, was spent on erecting new temples in three towns in the Territory, namely at Manti, Logan, and St. George. There was 3800*l.* given away to the poor, and over 1600*l.* appropriated to the Indians. The tithing-office salaries amounted in the aggregate to 3023*l.* 12*s.* 4*d.*, and 786*l.* 16*s.* was expended in telegraphic despatches. There was 94*l.* 16*s.* 6*d.* collected from unfortunate immigrants who had to camp out in the tithing yards in Brigham's Block.[4] The grand total receipts of the Church for 1879 amounted to 219,406*l.* 16*s.*, a sum which represents a tax of 1*l.* 19*s.* 3*d.* upon every man, woman and child in Utah! And where does all the money go to? As the Mormon priesthood would say, it all goes to "the Lord." "The amount of money," says the Rev. Mr. McNiece, of Salt Lake City, "paid to the priesthood by the hard-working people during the last twenty years, through the Tithing fund, the Temple fund, the Perpetual Emigration fund, the Relief fund, and other funds which only a man possessed of inspired arithmetic could enumerate, cannot be estimated at less than ten million dollars."

It is pleasant to turn from statistics such as these to those which can be afforded of the steady progress of Christian missionary work in Utah, as shown by the labours of the

[4] See page 174.

Episcopalians, Presbyterians, Methodists, and Congregationalists. Ten years ago there were only two public representatives of Christianity in the Territory, namely the two Episcopalian ministers, the Revs. T. W. Haskins, and G. W. Foote; now the Christian forces in Utah amount to twenty-four church organizations, twenty-two ministers, twenty-five mission schools, fifty-four teachers, 250 pupils (with about the same number in Sunday schools), twenty-two churches and chapels; and the total cost of buildings erected for church and school purposes has (in ten years) been 19,000*l*. The Presbyterians take the lead in the work of evangelization. They have ten church organizations in Utah, eight ministers, thirteen mission schools, eighteen teachers, 900 pupils, and nine churches or chapels. The Episcopalians come next with six church organizations, a bishop and five clergy, four mission schools, twenty-two teachers, 702 pupils, and five churches, with a cathedral (St. Mark's) in Salt Lake City which cost about 10,000*l*. The Methodists and Congregationalists are also doing a good work, joining hand in hand with the Presbyterians and Episcopalians in promoting the Christian reformation of the region. The churches and schools of these Protestant denominations are surely and gradually gaining ground and enlightening the masses, and as surely are they undermining the all-powerful influence of the priesthood. But in a Territory that is larger than England and Scotland put together, where there is already a population of nearly 112,000 unbelievers, whose ranks are being yearly increased by the addition of some ten or fifteen hundred, this little Christian army, fighting in the interests of civil and religious freedom, has a hard task before it, if it is to make any headway against the increasing tide of fanaticism and unbelief. What is sadly needed in Utah is more hands to help in the work of evangelization. And more sympathy in this work is required from the American people generally. More money, too, is needed, to establish a few free schools in the Territory. The leaders of the Latter-day Saints are naturally opposed to education—the priesthood can only maintain its influence so long as its dupes are kept in a state of superstition and ignorance. With all the money that comes pouring every year into the coffers of the Mormon Church there have been no free schools established in Utah, which is an anomaly such as does not exist in any other State or Territory in the Union. "One thing there is," says Mr. McNiece,[5] "that Mormonism cannot endure, and that is *the Light.*" Once get the people educated—once bring home to them the sacred and eternal truths of the Gospel of Christ—once convince them of the sensuality, the socially and morally degrading tendency of the doctrines of their religion, and refinement, self-respect, the realization of a higher intellectual and moral condition in life—all this will follow; and it is by planting schools in places where unbelief most abounds and inculcating the doctrines of Christianity in the minds of the *children* of the Latter-day Saints, that we can look for any success attending the praiseworthy efforts of the Christian missionaries of Utah.

It may not be generally known that the Mormons are using what influence they can so as to procure the admission of Utah into the Union as a State. The reason of this is obvious: Polygamy could then be practised with impunity, for Utah, as a State,—the Saints would give the new State the name of "Deseret,"—would have the management of its own affairs, and be altogether independent of Congressional legislation. The Territory could, and probably would, be admitted with a Constitution prohibiting polygamy; or it could be admitted upon the express condition that polygamy should be abolished. But it would be quite possible for the Mormons to annul the Constitution as soon as the rights of Statedom had been conferred, and it is more than we can reasonably expect that they would give up their pet institution when it would be within their power to introduce a State law distinctly permitting it. The National Government, moreover, would be powerless to interfere in the internal affairs of the State when created. Polygamy would then be unassailable, unless extreme measures were adopted, such as an amendment to the United States Constitution prohibiting the institution. The danger that lies in the future may be seen by the following remarks of Mr. J. M. Coyner,—an authority

[5] I am indebted to this gentleman for the above interesting statistics relating to Christian missionary work in Utah, as well as for several other important and interesting facts contained in this and preceding chapters.

already referred to,—who, writing to the *Boston Educational Journal*, says: "I am convinced that the plan of the hierarchy is to have Utah admitted as a State at the earliest opportunity . . . . . . This done—Utah as a State, and with all the peculiarities of the Mormon Church engrafted on its State Constitution, such as its polygamy, its union of Church and State, its priesthood control—two Senators and several Congressmen will be thus secured. Utah will then be divided into two States, with Salt Lake City for the northern capital, and St. George for the capital of the southern State. This accomplished, there will be four Senators. Then Idaho and Wyoming on the north, and Arizona on the south, will be so thoroughly colonized as to give the Mormons the balance of power in forming the State Governments of these Territories, so that they will undoubtedly ask for their admission as Mormon States. New Mexico will follow suit, making six Mormon States, which, when settled by this Mormon foreign emigration, can be carved into half-a-dozen more. . . . . . . Every influence that money and bargaining can command will be used to have Utah admitted as a State. The parties are now so equally balanced that a bribe of two Senators and several Congressmen, in the present condition of party morals, with the prospect of an increase of Senators and Congressmen as more Mormon States are admitted, may turn the scales of justice. . . . . Every Mormon is taught that his Church will ultimately overcome not only our own Government, but that all nations will become subject to the Mormon hierarchy; and unless something is done to check the progress of this sentiment by the strong hand of Government, there is serious trouble ahead of us."

But the Latter-day Saints can hardly be said to have merited such an extension of favours from the Federal Government if one may be allowed to judge by some of the utterances that are made by prominent Mormons in public, or through the medium of their official church organ, the *Deseret News*. Declarations not only dreadfully profane, but treasonable, are frequently made by members of the Mormon hierarchy. "What do we care for the Government of the United States?" said Brigham Young "Junior" (the deceased Prophet's second son), one of the twelve apostles, in Salt

Lake City on November 17, 1878. "If I had my way," he continued, "I would say to every Gentile in this city and Territory, You get out of here, or take the consequences!—and it is coming to this."[6] It was to the advantage of the Mormons that they should give the late President of the United States "a warm welcome" when he paid a visit to Salt Lake City on his way to San Francisco on the 5th of last September (1880), escorting him from Ogden in a special train,[7] and presenting Mrs. Hayes with "a fine bouquet of flowers." It would not have been good policy on their part to have acted otherwise. And yet this manifestation of loyalty scarcely harmonizes with the following atrocious statement of Elder Wilford Woodruff, also one of the twelve apostles, which he made in the course of an encyclical letter (addressed to the Mormon Church) published in the *Deseret News* of April 1, 1879,—a copy of which letter lies before me as I write,—where he says: "As an apostle of the Lord Jesus Christ, I will not desert my wives and children and disobey the commandments of God for the sake of accommodating the public clamor of a nation steeped in sin and ripened for the damnation of hell!" Again, in the same paper, on August 8, 1879, the following passage occurs in the course of an article severely attacking the Federal Government: "We settled in these quiet vales to serve God and build up Zion, and by His help we will do it, and we see no reason why we should bow our necks to the yoke and submit to be smitten and spit upon by the vile and despicable crew who have provoked one small act of retaliation, which, if they do not desist, will be the first drop of the drenching shower to come." Other

---

[6] *Letters on Mormonism*, by J. M. Coyner.

[7] The special train which conveyed President Hayes back to Ogden, at the conclusion of his official visit to Salt Lake City, was under the personal superintendence of Bishop (Mormon) John Sharp, the president of the Utah Central Railway Company. (The Mormons constructed the railway between Salt Lake City and Ogden.) Bishop Sharp is also one of the directors of the Union Pacific Railway, and the president of the Utah Southern Railway Company. He was a Scotch coal-miner, and is generally known among the Mormons and Gentiles in Utah as "the smartest man in the Church." Mr. Sharp rejoices in the possession of three wives—at least that was the number at the beginning of last May, as I was informed by letter from Salt Lake City.

statements, equally gross, might be cited. But I think that the three instances I have given are sufficient.

If the reader is shocked—as well indeed he might be—at expressions such as these emanating from the leaders of the Latter-day Saints, with what increased feelings of horror and disgust would he be filled were he informed of the nature of the secret ceremonies attending the marriages of Mormon men and women in the Endowment House in Salt Lake City! I cannot expose the scandalous proceedings which accompany these ceremonies,—they are far too shocking to print,—although I happen to be in possession of a full report of them, which has been forwarded me this year from Salt Lake City by a young victimized English lady; indeed, a sufficient exposure of the proceedings alluded to has already been laid before the public.[8] But there is one feature in the Endowment House ceremonies which ought, I think, to be noticed here, and that is the treasonable oath which every Mormon—whether man or woman—has to swear who is about to enter the marriage state. Every Mormon must swear that he (or she) will "obey the laws of the Mormon Church in preference to those of the United States!" There is a terrible penalty attached for revealing this secret oath. It is that you will have your throat cut from ear to ear, and your tongue torn from your mouth. The sign of the penalty is "drawing the hand with the thumb pointing towards the throat sharply across and bringing the arm to the level of the square, and with the hand upraised to heaven, swearing to abide the same."

No public record is kept of the Mormon marriages which are celebrated in the Endowment House. No marriage certificates are given, and, in some cases,—where, for instance, the woman is inclined to be perverse,—no witnesses are allowed to be present. "If occasion requires it," writes my fair correspondent (previously alluded to) from Salt Lake City, "and it is to shield any of their polygamous brethren from being found out, they (*i.e.* the Mormon priesthood) will positively swear that they did not perform any marriage at all, so that the women in this Church have but a very poor outlook for being considered honorable wives."

[8] See *An Englishwoman in Utah*, by Mrs. T. B. H. Stenhouse.

The interests of religion and morality demand that the power of the Mormon Church should be restrained at once. Mormonism has now flourished for fifty years—flourished through dire affliction and persecution—flourished in peace and tranquillity—until it has become a power not merely of importance to our Transatlantic friends, but one in which we as Englishmen are, or ought to be, as much concerned as are the people of the United States. It does not redound to the credit of Old England that she should allow such a scandalous institution as this to be fostered and strengthened by the proselytism of so many of her sons. Is it too much to hope that something will be done to put a stop to the evil?

THE MORMON TABERNACLE.
(*See page 166.*)

CHAPTER XII.

WESTWARD TO SAN FRANCISCO.

Further westward—A run through the Salt Lake Valley to Ogden—A warm spring lake—Mormon husbandry—Successful agriculture—Ogden—An uproarious greeting—Choice of three dinners—Scarcity of berths—Leaving Ogden—Brigham City—"Gentile" Corinne—Promontory Point—The "great railroad wedding"—A word for the poor Indian—The way he is treated—Census of the Indians—A wash and a breakfast at Elko—The American Desert—"All aboard, all aboard!"—A rush for the cars—Battle Mountain—Winnemucca—The "noble red man"—An oasis in the desert—Peaceful reflections—On the rampage again—Junction for Virginia City—The wonderful mines of the Comstock lode—Ascending the Sierra—A twenty-eight mile snow-shed—7017 feet above the sea—Californian mining names—Quartz mining and placer mining—Rounding Cape Horn—A run down into California—Sacramento—I become an object of attraction—A word about English tourists—The State Capitol of California—At the Oakland wharf—On board the ferry—San Francisco.

ON June 11, 1878, we left Salt Lake City for San Francisco, California, a distance of 920 miles.

Between the Mormon metropolis and Ogden, where we rejoined the Pacific Railroad, the line runs for some distance close to the Great Salt Lake. On the way we passed a warm spring lake, of about a mile in length, whose waters approached so close to the railway that they almost washed the metals as the train sped along. This lake is only separated from the Salt Lake by a thin strip of land.

The beach and flats about the Salt Lake are encrusted with alkali, which renders the earth barren, and vegetation, it would seem, entirely out of the question; but such is not the case. Mormon settlements are scattered over this "desert," and signs of careful husbandry around neat homesteads are seen by the traveller as he journeys along. Though the soil was at one time so alkaline as to hinder the growth of trees and plants, and to be a bar to all attempts at vegetation, it has been watered and brought under such an excellent system of irrigation by the Mormon settlers, that the alkali of soda or potash has been completely washed out, and thus the country has been made fertile and productive. Sagebrush, indeed, prevails everywhere, covering the mountain slopes and plains beneath, springing up naturally where no other plant can be induced to grow. But, as I have observed, where the Mormons have settled they have irrigated and prepared the land, and turned it to the best account, have successfully planted and cultivated it—and this is about the only good word that can be said on behalf of the "People of the Lord."[1] Along the beach there are in places thick, white layers of pure salt, the result of the evaporation of the water which has been washed up and has afterwards receded.

[1] In 1879 I received an invitation from a Mormon to look over his farm at Wood's Cross, distant about eight miles from Salt Lake City, on the Utah Central Railroad. The following facts which he stated to me concerning the produce from his land will show what can be done in this desert valley by the application of labour and intelligence—granted the possession of some capital to make a start with. His farm, which borders on the Great Salt Lake, comprises ninety-eight acres, or sixty-eight acres more than the average-sized farm in Utah; and he has irrigated it with forty streams diverted from the neighbouring mountains. He had been most successful with wheat, Indian corn, barley, and oats. Fifty bushels of wheat to the acre he considered a very fair (!) crop; but he had also raised as much as sixty bushels of wheat to the acre, also one hundred bushels of oats and fifty bushels of Indian corn. He told me that seventy-five to eighty bushels of oats per acre were regularly raised in the valley. He had raised thirty tons of beets and carrots to the acre, and once he raised a beet weighing thirty-six pounds, and sold 200,000 lbs. of carrots at 6s. per 100 lbs. Fourteen hundred bushels of carrots on four acres of land have been raised in the valley; but the average crop per acre is 250 bushels. He possessed a roadside fence of sixty-eight rods in length literally bowed to the ground with peaches, plums, pears, mulberries, etc., and this fence alone paid his annual taxes (territorial, county, and local), which amounted altogether to 12*l.* His tithe to the Church which he paid in for 1878 amounted in value to 58*l.* out of the yield from his farm, and included butter, eggs, corn, vegetables, fruit, etc.—a tenth in fact of everything raised on the premises.

After a run of thirty-seven miles, over ground we had already traversed, a distance which we managed to accomplish in two hours, stopping at four little stations on the way, we reached Ogden, and had to change from the cars of the Utah Central Railroad into those of the Central Pacific. Ogden, named after an old trapper who used to live in the neighbourhood, is a town of about 6000 inhabitants, is chiefly Mormon, and is the second town in point of importance in the Territory of Utah. Gentiles are fast pouring into the place, and the Mormons themselves are gradually getting "freezed out." Its streets are wide and regularly laid out, and have streams of pure water flowing at the sides, after the manner of Salt Lake City. Three times are kept here—Ogden proper, Laramie, and San Francisco times. The San Francisco time is 1 hr. 16 min. slower than Ogden, and the Ogden time is 30 min. slower than Laramie.

On reaching the station, we were received by such a clanging and banging and booming of gongs, together with such an uproarious and confused babel of voices from a number of excited individuals directly we stepped out of the train on to the platform, that it looked as if we had come to a place where everyone had taken leave of his senses. What did it all mean? In one word, it meant dinner. Yes, dinner it was, dinner and supper combined, and this is how the hour of the meal was proclaimed. There are four or five insignificant-looking little inns hard by the Ogden station, and the "runners" of these *hôtelleries*, each armed with a big gong, came forth with their satellites upon the arrival of our train, and made the most of such a windfall by intimating through the media of their gongs and their lungs how pleased they would be to see us inside their respective inns, where dinner was ready cooked and waiting for us, and how they would see us "fixed" for the meal with the smallest of amounts. Three out of the four or five came and pressed themselves on myself and my friend—they left off banging about their gongs and commenced vociferously haranguing us. As we had a couple of hours to wait before our train was due to leave for San Francisco, we began to turn a favourable ear to their vehement declarations; but so passionately did they address us, and so violently did they abuse one another, calling each other by the very choicest of American epithets in their anxiety to conclude with us a bargain which would at the same time be the most agreeable to themselves, that I thought more than once there was going to be a free fight. They called me "boss," and my friend they called "cap'n."[2] Hitherto I had generally been known as "colonel," particularly among the negroes. I rather approved of being called by this latter appellation. "To call a man 'colonel,'" says the *Philadelphia Post*, "is to convey the idea that he is of a mild, meek, and benevolent disposition."—But to return to these hotel touts. One of them promised us each a "clean" meal for the sum of seventy-five cents; another promised us one for fifteen cents less, and offered to get, in addition, some young ladies to wait upon us. A third promised us a fifty-cent dinner, young ladies to wait, and a good bottle of wine besides—all to be included in the bargain. It is needless to observe that we closed immediately with this last-mentioned offer.

Dinner over, upon which no comment need be made, except that it was served half cold, and what was served was half cooked, we returned to the station to see about securing a section in a sleeping-car, that we might be conveyed with ease and comfort to the far-distant end of our journey. But, as might have been expected, it was too late for us now to secure any berths. We ought to have made sure of these

---

[2] To be called "boss," "captain," "judge" (pronounced jidge) or "colonel" by the people you meet when you are travelling in the United States, is all very well, and you appreciate the good feeling that prompts the extension of such well-meaning compliments. But it is another matter altogether, indeed it is beyond a joke, when a letter comes addressed to you with some "bogus" title appended to your name on the envelope, or when the newspapers take you up and proclaim your name with a like spurious title attached to it, thereby causing you to become a laughing-stock to your friends, making you feel anything rather than "elevated." During my visit to the United States in 1879, I was twice dubbed a "Right Hon." (by letter), thrice was I knighted (in the newspapers), and once I was addressed (by letter) as "colonel." To give one instance,—In the arrival-list of guests staying at the Massasoit House, Narragansett Pier (a seaside resort on Rhode Island) on August 10, 1879, I found myself figuring prominently as "The Right Honorable," etc. etc.

before we left Salt Lake City. None were now to be had—all had been taken long ago. As it was, the Ogden station office for berth tickets was literally besieged with travellers, all anxious like ourselves to reach California comfortably, and everyone had to be similarly refused. So the prospect was before us of having to make the best of the situation for two nights in an ordinary car, where not only

OGDEN.

would there be no berths, nor indeed any proper accommodation for those who wished to have a comfortable sleep on the way; but no provision of lavatories, such as are in the parlour and sleeping-cars.

Ogden is finely situated, and as we pass out of the station for our run of 883 miles to the capital of the Pacific coast, mountains tower up grandly before us on our right and behind the town at our rear. We have now entered upon the second division of the Pacific Railroad.

Passing through a mountainous country, we come, in sixteen miles to Brigham "City," named after the late President of the Latter-day Saints. It is but an insignificant little Mormon settlement, where the "Church of Christ" is allowed to have full swing, for no "ungodly Gentiles" care to take the trouble to come here and set up their standard against it.

We now pass into a flat, desert region, and come within sight of the eastern of the two northern arms of the Great Salt Lake. We run first in a north-easterly direction, and then gradually curve round these two northern branches, keeping the lake in view, off and on, for seventy-four miles till reaching the settlement of Kelton, where we lose sight of it. But we must not omit to take a glance at the next settlement we come to after Brigham, six miles beyond. It is called Corinne —a very pretty name, and so indeed it ought to be, for here the Mormons are entirely "freezed out." No members of "Christ's Church" are allowed to have any voice in the counsels of *this* community. Corinne is the only town in the Territory where the Mormons do not preponderate. Its population is about 1500. Distant seven miles from the Great Salt Lake, a steamer used to ply between it and Lake Point, touching also at Black Rock. But the boat could not have paid very well, for it has now ceased running.

Twenty-nine miles beyond Corinne we pass a spot which is historically the most interesting on the whole of the overland route. It is Promontory Point, a headland jutting out into the Great Salt Lake, 1084 miles from Omaha and 832 from San Francisco. It was here that the two companies which engineered the Pacific Railroad—the one (the Central Pacific) commencing in California, the other (the Union Pacific) commencing in Nebraska—met and joined their lines, the Central Company having laid 692 miles of rail from Sacramento, the Union Company 1084 miles from Omaha. By an arrangement subsequently made, the Union Company gave up to the Central fifty-one miles of the portion they had laid, namely that between Ogden and Promontory Point, and again, in the same year (1869) which saw the union of the two lines, the Central Company purchased from the Western Pacific Company the 140 miles of rail which connected Sacramento with San Francisco. Thus we see how the length of the Union Pacific Railroad (from Omaha to Ogden) came to be 1033 miles, and the Central Pacific (from Ogden to San Francisco) 883 miles. This "great railroad wedding," as the union of the two lines has been termed, was celebrated with all the pomp and ceremony which the importance of the occasion demanded. Representatives from the principal cities of North America were present, and the ceremony of "driving the last spike" was performed by Governor Leland Stanford with a hammer made of solid silver, to the handle of which were attached telegraph wires that flashed, as he tapped the head of the gold spike, the news of the completion of the railway to San Francisco, New York, Boston, Washington, New Orleans, etc.

We were fast asleep when we passed Kelton, the nearest station on our journey to the present advanced scalping-ground of the Indian, where the detachment of fifteen had been sent from Fort Douglas, Salt Lake City, to look after the interests of the terrified population of the settlement. But almost the first thing we saw the next morning (June 12th) when we awoke was a camp of wigwams pitched close together in a meadow a few hundred yards distant on our left. We applied our field-glasses and gazed at them eagerly. The Indians have curious terms for the telegraph wire, and the railway train with its cars or carriages. They call the former the "whispering spirit," and the latter "bad 'medicine' (*i.e.* mystery) waggons."

I would here say a word on behalf of the poor Indian. We see him begging at the railway stations, looking dejected, miserable, dirty, and half-starved—but can we wonder at seeing him in this pitiable condition when we read of the way he is treated, and of the humiliations he has to endure at the hands of his pale-face masters? Driven from home, he has had to flee in the face of advancing civilization—nay, more than this. In Canada the Indian can truly say, This is all I have to complain of; but with the Indian of the United States the case is very different. Indians are not considered as "persons" in the eye of the American law. They are mere dogs; or at best "red imps, drunkards, and murderers of decent white men." Treaties can be made with them and can be broken at will. From the time that he first surrendered his roving hunting-ground to the American white man, and received in exchange for it a circumscribed tract of territory, in some cases utterly unsuited to his disposition and habits of life, the poor Indian has had to submit to a course of cruelty and rapine, injustice and deceit,—the whole history of the American's dealings with him reveals the same sad story of molestation and barbarism,—for, given these new lands to occupy, he has not been allowed to live and dwell in them peaceably; either he has been swindled out of them and forced to give *them* up and to "move on" elsewhere,—take the case of the Ponca tribe, for instance,—or else his allotted reservation has been encroached upon by mining "prospectors" or by settlers or others who have no business on his reservation at all. "The Utes must go," comes the bitter cry from Colorado; and why? Because the reservation that this tribe occupies has been found to contain mineral wealth, which the white man must have, and which the Indian has no right in keeping him from having; and so an organization has been started in Denver for the purpose of expelling the Utes from the Centennial State, in order that the white man may search for the gold and silver without being molested.[3] Other tribes have as much ground for complaint as the Ute tribe in Colorado. Ought we then to feel surprised when we hear of the Indian raising the war-whoop against his pale-face aggressors?

If the Indians were allowed to live upon their reservations in peace and quietness, we should, I fancy, hear less about Indian wars, massacres of white men, ambuscades, murder, and bloodshed: but something more than this is needed. Let the Americans increase their army by 50,000—it would then number but 75,000—and strengthen the military posts on

---

[3] "We do not want to fight the Indians," says a Coloradan prospector, "but we will do it in preference to being deprived of the privilege of prospecting a country which we are entitled to. . . . . We mean to go on that reservation and ascertain for ourselves what there is there. We know that there is an abundance of mineral, and believe it to be rich. Whether it is or not, we consider we have at least as good a right as the ndians."—*New York Herald*, Feb. 6, 1880.

the reservations of the wild and savage tribes, adding a few more of these posts, so as to overawe those Indians that are inclined to be troublesome. Not that the Indian cannot be civilized. With humane and just treatment he is capable not only of being won over to civilization from his wild and nomadic mode of life, but to Christianity as well, as we see is already the case with several of the tribes in the United States and Canada. (The Sioux tribe, for instance, which numbers about 40,000, have 8000 Christian members.) But, given his reservation, he should be left to live on it without being unduly interfered with, such as by compelling him to take to farming, with the object of rendering him self-supporting, for an experiment like this, if repeated, might result in another Milk Creek disaster.[4]

According to the census of 1870, there were 383,712 Indians in the United States, 96,366 of this number living on reservations and at agencies. The total number of Indians in the United States this year (according to the report of the Indian Bureau) is 256,000, all of them, with the exception of 18,000, being more or less under the control of the Government agents. There are about 7000 of their children in attendance at school.

At 8.30 a.m. we reach Elko, 274 miles from Ogden and 609 from San Francisco; altitude, 5065 feet. Elko is an "eating-station," and we turn out to have breakfast. A gong as usual proclaims loudly that the feast is quite ready, and we ash out of the train ahead of everybody past the gong-man into—not the meal-room, first of all, for we have our toilets to attend to after such a night as we have been obliged to put up with; but into a little room whither instinct leads us, where we find six leaden bowls filled with water standing in a trough containing

---

[4] Two reasons have been assigned for the Ute outbreak at Milk Creek, Colorado, on the 29th of September, 1879, which culminated in the massacre of Major Thornburgh, of the Fourth United States Infantry, and twelve of his men. One reason was the invasion of a gang of miners into the reservation and the refusal of the Government agent to grant any redress for the intrusion; the other was that the agent insisted on the Indians cultivating their land, and, upon their refusing to do so, very considerately undertaking to plough up their land for them. The latter theory has been the one generally accepted.

a sink, where there is also a piece of soap to wash with, and a long clean towel suspended on high from a wooden reel. We perform our ablutions and make ourselves clean and tidy before venturing into the meal-room. But everything had to be done in a hurry, for we had only twenty minutes allowed us before our journey would have to be resumed. So when we are "through" with our ablutions we hurriedly seek the meal-room, which the uproarious clatter of knives and forks

ELKO.

renders not very difficult to find. Politely conducted to some vacant seats by a womanish-looking Chinaman, we indulge in a repast that might be called sumptuous considering our position on the American continent, and pay a dollar for it. All the waiters here are Chinese, their pigtails coiled up round the backs of their heads, as the manner of some is. The Chinese, as waiters, are very brisk and attentive. Their style of pronouncing the English language seems at first to you rather strange, for they will add on "ee" to a number of their words, and, besides, will call you a "Melican man" before you are aware of it.

At Elko we are 280 miles within the State of Nevada. Utah Territory we quitted soon after leaving Kelton, crossing the boundary-line at 1.30 a.m. We have now 340 miles to cover before we enter California. It is needless to ascertain what we have missed seeing during the night, for we have been traversing nothing but desolate alkaline plains for the last 150 miles. We have, in truth, been crossing that dreary barren plateau known as the American Desert. It was lucky we were asleep during our journey across the desert. The white salinous dust brushed up by the train came sweeping in at the doors of the car intermittently opened during the night, and completely covered us, curled up though we were on the two seats of our section like a couple of dormice, with handkerchiefs tied round our necks and a rug thrown over us, making shift as best we could under the unpleasant circumstances in which we were unfortunately placed. Vegetation there is none in this dreary desert, except a meagre sprinkling of sage-brush. Water, too, is at a discount, for you would not find it even were you to dig for it ever so deep. The American Desert was once probably occupied by the waters of the Great Salt Lake. Early explorers have testified to the existence of immense sheets of solid salt extending over its surface, and the proximity of such a large body of salt water as the Great Salt Lake renders the theory all the more probable.

"All aboard, all aboard!" Hark! what is that? It is the warning of the conductor that we must be up and away. There goes the engine bell, too! So we leap up in the middle of our breakfast, though we have only half finished, and the first thing we do is to run straight into two "heathen Chinese," and nearly bowl them over, so great is our anxiety not to be left behind. The Celestials take it quite as a matter of course,—they are rather used, poor fellows! to being knocked and pushed about like this,—and seem not the least surprised. Perhaps they do not understand the apology we hurriedly make; but we cannot do more, for the train is already on the move. Some Shoshone squaws, or bucks,—I don't know which,—are squatting on the platform, begging; but we can only just glance at them as we rush quickly by, for as it is we have to run for it. If we miss the train now we shall have to wait till this time to-morrow for the next one.

Halting at seven unimportant stations, we come, in eighty-four miles, to Battle Mountain, a town so named from an engagement which took place some time ago on an eminence three miles distant from the railway, between the settlers and the Indians, when the latter had as many as 111 killed. The altitude of this place is 4508 feet. We arrive at 12.50 p.m., and wait half an hour. Meanwhile we have dinner, and Chinamen to serve us. Leaving Battle Mountain we continue to pass over a desolate sage-brush flat, and in seventy miles,—after letting the eastern overland train pass us on a short side track, which has been given the name of Coin,—we reach a place bearing the curious name of Winnemucca, which is the name of an old Puite warrior who is still (1880) alive, and who takes the side of the pale-faces in the present struggle. In the language of the tribe, Winnemucca means "chief"—being equivalent, I should say, to the American word "boss." There are more Indians begging on the platform, two groups of them this time, one group consisting of four men, the other one of ten squaws, the latter all squatting together in a corner by themselves,—Indian women never eat in company with the men,—eating something which appeared to us to be dried meat; whereas the four men boarded the cars the moment the train came to a standstill, and began asking us for "dimes." One word here as to the colour of the Indian. The "noble red man" is not red. He is a kind of copper colour, a sort of dusky, dirty brown, and such is his colour all over the country. Leaving Winnemucca, we proceed forty-one miles further, and at 5.25 p.m. reach Humboldt, called "an oasis in the desert," as we shall see in a moment. The distance from San Francisco is 424 miles; our height, 4234 feet. We stop half an hour and have "supper."

Humboldt is rightly called an oasis in the desert, for here we are in the middle of the Great Nevada Desert, and far away around us there extends an unbroken sea of desolate waste, backed up by cold, bleak-looking mountains; while here, round about the station hotel, is a sight which is at once refreshing to the traveller—an agreeable relief after the dull monotony of the last twenty-four hours. Here are fruit-trees in abundance, and an ornamental shrubbery. Here is grass as green as ever it was, and a garden of flowers tastefully laid out. A fountain plays in front of the hotel, close by the side of the line, and gold and silver fish swim about in the tank from which the fountain springs. Nestled in an apple-orchard at the far end of the platform is a pond, and geese are upon it. Look around and beyond this oasis and contemplate the desolation with which we are surrounded! In such a place as this, far away from everybody, thousands of miles from home, all so quiet around, you give way to reflection and your thoughts travel back to Old England, and you wonder—well, never mind now, for listen! "All aboard, all aboard!" There's that conductor at it again. Time's up, and we must be away. Immediately all is bustle and confusion, and a rush is made for the cars. We leave off looking at the pretty fish in the water-tank, and withdraw from the orchard with its pond and its geese. With a clanging of the bell, and a vigorous puffing of black smoke from the huge wine-strainer-shaped funnel of our engine, we advance further into the desert, but every mile nearer the Golden City—in eight hours we shall be in California, in twelve at San Francisco!

A ride of thirty-one miles brings us, in $2\frac{1}{2}$ hours, to White Plains, and, as its name might suggest, nothing can be seen for miles and miles around but a white, alkali waste. This station is 3894 feet above the sea-level, so that we have descended from Humboldt 340 miles, or rather 2290 feet in 322 miles from a place called Pequoq, 192 miles from Ogden, and the highest elevation on the Central Pacific Railroad east of the Sierra. But at White Plains we have reached the lowest elevation between Ogden and the Sierra, and from this station we begin again to ascend. The heat here is something fearful. Humboldt, with an elevation of 4234 feet, was one of the hottest places I ever was in.

Fifty miles further, at Wadsworth, we begin to ascend the Sierra Nevada (Snowy Range) Mountains. We also come across here for the first time a few trees growing in their natural state, the first we have seen for many a long and weary hour. It was a relief to look upon a respectable-sized plant once more. Every mile now we find the timber becoming more and more plentiful, and soon we are ascending through ravines densely clothed with magnificent forests of pine. At midnight we stop at a station which is an important one for one especial reason: it is Reno, the junction for one of the most celebrated mining regions in the world. A railway connects it with Virginia City, twenty-one miles distant,—though fifty-two miles by rail,—and at Virginia City are the wonderful silver-mines of the Comstock lode. Here are the famous Ophir, Gould and Curry, Savage, Hale and Norcross, Crown Point, Belcher (this the deepest mine in the United States, reaching a perpendicular depth of 3000 feet), Kentuck, Yellow Jacket, and Chollar Potosi mines. Virginia City, with a population of 20,000, and another mining town called Gold Hill, are both of them built on the top of the Comstock lode. This immense vein was discovered in the year 1859,—eleven years after the discovery of gold in California,—gold having been found two years previously in the neighbourhood of Gold Hill; hence the name given to that locality. The yield from this wonderful lode since 1859 is unprecedented in the history of all mining achievements. Whether or not it will continue to produce its prodigious amount of bullion every year is a question which the Fates must be left alone to determine. But it seems, from recent official returns, to have begun to swallow more money than it yields, for in 1878 the yield amounted to $21,295,043, whereas in 1879 it was only $8,830,562, a decrease of $12,464,481. The working expenses for 1879 came to $11,404,400, so that a deficit was incurred for that year of $2,573,838, or say 514,767*l.* sterling.[5]

Reno is 4507 feet above the sea, and distant 294 miles from San Francisco. Leaving Reno, we proceed along the bank of the Truckee River, and in the next nine miles rise 422 feet. We have determined to have no sleep to-night, but by the light of a full moon and of myriads of bright stars

---

[5] The gross yield of precious metals in Nevada during the years 1878 and 1879 respectively, was $47,676,863 and $21,997,714; in California, $20,134,068 and $18,190,973; and in Colorado, $9,820,774 and $19,110,882.

overhead, watch our progress as we wind up the beautiful cañons of the Sierra. Up we go, puffing and blowing away in fine style. We have two engines now, and their puffs are so strong and loud, so slow and yet so irregular, that there is no need to turn to "official guide-books" to tell us that we are ascending the Sierra in right earnest. We have yet to mount 2510 feet from Reno, and in forty-nine miles.

In eleven miles, between Reno and Verdi, we ascend 420 feet, and again, in the succeeding fifteen miles, between Verdi and Boca, we ascend 606 feet. Before reaching Boca we pass out of Nevada into California.

Still ascending through wild, precipitous ravines, the air becoming colder every mile as we rise, from Boca we come to Truckee, mounting 313 feet in nine miles. A grand view is obtained from this station—a panorama never to be forgotten. Snow-clad peaks rise from two to three thousand feet above us, springing from lovely forests of pine. As we stand on the steps of the hindmost car and look back upon the panorama we are leaving behind, the sun, which has just risen,—it is now four o'clock in the morning,—catches the tops of these peaks and gilds them with a soft pink glow, adding an inexpressible charm to the sublimity of the scene.

But our enjoyment is of brief duration. Our contemplation of the wonders of Nature is very suddenly cut short. Before we have advanced seven miles beyond Truckee we rush straight into a twenty-eight mile snow-shed! And a series of similar galleries, the breaks between each so brief as to be hardly noticeable, are built along this portion of the route for more than forty miles. These massive timber galleries are constructed along the flanks of the mountains, the uprights being huge solid pine-trunks of from sixteen to twenty inches in diameter. It is not in summer that the use of these sheds is required; but in winter, when snow-storms are often encountered, and when avalanches come crushing down from the heights overhead. It is said that in winter the snow lies on these galleries to a depth of twenty feet. So for many miles we have to put up with short, twinkling snatches of the lovely scenery for which this part of the route is famous, as we flit past the narrow openings in the wood-work of our shed, and the overwhelming smoke contributed by the combined efforts of our two engines certainly does not render the views in the distance any the more distinctive or attractive. However, there is no help for it, so we have to wait till the sheds are passed.

Fourteen miles beyond Truckee we reach the station of Summit (in a snow-shed), the highest elevation on the Central division of the Pacific Railroad, 7017 feet above the sea, or 1225 feet less than the elevation we attained at Sherman on the Rocky Mountains. We are now 245 miles from San Francisco. Snow lies all around us, and it is piercingly cold. Here the writer in a certain illustrated overland guide-book, which has for its frontispiece a picture of "Utah's best crop," is unable any longer to restrain his enthusiasm now that he has at last brought his readers to this "Summit of the Sierras." He looks around (from a snow-shed, remember) and contemplates the age of the "scattering groups of hardy fir and spruce" that grow in the vicinity of Summit station, and tells us that "they have lain, evidently, since Adam was a very small boy, or the tree sprouted from which our apple-loving ancestor, Eve, plucked that bedeviled fruit!"

From Summit the descent is rapid, for in the next thirty-eight miles we run down 3714 feet. We then reach Dutch Flat; height, 3303 feet; distance from San Francisco, 207 miles; time, 6.17 a.m. Dutch Flat is a famous "placer" mining district, where "hydraulicking" by means of water conveyed from long distances in "flumes" is carried on to a considerable extent. The country about here looks as if it had been suffering from convulsion,—as if an earthquake had been felt in the locality,—for miles of forest have been swept away, the ground has been bared, upturned, rent, and torn; everything lies in a state of confusion as if, I repeat, some great convulsion of Nature had suddenly overtaken the neighbourhood. But the fact is, Nature has had to give way before the violent efforts of man, in his eager desire to gain possession of the coveted treasure that lies hidden beneath the soil. And in like manner is the country denuded around every little mining settlement in this lively region. Gold Run, another mining town, is next passed; and some distance away on our right can be seen the villages of You Bet, Red

Dog, etc. You Bet, by-the-way, takes its name from an Americanism equivalent to our forcible expression "Rather!" or, "I should think so!" If you ask a man out West whether he likes whisky, he will immediately exclaim "You bet!"—in a manner there is no mistaking. This and Red Dog are nothing to some of the choice and elegant names that are given to mining localities in this part of the world. Chucklehead Diggings, Gospel Gulch, Ground Hog's Glory, Gridiron Bar, Greaser's Camp, Chicken Thief Flat, Shirt-Tail Cañon, Petticoat Slide, and Blue Belly Ravine, are among the most select that might be quoted. "When Americans strike new mines," says the *New York Herald*, "they do not sit up all night to find a fancy name for the new town. They take the first homely one that is thought of."

Gold-mining in the Western States is classed under two heads, placer and quartz. In placer mining the ore is found in alluvial deposits of gravel, sand, or clay, where it can sometimes be obtained by means of the simplest appliances; in quartz mining, however, the ore runs in lodes or veins of solid rock, when operations have to be carried on of considerable magnitude, and entailing great expense, such as sinking a shaft perhaps many hundred feet in depth, blasting the ore, extracting it and reducing the quartz to powder, etc. Placer mining prevails in California more extensively than quartz mining, whereas in Colorado the latter is by far the more important interest of the two. In the former process the "prospector" goes to work with merely his pickaxe, shovel, and pan, and so long as he is provided with plenty of water to wash away the earthy matter or "pay-dirt" in which the ore is imbedded,—which he does in his pan (made of sheet-iron or tin) by dissolving all the grit or gravel till the particles of gold are distinguished,—he has, it may be, everything requisite for his requirements. But sometimes, indeed in most cases, the precious metal has to be reached through immense masses of hard gravel, which would cause the prospector an endless amount of labour to remove did he not have resort to a more efficacious remedy than the mere pickaxe and shovel; and so he brings hydraulic pressure into play to tear down the rocky obstruction, which method of reaching the ore now forms part and parcel of the process of placer mining. The water for this purpose has often to be brought immense distances, fifteen or twenty miles in some cases, and this has caused the construction of "flumes," or wooden canals which are built over the country on trestle-work, at a considerable height above the ground,—sufficiently high so as not to be snowed up in winter,—with a grade of about thirteen feet to the mile; but iron pipes have to be used in the case of a deep depression to be crossed, such as a gap or ravine. The flume is carried to the top of the hill so that it just overlooks the "claim" or spot where the ore has been found, at a height of from fifty to perhaps 400 or 500 feet, and from this height is thrown a strong iron pipe down which the water pours with tremendous power, and is discharged against the gravel bank from a patent nozzle through an orifice from five to eight inches in diameter, whence it issues almost as a solid mass with, it is said, a force sometimes of 1300 lbs. to the inch. By this means enormous excavations are made, and the "fields" have become studded with blocks, mounds and pinnacles left standing, thus presenting that torn and ragged appearance which the traveller notices when approaching these mining settlements of the Sierra Nevada.

Between Gold Run and the next station, Colfax, is the sight *par excellence* on the whole Pacific Railroad. It is the view from Cape Horn over the American River Cañon. The construction of the railway at this point constitutes one of the greatest engineering achievements in the country. In rounding a precipitous bluff, the line is laid on the very edge of the cliff, and as you stand on the bottom step of the car and look over, you can see straight down into the gorge lying 2000 feet below. The line seems literally to cling to the mountain side. So inaccessible was the ledge over which it was intended to throw the railway, that the workmen had to be lowered down by ropes from the top of the cliff, at a great height above, in order that they might gain a foothold upon it. But glorious is the view that bursts upon us as we are rounding Cape Horn. Words are useless to convey an impression of it. Down into a deep gorge we look, down, far down beneath us. A silvery torrent is foaming at the bottom—it is the American River, and we pass along the brink of the precipice overlooking it. Forest ranges rise one above the other for miles

Westward to San Francisco. 255

and miles away, far away into California. Gorge after gorge can be traced winding their courses in the direction of the Pacific. This is but the bare outline of a sight that is indescribable.

After rounding the Cape we cross a lovely ravine, called Rice's, by a trestle-work bridge 113 feet high and 878 feet long. Then we reach Colfax, where we stay twenty-five

THE AMERICAN RIVER CAÑON,
View from Cape Horn.

minutes for breakfast. Several Chinamen, workmen on the line, are visible now, and the notices here and at the succeeding stations are posted up in two languages, English and Chinese. Leaving Colfax, we continue to descend rapidly, and in twenty-three miles, on reaching Newcastle, find we have descended from Summit 6047 feet in seventy-four miles. As we run down into California the scene completely changes. We leave the mountains behind us, and in their place we have rich cornfields, vineyards, orchards, orange-groves, fig-groves, and hay-fields—in a land that knows not rain from March to November. We are now travelling fast through the Golden State.

At eleven o'clock we reach Sacramento. It is the political capital of California, and has a population of about 23,000. San Francisco can be reached from this city either by rail, or by boat down the Sacramento River. The train waits twenty minutes, and I employ this interval in patronizing the *buffet*, and being helped to all manner of good things by a "heathen Chinee." I happen to be wearing knickerbockers, and as they disclose a fine view of my calves, I soon discover that I am the object of considerable attention. A crowd assembles around me, and gazes in wonder at the remarkable costume of the "Britisher." Perhaps my admirers had caught sight of some remarks about English tourists that appeared in this morning's *San Francisco Chronicle*, which are, I think, worth quoting. They are contributed by a "special," and run as follows:

"English tourists are easily known all the world over, rather, I think, from a capricious and various fancy in the article of travelling-hat than for any more marked peculiarity. A large number of them came over in the last Australian steamer, and every individual one has an individual style of head-gear. Some wear the shelterless Glengarry bonnet; some a little round flexible cap; and many of them various modifications of the Derby, with long, light veils draped thereon with studied carelessness. San Francisco is the first American city upon which many of them set foot, and they are continually amazed at the size, the bustle, and the civilization of a city so far upon the outposts of the known world. . . . . The passer-by has the full benefit of an Englishman's curbstone discourse. His lungs are always sound, his views are positive, and his self-possession is impregnable. He has a faint idea that the American language is as foreign as Greek or Italian, and the accompanying impression that all foreigners are slightly deaf. He gives his order at the *table d'hôte* in a voice distinctly audible to everyone in the room. He looks at the women as if they were a portion of Mme. Tussaud's exhibition. He is more careful of the *convenances* than when at home. But he is withal an exceedingly intelligent observer, and if he remains with us any length of time, carries away with him a very fair general impression."

Sacramento possesses amongst its public buildings one of the finest in the Western States. This is the Capitol, where the State Legislature assembles. Its lofty metallic dome—surmounted by twelve Corinthian pillars supporting a lesser dome, which is crowned with a bronze statue of California—is a conspicuous object for several miles around. The city is laid out regularly in the usual right-angle American fashion. Those streets running north and south are numbered one, two, three, etc.; those running east and west, A, B, C, etc. A very simple arrangement.

Only 140 miles now before we reach the shores of the Pacific! We take on two cars, and quit the Sacramento station with quite a trainful of passengers. As we thread our way through this the second city (though the capital) of California, we take note of the elegant villa residences of its citizens, covered as they are with vines, and standing in beautiful gardens bedecked with semi-tropical plants, approached by smooth grassy lawns that look indeed as if they were verily made for lawn-tennis and croquet.

After leaving Sacramento, we run almost due south for forty-eight miles to Stockton. Orange-trees grow by the side of the line, and fig-trees take the form of little horse-chestnuts. Apple-orchards are abundant, and the country seems to be fairly populated. The air is deliciously fragrant. No imaginary odour is it that we are sensitive to, such as is only too apt to be conceived and made the most of by two weary travellers like ourselves upon their first arrival in this " Land of Setting Suns," as California has been peculiarly and distinctively named. But it is an air rendered fragrant by the presence of flowers, by the scent from the hayfields as we pass through the midst of them, by the breeze from the ocean that is wafted up the valley. The sky above is a deep cloudless blue, the day is as fine as it can be. Our entry into the Golden Land could not be made under more favourable auspices.

S

Stockton we shall see more of when we return to it from San Francisco, as it is the point of departure for the groves of "Big" Trees and the Yosemite Valley; so we will now pass it by. We come to Lathrop, next station to Stockton, and then turning nearly due west run so for sixty-two miles, across immense cornfields, as far as Niles, where we are thirty miles from San Francisco. Then we turn north-west and continue in this direction till reaching Oakland, which lies on the Bay of San Francisco. Oakland has a population of 48,000, and occupies the same position to San Francisco that Brooklyn or Jersey City does to New York. The Golden City is not reached by train (except from San José by the Southern Pacific Railroad), but, lying on a peninsula five miles across the bay, is approached from Oakland by means of a ferry, which conveys passengers and baggage, all except the train itself, over to the metropolis of the Pacific coast.[6]

So, skirting Oakland, we make for the wharf, which lies at the end of a two-mile pier running out into the bay; and on reaching the wharf, the termination of the Pacific Railroad, we transfer ourselves and belongings as quickly as we can on board the ferry, amid the bustle and commotion of as cosmopolitan a crowd of people as is to be found in the Western Hemisphere. Mounting to the upper deck of our ferry-boat,—it is a wooden two-decker we are in, painted white and called the "Oakland,"—we find ourselves in a large saloon decorated with paintings of the principal sights of this part of California, and a rich Turkey

[6] A monster ferry-boat has now been built to convey the trains of the Central Pacific Railroad across the bay to San Francisco. She is called the "Solano," and her length is 424 feet, and her width 116 feet. *Harper's Weekly Journal*, of August 2, 1879, describing the boat, says : " She will have two vertical-beam engines and eight steel boilers (weighing twenty-one tons each), and four rudders at each end worked by hydraulic steering apparatus, operated by an independent steam-pump. The engines work independently, each moving one wheel. The boilers are placed upon the deck, to prevent escaping steam from rotting the wood. The hold is divided into eleven water-tight compartments, which render the boat less liable to sink, and also strengthen her. Four tracks will be placed upon her decks, which will accommodate forty-eight freight cars, or twenty-four passenger coaches. Her slips will be provided with aprons 100 feet in length, which will admit of cars being taken aboard without uncoupling from the engine."

carpet and cushioned sofas and ottomans take the place of the usual hard boards and benches. Below, on the lower deck, is the passengers' luggage, and vehicles of various descriptions— carriages-and-pairs, market-carts, many horses, and two mules and a donkey. All is commotion above and below till we have weighed anchor, and then everyone begins to settle down and many ladies and gentlemen in the upper saloon to compose themselves and diligently study apricots, peaches and daily papers sold by three little boys. But who are

LEAVING THE OAKLAND WHARF.
San Francisco in the distance.

those men searching about and asking questions among the passengers, wearing gold-banded caps and having an air of importance about them as if they were officers on board one of the Cunard steamships? They are hackmen and hotel-runners touting for patrons, each for his respective master's hotel. " Palace Hotel, yer 'onor?" said a fat, joyous-looking individual to me as I sat contemplating a Californian beauty on the other side of the saloon. I answered him in the affirmative. (There was no mistaking the man's nationality.)

"Then give me your bhaggage checks, and, bedad, we shall be rhight glad to see ye," he said, putting his hand on my shoulder and gazing on me fondly, as a father does his son. "But first tell me where I can find a bird-stuffer to whom I can take all these birds to be skinned," I replied, showing him the contents of a satchel I wore—they were some birds I had shot at Salt Lake, which I had not yet had time to skin. They had already begun to give undoubted proofs of their antiquity. "Shure, then, and you'll get the birrds claned rhight undernath the hotel," was the hotel-runner's answer. I thanked him and withdrew, but little thought he was deceiving me, for I afterwards found that there was no taxidermist of any description under the hotel. I had to go running about over the city for an hour before dinner before I found what I wanted.

We are now in full view of San Francisco, which is spread out before us over its several hills. We are a little reminded of Leith and Edinburgh, as seen when approached from the sea. Here, however, the shipping is few and far between, and the houses which are seen are nearly all wooden, and there is no vegetation of any kind visible, and the sand-hills over which the Golden City is spread are the colour of brown paper; so that a good deal has to be left to the imagination to fill in the picture. Soon we are alongside the landing-place and are bundling ourselves out of the ferry. What a motley crowd below! Palefaces, negroes, Chinese; white, black, and yellow. Through this bustling throng we force our way under care of "ould Ireland," and are soon in a 'bus rattling away to our home for the next week, the "Palace Hotel of the world."

Palace Hotel.   SAN FRANCISCO.   Jewish Synagogue.

CHAPTER XIII.

THE GOLDEN CITY.

The Golden City—Its rapid growth—General plan of the city—Its principal thoroughfare—Monster hotels—Curious street conveyances—The balloon car—The dummy cable car—Boot-blacking—Champion boot-blacks—A champion boot-black's challenge—A rush for wealth—Hoodlums—Their vocation and operations—The hoodlum alphabet—Instance of rough handling — A Californian fruit market — A treacherous climate—Wet days and cold days—The great hotel of America—Its form and general appearance—Its Grand Central Court—"Barbarism" with a vengeance—Our suites of apartments—To the Cliff House—Irrigation in California—The windmill system of irrigation—Oakland—Marvellous rapidity of growth—University of California—An anomaly in railway travelling—The white-paint nuisance again.

THE commercial metropolis of California and the Pacific coast lies at the northern end of a narrow peninsula extending north between the Pacific Ocean on the west and the Bay of San Francisco on the east. This peninsula is bounded on the north by a strait called the Golden Gate, which is a mile wide, and five miles in length, and which separates it from another peninsula running south towards it from the northern mainland, thus forming the outlet from the bay to the ocean. San Francisco faces its bay, and not the Pacific, from which, indeed, the city is distant some six or seven miles. The road to the sea is one of the dustiest roads in the United States, as the traveller will find should he happen to make the trip any time between March and November. The Bay of San Francisco is very capacious, so much so that there is a popular saying that it is capable of finding accommodation for all the navies of the world. It is also very beautiful. San Francisco lies in lat. 37° 46′ N., long. 120° 23′ W.,—in about the same latitude as Palermo and Athens,—and is the chief city of a State whose area is 100,200 square miles more than that of Great Britain. The area of California is 188,981 square miles. It is 1800 miles long and 190 miles broad, and it has a coast-line of 1097 miles.

The history of San Francisco dates from the year 1776. when two Spanish monks—Benito Cambon and Francisco Paulo—of the order of St. Francis, established in the locality the Mission Dolores. The settlement thus founded was called Yerba Buena ("good herb"), and it remained under that name till 1847, when it was changed to San Francisco. In 1847 we find the place consisting of a collection of a few wooden shanties, with a population of 450. But in the following year the gold fever broke out—then was made the lucky discovery of the golden ore in the bed of the stream flowing from General Sutter's mill near Sacramento,[1] and the city sprang into existence in place of the wooden shanties which had formed the earlier settlement. The rapidity of the growth of San Francisco from this date affords one more instance of those extraordinary building exploits which will probably astonish a visitor from the Old World, whose towns have become developed by slower degrees; and the rapid development of the great Western city will seem all the more remarkable when it is remembered that on six different occasions since 1848 has it narrowly escaped being completely destroyed by fire. In the year 1847, as we have just seen, its population numbered 450 souls; whereas now (according to the estimated census returns of 1880) it numbers 233,956. Included in this are 20,549 Chinese.

The city is built mainly upon three hills of an average elevation of 350 feet, and is spread over an area of forty-two square miles. There is a certain wearisome regularity in the arrangement of the streets, such as is to be noticed in many other cities and towns in the United States, the thoroughfares being laid out at right angles to each other, and con-

---

[1] Gold was discovered in California on January 19, 1848, at Coloma, forty-five miles north-east of Sacramento, by a workman—one James W. Marshall—employed in building a saw-mill to be driven by water the gold being found in the race or ditch beneath.

sisting of set blocks, so many houses to each block. In San Francisco, however, this does not strike one so forcibly as in New York, Chicago, Salt Lake City, St. Louis, New Orleans, etc., for here the Market-street, which is the principal thoroughfare, runs athwart the city for nearly the whole of its length, from north-east to south-west; and on one side of this thoroughfare the streets branch from it obliquely, and this half contains small blocks, whilst from the other side they branch at right angles, and this part is laid out in large blocks. This well and handsomely built (but villainously paved) Market-street, containing as it does such palatial edifices as the Palace, Baldwin, and Grand Hotels, is laid with four lines of tramway; and no livelier street scene could well be imagined than the sight of such a number of cars visible at a time,—once I counted as many as thirty-eight,— of so great a variety of private carriages and 'buses, and so many bustling crowds of people, as are to be found all day long in front of, for instance, the Palace Hotel. Public conveyances in the form of cabs there seem to be none, as the roads are too unevenly paved—or "cobbled"—to admit of travelling with comfort in this sort of fashion. Railways, therefore, are laid along the principal streets, and transfer tickets take you from one line of cars to another. Go about the city where you will, the fare, I believe, does not exceed five cents.

Besides the Roman Catholic Cathedral (St. Patrick's) in Mission-street, and the Jewish Synagogue in Sutter-street, and ninety other churches of various denominations, there is a Greek Church, and a Chinese Roman Catholic Church with a school attached. The Episcopalians, Methodists, Baptists and Presbyterians have each established mission-houses among the Chinese in San Francisco, to which schools are attached. The services in each case are conducted in the Chinese language. The Jewish Synagogue, standing as it does on rising ground, is the first building one notices when approaching the Golden City from Oakland. Amongst the public buildings may be mentioned the United States Mint, the Bank of California, the Merchants' Exchange, and the Post Office and Custom House combined. But San Francisco is very badly off for public buildings, those I have mentioned being about

the only ones of any importance, although when the new
City Hall is completed—for there is here, as usual, some
great building in course of erection which has already
taken several years to set up, and which will be completed at some indefinite period in the future—the people
of the Golden City will have a public building which
they may justly feel proud of. Undoubtedly the most imposing structure in San Francisco is the Palace Hotel,
which may be considered one of the sights of America.
Other hotels there are, however, which are wonders in
their way, some for size, others for the luxurious and
costly style in which they are fitted. Indeed the hotel
system of San Francisco is unrivalled. One is simply
astounded at the sight of such extravagance as has been
lavished upon the fittings and decorations of Baldwin's Hotel,
for instance, which cost Mr. Baldwin three million five hundred
thousand dollars, or 700,000*l.*, and is located on the top of
quite a little town of shops. A noteworthy feature in the
form of architecture of a number of the buildings is the
prominence given to bay windows. Hotels, private residences
and shops are most of them built in this style. Many of the
houses are built of wood,[2] so that one is led to think that
should a conflagration arise there would be no putting an end
to it, despite the united energies of the Corporation's Fire
Brigade and the Underwriters' Fire Patrol of the insurance
companies. But the wood now used for building purposes
is that of the *Sequoia sempervirens*, or redwood, which burns
so slowly that there would not be time—so people say—for
the flames to make any considerable headway before they
could be got under. The "sidewalks" or pavements are also
of wood, and herein lies a nuisance, for the nails project in so
many places that one has to be always on the look-out lest
he should trip and tumble. I once did do this, when I was
walking along down Market-street (reading a letter). My
foot suddenly struck against a projecting spike, and down I
came on "all fours" before I could tell what had become
of me.

There are some remarkable street conveyances in San

[2] A Californian writes, "Nine-tenths of the houses in the State are
built of wood; the others are built of adobe."

Francisco. Besides the ordinary "bobtail" tramway car, or one without a conductor, which is common enough in every American city, there is the "balloon car" and the dummy cable car, the two last unique in their construction and peculiar to the Golden City. The balloon car is a curious-looking device, reminding one more of a spread-out umbrella than a balloon, though either name would do for it. Very like a circular box placed upon wheels, it has a large projecting roof quite out of proportion with the rest of the design, and this has caused it to look like an umbrella—a great spread-out family

THE BALLOON CAR.

umbrella, and one cannot avoid making the comparison. The top part is moveable, and able to be pulled round by the horses or mules at the end of a journey, thereby saving the inconvenience of having the animals taken out and hitched on at the other end; the driver, too, keeps his seat and is pulled round with the rest of the vehicle. But the "dummy car" is stranger still. Not drawn by horses or mules, nor propelled by any visible machinery, it is worked by an endless-wire underground cable of an inch and a quarter in diameter, by an engine of 500 horse-power,—there being an engine to every street provided with this sort of locomotion,—and the force of its speed is controlled by a system of cog-wheel machinery. This latter method of locomotion is used only up and down the hills, which are very steep—too steep to allow of any other sort of rapid conveyance, unless a regular train with steam-engine were introduced, as is the case on Mount Washington in New Hampshire, and on the Rigi near Lucerne;

VIEW IN CLAY-STREET,
Showing the dummy cable car.

or unless a locomotive were employed like that used with the train which now makes the ascent of Vesuvius. Each dummy-car arrangement consists of, in fact, two cars, the front car being an open one, unprotected at the sides, so that one can jump up on to it while it is in motion, and from whichever side one pleases. This front car might not unreasonably be termed the engine, for though there is no appearance of an "engine" at all, nor of anything approaching a compound machine of this description, yet the driver stands in the middle of it and controls the progress of his car, and the one behind it, by means of a "gripping clamp" or large lever, which grapples the cable underground, the cable lying beneath a slit in the track between the two lines of rail. At the top of every hill the cable passes over a wheel or set of wheels, and at the bottom of the hill a pulley, and it is kept taut and prevented from slipping by the heavy strain of the several cars passing along upon it overhead. The hinder of the two cars is a covered one, and intended for those who object to smoking, or who find the rays of the sun too powerful for them. As the open car—that is the smoking car in front—has always to be the foremost of the two, a difficulty might seem to occur at the end of a journey as to how it could be brought back again into its position as the foremost car, so as to lead on the return journey; but by an ingenious method of double shunting lines, the positions of the two cars are quickly reversed. The pace whether up or down hill is uniform throughout. You step up on to one of the front or side seats, and you have barely had time to sit down before you find yourself moving over the ground at full speed. And the pace is not gradually attained, as with a railway train; but you pop off all at once as if you were a wound-up bit of machinery, and had been suddenly let loose. Your feet are only twelve inches above the ground, and you experience a delightful and comfortable sensation as if you were sailing over water. The idea is an ingenious one. It is a contrivance for quickly and comfortably mounting the steep hills, having been invented by a German resident in the Golden City. The Chinese describe this kind of locomotion in language as graphic as it is terse. "No pullee," says John, "No pushee. Melican-man go like hellee!"

Of course a ride in the cable car is "the thing" to do during a stay in San Francisco. Besides the novelty of such a ride, it is advantageous for the reason that as the several lines are laid up and down the hills for the distance of some miles, splendid views can be obtained over the city and bay; and many of the costly private residences of California's millionaires, and her lesser monetary magnates, are passed, and are able to be seen with comfort. A movement is on foot to introduce steam cars on the tramways, so that there will be a great variety of conveyances in San Francisco what with bobtail cars, umbrella cars, steam tramway cars, and dummy cable tramway cars.

A noteworthy feature in the streets of San Francisco is the sanctum of the boot-black. This is a little room leading out from the street, devoted to the cleaning and the polishing, into which you enter to have a "shine." You find four, sometimes six little chairs placed in a row on a daïs, with two steps to mount up to them: you seat yourself in one, and the boot-black will hand you the day's newspaper to look over, and then set to work and give your boots the necessary "tone." There is sometimes considerable difficulty experienced in getting one's boots blacked in the United States. In some of the hotels it is impossible, so that you have to wait till you can find a boy in the street to do them for you, whose method of polishing them will be simple enough, but not the most agreeable—should you watch him. I remember one morning when I came to open my door to look for my boots,—when staying at an hotel not 150 miles from New York,—that I found them lying outside my room on the corridor in the same uncleaned state in which they were left the previous evening. Hearing a domestic sweeping up on the stairs opposite, I hailed her, and inquired how I could get my boots cleaned? She replied curtly, resting her arm on her broom and looking up at me; whereupon I thanked her, and withdrew. Seeing no other alternative, I took the boots downstairs, but found, when I reached the bottom, that there was no such institution as a boot-black belonging to the establishment; so I was obliged to call in the services of a boy from the street, who by spitting on them and rubbing them made them "shine" in ten minutes—for the sum of five cents. I have frequently seen notices fixed in the bedrooms of the hotels to the effect that "The Prop'r of this hotel will not be responsible for the safety of gentlemen's boots which are left outside their bedrooms at night."—But to return to boot-blacking as it is carried on in the Golden City. This is a "luxury" most assiduously indulged in by those who can find nothing better to do, and as there is a mania among the better classes for having their boots resembling looking-glasses at all hours of the day, the street boot-blacks have established their little private apartments, so that they may entertain their well-to-do patrons in a fit and becoming manner. Some of these blacking rooms are elaborately fitted up. Pictures hang against the walls, and the chairs that are provided for sitting upon are comfortably cushioned. There is a champion boot-black to every principal street in San Francisco. The champion of Market-street, for instance, resides at No. 828, near Baldwin's Hotel, and he has affixed the following notice at the entrance of his sanctum :

> Boots blacked, quick ! quick !
> I am champion of this street.
> Make good shine,
> Cost half a dime.

But the chief boot-black of all, the one who has reached the highest pinnacle of fame in his profession, has his location in Bush-street. An Englishman, and twenty-two years ago (in 1858) a member of the London "City Reds," or the Ragged School Boot-black Society (of Saffron-hill, Farringdon-road, E.C.), he has become such an adept in the business that he has thought fit to throw down the gauntlet to all the boot-blacks in the United States, and to challenge them to a "trial of skill," as will be seen by the following notice which I took down one morning while the champion himself was engaged in polishing my boots :

> BOOT BLACKING
> CHALLENGE !
> The undersigned, claiming to be the
> CHAMPION BOOT BLACK OF THE UNITED STATES,
> and hearing his right to the Title disputed, for the purpose of friendly disposing of all controversy upon the subject, hereby challenges any man in the United States to a trial of skill, the result to be decided by a mutually appointed Committee.
> I propose to Black from 5 to 10 Pairs of Boots
> for from
> FIVE HUNDRED TO ONE THOUSAND DOLLARS
> a side, United States gold coin,
> the test to be the time employed and the quantity of polish.

Should any man outside of California accept the above challenge, I will pay his reasonable expenses to and from California. The above challenge to remain open for ninety days from date.

The Profession are respectfully invited to " Put up or Shut up."

Address . . . . . . Cornelius Lyons,
Champion Boot Black of the United States,
Bush-street, between
Sacramento and Cosmopolitan Hotels,
San Francisco, California.
February 1st, 1871.

At the junction of California and Montgomery streets is the medley of all things. Here men and women meet to bargain and barter for everything on the face of this earth—and off it, perhaps. Everyone speculates in San Francisco. It is a mania pervading all classes of society, nor indeed does sex, nor age, nor any degree of wealth make any difference to the votaries of Mammon. The poor Irish servant girl blindly indulges in some likely investment together with her rich master and mistress; boys and girls still in their teens resort to the stockbroker to put their savings into some mine that seems likely to "pay." A fortune is made in a day, a fortune is lost just as quickly. All is money, money, money. No serious thought of religion or of anything save what is purely temporal and transitory. This is one of the characteristic features of life in the Golden City.

Now the Golden City enjoys a monopoly among the votaries of crime which is not shared by any other city in America. I allude to a species of the rough or rowdy type, called a "hoodlum." The hoodlums of San Francisco are young embryo criminals—regularly organized gangs of boys and girls, whose ages vary from fifteen to twenty or twenty-five, their business being to waylay unoffending citizens during the hours of the night, and get as much as they can out of them, and, when found necessary, speedily despatch them to happy hunting-grounds by means of knives or revolvers, with which they are well provided. The freaks of these young rascals are multifarious; but a common one is to enter a grocer's store, or a beer saloon, and compel the proprietor to hand over what is wanted by threatening him with a sound thrashing, or by the sudden presentment in his face of an irrepressible six-shooter. "Hands up!" shouts the hoodlum; and if Mr. Grocer does not immediately throw up his hands, he is popped off *instanter*. Another employment of the young vagabonds is to follow people and annoy them by telling them lewd stories, for which they ought to be caught and well flogged. Unless a change is made for the better in the police organization of the Golden City, the hoodlums are likely to have a very merry time of it, for there are not more than 400 police officers,—prior to February 24, 1880, there were less than this number, for on that day the Board of Supervisors passed an ordinance increasing the police force to 400 men,—and what with the constant attention which has to be bestowed in looking after other classes of rogues with which the city abounds,—for crime in San Francisco takes a variety of forms, and has many votaries, as in other large cities,—this comparatively small body of men has been found to be quite inadequate to cope with the audacious freaks of these juvenile offenders, whose brutal operations against the poor hated Chinese are about as cowardly as they are entirely unprovoked and uncalled for, notwithstanding the ill-feeling engendered by the outcry against Chinese cheap labour. There are twenty or more gangs of these hoodlums, comprising altogether some 500 or 550 members, who, before sallying forth on their nocturnal expeditions, will mask their faces and then exchange and dress up in each other's clothes, and, above all, take care that no one among them, be it boy or girl, ventures forth without being provided with such a six-shooter as is becoming to the sex of the wearer. These gangs are named according to the several districts of the city wherein they carry on their operations, each after its respective district. Thus there is the Bernal Heights gang, commanded by a youth who answers to the *soubriquet* of "Mountain Jack;" also the Fifteenth-street, a gang having for its leader one Dave Condon, a young man who has been tried for various felonies, including one for murder, but who nevertheless is allowed to actively head his gang and at the same time live quietly at home with his parents in West Mission-street! Dave Condon is an adept in the art of boxing. He is the "boss" pugilist of San Francisco. Two more of the gangs I will mention. They are the Hayes Valley and the Beach Combers. The former chiefly confines its raids to grocers' stores.

Now in order that they may evade the police or make themselves scarce at any critical juncture, the hoodlums have invented an alphabet, from which they acquire their passwords and slang phrases, etc., and this alphabet is as follows:

A . . . A	G . . Gug	M . . Mum	S . . Sus
B . . Bub	H . . Hash	N . . Nun	T . . Tut
C . . Cus	I . . . I	O . . . O	U . . . U
D . . Dud	J . . Jug	P . . Pup	V . . Vuv
E . . . E	K . . Kuk	Q . . . Q	W . . W
F . . Fuf	L . . Lul	R . . Rer	X . . . X
	Y . . Yoke	Z . . Zud	

It will be seen from the above that all the letters, with the exception of the vowels, and Q, W, and X, have their distinctive hoodlum pronunciation. Thus can a strange and remarkable language, indeed, be produced by the very simple method of stringing together into sentences the pronunciation of the letters required, as will be seen by the following examples which may be given by way of illustration.— Thus, "Mind your eye, Tommy," becomes *Muminundud yokeourer eyoke, Tutomummumyoke;* "Look out for yourself," *Lulookuk outut fuforer yokeourersuselulfuf;* "Give him the slip, Charley," *Gugivuve hashimum tuthash suslulipup, Cushasharerluleyoke;* and "Here comes Bobby round the corner," *Hasherere cusomumesus Bubobubbubyoke rerounundud tuthashe cusorernunerer.*

But it must not be thought that such mouthy, protracted sentences as these are used by the hoodlums when they find themselves in a fix, and obliged to "cut and run" for it, for if that were so, "Robert" would be upon them long before the note of alarm could be successfully communicated. One password is quite sufficient, and would be given in accordance with the sort of danger apprehended.

I myself came across a good illustration of the rough handling a poor fellow is subjected to who happens to be attacked by these audacious young scamps. One day, when near the Lone Mountain Cemetery, I happened to step into a lager-beer saloon to ask for a glass of that beverage before entering the beautiful burial-ground. The keeper of the saloon was standing behind his counter. His head was bandaged up, his arm was in a sling, and he looked altogether as if he had just fallen into bad hands. I asked him what was the matter? He told me that the evening before, about eight o'clock, two young boys, aged apparently twelve or fourteen, entered his saloon and asked for some whisky. They then enticed him outside his door, when the moment he had stepped beyond the threshold he was set upon by five or six more juveniles, one of whom was a girl, and before he had time to get out his six-shooter he was felled to the ground with a sharp crack on the head, after which he was kicked and beaten about the head and body till he was well nigh dead. His revolver was taken from him, for this was what they really wanted after all. I asked him if he expected to catch the young rascals and bring them to justice? But he laughed at the idea, and said it "couldn't be done."

One of the great sights of the Golden City is its fruit-market, and this is a sight indeed! Here are gathered together the fruits of all America. Not collected, indeed, and brought to this market from various parts of the country; but all grown within the State, for sub-tropical fruits and those of the north temperate zone here grow side by side—the climate is suitable for both. Amongst an immense variety will be noticed figs, plums, pears, apples, olives, medlars, pineapples, strawberries, peaches, apricots, nectarines, native lemon-coloured oranges, the ubiquitous banana and water-melon, all of which lie about the market in the greatest profusion. The peaches are the first that rivet the attention. Each is as large as one's two fists put together. Grapes lie about here in the season in veritable heaps, and no wonder, for enough can be found in this vine-growing State to be cast away as waste to the dogs and the pigs. There are 30,000,000 grape vines in California: her vineyards are spread over 60,000 acres. Many vineyards are planted with 800 vines to the acre.

The word California is said to be derived from the Spanish *caliente fornalla*, a hot furnace; but it is not in San Francisco that this derivation of the word is applicable, for the mean temperature of the Golden City all the year round is but 54°.³ Inland, however, where the winds and fogs of the Pacific do not penetrate, the country may in very truth, be likened unto an oven; and this we shall have good reason to notice later on. But the climate of San Francisco will be found very treacherous by those who are unaccustomed to such sudden changes of temperature as occur, even, during the course of a single day, for in the morning it will be very chilly, in the middle of the day it will be very warm, and in the evening it will have become quite cold again, so that coming from the East you cannot be certain what kind of clothing to put on, and to keep to, and you find when you come to go to bed at night that you want an extra blanket to keep out the cold. As a writer in a Stockton journal once remarked concerning the Golden City: "You go out in the morning shivering, notwithstanding the fact that you are dressed in heavy woollen clothing, and under-clothing, and have a thick overcoat buttoned up to your throat. At 8.30, you unbutton two of the upper buttons; at 9, you unbutton the coat all the way down; at 9.30, you take it off; at 10, you take off your woollen coat, and put on a summer coat; at 11, you take off all your woollen and put on light summer clothing; at 2, it begins to grow cool, and you have to put on your woollen again; and by 7 o'clock your overcoat is buttoned to the chin, and you shiver till bedtime." ⁴

The rainy season commences about the 1st of November, and continues to the end of March. Little or no rain falls during the other months—from the beginning of April to the end of October; indeed it is said that during the last fifteen years the average number of rainy days each year has been but sixty, together with 220 clear and eighty-five cloudy days. Taking the temperature of 30° to represent a cold day, there were no cold days registered in San Francisco during the winters of 1852-53, 1864-65, 1866-67, 1868-69, and 1871-72. In the winter season of 1853-54, there were three cold days; in 1854-55, one cold day; in 1855-56, seven cold days; in 1856-57, five cold days; in 1857-58, four cold days; in

---

³ The mean temperature of September, the warmest month, is 58° Fahr., and that of January, the coldest month, 49°.
⁴ *Resources of California*, by J. S. Hittell.

1858-59, nine cold days; in 1859-60, one cold day; in 1860-61, one cold day; in 1861-62, twenty-one cold days; in 1862-63, three cold days; in 1863-64, one cold day; in 1865-66, one cold day; in 1867-68, eight cold days; in 1869-70, three cold days; and in 1870-71, seven cold days.

The Chinese have their location in "Chinatown"—a part of the city exclusively inhabited by the Celestial People. Here, within a small area of back slums, about 10,500 of these people live after Chinese fashion, and the remaining 10,000 are scattered over other parts of the city. We have spent two evenings—or rather nights—in their quarters, and have made ourselves familiar with the theatres, opium-dens, joss-houses, thieves' retreats, etc.; indeed we have seen many phases of Chinese life in a very short time. I propose therefore, later on, to describe a night's experiences in Chinatown. But meanwhile a word or two may be said about the Palace Hotel, and perhaps one or two other matters of interest.

The Palace Hotel forms an entire block by itself, in the commercial centre of San Francisco. It was built at the instance of a certain Mr. W. C. Ralston, a banker and a "representative man" of California, with the intention that it should eclipse in size every other hotel in the world, just as Baldwin's was built to surpass in elegance and finish, and in the luxuriousness and splendour of its internal fittings, also every other known building of the kind; and I think that each projector has well-nigh succeeded in attaining the realization of his heart's desire. Mr. Baldwin was certainly not long in realizing *his* heart's desire, for he was but a poor man only a few years ago. However, he suddenly took to keeping a livery-stable, made a little money, went on 'Change, speculated, and the result is seen in his splendid hotel of three million dollars built entirely out of his own pocket! *Sic est vita.*—But to return to the Palace Hotel.

Rearing itself seven stories above a deep and lofty basement, this giant pile covers nearly two and a quarter acres, or 96,256 square feet; and if the sub-sidewalk extensions are taken into account, the entire basement will be found to cover the enormous area—for an hotel—of three acres. The height of the lowest story measures over twenty-seven feet, and the uppermost story is sixteen feet. The building is bounded by

New Montgomery, Market, Annie, and Jessie streets, and its main front lies on the first-named of these thoroughfares, facing south—a vast, rich front of immense bay windows, stretching to a length of 350 feet. Bay windows cover the entire edifice from top to bottom, whilst the ground floor is almost wholly devoted to shops. A glance at the prospectus of the hotel—a copy of which is presented (with a photograph) to each individual guest—will reveal certain details which I should not otherwise be able to give. "Its general form," it

THE PALACE HOTEL.

says, "is an immense triplicate, hollow quadrangle, including one grand central crystal-roofed garden court flanked by a lesser and parallel court on either side. . . . . . The deep foundation wall is twelve feet thick; stone, iron, brick and marble are the chief materials. Of the brick alone, its construction consumed thirty-one millions. All outer, inner and partition walls from base to top are of solid stone and brick, built around, within, and upon a large skeleton of broad iron-wrought bands, thickly bolted together and of such immense size as to have required 3000 tons for this purpose alone. Thus the building is really duplex—a huge self-supporting frame of iron, of enormous strength, within massive walls of firm-set brick and solid stone. The outer and visible walls are proof against fire; the inner and invisible frame secures against earthquake.[5] The supporting columns, within and without, are of iron; the cornices of iron and zinc. Four artesian wells having a tested capacity of 28,000 gallons an hour, supply the great 630,000-gallon reservoir under the central court, besides filling seven roof tanks holding 130,000 gallons more. Three large steam fire-pumps force water through forty-five 4-inch wrought-iron upright fire-mains, reaching above the roof, distributing it through three hundred and twenty-seven $2\frac{1}{2}$-inch hose-bibs and 15,000 feet of fire-ply carbolized fire-hose, thus doubly and trebly commanding every inch of the vast structure from roof to basement, within and without." There seems to be every precaution taken to prevent a fire spreading, should it once arise, as the prospectus proceeds to show.—"Electric fire alarms, self-acting, instantly report at the office the exact locality of any fire, or even of extraordinary heat in any parlour, bed-room, closet, hall, passage, stairway or store-room. Special hotel watchmen regularly patrol all parts of the building every thirty minutes, day and night. . . . . . Besides all these precautions a fire-proof iron staircase, enclosed in solid brick and stone and opening through iron doors upon every floor, ascends from basement to roof. . . . . . Every floor has its exclusive annunciator, and its own tabular conductors, carrying all letters for the post-office directly to the main letter-box in the general office. A pneumatic despatch tube instantaneously conveys letters, messages or parcels to and from any point on the different floors. Two thousand and forty-two ventilating tubes opening outward upon the roof from every room, bath-room, and closet, ensure constant purity and thorough sweetness of air in every part."

Entering the hotel from New Montgomery-street, a carriage-

[5] The Palace Hotel is not the only building in San Francisco that is braced together with iron bands, so as to keep the whole structure compact and proof against a convulsion of Nature. Many of the shops and warehouses are similarly built, and, moreover, are built entirely of iron, which is painted the colour of masonry.

way of 44 feet in width (and a sidewalk) expanding into a circular driveway 52 feet in diameter, brings us into the Grand Central Court, 144 feet by 84 feet, which is surrounded by colonnades. Standing in this court and looking up and around

GRAND CENTRAL COURT, PALACE HOTEL.

the sight is most imposing. Story upon story does the giant structure tower aloft, broad open balconies facing each story, till an immense iron-framed glass roof is reached, which covers in the whole court. Palms and other exotics grow in pots around this court; many rocking-chairs (and spittoons) lie concealed amongst the palms; a music pavilion, too, there is, where the hotel band occasionally plays on an afternoon, discoursing "Nancy Lee," "Pinafore," and other popular selections from the Old Country. From the central court broad passages lead to the two outer courts, each of these passages measuring 22 feet by 135 feet,—each, too, having a carriage-way from the street measuring 20 feet in width. There are several shops in the hotel. Thus we have, inside, an establishment for cleaning, scouring, dyeing and repairing gentlemen's clothing; a tailor's store, by one J. Kavanach; ditto, by one W. Roberts; a book and newspaper store; a Japanese store; a bric-à-brac collection, with many fossils and old clothes; a trunk and portmanteau store; another book store; another tailor's store, by one J. Roberts—probably rival brother to the other Roberts; besides a tourists' agency or office for obtaining round-trip tickets for visiting the Yosemite Valley and Big Tree Groves; and a telegraph office. Then there are billiard rooms and bath-rooms, and rooms devoted to perfumery and hair-cutting, where cropping is done on an expensive and lordly scale—where you can, if you choose, go and pay a dollar-and-a-half for being shaved, cut, and shampoo'd! I never was more surprised in my life than when I was asked to pay one dollar for subjecting myself to the first and last of these operations. And after my locks had been arranged to the barber's satisfaction, I had to take up the brush and spoil all his little game by re-arranging my hair Christian-like in the manner that I am generally accustomed to wear it, instead of having it all stuck up in front like a fan—much to the barber's mortification, no doubt.

Returning to the Grand Central Court, large folding doors on the left lead into the hotel office—a wide, free and open space 65 feet by 55 feet; and this is the part of the building that a new-arrival will first seek out in order that he may report himself and be allotted his apartments. Here, behind a long counter, he will find stationed the "boss" gentlemen of the hotel, such as the proprietor, the chief clerk, etc., who will hand him the visitors' book and request him to write his name in it. This done

and the apartments allotted and the key presented, as many
negroes as are required will seize hold of his baggage and
bear it away to the lift, so that it may be conveyed upstairs,
while another negro will attend on the new-arrival personally,
conduct him to the lift and ascend with him to his apartments.
There are five lifts or "elevators" communicating with the
different floors, ascending rapidly and noiselessly to the top of
the building—even to the roof, where are promenades for
obtaining a bird's eye view of the city. We found these elevators the greatest possible convenience, for the staircases,
though plentiful, dodge all about the building. Twice did we
assay to descend by the stairs from our rooms, and on both
occasions we became utterly bewildered. The domestics upstairs consist of Chinamen and negresses. The former dust
about and keep the passages clean, the latter attend to the
cleansing of your chamber. Chamber, did I say?—We have
each a suite of six apartments; and in this hotel there are
exclusively for guests, seven hundred and fifty-five suites
of apartments above the ground floor! Not seven hundred
and fifty-five *single* apartments, as the hotel prospectus would
lead one to imagine when it says there are so many hundred
rooms. But here your "room" means so many apartments;—
to take our own case, for instance. We have each a large
sitting-room, also another room in which to receive friends, a
bedroom, a little lavatory, a closet, and a bath-room. Our
bedrooms have each a marble fireplace and a 6-ft. pier-glass,
besides two gas lamps, a large dressing-table fitted with
drawers, and a 5-ft. looking-glass. In our sitting-rooms are
blue, velvet-covered arm-chairs, mahogany writing-tables,
3-jet chandeliers with gas reading-lamps attached, etc.
Many of the sitting-rooms are 20 feet square, and there are
none less than 16 feet square. Every room has its electric
bell, and is liberally supplied with gas.

There are, altogether, thirteen dining and breakfast-
rooms. From the Grand Central Court access is obtained to
the main breakfast-room, which is 110 feet by 55; and this
leads into the grand dining-room, which is 150 feet by 55.
Other dining-rooms—including the children's—are upstairs,
on the second floor; also the ladies' drawing-room, 84 feet
by 40. The waiters at table are all "colored," and are

presided over by a generalissimo, who, himself a darkie, sees that the darkies under him are brisk in their movements and zealous in their attentions. He also graciously receives the guests as they enter the room, and conducts them to seats according to his fancy. There are 156 coloured waiters in this hotel—that is, more than in any other hotel in America, except the Grand Union at Saratoga.

The charges of the Palace Hotel are as follows: Room with board, 16*s.* or 12*s.* per day; room without board, 4*s.* per day. If you select the first of these amounts you are given a splendid suite of apartments on the first, second, or third floors. If you select the second or last, you are put on the uppermost floor, or, if not on this, on the one below it. But in neither of these cases do you pay for anything extra— unless you like to play billiards, or have your hair cut, etc.; and then you will have to pay pretty dearly!

Pleasant walks and drives in the immediate vicinity of San Francisco are few and far between; indeed there is only one, and this, again, can scarcely be called pleasant at this time of the year, when the dust lies about the roads some inches in depth, rendering it impossible to move very far without incurring the risk of being completely smothered. The excursion referred to is one of seven miles to the Cliff House, which is an hotel built on a cliff overlooking the sea, where are to be seen some hundreds of seals sprawling about on rocks close in shore. As this excursion is a favourite one of the people of the Golden City it may be as well to say a little about it. The horse-car can be taken for some miles, the rest of the distance being completed by "stage." The last part of the journey is mostly up hill, along the very dustiest of roads, and several large cemeteries are passed on the way. It is worth while walking through one of these cemeteries if it is only to see the magnificent fuchsias and geraniums, the palms, cactuses, etc., which grow in them so luxuriantly. As the Cliff House is approached, a fine view is obtained of the rockbound coast in the direction of the Golden Gate. Fogs are very prevalent here, and when one does arise it is hard indeed for a vessel to hit upon this narrow, one-mile-wide inlet to the bay, even with lighthouse assistance. The Cliff

House reached, about a couple of hundred yards from the shore can be seen the object of one's visit. A few low rocky islets, and upon them hundreds of seals, some lying motionless, basking in the sun, others wriggling themselves one over another, more, too, struggling in the water with the tide in their endeavours to reach their companions on dry land—an ugly collection of brown ungainly monsters, silent amongst themselves, except now and then when a solitary "bark" is heard from some creature who happens to be roughly pushed about by his sleek, unmannerly neighbour. These seals are protected by legislation, no person being allowed to fire off a gun in the vicinity of the rocks under a penalty of 30*l*. Should anyone be caught killing one of them, the fine imposed is 100*l*.

On the way to the Cliff House one is able to see the system which is commonly adopted in this State for irrigating the country. First, however, let me mention that California is not the farmer's paradise that some people have imagined it to be. The frequency of long-continued droughts renders irrigation a matter of necessity,[6] and puts the farmer annually to con-

[6] "Many millions of land in the far West are almost entirely without value unless they can be irrigated by water supplied by artificial means. The arid region of the United States embraces 900,000,000 acres, lying in the Territories of Arizona, Dakota, Idaho, Montana, New Mexico, Utah, and Wyoming, the States of Colorado, Nevada, California, Kansas, Nebraska, Oregon, Texas, and the Indian territory. Not one per cent. of this vast area has been sold. It has been ascertained that about 200,000,000 acres are mountainous land, upon which agriculture cannot be successfully carried on, even with an abundance of water. Of the remainder, 200,000,000 acres are lava lands, covered with cinders, etc., lands without soil or vegetation, and desert plains of drifting sand. On the greater part of the 500,000 acres not included above, valuable crops can be raised by the aid of water. By spreading the water of streams over the land while the crops are growing, several thousands of acres of this area have already been reclaimed, but these methods can be applied to no more than 15,000,000 acres. There remain 485,000,000 acres which are now used only for pasturage, and on which the vegetation is so scanty that they are almost worthless. It has been shown that the introduction of water is all that is needed to make these lands fertile. The Government is asked to provide for the sinking of two artesian wells east of the Rocky Mountains, and three west of the Rocky Mountains, as an experiment towards the solution of a great problem—the reclamation of what used to be described on maps as the Great American Desert."—*New York Times*.

siderable expense,—a field of grain requires to be irrigated three times a year,—sometimes indeed when he can ill afford the outlay. The rainy season, too, when it does come round, does not bring him a regular supply of rain, for one month will be wet throughout, and the next, perhaps, will be one of drought. In the neighbourhood of San Francisco is some of the worst land in the State.[7] Sand-hills predominate ; but by taking a ride over those which lie at the back of the Golden City, between it and the sea, one can obtain some idea of the means which have to be resorted to here to get things to grow. Pass through this region on a windy day, and you will see dotted over the country a number of wheels in motion, so many that you will find it a matter of difficulty to count them. They are windmills for pumping up the water, which lies underground at a depth of twelve or fourteen feet, and to every windmill is attached a long wooden trough or " flume," which, with a fall of from three to five feet to the mile, conducts the water over the land which requires to be submerged, and in this way is water procured to irrigate the market-gardens and farm-lands in the vicinity of the Golden City. This system of irrigation is also extensively employed in other parts of California. In the Sacramento Valley its adoption is general. Stockton, which is passed on the Pacific Railroad between Sacramento and San Francisco, is called the " City of Windmills" on account of the vast number of mills of this description to be found in and about the place.

Another excursion is one to Oakland. This city lies five miles across the bay, and is connected with the Golden City by constant communication, commodious and luxuriously-fitted boats conveying passengers, with their horses and carriages, over the water every twenty or thirty minutes from the foot of Market-street, landing them at the end of the two-mile pier which is thrown out from the Oakland shore into the bay, the rest of the distance being completed by train. Deep water lies about this pier, for vessels can lie alongside and ship their cargo direct from the railway-trucks without need of further trouble and change. Thus, supposing goods are started in a baggage-van from New

[7] "We must go twelve miles before we reach any large body of tillable soil."—Mr. J. S. Hittell, in *Resources of California.*

York over land, bound for Yokohama in Japan, distance 8125 miles, they could be despatched the entire distance with the need of only one change, and that would be from out of the van into the ship lying alongside the Oakland pier.

Oakland is more like a suburb of San Francisco than a separate city of itself, for here a great number of the business men of the Golden City have their private villa residences, since the climate is so much milder and more equable, and there is less chance of exposure from the trade-winds of the Pacific. Yet Oakland possesses a history of its own apart from that of its great sister-rival, and it is one equally as marvellous. We have seen that the population of the Golden City numbers 230,000, and that thirty-three years agone it numbered but 450. Oakland cannot quite boast the antiquity of the Golden City, yet during a space of seven years it increased nearly 36,000, for according to the census of 1870, its population was in that year 11,104, whereas in 1877 it had risen to 47,000. Its population is now (December, 1880) 34,550. It is a city of detached houses, one almost wholly devoted to private residences, and every house more or less has its garden attached. These gardens consist for the most part of scarlet geraniums, which deck the city in gayest attire. Evergreen oaks spring up thickly around; in short, it is a "city of oaks," as its name implies. At Berkeley, a few miles out of Oakland, is the University of California, which receives students of both sexes, giving them a free education. Care is taken to prevent any "tippling" amongst the students, as no intoxicating liquors are allowed to be sold to anyone, whether student or non-student, within a radius of two miles of the institution. The local railway in Oakland is laid along the middle of the streets; and since the train proceeds very slowly, people who are engaged in shopping or otherwise jump on and off the cars whilst they are in motion, just when and where they please, for they pay nothing for their ride. All travelling on the local railway is free of charge!

I may perhaps be allowed to draw attention once more to the white-paint advertisement nuisance—by alluding to some of the notices that are so conspicuously daubed about the environs of San Francisco. The allusion to them may be considered trivial; but when one can hardly travel over a mile of ground in the States where the country is well settled and populated, without being compelled to associate oneself with some sort of mixture or cure, or recipe of some kind or other, I think another word or two on the subject, beyond what has already been said in the earlier part of this work, will not be found to be out of place or superfluous. These advertisements are similar in size, colour, style and tone to those that are found in other parts of the country; in fact, America is simply white-washed with the nuisance, the whole country from one end to the other being disfigured with what must seem to the foreigner nothing but a blotch and an eyesore. When we come to look back upon wonderful Niagara, we cannot help associating it with the "Rising Sun Stove Polish," which, we are told, is the "best in the world." We have seen the beautiful Hudson River, too, mixed up with seltzer aperients and gargling oils. Chicago we have found the most extensively daubed; Omaha and the little settlements we passed on the Plains, are daubed in a similar manner. Thus the country is completely surfeited and gorged with this common, inelegant mode of advertising, a means employed—and so universally, too—which I have not seen in any other country I have visited. Now the road to the Cliff House is just one instance out of a million of what I mean, for here, for some miles, one finds a splendid and judicious assortment of notices repeatedly daubed in white paint on the palings by the side of the public way, and now and then on such a conspicuous location as is afforded by the blank wall of a house, as one drives along towards the coast in order to have a look at the seals. The most interesting piece of information that arrests the attention of the stranger as he approaches the seals, is, "VINEGAR BITTERS IS ALL THE GO FOR LOVE!" (This mixture is sold in bottles of various sizes.) Other white-paint notices are as follows: "ONE WORD TO THE WISE—BUY CONDENSED EGGS;" "CONDENSED EGGS IS BETTER THAN FRESH;" "CURE YOUR PAINS AND LAMENESS WITH PRATT'S ABOLITION OIL;" "BUY THE HOWE AND YOU'LL B HAPPY;" "CHEW JACKSON'S BEST PLUG;" "SAY, HAVE YOU SEEN THE GREAT CROCKER?" "TRY ONE BOTTLE OF YOSEMITE BITTERS;" "YOSEMITE BITTERS GOOD FOR BELLY AKE;"

"Yosemite Bitters never fails;" "Yosemite Bitters will do you good;" "Pacific Stomach Bitters the finest in the world;" "Pacific Stomach Bitters beats them all, Try 'em," etc., Another white-paint notice frequently seen in and about San Francisco is, "If you feel very bad and want money go to Uncle Harris." But perhaps the most extraordinary advertisements occur on the Oakland pier, though the like is repeated over and over again in the streets of that city, and all about the surrounding country as well. One is continually reminded that there is in the world such a person as one Van Shaack, who, hailing from "708 to 716, Kearney-street, S.F.," endeavours to impress on you the varied character of his merchandise, as also that he is in urgent need of your patronage and support. He blows his trumpet in white paint after the following remarkable fashion:

    C. P. Van Shaack & Co.
    Van Shaack & Co. sell klose.
    Van Shaack & Co. sell haats.
    Van Shaack & Co. sell toys.
    Van Shaack & Co. sell jewelry and notions.
    Van Shaack & Co. sell white shirts.
    Van Shaack & Co. cut corns.
    Van Shaack & Co. cure bunions.
    Van Shaack & Co. are bully.
    Van Shaack & Co. dont teach school.
    Van Shaack & Co. dont you forget it.
    Van Shaack & Co. are not quacks.
    Van Shaack & Co. dont belong to the ring.
    Van Shaack & Co. dont keep hotels.
    Van Shaack & Co. dont practise law.
    Van Shaack & Co. darned cheap.
    Van Shaack & Co. wont cheat you.
    Van Shaack & Co. want you bad.
    If you want any money go to Van Shaack & Co.
    Ye Gods! what bargains at Van Shaack & Co.'s.

CHAPTER XIV.

A NIGHT IN CHINATOWN.

Preparing for Chinatown—Setting out for the quarters—A walk down Montgomery-street—An anti-Chinese demonstration—A troublesome problem—"The Chinese must go"—We arrive in Chinatown—Novel street scene—Popular Chinese restaurant—Choice articles of food—A ceremonious little grocer—Buying shoes—Very tight fit—A Chinaman's signature—Visit to a joss-house—Popular Chinese gods—Examining a Chinaboy's head—The "Royal China" Theatre—A Chinese opera—Music of the past—An acrobatic performance—"All aboard" for an opium-den—Double guard—A disreputable locality—Inside an opium-den—Very close quarters—How to smoke opium—We turn opium smokers—The way John Chinaman smokes himself to sleep—Saving expense—A man of delicate birth—"Old Johnny" counts up.

I WILL now proceed to relate a night's experiences in the Chinese quarter of San Francisco, or "Chinatown," as that part of the city which is densely populated by the Celestials is called. It lies within the compass of a comparatively small number of "blocks," but it is a perfect maze of some of the dirtiest and narrowest alleys to be found in all Christendom or heathendom. This used to be the old Spanish quarter, the aristocratic centre of the Golden City—till the Chinese came trooping in and drove all respectable people away.

As we determined that our visit should include, besides theatres and joss-houses, a peep into the opium-dens, where, had the authorities caught us, we should have been liable to be fined a sum of fifty dollars apiece,—for not only is a heavy fine imposed on a Chinaman who is found keeping an opium-den, but a penalty also attaches to a white man if he is found entering one,—we placed ourselves under the ægis of a cicerone, whose business it was to conduct strangers over the quarters; and at half-past eight o'clock on Friday evening,

June 14, 1878, we started forth, a party of five, under the protection of a policeman, to look up the Chinaman in his den. Besides my fellow-traveller, myself, and the guide, our party included Dr. Terriberry, of Paterson, New Jersey; and a Scotchman who had pushed on to San Francisco after hunting buffalos on the Kansas prairies.

Proceeding down Montgomery-street from the Palace Hotel, we had not walked many hundred yards before we had to pull up in order to allow a procession to pass us. It was a demonstration of 10,000 workingmen returning from Chinatown, after menacing the Celestials by marching through and parading their quarters. This was a bit of "Kearneyism," —that is, a mischievous agitation got up at the instigation of a revolutionary demagogue of the name of Dennis Kearney, an agitator of the very worst type, the champion and friend (?) of the working classes of California,—and meant the rooting out of John Chinaman neck-and-crop from the land, because by fair and honest means he had succeeded in reducing wages; because by his industry and frugality, his patience and perseverance, his skill, his dogged devotion to the performance of any work to which he applied his hand or his brain, he had proved his superiority over the Californian workingman; and for the bringing about of such a state of things John had been called everything that was vile, he had become to the workingman of California an object of the direst calumny and hatred, whilst in the Golden City he was the butt of hoodlums, and the subject of oratorical explosions at frequent mass-meetings of its indignant citizens. The Chinese question is still the great problem affecting western North America. The Chinese come pouring into the country and underbid the American labourer for wages. They cheapen wages, hiring themselves out for next to nothing—and why not? The presence of the Mongolians cannot but exercise a powerful influence for good in such an advancing, rapidly growing State as California, one of the least developed in the Union, where railways have still to be built, land has to be reclaimed,[1] labour well-nigh incalculable must be expended

---

[1] There are between two and three million acres of swamp-land in California waiting to be reclaimed.

to develope the country as it should be developed, and the necessary work can be done at a considerably less expense by the employment of the Chinese than by the utilization of native labour; and the community at large, instead of being the losers, are, on the contrary, the gainers thereby. But many persons take a different view of the matter. Indeed there are certain agitators who stump the country to try and excite general indignation, and to procure legislation against the heathen,—against the Chinese first, to get them turned out of the State, and then against all owners of real estate, who "must go" likewise,—and amongst the foremost of these agitators is Mr. Dennis Kearney. "The Chinese must go," is the war-cry of these agitators. "They poison the earth, they suck the richness, the nourishment out, and leave the impoverished dust, while they return to China to jingle their pockets and laugh in their sleeves at us like Yankee clock-peddlers"—says a certain indignant American writer. Not a cent of the money that the Chinaman acquires re-circulates in the States, but all goes to China to pay for the bringing over of more of his countrymen. But to give John his due, he is adroit, and industrious withal. He shows a wonderful aptitude for imitation, and he will learn a new trade and excel in it as quickly as any man to be found in the country. His morality is not exactly "high-toned;" but the difference between the Anglo-Saxon and Mongolian races—races which will never assimilate—is too distinct for the morality or otherwise of the Chinaman to make any material difference. He is rather given to prevarication, and now and then a fit of kleptomania comes upon him; but he is peaceable and law-abiding, and seldom or never is found drunk. Thousands of the Chinese are employed as indoor servants in San Francisco alone; thousands, too, are employed about the State as labourers in the field. Why then is John told that he "must go" when his services are accepted and paid for to his satisfaction? There are less than 100,000 Chinese in the United States, so why this terror over such a handful of Celestials?

But to return. The procession we met was a most orderly one, considering the circumstances. Many of the workingmen were singing a plaintive sort of melody, which sounded more like a psalm-tune than war against the Chinese. They carried a number of flags and banners, whereon John appeared in effigy in a variety of ingenious portraitures. They also had a quantity of Hibernian green ribbon bound about their hats and coats. We forced our way through the crowd, crossed over into Kearney-street and continued our walk towards Chinatown.

Traversing several cross-streets, we soon reached the quarters of the Chinese. We had come to Jackson-street, one of the "fashionable" thoroughfares of Chinatown, and here the scene was completely changed. A moment before we were walking amid a fine blaze of gas-light: now we found ourselves in comparative darkness, the only relief from the general gloom being a murky kind of light afforded by grotesquely-designed, coloured lanterns depending outside balconied houses. The road was well-nigh impassable, such crowds of people were thronging it—a silent, voiceless concourse of expressionless, moonfaced Celestials; all men, not a single woman among them; all Chinese, for not a white man was to be seen. "I reckon," said our guide, "you'll not see ten white men to-night, till you leave Chinatown and go home to your hotel;" and he reckoned not inaccurately. Pigtailed John was here in his glory—there was no one else but pigtailed John. Every individual we met wore the caudal appendage, and in every case it was allowed to drop down the back and legs, for when the Chinaman is not engaged in manual labour he carries his hair in this manner, but it is coiled around the back of the head when it would be likely to interfere with the movements of the wearer. All the men might have been women, for aught we could tell, for the countenances of the two sexes are very much alike, and the habiliments of both are very similar. But our conductor positively assured us that there were none of the fair sex in Jackson-street to-night.

The houses in Jackson-street were all built of wood, and many of them had balconies, and from the balconies we found coloured Chinese lanterns depending; and curious devices, such as gold-gilt and red paper dragons and "flying" serpents, and countless other extraordinary designs, were pasted about the buildings, and incomprehensible Chinese characters met the eye wherever it turned. Some of the shops were lit up inside with lanterns, others with gas, and business seemed to be carried on actively in every one we went into. Tuck Wo kept a provision store, a kind of grocery, with balconies around. Yven Hong was a jack-of-all-trades. He kept clothes, candles, sweetmeats, tobacco, etc. Choy Yan Low kept a restaurant, a three-storied, balconied corner house, with "high-toned" supper-rooms upstairs, well lighted with lanterns, crowded with Celestials both inside and outside upon the balconies—eating, drinking, and smoking. We went in and sought out the proprietor, Mr. Low. This Chinaman is the Gunter of Chinatown, and his restaurant the popular resort of pigtailed Epicureans. Having mounted a stairway, we found ourselves in a long, low, narrow room, at one end of which was a counter supporting a variety of eatables, which were presided over by a stout, pigtailed old man, who was smoking a long clay pipe and was bare-footed and bare-legged. Several small tables were distributed about the room, and at these were seated about twenty Chinamen, likewise pigtailed and barelegged, who smoked their long clay pipes or were engaged in eating and drinking, or both. The stout old gentleman afore-mentioned came forward upon our appearance, and introduced himself as Ah (*i. e.* Mr.) Chung. He was not the proprietor of the restaurant, as we took him at first to be; but he was Mr. Low's head man. Mr. Chung introduced himself in the most perfect and graceful manner possible. First he took his pipe out of his mouth and spat on the floor. Then he went through an elaborate series of bows and scrapes, bending his body into a variety of forms, bringing his right arm across his chest and his head almost down to his knees, in respectful obeisance; and then he asked us if we would take some tea, or anything at all to eat, and he also made a motion with his pipe towards his guests who were eating at the tables, signifying that we should do the same; but we politely declined. These Chinamen were eating garlic and greens, rice, gizzards, dried shrimps, dried sharks (unsalted), "ham tan" or dried ducks' eggs, etc. There seemed to be a scarcity of knives and forks, for nearly every Chinaman ate his meal by the aid of two little pieces of stick, called "chopsticks," though we noticed a few who adopted the fashion of our first parents before knives and forks were invented, and simply used their fingers. An indescribable odour filled the room, one that was particularly objectionable. When we came to take leave of Mr. Chung, he presented each of us with a card, upon which was printed in English, "CHOY YAN LOW, FIRST CLASS RESTAURANT AND DINING SALOON, SOUTH EAST COR. JACKSON STREET, UP STAIRS, ENTRANCE ON WASHINGTON ALLEY, MEALS IN FIRST CLASS STYLE, FURNISHED AT ALL HOURS." We asked Mr. Chung to write his name in Chinese on the back of his card, which he did. As we were leaving, he said, "Willee comee see me again?" I fear we answered him rather evasively.

It was now eleven o'clock—time to be thinking of going to the theatre, but not time enough yet for visiting an opium-den. There are two theatres in Chinatown, one of them nearly opposite Mr. Low's restaurant. So we crossed over the street, intending at once to see the play. We found, however, that the doors of the theatre were closed, and would not be opened for half an hour at least. This was owing to the alarm caused by the recent parade of the 10,000 workingmen, which seemed to have quite scared the Celestials. So we turned into a shop to buy caps and shoes. It was a grocer's store that we entered, No. 636, Jackson-street, kept by one Sun Kee, wholesale and retail dealer in tea, sugar, rice, dry goods, and Chinese provisions; also in ladies' and gentlemen's shoes, ready-made clothes, candles, confectionery of all kinds, opium, pipes, and tobacco. The premises were lighted by means of fanciful coloured oil-lanterns, though gas was also employed. Mr. Sun Kee was smoking a clay pipe behind his counter, bending down and making up his accounts for the day. Judging by the neat little performance he went through directly he caught sight of us entering his establishment,—he divined, I suppose, that we were come to make purchases,—he was evidently pleased at the prospect of such a windfall, for he quickly doffed his "wide-awake," came forth from his retreat, and commenced bowing and scraping, backing all the while, keeping his head down and his legs and body in continual motion; and then he most graciously extended his little yellow hand, and gave us a gentle squeeze all round. He spoke "pigeon English," as all Chinamen do, so that he was hardly understood.[2] We told him what we wanted—or I should rather say I did; and he thereupon fetched down from a drawer a pair of the well-known cork-soled shoes for my inspection. Now a Chinaman's foot besides being peculiarly round is also peculiarly small, so that I knew there would be a difficulty in getting a pair to fit. The first shoe he gave me to try on measured scarcely half the length of my boot. I said to John, "Bring me a larger pair." John did so, but with no better result. "I must have a larger pair still," I said. John therefore looked me out another pair. But when I came to try this on it was still impossible to get my foot in—it was scarcely larger than the other pair. "Bring me the largest pair you've got," I exclaimed, getting somewhat impatient. After a good deal of searching about, Mr. Kee found me a pair that certainly did seem somewhat larger than the other three, and had all the appearance of being likely to fit. I tried to get my foot in, I squeezed away with all my might, and at last succeeded in forcing an entrance; but to walk about with the shoe on was quite out of the question. I asked for a still larger pair, but John laughed in my face, and told me that it was the largest he had ever seen, and that there was not a larger pair in Chinatown. The men's shoes were small enough, in all conscience; but the ladies'! Such tiny little bits of things, so narrow, so heavy, so very like boats

---

[2] "Choy Awah is a young Chinaman, and a Sunday-school scholar at Washington. Choy Awah recently set himself to work at the English language, and succeeded admirably. He wrote out the parable which is to be found in the twenty-fifth chapter of Matthew, and this is what he made of it:

"'The kingdom like ten girls; never marry; they bring some lanterns; come out till some new married man come that way. Have got five wise and five foolish. Five hold lanterns with no oil. Smart five all have oil inside. The new married man come late; they sleep. By-and-by they all say, "New married man, come." All go out to him. Five makey nice lanterns. Five foolish say, "You give my oil; lamp no oil, you give me some." The smart say, "I no give you; I not enough; you go market buy." Foolish go market to buy. The new married man come. All come in to dinner. Shut the door. By-and-by the foolish come and say, "Boss, boss, open door." He say, "I no key you; you no my. Must be smart, no understand the day."'"—*Detroit Free Press.*

in their shape, without any soles—fashioned, too, for feet fully developed, I had really never imagined till Mr. Kee showed me a pair. They fully illustrated the riddle, Why is wit like a Chinese lady's foot?—Because brevity is the sole of it.

Before leaving, we asked Mr. Kee for his card, which he gave us with the greatest pleasure. Like Mr. Chung, he gave one to each of us, and wrote, or rather painted, his name on the back. This he did in an instant. He took up a small paint-brush, held it vertically between his fingers, and, as quickly as I could write my own signature, with a few rapid twists and turns of the brush he produced a pile of four little squares lying one on the top of the other, each square containing such a confused collection of strokes and cross-strokes, that we were quite surprised how John could ever have accomplished his signature—and such an intricate one, too—so cleverly, as it seemed, and in so short a time. We one and all thanked John for painting his name, and withdrew.

We then entered a few more shops, notably a jeweller's, where we watched John hard at work, late as it was, fashioning gold rings. Then, before returning to the theatre, we went into a joss-house, or Chinese temple of worship, a description of which I will now attempt to give.

The temple we were taken to was situated "on" Dupont-street, or rather *off* that thoroughfare, for we had to grope our way along a dark narrow passage which led out of it, then pass into a small square full of Celestials living in dirty higgledy-piggledy, apple-pie fashion; and then we had to ascend the outside of a house by several rickety flights of stairs, to a room on the third story. This joss-house was dedicated to Kwan Tai, the god of war, and consisted of two rooms, one a little larger than the other, both of them devoted to the worship of the Chinaman's popular gods. The door was fortunately open, and we entered; but we became immediately sensible of such an abominable odour that we were almost compelled to beat a hasty retreat. However, we aroused the keeper, who was sound asleep inside, in a corner near the doorway; and he lit a few lanterns for us, which threw a pale glimmer on the objects around. It was a singular, tawdry arrangement that we looked upon, a gaudy spectacle, grotesque in the extreme. Red and gold paper dragons, and ingeniously devised, hideous-looking birds and beasts, were pasted about the apartment, covering walls and ceiling. At one end of the room were the images of three of the more important deities, placed in separate little recesses or alcoves, and before each god a small red oil-lamp was depending, which, although burning, emitted little or no light. In the centre was the figure of Kwan Tai himself—a most hideous and frightful object. He had a face as red and shiny as a billiard ball. He wore an immense black beard reaching down below the waist; peacock's feathers stuck out from his head, and he was robed in scarlet and gold. The expression of his countenance was terrific. The Chinese hold this particular deity in the greatest reverence and esteem, and claim a correlative feeling of regard on the part of the deity himself. "Chinaman he likee him heap muchee," says John, "and he likee Chinaman heap muchee too." At the feet of Kwan Tai were placed three little cups of tea, in case he should get thirsty and want to take a drink. On the right of this deity was a figure of the god of finance; on his left was the god of pills—the medicine god, whose name is Wah Tah. He held a pill in his left hand. The walls of this room were decorated with battle-axes, spears, and shields, all brought over from China. There was a bell and a drum suspended just inside the doorway. These are used for wakening up the gods when they get sleepy, and do not properly respond to the invocations of the worshippers. Besides the gods already mentioned, there was, in this room, a figure of Ham Nai Hung Shing Tai, the god of fire. The colour of his complexion did not belie his name. In the centre of the room was a very interesting and valuable curiosity, namely a large iron-framed glass cabinet, covered over with wire, containing hundreds of grotesque little gold-gilt, carved wooden figures representing Chinese men of mark, such as great historical personages, heroes, warriors, etc., from the earliest ages down to recent times. Many of the figures represented mythology as well. The Chinese attach the utmost importance and value to this collection. It had been brought hither from Pekin. Passing into the other or smaller room we found the images of three more deities, similarly posed in separate alcoves. First there was the Woman Warrior. She was red-faced, and looked very masculine. She had been given one cup of tea. On her left was a small figure of the Tiger Slayer, with a small tiger looking fierce by his side. On the right of the Woman Warrior was the Great Religious Woman, or Goddess of Mercy. She had been given three cups of tea. There was the image of a baby let into her forehead. In a corner of the room was a figure of the Bad Joss, or Wicked Fellow, put out of sight as much as possible.

We were shown over the temple by the keeper aforesaid, a stout, pigtailed old Chinaman. He had a youth with him, aged nineteen, who also wore the caudal appendage. As we were going out, I explained to our guide that I should like to examine the youth's head. I felt interested in the lad, and wished to prove by ocular demonstration how he managed to arrange his long twisted rope of hair. So we got him to stand still, and then we asked him if he would kindly favour us by showing us his head. He uncovered it—lo, what a blue pate it was! It was literally shaven blue all over with the exception of a small circular patch at the back, from which sprouted a luxuriant bunch of a healthy crop of hair, which had been allowed to grow freely while the rest of the head had been continually shaved, and was plaited and twisted and let fall over his back in one long, extended cord. I applied my hands and my eyes to a minute examination of the head, and carefully tugged away at the hair to see if there was any deception in the matter; but it was not necessary—there was no chignon nor any false pretence or vain show of the kind. All the hair he wore was his own. We were standing at the doorway, and the young man answered, "Al' right, go' bye. An' willee comee see me again?"

We also went into the Clay-street joss-house; but as a description of this would be found similar to that of the Dupont-street temple, I will pass it over. There are several of these idol-houses in Chinatown. Besides the two already mentioned, there are the Pine-street, the Jackson-street, and the Brooklyn-place temples; and others. Of these, the Pine-street—as also the Clay-street—is dedicated to Kwan Tai; and the temple in Jackson-street is dedicated to Ma Chu ("Grandmother" Ma Chu), the goddess of sailors, who is also called Tin Tan, or the Heavenly Queen.

As it was past twelve o'clock, we returned to the theatre in Jackson-street. It is known as the "Royal China" Theatre, or the "Chinese Royal." The doors were now open, in fact the play was in full swing. Performances at this theatre commence ordinarily at 8 p.m., and terminate at 4 a.m. During these hours there is a cold collation spread in the dressing-room of the theatre, of which each actor will partake, without ceremony, at that time of night when he feels most able to do justice to it. Threading our way along a dark passage crammed almost to suffocation with Celestials, the nauseating odour arising from the hot stuffy atmosphere being almost more than human nature could stand, we at length reached the entrance-door, where were two Chinamen presiding over baskets of fruit, sugar-cane confectionary, peanuts, cocoa-nuts, almonds, rice, and other refreshments. Here we had to pay before entering the theatre. We were charged four "bits" apiece, *i. e.* two shillings; but a Celestial has to pay only half this amount. We could have had a private box if we liked, by paying ten shillings for it; but we preferred going into the "pit," along with the ordinary run of Celestials. Inside, the theatre was bare and gloomy in the extreme. There were a few private boxes and a small gallery aloft, the latter exclusively devoted to the use of the fair sex, who were not allowed in other parts of the building. A circular pit, capable of holding some 300 or 400, led up to the stage, which was simply a raised platform devoid of any surroundings, without "flies" or "wings" or scenery of any kind—only a wall at the back placarded over with paper dragons and shapeless beasts, and the usual incomprehensible characters. Two doors at the rear, concealed behind curtains, allowed of exit from the platform, which was approached from the pit by a flight of steps at either end. There were no footlights; but lanterns were hung about the walls, and depended from the ceiling above. An "opera" was being performed, and two persons were acting, a man and a woman; but as Chinese women never act on the stage, the woman was a man dressed up as such. The costume of the male proper was very rich. With a face like Kwan Tai's, namely red and shiny, and with a very long black beard, and a bandage tied over his eyes as if he were having a game of hide-and-seek, he was attired in a gorgeous blue dressing-gown with large white sleeves. He had a gold-tasselled pink girdle tied around his waist; high-peaked

AN ALL-NIGHT SUPPER AT THE CHINESE THEATRE.

shoes were on his feet, and peacock's feathers a yard long were sticking out from his head. Four red flags, fringed with gold, were strapped on to his shoulders like wings; and when we entered the place he was capering about the stage by himself with a wand in one hand and a spread-out fan in the other, and with this hand he kept endeavouring to fan himself as he leapt about and contorted his body like a lunatic just escaped from Bedlam. While he went through this performance, the made-up woman maintained a kneeling attitude at the extreme end of the platform, fanning herself with her left hand while she extended her right in the direction of the wizard—for such her companion appeared to be—as if imploring his pardon, indeed she looked as if she were suffering from a nervous fear that he was about to do her some grievous bodily harm. For twenty minutes these two creatures kept up alternately between them a wild singing dialogue, with " musical " accompaniment, the wizard every now and then, when a fit of lunacy seized him, jumping up from a kneeling posture close beside the woman, and kicking his heels about the stage and trying to make himself look terrific, and, while he so diverted himself, the woman singing in squeaky treble, fanning herself and gazing bewitchingly down on the audience with a side glance, when the wizard was not looking, while the wizard himself took up the same strain in a lower key when he had done his leaping about for the time being; till at last a crisis was reached in the performance, the man vigorously applying his wand and driving the young " woman " off the stage, and disappearing with her, and then in a few seconds reappearing with a hop, skip, and a jump across the platform, with his mouth wide open and his arms spread out in the air, which latter performance constituted, I suppose, his final bow to the audience. Then the made-up woman came forward from behind the scenes and made her final bow likewise, but with far more elegance and grace, for this is how she managed it. She gracefully approached the edge of the platform and went down on her knees, facing the audience. Then she neatly arranged her dress before and behind, and leaned forward towards the audience, bowing her face in her hands on the floor. After this she got up and sidled out with a kind of Grecian bend, fanning herself proudly like a Dolly Varden. And this concluded the first part of the entertainment.

This was by no means a comic performance, from a Chinese point of view, but a genuine and serious piece of acting, and probably considered by the audience as very high-class and artistic. I noticed particularly that none of the spectators were moved to laughter, but that all looked on in wonder at the leaping and the capering which seemed to us so thoroughly absurd, nor was there any applause whatever either during the piece or after it was concluded. As for ourselves, we were simply overcome at the utter absurdity of the whole thing.

The music that accompanied the performance was of a strange and remarkable description. The band, posed behind the actors against the wall, consisted of seven performers seated in a row (on chairs) conducted by a bare-legged Celestial, who sat on a stool in front of his colleagues with his coat off and his

A PERFORMANCE AT THE CHINESE THEATRE.

arms bared up to the shoulder, and who rapped violently all the while upon a circular piece of stone with two bits of stick. His brother musicians played instruments of various descriptions. There was a gong, a kettle-drum, and a huge pair of cymbals; a violoncello, and an instrument in the background that I could not quite succeed in obtaining a view of, but which produced a sound not unlike the popping of corks; and there were two Chinese fiddles, neither of them in the slightest tune—in fact, what with the clanging of the cymbals and the constant popping of corks, the banging about on the gong and kettle-drum and the grating of the stringed instruments, such an excruciating medley of din and discord I have never before heard, and I certainly never wish to hear again. No time was kept and no regular tune was played, but there was a continual repetition of some strange, meaningless dirge, which had to be often repeated before it could be properly understood. Every player seemed thoroughly in earnest, and worked away at his instrument as if his very existence depended on the amount of noise he could add to the general din and confusion. But if one performer got tired, he would put down his instrument and smoke his clay pipe, and then resume his playing when he felt inclined. Not a single man among the players had a pair of shoes or stockings on.

The second part of the entertainment consisted of a tumbling and acrobatic performance. Preparations for this had been made before the close of the "opera," for during the singing and the capering, while the actors were engaged in their final trial of lungs and legs, some pigtails were busily employed in erecting poles and horizontal bars, and in tying up ropes for performing on, so that directly the made-up female had disappeared behind the scenes after she had made her final bow to the audience, with scarcely a moment's pause—for everything was now ready—the stage was filled with clowns and sprites, tumblers and turn-inside-outers, many of them bared to the waist; and I must say that the performances they went through were executed in first-rate style. A fearful yelling and screeching was kept up the whole time, without intermission—in short, the whole performance seemed to us nothing but a hideous Chinese nightmare. Each tumbler had his fan, and he often managed to tumble with it.

We will now peep into an opium-den. It is the Chinaman's elysium, his heaven upon earth. Here he finds a solace from the cares and anxieties of a wicked, persecuting world. He comes here to revel in transitory bliss, to absorb for a while the somniferous juice that causes him to forget his earthly state, creating for him visions of ethereal splendour and happiness never to be realized.

It was past midnight when we came out from the theatre.

The first thing we did after we emerged again into Jackson-street was to take unto us a second guide—a Chinese policeman, and yet not quite a policeman in the ordinary meaning of the word, for we were about to be taken into the prohibited den. But this person, who had been forewarned by our guide that his services would be required on this occasion, was one appointed by the Chinese to look after and protect their interests, who for a small fee conducts strangers over the opium-dens, and introduces them to prominent smokers. Without him, or some such person duly recognized by the heathen, it would not have been safe to have visited these places. So we found him waiting for us in his house in Jackson-street, ready to escort us immediately below.

The first den we were taken to was a respectable or "high-toned" one. It is the only one that shall be described, for it shall be left to the imagination what the others we went into were like—those not quite so "high-toned"—from the description of the one that I will now proceed to give. Where it lay I cannot exactly tell, indeed I have not now the remotest idea. But I remember that it was somewhere underground, and that in order to reach it we had to feel our way along narrow, dark smelling passages, and down rickety flights of stairs, our guide's guide leading the way with a lighted tallow candle, till at last we came to a quarter known as the Ragpickers' Alley, the haunt of some of the most desperate characters in Chinatown. Our path came to an abrupt termination at a low door at the end of a passage where there was scarcely room to turn round; and a knock upon the door provoked a squeaky response from within, and we entered. The dreadful stench which followed immediately upon the opening of that door well-nigh clean knocked us all down. It was the most incomprehensible odour we had yet experienced in Chinatown. Bottling, however, our aversion to it, we gazed in surprise on the scene which was before us, and the following is what we saw. In a room not more than ten feet square, and scarcely lofty enough to stand upright in, were ranged two rows of hard board beds or bunks, —an upper and a lower row, the lowest row raised three feet above the floor,—and seven bare-legged Chinamen were lying outstretched upon them. Six out of the seven had smoked themselves to sleep, and the other one was about to do so. Under all, upon a bit of matting spread on the floor, was lying the owner of the den, "Old Johnny," well known to our guide's guide—a fat, iron-grey, pigtailed old Chinaman, who cleaned the pipes and sold the opium to smoke. The other Celestials lying about the apartment were his guests for the night. The room was utterly foul and filthy, and was chokefull with smoke; and a single tallow candle on the floor by the side of

INTERIOR OF AN OPIUM-DEN.

the proprietor of the den, spread but a dim light over the apartment, so counteracted was it by the thick fumes of smoke lately produced by the six Chinamen who were lying on their beds in a state of stupefaction. The only attempt at ornamentation was some red and gold paper strips pasted about the walls—the Chinaman's prayers, forsooth, so pasted that he might gaze upon them and invoke his gods while committing himself to bliss. The smokers were given little boxes containing the crude extract of opium, price twenty-five cents per box, and they paid ten cents each for the privilege of a pipe and a bunk. The opium could also be bought in larger measure, at the price of nineteen dollars per pound. The pipe used for smoking the opium is not an ordinary one. It has a thick reed stem of twenty-two inches in length, and the bowl, seven inches from the end of the stem, is an inverted hollow cone of baked clay (coloured to resemble bronze), two inches in diameter at the top, which is flat, and has a small hole about the size of a pin's head bored through the centre. The Chinaman who was still in the possession of his senses we addressed, and having purchased from "Old Johnny" a box of the opium, we asked him to prepare us a pipe, which he willingly consented to do. Given a lighted candle, he took a steel wire of five inches in length, and gathered with it a small quantity of the inspissated juice which was in the box, and held up to the flame what he had so gathered, and kept it there till the glutinous substance became thoroughly roasted and began to frizzle. Then he took his pipe and smeared the hot roasted opium over the flat surface of the bowl, spreading it out like butter, and into the small hole in the centre he inserted the opium as well. Within two minutes after he had commenced this preparation the pipe was ready, and it was handed round to each of us in turn to smoke. My turn came last but one. I took one whiff, then another, then a third, for it was not so bad after all. So said all of us, for the taste and the odour were far from disagreeable. The taste was not unlike that of burnt treacle, and the more one indulged in it the more one liked it. At first it was rather unpleasant, but in time it became savoury and agreeable. We gave John back his pipe and asked him to finish it off for us. He seemed highly pleased, and proceeded to warm up afresh the sticky mass that covered the bowl of his pipe, by holding it to the candle, puffing away vigorously while he did so, and then he fell back on his bunk in a comfortable outstretched position, having evidently made up his mind to enjoy himself thoroughly and go right to sleep. Watching him as he lay, we noticed that he did not, after inhaling, emit the smoke from his mouth; but after several prolonged "draws" it came forth in one long steady puff from his nostrils. Then he took another prolonged series of inhalations, and after a while the smoke was again emitted, and so he continued for a quarter of an hour or more. Meanwhile his eyes were fixed upon us with an imploring, withering stare. He inhaled long and deep, till at last his eyes began to close; we could see that a state of stupefaction was fast creeping upon him; his pipe dropped at last from his clutch—the narcotic poison had now filled him through and through; he lay perfectly stupefied—the opium-smoker was asleep. He dreamt of—bliss of some sort, undoubtedly, from a Chinaman's point of view. But he little knew, or, if he did, little heeded the fact that he was killing himself by slow degrees in order to attain such enthralment; he forgot, too, that he was lowering his whole moral nature by indulging in so filthy and degrading a luxury. But it would have been better to try and reason with a pig than with John Chinaman on the subject of his opium-smoking. And this fellow whom we had watched, smoked, we were told, his dollar's worth a day! When any one of his guests had done his smoking for the night, the dodgy old proprietor took the charred residue of the opium which was left clinging to the pipe, and had it rebaked, and after he had made it up again into fresh opium he re-sold it to the next comer—to save expense.

Now the proprietor, "Old Johnny," was a sight worth noticing. He looked the very essence of good temper, his face beamed with smiles. Upon seeing his little round eyeballs peering forth merrily from the almond-shaped slits, it was impossible to resist feeling a sort of liking for him, even though he looked so yellow, and wore nails on his slim, tapering fingers an inch long at the very least. They (the nails) were the longest I ever remember seeing; but they only showed what a gentleman he was, how delicate was his birth, and how high-toned was his caste, else he would have decently and properly pared them. He had a splendid set of teeth, as white as the purest ivory, as regular as the incisions on a saw, and when he parted his lips to address one they (the teeth) did not project too prominently. His garb was very simple.

Before quitting the premises we asked "Old Johnny" to

show us the method of Chinese counting. He had been busily employing himself while we were standing, watching the smoking, in balancing his accounts, and he did this after the fashion peculiar to all Chinamen. At his side lay a small square piece of framework, and across it were stretched several wires, and upon these were strung several beads

CHINESE MERCHANT BALANCING HIS ACCOUNTS.

representing units, tens, etc. By arranging and re-arranging the several beads in their sets, the Chinaman is able to work out the most difficult arithmetical calculations, and having a good head on his shoulders he generally manages to do so in the shortest space of time. No resort is had to paper, pen, or pencil. We therefore asked him to show us how he worked his machine, and he kindly explained to us the process in the prettiest pigeon-English he could possibly muster. Then we tried to puzzle him by giving him a sum requiring considerable calculation, but instead of this we nearly got puzzled ourselves. Away flew his hands over the board, and the beads in a few seconds had shown the result to his satisfaction before we had ourselves finished the sum we had propounded. As we were leaving, he shook hands with us, and said, " Go' bye. Comee see me again." " No, thanks," said I—in an undertone to my friends. " One visit here is quite enough for a lifetime."

It was a pity the hour was so late, or I might say so early, —it was now 3 a.m.,—as we wished to see a head-shaving operation performed, and to have made ourselves acquainted with the delicate little instruments that are used by the Chinese for removing the hairs from the insides of their noses, and for purging their eyes and ears. But perhaps it is sufficient to know that there are such inventions rather than to see them put into practice.

There is no need to give an account of the other dens we visited, the above description, which will serve for all, being quite sufficient. It was daylight when we got back to our hotel. The adventures of this night now seem like a dream —a very hideous and disturbed dream, quite a nightmare in fact. And no one of our party is likely ever to forget his experiences in Chinatown.

CHAPTER XV.

A TRIP TO THE GEYSERS.

Setting out for the Geysers—A sail up the bay—A barber afloat—Bird's-eye view of the Golden City—The Bay of San Francisco—From Donahue to Cloverdale—The Road to the Geysers—Smothered with dust—Dexterous driving—The Geysers Hotel—Pretty crowded—A rush for beds—Setting out to survey the premises—A foolish adventure—A remarkable spot—Devil's conveniences—The "Steamboat Geyser"—The "Witches' Caldron"—The Geysers mis-named—An early-morning walk round the cañon—Returning to San Francisco—Splendid ride over a mountain pass—Luxuriant growth in a Californian forest—Bark-shedding trees—Fossville—The abode of a veteran driver—A great man with a Californian reputation—Preparing for dinner—A gushing matron—A father reproves his son—Geological curiosity—A forest of stone—The "Pride of the Forest"—How Charlie Evans became a rich man—Average weight of the ladies of Calistoga—Back again in the Golden City.

ON the morning of June 18th we started for a trip to the celebrated hot springs known as the "Geysers" of California. After visiting Iceland together in the summer of 1877, we, my friend and I, could hardly have chosen a more interesting trip. It is a two days' excursion from San Francisco, and available by two routes. By one route the distance is 85 miles, and by the other, 106 miles. We chose of course the round trip, going by one route (the longer one) and returning by the other, thus seeing more of the country.

First we took steamer up the bay for thirty-four miles to a place called Donahue, putting ourselves on board a boat of the North Pacific line at the Washington wharf, which lies near the foot of Market-street. Our boat, the "Donahue," was commodious—was built of wood and painted white as usual. Tea and coffee were obtainable on board, and two small boys were very importunate with baskets of fine ripe peaches, pears and figs. There was a barber's stand on deck, and more than one availed himself of the privilege of being publicly shaved. The weather this morning was highly favourable for the successful performance of an operation requiring such delicate attention, for the boat skimmed over the water without sway or motion, otherwise the consequences to a poor victim at an unlucky moment might have been unpleasant, not to say disastrous. No door or curtain to screen the "patient" from the vulgar gaze, but shaving and hair-cutting were performed alike in full view of everybody. Besides the usual bottles of bay-rum and lime-juice, the barber had for sale many paper collars, hats, ties, and cotton shirts.

When we had got a little out into the bay we obtained a fine bird's-eye view of the metropolis of the Pacific coast, as it lay spread out before us over its several hills. Bathed in the rays of the early-morning sun, the Golden City looked grand indeed. A lively scene it was, too, in the harbour before the city. We threaded our way among a gay collection of craft, vessels from all parts of the world rode at anchor within the bay. Conspicuous amongst all was a British man-of-war (H.M.S. "Shah"); also a Russian man-of-war, and a French schooner. A steamer was pointed out to us getting up steam for Yokohama. It was one of the ten that ply regularly between San Francisco and Japan, and forty other steamships run from the Golden Gate to Australia, New Zealand, Panama, and various ports in South and North America.

Even dry land is not enough to contain this wonderful Golden City of the far West. She must needs encroach into the bay and, Venice-like, build her houses on piles even in water of no moderate depth. It is affirmed that where we now see half a mile of the city—as far back as the Palace Hotel—fronting the open bay, covered with warehouses of iron and granite, ships used to ride at anchor only a few years ago. But now they have been compelled to retire before the advance of the Golden City, which has gradually extended its limits into the bay, having reared itself out of the water upon a foundation of closely-riveted stakes. This encroachment has caused a sea-wall to be built along the water-front of the city, which is sixty-five feet wide at the top, and has its foundations laid at a depth of twenty-six feet below low water mark. New York might take a lesson here from San Francisco.

Our ride to Donahue enabled us to comprehend the splendid capaciousness of this great landlocked bay, though we traversed only about half of it. Approached from sea solely by a deep, narrow strait,—this strait, as we have seen,

THE BAY OF SAN FRANCISCO.
View from Telegraph-hill.

being five miles in length and one mile in width,—the Bay of San Francisco stretches from north to south a length of sixty miles, with an average breadth of eight to ten miles; and a grand sheet of water it is, too, set in the midst of scenery the most beautiful and diversified. Islands are dotted over the bay, and mountain ranges shut in the view to the east, north-west and south. To the west, forty miles beyond Oakland, looms the Contra Costa range, with Monte Diabolo, 3870 feet above the sea-level, its culminating point.

To the immediate north of the Golden Gate, scarcely twelve miles out of San Francisco, is Mount Tamalpais, 2600 feet high, one of the higher peaks of the range which bounds the coast. Of the islands, one, an islet called Alcatraz, guards the entrance to the harbour from the Golden Gate, and is used as a military station, a fort and batteries being erected upon it. Angel Island, north of Alcatraz, is another military station, and rises 800 feet. Goat Island—called also Yerba Buena, which it will be remembered was the old name of San Francisco, or rather of the settlement of the Mission Dolores just beyond the city—we passed on our left soon after weighing anchor. It is also used as a military station, contains about 350 acres and is about 350 feet high. Other islets there are, most of them rocky and bare, which are known by such names as "Old Man and Woman," "Two Sisters," "Grandfather," and "Two Brothers." But they do not require anything further to be said about them.

In two hours and a half we reached Donahue, and changed into the cars of the North Pacific Railroad, which were drawn up in a shed close beside the water's edge. A dusty ride in the train of fifty-six miles brought us to Cloverdale, which is sixteen miles from the Geysers, the latter being reached by road, by the stage line of Messrs. Van Arnam and Kennedy. Apple orchards and apricot groves were numerous along the route between Donahue and Cloverdale, and one place we passed, namely Santa Rosa, had its streets planted with *eucalypti*. Cloverdale rejoices in a population of 500, and can boast of about half a dozen shops and two humble hotels. To one of the latter we repaired, and as the stage was not due to leave for the springs for an hour, we employed the interval in having a wash and a meal. The landlord was an Englishman, and appeared glad to make our acquaintance. At two o'clock —for it was one o'clock when we reached Cloverdale—the coach, a four-in-hand, drew up at the door, and we started away for the springs, driven by Mr. Kennedy himself. The scenery throughout this ride was extremely picturesque, the road leading almost the entire distance up a grand forest gorge, where vegetation abounded in profusion, and an immense variety of lovely plumaged birds flitted about merrily from tree to tree. But leaving out of the question the excessive heat of the sun, which we were now beginning to get accustomed to, we were deprived of all enjoyment of this beautiful ride by the fearful amount of dust that we raked up, which not only blinded and powdered us—got into our eyes and mouths and found its way down our backs; but it is a fact that often for several minutes at a time I could see absolutely nothing of my friend who was sitting barely two feet in front of me, so thick were the dust-clouds we gathered as we proceeded. Our road for some miles lay on the verge of a precipice, the Pluton River foaming about 300 feet below; and never shall we forget the last few miles of the journey, during a gradual descent towards the end of the gorge, how persistently Mr. Kennedy *would* choose just the very edge of the cliff and make our flesh creep as he whirled us along within only a foot or two of death and destruction. However, he was a crack whip, and managed his team splendidly.

On reaching the end, or I should say the head of the cañon, a strong smell of sulphur betrayed the presence of the springs. This odour increased as we approached the hotel—a frail, wooden, two-storied building, almost entirely given up to bedrooms and a balcony, with a good deal of balcony at the expense of the bedrooms. The hotel stands on the mountain side on elevated ground facing the springs, which are seen steaming away in a burnt, bare hollow a quarter of a mile off on the other side of a wooded ravine,—down which flows the Pluton River,—which intervenes between them and the hotel. With the exception of two beds, which were fortunately not engaged, the house was quite full, chiefly with young married couples, for this, the Geysers Hotel, is a favourite summer resort of the San Franciscans and people of California, many of the *élite* coming here and making a prolonged stay. We were not long in securing the two vacant beds, though we were only just in time, as the coach arrived soon after from Calistoga bringing many more visitors, who of course all wanted beds; and as this hotel was the only establishment in the locality that sported such luxuries, the unfortunate new-arrivals had to do as best they could till morning by sleeping outside on the balcony—or by resorting to the meal-room after supper.

When we had made ourselves clean and respectable-looking

once more after such a terribly dusty drive as we had just been through, it wanted about an hour to dinner-time. We had therefore time enough to take a look round and survey the premises. We did so; but we began, after we had crossed the ravine, by taking a wrong path, or I should say no path at all, and almost breaking our necks in endeavouring to clamber up the steep, charred side of the cliff on the opposite bank, where the surface was loose and bare, and where there was nothing to hold on by, as we thought we would strike a trail of our own and so reach the springs by a roundabout way, instead of making for them direct. However, it was my lot to experience, in a marked degree, the uncomfortable sensations of gradually approaching death, for when I had nearly reached the top, and with little short of a hundred feet to tumble down if I should have unhappily lost my balance and fallen, I found myself slipping away each time I moved, unable to advance or retreat, owing to the steepness of the incline and the absence of anything firm to cling on to; and it was only by "hanging on by my eyelids," as the saying is, and supporting my balance with the tips of my fingers and my knees planted firmly into the gravelly surface, that I effected at last a successful crawl to the top, and was able to look back upon the scene of an adventure that was extremely foolhardy, and void of any advantage whatever.

The Californian "Geysers"—or fumaroles, as we shall presently see they ought more properly to be called—lie in groups in a mountain hollow of about a mile square. There must be some thousands of them, even in this small area, for the bottom and steep sides of the hollow or cañon are completely riddled with holes, and so thin is the crust of sulphur forming the surface of the ground, that as you walk you can press up in places the boiling water that lies beneath your tread, which causes you to be on the constant look-out and to watch where you really do place your foot for fear it should inadvertently be lodged in a little boiling pond. From a number of these orifices proceeds a hissing, fizzing sound, and the air emitted from them is so hot and scalding that you cannot place your finger at their mouth and keep it there for more than a second at a time, for it is just like putting it in the fire. The smell of the sulphureous vapour ascending from these holes is sometimes quite overpowering.

In this small cañon are springs of various temperatures and impregnated with various minerals. Here extremes meet. Hot springs lie next to the cold, sweet springs next door to the acid and the bitter. Here is sufficient to cure all the diseases in Christendom. Springs of Epsom salts, ammonia, magnesia,

THE CALIFORNIAN GEYSERS.
View of the cañon.

tartaric acid, soda, sulphur, iron, alum, copperas, and cinnabar. An "eye-water" spring to cure bad eyes, a "lemonade" spring to remove freckles from the skin and make one beautiful for ever. A spring specially warranted to cure rheumatic gout, another strongly recommended in cases of asthma. A boiling black sulphur spring and a boiling black ink spring. A cold soda-and-iron spring and a tepid iron-and-soda spring. A "Devil's Inkstand," a "Devil's Caldron," a "Devil's Tea-kettle," a "Devil's Kitchen," a "Devil's Grist-mill," and a "Pluto's Punch-bowl."

There is the "Steamboat Geyser" and the "Steam Iron Bath," the latter with a temperature of 183° Fahr. The "Steamboat Geyser" is the greatest "roarer" in the whole collection, the sound it produces being perfectly deafening when you are standing close beside it. It is so named because the loud fizzing noise that it produces is supposed to resemble that of steam escaping from the boiler of an engine. The lion of all, though, is the "Witches' Caldron." This is a deep, bubbling, circular pool of eight feet in diameter, as black as the blackest ink, horrible to look at, its waters semi-liquid and strongly impregnated with sulphur. The temperature of this spring is 212° Fahr. A short distance above the hollow, over the shoulder of the cañon, are some beds of lava, thus showing to anyone who looked for a tangible proof, that the whole of this locality once suffered from the effects of volcanic eruption. Close to these lava beds is the "Indian Sweat Bath," where the Indians used to bring their sick to be cured by the process of sweating. The temperature of this spring is also up to boiling point. Within only a few yards of many of the springs there are trees—such as the oak, laurel, pine, and alder —growing in richest luxuriance ; and this, considering the extreme heat of the earth in such close proximity to them, seems to me one of the most extraordinary features of the cañon. Indeed the whole of this region, bare and charred as it is, hot and perforated throughout with thousands of orifices and steam-vents, smoking and perpetually resounding with an uproar of mechanical noises, is surrounded with the loveliest of forest scenery, the smoking hollow and the wooded glen forming together a striking natural contrast.

It would be hard, I should think, to find another spot where there is, in so small a compass, such a number of springs containing so many varieties of minerals, and where extremes meet so singularly ; but that these springs are not veritable geysers will be seen if we turn to Iceland for one moment. "Geyser" or "geysir" is from the Icelandic word *geysa*, (the modern form of the old Scandinavian root *gjosa*), meaning, according to Vigfusson, to " rush furiously," or to " gush ;" or, according to Paijkull, to "ascend violently." If then, by "gushing" or "ascending violently" is meant the strong ebullition of hot air accompanied by a loud fizzing sound but *un*accompanied by the eruption of water, then nothing further need be said on the subject. But I believe I am right in affirming that there is no actual eruption of water from any spring in the cañon, except from that of the "Witches' Caldron," and the water of this spring ascends only a foot or two at the most. In Iceland, however, the term "geyser" is applied by the people of that island to one erupting spring only, namely the Great Geyser in Haukadalr, near Reykjavik; and surely all those springs in the island which send up volumes of water—and how many there are it would be impossible to say—would certainly with more reason come under the term "geyser" than any one of these so-called "geysers" of California. The Californian Geysers are rather fumaroles—an immense collection of vents from which hot air is emitted. But it is wrong to give them a name which implies they are a collection of boiling fountains.

Before starting the next morning (June 19th) on our return to San Francisco, we got up early to see the springs in company with the hotel guide, who called a large party of us at four o'clock. He was the boots, milkman, and general gardener of the establishment, and he had an original explanation to offer as to the cause of the impregnation of each spring that we came to, when we asked for an explanation to be given. I hope he knew more about milk and blacking than he did about the springs. The reason we got up at such an early hour and revisited the cañon was because the springs are seen to best advantage at that time of day, before the steam ascending from them is eaten up by the heat of the sun. Thus the "Witches' Caldron," which, when we saw it the day before, emitted very thin clouds of steam, was this morning so enveloped in its own thick white vapour, that when we came and stood on the brink and looked down into it, though the water was nearly bubbling over the top of the basin, we could see nothing; and yet the belching, seething fury of waters gurgled and frizzed away beneath us in grand style.

At eight o'clock we left the Geysers to return to San Francisco, taking a different route to the one we had come by, in order to see, more especially, one of the most interesting natural curiosities in California, namely a petrified forest near Calistoga. First twenty-two miles' staging up a pass and down again, to Calistoga; then by rail thirty-eight miles to Vallejo; from thence by steamer twenty-five miles down the bay to San Francisco.

To day's was a splendid drive, a grander—or rather a more picturesque—it would be hard to call to mind. The scenery was Norwegian, but equal if not superior to some of the finest parts of that forest country. Here, too, the atmosphere was clearer, the pines taller, the foliage more varied, trees beautiful and new, wild flowers strange, lovely birds numerous —roads dustier than ever. First we made a steep ascent for several miles through forests to the summit of a magnificent pass, obtaining, as we ascended, such glorious views on our left over the luxuriant and seemingly interminable forests covering the sides of the mountains that rose on the other side of the valley, the mountains, too, of such rich and exquisitely striking colours, and the foliage around so beautiful and diversified, that it now seems more like a dream, when we come to look back upon such a lovely combination of natural landscapes as are to be seen on the road between the Geysers and Calistoga. Trees we had never before seen grew around us here in the greatest profusion. There was the madroña (*Arbutus menziesii*), a tree often met with in the forests of California, growing to a moderate height, about fifty feet; and whereas most other trees shed their leaves only, it has the peculiarity (like the planes) of shedding both bark and leaves. The bark before it is shed is of a dark, reddish-brown colour, but after it is shed the tree is the colour of bright salmon, which gradually becomes darker as the next shedding time comes round. Then there was the buckeye, or Californian horse-chestnut (*Æsculus californica*), with blossom and leaf resembling our English horse-chestnut's; but the tree is more stunted in growth, for it seldom exceeds fifteen or twenty feet in height. There was also the manzinita (*Arctostaphylos glauca*), or "little apple," a dwarf tree or shrub also shedding its bark, like the madroña. It has twisting, curling branches, and a small oval-shaped leaf, the shape of a walnut when cracked open. A walking-stick fashioned from the wood of the manzinita is considered a curiosity, for the branches of this tree curl and intertwine in such a way that it is difficult to find a piece of wood sufficiently straight to make one. Indeed the branches have to be straightened out by steam, and by hanging weights at the bottom. The wood polishes up finely, so much so that when polished it has the rich, dark appearance of mahogany. The root is much sought after by stick and umbrella makers. A parasol with a manzinita handle made from the root, or a workbox of the same, is considered a very appropriate present for a young lady "out West." Some of the pines grew to enormous heights. These were mostly the sugar-pine (*Pinus lambertiana*), one of the monarchs of the Californian forest, growing abundantly everywhere, and often attaining the height of 250 feet. We noticed that many of the trunks had vines clinging to them, to the height of fifty feet or more. Apricot-trees, with plenty of fruit on them, too, grew in the woods in profusion close beside the road. The forest teemed with life—never before have I seen such a splendid collection of the feathered tribe. We chased Californian quails along the road. There were scores of them on the banks, always in pairs, cock and hen together. It was interesting to watch a pair of these black-topknotted, perky little creatures scuttle away ahead of us as we approached them, first quickly pattering their feet for a few yards like bits of machinery, then suddenly stopping short and looking round, then moving on some more yards another pattering, then pulling up again, then on once more when we got too near to be pleasant—till at last, being fairly out of the way, having, perhaps, run up on to some bank, and the cock having scuttled off in a different direction to the hen, they would both stand still where they were and jerk their heads backwards and forwards, and continue to do so until all danger was past. Woodpeckers were the most numerous of the birds we noticed. We must have seen hundreds of them hard at work boring their holes in the pine-trunks, into which they would store away the acorns or hazel-nuts for their winter and spring supply. Every trunk selected was peppered full of these holes. Squirrels abounded in the woods; but these were the only animals we saw from our coach.

At the top of the pass we obtained a glorious, sweeping

view, embracing both land and sea. Westward we could see the Pacific, and southward we could trace the Coast Range Mountains stretching far away into California. We came a slashing pace down the mountain into the open country, till we reached Fossville, five miles from Calistoga. At Fossville —a collection of a few wooden shanties—lives Clark Foss, the celebrated crack whip, who has given his name to the locality. Foss and his son drive the stages between Calistoga and the Geysers, and the rivalry between them and the drivers on the Cloverdale route is as keen as might be expected. The father has a Californian reputation, for he always drives his passengers with a team of six horses, thus creating a sensation. The pace he is said to take his six-in-hand down the mountain along a not so very wide road—bordered as it is most of the way with a precipice inclined at times to be rather too abrupt, and with its edge too unpleasantly close to the wheels of the coach as you are helplessly spun along—has no doubt gone a good way towards gaining him the reputation he has been so successful in establishing. At his house we stopped for dinner, and were entertained by his spouse, a clean, tidy, fresh-looking buxom matron, a fitting mate for so great a man. She took us to a pump in her verandah at the back of the house, and presented us each with a piece of soap, at the same time intimating that we had better wash and get ready for dinner. This pump seemed to serve as the public lavatory of the neighbourhood, for others after we had finished came and washed themselves likewise—three workmen in the village, forsooth, who, unasked, walked into the house and into the verandah and gave themselves a wash and a brush; and the poor fellows seemed to sadly need the washing and the brushing they gave themselves, for the day was very warm,—the mercury pointing to 95° in the shade,—and the dust lay about the roads several inches in depth. The men walked into the house the colour of brown paper; but it was difficult to recognize them as they walked out, such a thorough cleansing had they undergone. We were sorely disappointed at not seeing the crack whip himself, for he was away from home, having taken a holiday and gone on a shopping expedition in Calistoga. His good lady, however, to whom we revealed at dinner our interest in her "old man," as she called him,—thus bringing the blushes to her face and causing her to look pleased,—was kind enough to say, " Foss will be home in a few minutes, and will be pleased to give you his photograph!" This was really too much ; such liberality was more than we expected. But the few minutes came and went, and yet no Foss arrived. And now the stage was waiting at the door, waiting to take us on to the petrified forest. We said, "We cannot wait any longer, Mrs. Foss, so will you tell your husband how sorry we are we have missed the pleasure of seeing him?" "I'm proud, gentlemen, I'm real proud," exclaimed Mrs. Foss. "But no doubt you can get his likeness in Calistoga. Foss keeps all his photos locked up." So with a hearty shake of the hand we jumped into the stage, and were out of sight of Fossville in a twinkling. We had not proceeded far before we met the veteran himself, driving home from market in a buggy. He pulled up, and so did we ; but as we were alone in the stage,—the other passengers having stayed behind at Fossville,—the son of Foss, who was driving us, happened to be taking liberties at the time, urging along his four-horse team at a flying gallop. " Now ease them horses and drive at a Christian pace, can't you, boy?" thundered out the father to the son. The "boy" did as he was told, and eased them immediately. And now father and son were face to face. " Now didn't I tell you that that mare was to be handled gintly, so what d'ye mean by going the like o' that?" There was no help for it, the "boy"—he was at least twenty-five years of age—was in error, and expostulation useless. As for ourselves we were held in speechless amazement at the sight of so great a man. Instead of asking him for his photograph we simply gave him two of our blandest smiles, said " Good afternoon " with hats raised, and passed on.

We drove to within a mile of Calistoga and then diverged to the right, leaving the main road and the corn-fields that bordered it, and ascending through forests the spur of a mountain, till, in five miles, we came to the wonderful geological curiosity which I will now attempt to describe. Within an area of about thirty acres, mostly on sloping ground, were lying prostrate and plainly visible one hundred or more petrified trunks and stumps of trees, the majority if not the whole of them lying in one direction ; and besides these there were many more, all of them also petrified, which, covering a larger area, had been simply outlined or partially excavated from the earth and volcanic matter in which they had become imbedded—for as yet they had only been traced, the work of excavation not having proceeded far. Judging by the dimensions of some of the more exposed trunks, these trees must indeed have been veritable monsters. One of them, which has been appropriately designated the "Pride of the Forest," measured eleven feet across the stump, and thirty feet up the trunk the diameter was seven feet. The tree reveals its own growth, for by the grain of the wood its age has been traced to 1100 years—that is, of course, its age before it became thrown and turned into stone. This great fellow lay thoroughly exposed, and, apart from its size, was a geological curiosity in the fact of its having an almost perfect petrified bark; and a portion of its wood was not wholly petrified, but was just in its original state as if the tree were alive. The ground around the trunk glistened with deposits of crystallized silica; and chips of petrified charcoal, so crisp as to break in pieces with the slightest amount of pressure, were lying scattered about, showing that heat had in some way been brought to bear upon the wood before petrifaction set in. Some terrible convulsion of Nature, possibly a volcanic eruption, must suddenly have overturned these once monarchs of the forest, and have buried them out of sight; and as there is an extinct volcano in the vicinity, namely Mt. St. Helena (which rises to a height of 3700 feet above the sea-level), it does not seem improbable that such was the case, and that Mt. St. Helena had something to do with it.

Though this splendid forest of petrified trees had, when we visited the collection, only been excavated and outlined to the extent of thirty acres, it is probable that it extends over a much larger area, as fresh specimens were then being continually unearthed. Many of those which had been simply outlined lay covered with gravel and brushwood about three feet or so in depth. All the trees, as I have already mentioned, were prostrate, and lying in one direction—from north to south.

This forest was, I believe, discovered in 1867. To the credit of one "Charlie" Evans, a Swede, is due its excavation and disclosure, though whether he was the actual discoverer of it I am unable to say. However, he became an early possessor of the forest by obtaining a grant of the land from Government—before it was known that there were any petrified trees underground; and now he is complete master of the situation. He has set up a shanty at the entrance to his demesne, which serves as a toll-gate, for Charlie Evans knows well indeed how to charge those who come to pay his trees a visit, and thus does he reap a very considerable income. In appearance a common farm-labourer, we found him in a high state of glee, as he was expecting his sister from Stockholm, for, not having seen her for many years, he had sent for her to come out to him and become a sharer in his profits. He became hilarious when we told him that we had been in the "Venice of the North," and he endeavoured to explain to us the exact position of his sister's country shanty; but in this he did not succeed. He very kindly allowed us to pick up and carry away as many specimens of the petrified wood and charcoal as we liked, whatever there was lying about, charging us half a dollar for doing so. In his cabin he had many fine polished pieces of petrified roots of the trees, as well as some splendid agatized specimens, all obtained from this forest.

The petrified forest explored, we came on to Calistoga, a town with 1700 inhabitants, chiefly famed for its hot sulphur springs. We learn from the *San Francisco Chronicle* that the ladies of Calistoga weigh, on an average, 120 lbs. each.

Calistoga is the terminus of the California Pacific Railroad. We took the train for thirty-eight miles to Vallejo, passing the town of St. Helena (1200 inhabitants), famed for its white sulphur springs, and the "city" of Napa (5000 inhabitants), famed for soda as well as for sulphur springs. From Vallejo, which is a small port lying at the extreme north-eastern end of the Bay of San Francisco, we took steamer twenty-three miles back to the Golden City, and reached the Palace Hotel at 9.30 p.m.

CHAPTER XVI.

THE GIANT TREES OF CALAVERAS.

Leaving San Francisco—Visions of the Yosemite Valley—How to reach it from the Golden City—Stockton—A night with a mosquito—A Chinese family—On the road to the Giant Trees—A refreshing draught of cold water—An army of small frogs—Dinner in the thick forest—A cosmopolitan mining district—Murphy's—Grand drive through the woods—The Calaveras Mammoth Grove—Passing between the "Two Sentinels"—Fashionable quarters in the wild forest—Wonders of Nature—The "Father" and "Mother of the Forest"—Other fine trees—The Three Graces—A "mother" fifty feet in circumference—A pair of Siamese Twins—The greatest wonder of all—A novel ball-room—"John Bright" and "Richard Cobden," etc.—Monster pitch-pine cones—Lovers again—Other mammoth groves.

ON June 20th we left San Francisco and commenced our homeward journey. We took "through" tickets to New York, and with the same tickets we could break our journey at whatever place we liked on the route that we chose, though it comprised almost the whole breadth of the United States. We intended, in the first place, to break the journey at Stockton, in order to make an excursion from that city to the "Big" Trees and the Yosemite Valley, both lying in the heart of the Sierra Nevada Mountains.

There are four routes by which the Yosemite Valley can be approached from the Golden City. Neither of these is very direct, and each necessitates a rough "stage" drive of at least eighty miles. One can either take the Mariposa route, namely by way of Lathrop and Merced, and the Mariposa grove of Giant Trees, in which case there are 151 miles to accomplish by train (to Merced), and a stage drive afterwards of 97 miles—total 248 miles; or one can go by way of the

Coulterville route, that is, to Merced 151 miles by train, after which there are eighty-eight miles to accomplish by stage—total 239 miles; or one can go by the Madera route, namely 173 miles by rail to Madera, and eighty-two miles afterwards by stage—total 255 miles, this route affording the opportunity of seeing the Fresno Mammoth Grove; lastly, the Big Oak Flat and Calaveras route may be taken, in which case there is a railway journey of 120 miles followed by a drive of 150 miles, including fifteen miles' divergence from the main road to the Calaveras Grove and fifteen miles back—total 274 miles. Though the longer and more tedious route, we chose the last-named, as it would enable us to see some of the largest specimens of the giant *Wellingtonias* growing in the Sierra Nevada. Of these there are a few " groves "—I believe seven in number. The Calaveras and the Mariposa are the two finest, and between these there is not much to choose, for though there are more specimens in the latter grove, in the Calaveras the trees are generally taller. It was therefore the Calaveras Grove that we decided to see on our way to the Yosemite.

Bidding final adieu to San Francisco, we crossed the bay to Oakland, and took the Pacific Railroad for ninety-two miles to Stockton. Reaching the "City of Windmills" at 9 p.m., we put up at the hotel called the Yosemite House. Stockton is famed more for its mosquitos than its windmills. This part of California is full of these tormentors, and, like Van Shaack, they "want you bad." We knew we should suffer here, we had been told we should; but we never expected—at least I did not—that our sufferings would last through a whole night. I had not only a mosquito curtain to my bed, but the whole of it was mosquito-curtained, at the sides and overhead. I laid myself to rest beneath a canopy of muslin, and great was the care I took when I came to slip myself in between the folds of muslin at the side so as not to admit an intruder at the same time. I had been bitten quite enough whilst undressing, for the brutes made such an onslaught on me, and with such signal success, that my face and hands soon became covered with little swellings, though I rejoice to say that I succeeded in killing a fair number of victims before I came to take to my rest. Judge then my mortification when I found just as I was comfortably snoozing away that there was one inside the muslin curtains! There was no mistaking him—there he was, buzzing away around the top of my head. "This creature must be caught," said I; and I thereupon proceeded to catch him. Owing to the darkness —for I had unfortunately turned off the gas—the most I could do was to allow him to settle quietly, and then bring my hand down with a good hard rap on whatever part of my head he selected for his meal. This I did several times, but am bound to say without experiencing that success which I think was my due considering the lateness of the hour. At length I gave up the attempt in despair, and withdrew my exposed head far down under the bedclothes, feeling sure that even if I were nearly smothered in the endeavour to obtain some sleep, I should at least be safe from the attacks of my enemy. "Now what's that?" I soon exclaimed, feeling a sort of tickling sensation just below the right hip, as if something was taking a walk towards the bottom of my leg. "Whow —ugh!" I screamed in pain. I had been bitten, the mosquito had got into bed with me! What was I to do? Ring the bell?—no, that would be foolish. I must try again and terminate this little beast's existence. After many vain attempts to do so, prolonged even unto daylight, I was at last successful, for at a lucky moment I managed to settle my enemy for ever—he settled again and I settled him. I was now able to snatch an hour's sleep before breakfast.

As we intended to return to Stockton after the Yosemite trip, before proceeding East, we deposited at the hotel all our baggage, with the exception of what we should want to enable us to travel comfortably for a short time, and arranged to call for our paraphernalia in ten days. So at eight o'clock on the morning of June 21st, we left Stockton, taking the train to Milton, a distance of twenty-eight miles. In our car was a Chinese family—father, mother, two small boys, one little girl, and a baby-in-arms. The father had a magnificent caudal appendage, and his head was shaven blue as usual, save from where the pigtail sprouted. The mother wore the full complement of hair; but she was a curious, diminutive-looking little body, and her skin was the colour one's fingers get after handling unripe walnuts. The two sons wore queues like their father's—very fine ones, considering the ages of the lads; but their heads were otherwise shaven blue. In the little girl and the baby there was nothing particular to notice, save that their complexion very much resembled that of their mother.

At Milton, a small place, we found an open four-in-hand break waiting to take us to the Calaveras Grove, which lay forty-five miles distant; and as it was "All aboard, all aboard" directly we got out of the train, we started off immediately without loss of time. The first dozen miles—a gradual ascent out of the plains of the Sacramento River—were over a bare, monotonous country, though fine oaks grew here and there in their solitude. The first halt we made was to get water, for both passengers and horses. In such a hot climate as this, water is necessary, and is always at hand; and in nine cases out of ten it is iced, as it was in this case. The mercury here was 102° in the shade. It was a solitary farm-house where we pulled up to drink, but around it were growing some very fine fig-trees laden with fruit, and an apple orchard. Indeed it was a little oasis in what was almost a desert, the country for some miles around being sparsely clothed with oaks growing out of the brown, burnt-up grass; but the forests of the Sierra rose before us in the distance, into which we were about to penetrate. Just beyond the farm we came to a large reservoir, and overhead there were hovering several black hawks. Keeping along the bank of the reservoir, we drove into a host of small frogs. There must have been millions of the little creatures, and I am sure we killed thousands as we dashed straight into the middle of the thick brown mass.

In a few miles we began to ascend the high country in earnest. The road was very steep and badly made—the dust dreadful. The jolting we now had to endure was almost unendurable. Passing through dense forests of pine, we reached, at one o'clock, a lonely little shanty, kept by a German, where we stayed to have a wash and a brush, and then dinner. We sat down to dine, a party of six, and we were each given a plateful of roast mutton, with the addition of some fig-jam, this being followed by whortle-berry pie and sago pudding. Our host was short of plates, for we were

THE "TWO SENTINELS," CALAVERAS MAMMOTH GROVE.

Page 326.

allowed only one apiece to make use of during the repast; besides, the knife and fork we devoted to the mutton and jam had to be used for the sago pudding and whortle-berry pie as well. I noticed here an instance of a Yankee's want of refinement which, though exceptional, I grant, surpasses anything I have yet seen at table. We were short of plates, as I have said; but an American, who was sitting opposite me, soon settled this little difficulty—when he came to help pudding on to his plate which had lately been filled with mutton and jam—by taking his handkerchief out of his pocket and wiping over his plate with it!

Starting once more, we passed through an extensive gold-mining district,—where were Americans, Chinamen, Frenchmen, Italians, and probably Englishmen, diligently seeking for the hidden treasure,—and reached Murphy's, fifteen miles from the Calaveras Grove, where we changed horses and coach. Murphy's is a little place consisting of a single street planted with an avenue of acacias, and is called after the name of the former proprietor of the inn we drove up to, who was one of the first discoverers of gold in the locality.

We continued to drive for five hours after leaving Murphy's, the road traversing, as it seemed, the wildest and thickest part of the forest, the sugar pines (*Pinus lambertiana*) around us growing to exceptional heights, and other majestic trees such as the redwood (*Sequoia sempervirens*), the yellow pine (*Pinus ponderosa*), the red fir or Douglas spruce (*Abies douglasii*), —besides sycamores, cedars, evergreen oaks, and laurels,— springing up thickly with the sugar pines, each contributing to the splendour, luxuriance and variety of foliage which constitute the characteristic features of a Californian forest; till at last, when it became so dark that we could scarcely find our way owing to what little light there was being shut out by the denseness of the foliage overhead, we reached the Calaveras Grove at 9.15 p.m., and were just able to catch sight of two monster trunks—the "Two Sentinels," which guard the entrance to the Grove—as we dashed past them into the open space which has been cleared away in the forest to make room for the hotel and premises. In front of the hotel a large bonfire was burning; and before we had pulled up and got down from the coach, we could see, by the number and the "style" of the people who crowded out of the building to inspect us new-arrivals, that we had come to another fashionable resort of the Californians.

The Calaveras Grove contains between ninety and a hundred " big " specimens of the *Wellingtonia* or *Sequoia gigantea*,[1] which spring up in the thick forest comparatively close to each other, all within an area of fifty acres. Running up as straight as arrows to the height of some of the loftiest buildings in the world, these vegetable monsters are, we shall see, no less remarkable for the prodigious girth of their trunks. There are trees in this grove over 300 feet high, and one prostrate trunk measures more than 400 feet. Let us take the last-mentioned. It has been called the "Father of the Forest," and measures 430 feet in length,—that is, it is 102 feet higher than is the top of St. Paul's Cathedral above the ground, or but thirty-eight feet lower than the top of the spire of Strasbourg Minster. This veteran measures 110 feet in circumference at the base, and the trunk runs for 210 feet before the first branch is thrown out. Three hundred feet up the trunk there occurs a break, owing to the tree having come into collision with another as it fell to the ground. The girth of the trunk at this point—300 feet from the roots—is eighteen feet. The trunk is mostly hollow, for there is a tunnel inside extending for 200 feet, and along thirty-five feet of this there is height and room enough to ride about on horseback, right inside the tree. By means of a ladder an ascent can be made to the top of the fallen trunk, and here one can enjoy a walk before breakfast

---

[1] The *Wellingtonia gigantea* of scientific nomenclature was so named by Dr. Lindley in 1853, three years after its discovery; but the *Sequoia gigantea* was so called from a chief—Sequoia or Sequoyah by name—of the Cherokee tribe of Indians, who made himself famous by inventing an alphabet for his tribe. American botanists claim that this tree is closely allied to the redwood or *Sequoia sempervirens*, which grows freely in the forests of the Sierra Nevada and Coast Range Mountains. "It is to the happy accident of the generic agreement of the Big Tree with the redwood, that we owe it that we are not now obliged to call the largest and most interesting tree of America after an English military hero. Had it been an English botanist of the highest eminence, the dose would not have been so unpalatable."—J. D. Whitney, State Geologist of California.

THE "FATHER OF THE FOREST," CALAVERAS MAMMOTH GROVE.

of a morning, and acquire a good appetite for it by pacing backwards and forwards. Care, however, must be taken to

THE "MOTHER OF THE FOREST."

keep on the move all the while, for the bark is so rotten that swarms of earwigs and stinging insects have made themselves a home upon it; so that if you loitered at all, the consequences would be serious. After the "Father" we will take the "Mother of the Forest." The tree so called stands at the far end of the enclosure away from the hotel, and is 327 feet high, being the tallest standing tree in the grove. Not a vestige of foliage is there upon it, for it rears itself a gigantic dead trunk, mostly bare, since the bark has been stripped to a height of 116 feet, and nearly all the remainder has been destroyed by the ravages of fire. The bark so removed was taken to the Crystal Palace, Sydenham, and there set up; but it was unfortunately destroyed by the fire which consumed a portion of that building in December, 1866. This tree, barkless as it is, has a circumference of seventy-eight feet, and it throws out its first branch at a height of 137 feet. A great living wonder is the "Pioneers' Cabin," which stands over 300 feet high, and is so called from a large recess or cavern in the lower part of the trunk, which is capacious enough to comfortably seat a large family party at breakfast. The circumference of this tree five feet above the ground is ninety feet, by our admeasurement. There is a grand prostrate monster, called the "Burnt Tree," which measures 330 feet in length, and has a circumference of ninety-seven feet. It is hollowed from repeated fires, and one can ride on horseback into the trunk for a distance of sixty feet—in one way and out the other. "Keystone State" and "General Jackson" grow respectively to heights of 325 feet and 319 feet, and "Daniel Webster" has a height of 307 feet. Perhaps one of the most striking sights in the grove is the "Three Graces," or "Em, Carrie, and Belle," as they are called. They stand but a few feet apart, and with their branches intermingling run up to an almost equal height of 262 feet, this being the height of the tallest "Grace." The same with the "Mother and her Sons." Running up to about the same height as the Graces, the trio stand in close proximity to each other, and one of them, the Mother, is fat and bulky,—she is over fifty feet in circumference,—but her children beside her are slim and "lanky." The "Siamese Twins," too, are great curiosities. There are two sets of this particular species of twins in this grove, the specimens in each being a little under 300 feet high, both sets of twins having the peculiarity of union some forty or fifty feet above the ground, which makes them, indeed, very wonderful curiosities. The greatest wonder, however, has yet to be mentioned. This is a big monster which has been purposely thrown, having been severed six feet above the ground and a pavilion built on the remaining stump, which has been converted into a theatre and a ball-room. On this stump dramatic performances have been held; and the surface having been properly smoothed over, upon it a dance is indulged in occasionally by the guests at the hotel, sixteen couples having danced upon it at one time; and again, the *cotillon* has been performed upon it by twenty couples! We measured the dancing space across, and found the exact diameter 28 ft. 8 in. This stump has also been utilized as a newspaper office, for upon it, in 1858, the *Big Tree Bulletin* used to be printed. It took five men twenty-two days to cut in twain this monster tree, by boring it through with pump augers, and even then it would not fall, for it required three additional days before it could be induced, by means of bolts driven in at the side, to quit its ancient foundation. This tree is said to have been over 300 feet in height. The girth of the stump is ninety-six feet.

Besides those already mentioned, there are other gigantic specimens, all more or less remarkable for their immensity of height as for their hugeness of bulk, and to some the Americans have given the names of their worthiest men, past and present, and have also been good enough to honour our nation by affixing to a few the names of some of our well-known people. Thus there is "John Bright" and "Richard Cobden" standing side by side. "Miss Burdett Coutts" and "Florence Nightingale" are also fine trees. (The last-named was originally called the "Nightingale," simply; but in 1865 the word "Florence" was added, to perpetuate the memory of Miss Florence Nightingale.) The following is a list of a few other trees we noted: "George Washington;" "Abraham Lincoln;" "Lafayette;" "U. S. Grant;" "W. T. Sherman;" "J. B. McPherson;" "Henry Ward Beecher;" "Columbus;" "Sir John Franklin;" "Humboldt;" "Dr. John Torrey;" "Prof. Asa Grey;" "Longfellow;" "Wm. Cullen Bryant;" "Prof. James Dana;" "Sir Joseph Hooker;" "John Lindley;" "Phil. Sheridan;" "Elihu Burritt;" "General Sutter;" "Bishop Kip;" "General Scott;" "Major Gen. G. A.

Thomas;" "Dr. Kane;" "Andrew Jackson," 'Daniel O'Connell;" "Henry Clay;" "Uncle Sam;" "Uncle Tom's Cabin;" "Old Maid;" "Old Bachelor;" "Old Dominion;" "Old Republican," etc.

Sugar and pitch pines, Douglas spruces and cedars, spring up thickly in this grove, growing to immense heights; but they seem entirely dwarfed when regarded by the side of the Giant Tree. Throughout the enclosure the ground is be-

THE "JOHN TORREY" GROUP.

strewn with cones of an enormous size, some eighteen to twenty inches in length—these being the cones of the pitch pine, not those of the *Wellingtonia*, which, curiously enough, are very small, not much larger than a hen's egg. Paths have been cut through the grove for the convenience of the guests staying at the hotel, which is within a stone's throw of the nearest Giant Tree, and between many of the trees we found chairs and forms placed for the convenience of lovers, of whom there appeared to be—judging by their conversation and manners—a good number of pairs tarrying here for a season.

Now concerning the age of these giant *Wellingtonias*, it seems hard to comprehend their antiquity even with such facts before one as are to be found in the immense number of rings that can be counted on some of the severed, prostrate trunks. My friend counted on one tree as many as two thousand rings. If each one of these rings represents a year's growth, then this tree is two thousand years old at the very least. Report goes that a tree has been found in the Mariposa Grove with six thousand rings in it. If such is the case, though I rather doubt it, can this tree be six thousand years old?[2]

The Calaveras Grove lies about 4700 feet above the sea-level. It was first sighted in the year 1850, by Messrs. Wooster and Whitehead; and as it was the first collection of these trees discovered, it may be said that it was in this year that these giant specimens of the taxodium family became known to civilization. Since then six "groves" have been discovered, all lying in the Sierra Nevada. In the Mariposa Grove, already mentioned, there are 365 Giant Trees, and 125 of them have a girth of forty feet. The other groves are the

[2] The following remarks on the Giant Trees by Sir J. D. Hooker, which appeared in the *Gardeners' Chronicle* of August 17, 1878, may be read with interest: "So little that is trustworthy has hitherto been published regarding the age, size, and durability of the Big Tree trunks when fallen, that I shall offer you some accurate data which I obtained on these points chiefly from Mr. Muir. A tree felled in 1875 had no appearance of age; it was sixty-nine feet in girth inside the bark, and the number of annual rings counted by three persons varied between 2125 and 2139. Another was 107 feet in girth inside the bark at four feet from the ground; its wood was very compact, and showed, throughout a considerable portion of the trunk, thirty annual rings to the inch. This, if the rings were of uniform diameter in the rest of the trunk, would give the incredible age of 6400 years; but as the interior rings of such trees are much broader than the outer, half that number to the inch is a more conceivable estimate, and would give an age of 3500 years. The only other instance of careful counting which I can find is that of the felled tree in the Calaveras Grove, which measured seventy feet in girth inside the bark at six feet above the ground, and which at forty feet above the ground had 1255 rings. In this case the rings next the bark were thirty-three to the inch, a number which at five feet inward had diminished one-half."

South Park, with 1380 trees; the South Tuolumne, with thirty trees; the San Joaquin, with 700 trees; the Fresno, with 500 trees; and a long belt extending for fifty miles between the King's and Kaweah Rivers, where there are several thousand. The South Park Grove is only five miles from the Calaveras Grove. The South Tuolumne Grove lies on our route to the Yosemite.

THE "PIONEER'S CABIN."
(*See page* 330.)

CHAPTER XVII.

THE ROAD TO THE YOSEMITE.

On the road to the Yosemite—A "Digger" Indian—No accounting for taste—Columbia gold-diggings—Slightly warm—Dinner at Sonora—The white-paint nuisance again—Chinese camp—A Polish count—A Jehu madly drives—"Wouldn't you like a wash?"—Driver and passenger take a drive together—Crossing the Tuolumne River—Up Rattlesnake Hill—Under the tender care of Mrs. Priest—We rise at four o' the morning—A Jehu madly drives—A mixture of everything—The village of Big Oak Flat—Colfax Springs—Hodgson's—An ostler's ditty—The charm of a ride in a Californian forest—The Tuolumne Mammoth Grove—Driving through a Giant Tree—Siamese Twins—Almost a collision—Narrow escape—Magnificent view—Our driver's laundry in the Valley—Shakespeare in California—The Yosemite Valley.

AFTER remaining a couple of days at the Calaveras Grove, we set out—on the evening of June 23rd—for the Yosemite Valley, first driving back the fifteen miles through the forest to "Murphy's," where we put up for the night, so that we might make an actual start for the Valley by the coach which would leave that place early on the following morning.

June 24th.

Murphy's is ninety miles from the Yosemite Valley, or two days' staging. We started away at six o'clock this morning in a four-in-hand break to accomplish just half that distance, namely forty-five miles to "Priest's."

Three miles on our way we met an Ute or "Digger" Indian, who stood and made a horrible face at us as we dashed quickly past him. This Indian, we noticed, had an exceedingly large mouth, and a very square head. His skin was a dusky dark-brown,—he looked as if he had never had a bath in his life,—and his face put one in mind of a shrivelled-up old witch. His hair, as black as coal, hung down below his ears and neck like a mop or the thick mane of a horse. The Ute is the lowest of all the Indians. His diet is simple, and varied. Grass, clover, acorns, fish, grasshoppers, lizards, and snakes form his favourite articles of food. The grass and clover he eats raw, the acorns he grinds and boils, the fish he broils, and the grasshoppers, etc., he roasts. He is also fond of eating the roots of certain plants, for which he will dig; hence the name "Digger," by which he is commonly known. He is an ardent fisherman, and he goes on his fishing expeditions carrying the worms—the bait he uses—in his mouth. But the worms will have found their way down his mouth and into his stomach before he has caught many fish.

For fifteen miles we passed through an extensive mining district, called the Columbia gold-diggings, and at different points, on the flats and in the excavated hollows, we could see many poor fellows—mostly Chinamen—boring, blasting, picking, digging, and "pickaxing" in the fervent heat, as if very life depended on the result of their exertions, as no doubt in a good measure it did. And hot it was, too! At 11.45, when we reached the town of Sonora, the thermometer stood at 110° in the shade. We all declared it was the hottest day we had ever experienced. And yet it was a dry heat, causing no perspiring or feeling of exhaustion and fatigue. But it made us drink wherever we stopped—iced water.

Sonora is a little mining town consisting of a single street of wooden shanties, planted with shade-trees, and it has a very picturesque appearance. I forget how many lager-beer saloons I counted in the one single street, but the number was excessive; indeed every other house in the town seemed to be a liquor saloon or a gambling saloon of some sort or other. We stopped to have the mid-day meal at the hotel of the place, and had it in company with mine host and hostess, together with our driver from Murphy's, our new driver who was to take charge of us after we left Sonora, and a few miners—rough-looking customers these latter, who dropped in just casually to see what was going on. The miners ate like hounds, and behaved as if they were altogether ignorant of the primary conventionalities of ordinary decent society. As might be expected, the conversation turned chiefly upon mining; and information was imparted to us in pure, simple, ungarnished, though thoroughly racy mining language, characteristic of the locality. The men meant well in what they had to tell us, but they had a very questionable way of putting it.

These two mining settlements, Sonora and Columbia, were, in 1855, the largest towns in California outside San Francisco. Sonora had at that time a population of about 5000: its population now is scarcely 2000. We found about 300 people in Columbia.

The country around Sonora is largely whitewashed with a strange medley of medicinal recipes—all no doubt very good in their way, but it cannot be said that the landscape is beautified by their repeated appearance. Our old friend "Bitters," which had been with us ever since we first set foot in the New World, figured here in great prominence and in much variety. Some of the more frequent, yet withal useful announcements that we noticed, were the following: "TRY FIG BITTERS;" "FIG BITTERS FOR INDIGESTION;" "WE TAKE WAHOO BITTERS;" "IF YOU HAVE THE AGUE AND FIND NO ENJOYMENT TRY HIERAPICRA BITTERS;" "TO PREVENT FEVER AND AGUE TRY HIERAPICRA BITTERS;" "USE MARSHALL'S COOKING EXTRACTS;" "TRY MARSHALL'S HORSE LINIMENT;" "MARSHALL'S HORSE LINIMENT GOOD FOR MAN AND BEAST." And so on *usque ad nauseam*.

There is a limit to everything, even to these hideous whitepaint advertisements. But on the road to the Yosemite Valley this limit is over-stepped, for one passes certain conspicuous white (and yellow) paint notices that are really not fit to meet the eye of the man or woman who has the least regard for any decency or propriety.

Starting from Sonora with fresh horses and driver, we rattled away for twelve miles to Chinese Camp, the next place for halting and changing our team. Chinese Camp we found to consist of an inn, a grocer's store, a chemist's, two other stores, and a few more wooden shanties. The inn, called the Garrett House, was kept by Count S——, a festive Pole, who hated Russia like poison, and told us to our face that he considered the English "thorough" people. He also said other complimentary things, which I cannot repeat. But let an Englishman travel where he may, he will always find that he is respected and considered—a gentleman. So let him not forfeit when he is travelling the good name which has been given him!

"All aboard, all aboard!" This is the universal warning, on the road and on the rail, that time's up and the journey must be resumed. So we leave off talking to the Polish count over the counter, and obeying the "all aboard" of our new coachman we start again "on the rampage" for more miles of jolting. We now had a team of five horses; and evidently our driver had taken leave of his senses, or wished to show us how near ruin and destruction he could bring us without actually causing our death, for off we started at a flying gallop and away we banged up and down the hills and round impossible corners, along the edges of precipices and slosh through deep stony streams,—we were the only passengers in the coach,—till at last we pulled up suddenly by the side of a river, when the driver said to me, "Wouldn't you like a wash?" No suggestion could have been propounded more to my own liking; but, thinking him joking, I inquired, "Do you mean it?" "Why of course I do," was the reply. And suiting the action to the word he threw up the reins to his companion on the box, jumped down and commenced disrobing himself; and I, not to be outdone, commenced following his example. His "wash" consisted in floundering about in water reaching up to his knees, and every now and then besprinkling his head with a bit of wet. But I indulged in an enjoyable swim in a smooth piece of water, for the river was wide—though the current out in the middle was, I confess, running rather unpleasantly strong.

This river, which is called the Tuolumne (pronounced Tuollumé), we found we were obliged to cross, for the road soon came to an abrupt termination in its waters. Our passage over was effected by means of a raft or barge, on to which we drove, and the coach and five horses stood upon it with plenty of room to spare. The method of working the ferry across-stream was simple and ingenious. Stretching over the river from one bank to the other was a strong, taut, iron-wire cable, and at each end of the raft was a movable pulley, which slid along the cable. By shortening the rope at one end and letting it out at the other the mere force of the current urged the raft across the stream. We had crossed the Stanislaus River in the morning in a similar manner.

Bumping along up Mocassin Creek, we came to a steep hill, called Rattlesnake Hill, on the top of which lay our destination for the night—a solitary little wooden inn called after the name of its present proprietor, Priest's. Rattlesnakes abound here, hence the name of the hill. So also do quails, as they do along the road all the way from Murphy's but here more especially. We had given chase to many of them. We ascended this hill during a magnificent sunset, and found it a very stiff pull-up, as the rise of the ground was from 16 to 20 feet in 100, and we had to ascend for 2000 feet before we attained the summit. However, the little inn reached, we put ourselves under the tender care of Mrs. Priest, who hailed from Scotland. She showed us clean-looking bedrooms, and gave us an excellent supper, and we were soon afterwards in comfortable beds enjoying a comfortable sleep.

The next morning (June 25th) we rose at four o'clock, had breakfast, and started away at five. We had a fresh driver to-day, who, if anything, drove more furiously than our driver of the day before. With a five-in-hand we went the killing pace. We were obliged to hold on to the sides of the coach for very life, else we should certainly have been pitched out, in rounding the corners so suddenly. As for our articles of baggage they were sent flying about over the place in an uncontrollable sort of fashion, the result being a general smash-up of pomade bottles, pots of shaving-cream and tooth-paste, in so ruthless a manner, that we had to cry out to our driver to spare us and our bottles too. Things got a little mixed, for when I opened my bag later on I found the razor had broken through its case and was folded in the embrace of the Areca-nut toothpaste. We were the only passengers on the coach, and so the driver took liberties, and brought us along as hard as ever he could.

A mile beyond Priest's we came to the mining village of Big Oak Flat, so named from the fine sturdy oaks growing in the locality; or perhaps from one oak in particular, which we passed on our right, whose trunk measured eleven feet in diameter. This little place is inhabited, of course, by people of various nationalities, who have been attracted hither to dig for the quartz, the copper, and the gold. We noticed the following announcement over the door of one of the houses: "English and Spanish newspapers taken in here."

A long and glorious drive through dense forests of pine and fir brought us to a collection of a few little shanties, all included under the name of Colfax Springs. We pulled up for a few minutes at a cottage, in order to bait the horses.

A few more miles and we pulled up again, this time at a cottage called Hodgson's (? Hodgeden's), where we had dinner. We also, after dinner, took on fresh horses—a team of four this time—and a new coach and driver. The ostler here was musical, and withal a poet. He sang us a song of his own composing, while managing the horses, the first two lines of which ran thus:

> "O how'd you like to be
> Roll'd up in a blanket with me?"

We continued to plunge through the thick forest after leaving Hodgson's, and for the rest of the journey, till we sighted the Yosemite Valley, we were simply kept in a fever of rapture and delight. It is not within the power of imagination to enable one who has not visited California to understand at all the stately grandeur of its forests, more especially the exquisite charm of a ride in them for many miles. Neither in a Swiss, nor in a Norwegian forest could one see such glorious pines, such a carpeting of beautiful flowers, and such bird and animal life. Here, for example, during this portion of our drive, the immense height of the pines and firs growing so thickly around, seemed to us remarkable, even after a sight of the Giant Trees of Calaveras. Rhododendrons, wallflowers and azaleas grew in great profusion, tinging the forest with richest hues. Ferns, too, were in wonderful variety. It was a paradise for botanist and naturalist. Splendid gorgeous-coloured butterflies flitted around us in great numbers; blue, silken-feathered jays hopped about among the branches of the trees that overshadowed us; woodpeckers abounded—drilling holes into the trunks of the nut-pines that we passed; and upon many a stone was a lively little ground or "chipping" squirrel (*Spermophilus douglasii*), which with a whisk of the tail would suddenly vanish out of sight, underground or somewhere, when we approached too near, but only to reappear in a moment or two and cautiously look about, and then resume its gambols on the stone when it found we were well out of the way. The coat of this little creature is most beautifully marked. In Colorado, in 1879, I secured several of these "chipmunks"—as they are popularly called —and brought them back to England. Since their arrival they have increased and multiplied, and have become a very numerous family.

Pursuing a helter-skelter pace for some miles, our new driver from Hodgson's having the same unfortunate tendency to take us "the pace that kills" as the rest of his fraternity in California, we were soon obliged to slacken our speed, for we commenced a steep ascent of 3200 feet—an ascent during which we obtained extensive, glorious views over forest-clad valley and mountain; till at length we came to the Tuolumne Big Tree Grove, and at the same time upon a novelty such as one does not come across every day. This is a tunnel through the stump of one of the largest *Wellingtonias* in the grove, through which the road passes and the stage-coach is driven! The stump so standing—the trunk has been severed about ninety feet from the ground—is entirely barked, and measures 30 ft. 8 in. in diameter; but the diameter of the trunk with its bark is said to have been over forty feet. In height the tunnel measures twelve feet, and it is ten and a half feet wide at the base and eight feet wide at the top. When we reached the middle of it we pulled up, of course, for here we were with coach and four horses standing *inside* one of the mammoth trees of California! We waited a considerable time within the tree. The tunnel had only been completed a week before our visit to the grove, the first coachful having passed through the stump on the afternoon of Tuesday, June 18th. We found the names of the parties who first performed this extraordinary feat pencilled up inside against the wood. The road, in order to reach this tree, has been diverted a short distance from the old one, which it rejoins soon after the tree is passed. This road will now become a relic of the past, untrodden and grass-grown, for no one will care to traverse it when there

ROAD-TUNNEL THROUGH A GIANT TREE.

is the alternative of a free passage right through a "big" tree. It is a wonder that there was no toll to pay at the entrance, and that a collection was not made for expenses by the sending round of a hat. Indeed the omission of such an opportunity on the part of the authorities is unaccountable.

The Tuolumne Grove, as already mentioned, contains about thirty "big" specimens of the *Wellingtonia gigantea*; but there are here, as in the Calaveras Grove, several young ones growing around, which are "coming on," and should the world last long enough will in their turn grow "big" and become a surprise to future generations. Pines and Douglas spruces, also the redwood and the white fir (*Picea grandis*), spring up thickly side by side with the *Wellingtonias*; in short the Tuolumne Grove, small as it is, is but part and parcel of the dense forest that clothes the mountain we are ascending. There is a set of Siamese Twins in this grove, which are similar in character to those in the Calaveras Grove, two *Wellingtonias* springing up from the same root and coming together again some feet above the ground. The bark of each is said to be twenty inches thick; their circumference at the ground, 114 feet.

Still ascending the mountain, the road very steep and narrow in places, a sudden turn of the road brought us face to face with a four-wheeled vehicle, with three people in it, who had lost their drag, and having no heavy weight with them to check the impetus of their fast descent, used by way of substitute a square piece of board, which they tied to cord, and got a small boy to stand on the board so attached and catch hold of the cord while he was being dragged down the hill and banged about over the stones in so unmerciful a manner, that we thought that if he had held on much longer there would have been nothing at all of him left. But they were coming straight into us at full speed when we sighted them, just after we had rounded the corner, and they had to come to such a sudden halt in order to prevent an actual collision with us that they were all three almost thrown out. Our driver became exceeding wrathful, and freely made use of some of the very choicest expressions to be found in the American version of our English language. It might indeed have been a very awkward business—it was touch-and-go as it was. On our right lay an ugly-looking precipice, which was unfenced and altogether unprotected: on our left was a wall of rock rising abruptly several feet above us. The road was at that place particularly narrow, so much so that with the most careful steering we were only just able to creep past the carriage, which was held stationary to allow us to do so. And as the rules of the road obliged us to keep to the right, our precarious position may be appreciated when I mention that we were but an inch or two off the edge of the precipice as we cautiously crept past, whilst the wheels of the carriage were forced up some feet against the wall of rock on the opposite side of the road.

Crossing here and there a bit of grass-land forming a break in the grand, interminable forest, we mounted higher and higher, till at length we reached an elevation of 6600 feet, and superb was the view we obtained from this point of the main forest-ranges of the beautiful Sierra! Peak rose high above peak, range above range. There were heights of 13,000 feet and more, forest-covered mountains rising one above another till at last they became capped with perpetual snow.[1] But we could not stop to admire. We were fast approaching the wonderful Yosemite Valley, when all our energy would have to be concentrated in order to comprehend, as we should, the great sight of the North American continent, one of the natural wonders of the world.

We came to a notice-board fixed against a tree, on which was the following:

TO
PIONEER'S LAUNDRY
8 MILES.
WHAT WOULD YOU DO IF YOU GOT YOUR NECK BROKEN
AND WORE A DIRTY SHIRT?

On seeing this we began to question among ourselves what it could mean? Our gray-bearded driver, hearing us, leant back from his seat, quickly touched his hat to us, and said, "I'm the man as runn'd the Pioneer's Laundry." We asked for an explanation. He then told us that he used to keep a laundry in the Yosemite—a general wash-house for tourists camping out in the valley, who wanted their linen attended to. "But," he added, "it's now busted up and goes unkimmon 'ard with me. Them 'otels 'as come and skeared away all my trade." He further informed us that he had put up the notice "to 'tract 'tention" to his laundry, and that he had fixed a similar notice at the top of the Sentinel Dome, one of the mountains rising on the other side of the valley which, he said, ran thus:

---

[1] Thus the Sierra Nevada, or the "Snowy Range."

'TIS BETTER TO BE LOWLY BORN AND RANGE WITH DIGGERS
IN THE DIRT
THAN TO BE PERCHED UPON A MULE AND WEAR A DIRTY
SHIRT.
8 MILES TO PIONEER'S LAUNDRY.

We asked him what he had put *this* up for? He replied again, "To 'tract 'tention." He was also good enough to inform us that this was "a bit of Shakespeare!"

"Shakespeare?" we exclaimed in astonishment. "Where?"

The man could not tell us. But if the reader will turn to *Hen.* VIII., Act ii., Scene 3, he will find the following passage:

> "Verily
> I swear, 'tis better to be lowly born
> And range with humble livers in content,
> Than to be perk'd up in a glistering grief,
> And wear a golden sorrow."

A few hundred yards further, and we came upon the Yosemite Valley in all its unapproachable, unspeakable magnificence. But it will be better to commence a description of this remarkable spot with a new chapter.

THE YOSEMITE VALLEY.
Bird's-eye View.

CHAPTER XVIII.

THE YOSEMITE VALLEY.

Our descent into the gorge—A wonderful sight—El Capitan Rock—The Spires and Cathedral Rock—The Bridal Veil Fall—Our first view of this fall—At the bottom of the gorge—The Ribbon Fall—The Three Brothers—Sentinel Rock—The sight *par excellence* of the Valley—The deepest plunge in the world—North and South Domes—At the door of Black's Hotel—Our driver a nuisance—The Yosemite Falls Hotel—Discovery of the Valley—Action of Congress—An hotel largely advertised—Seclusion of the Valley—The word "Yosemite"—How to pronounce it properly—A walk up the Valley—A camp of tourists—The Mirror Lake—Curious rock formations—Reflections in the lake—Breakfast at the hotel—An agile waiter—An Englishman and a cricketer.

WE are on high ground, and the Valley lies deep down below us. As we descend into it, a descent of six miles down the steep mountain side, along a road admirably engineered,

—here carved out of the face of an almost vertical wall of rock, there necessarily supported by a mass of solid stone

EL CAPITAN.

work,—the elements of grandeur of which this famous region consists become gradually unfolded to us. Beneath us is a valley or trough seven miles long, barely a mile and a half wide, and from 3000 to 4000 feet in perpendicular depth, with stupendous cliffs of gray granite enclosing it throughout

THE CATHEDRAL ROCKS.

its entire length. The softness and exquisite loveliness of the scene, and its incomparable majesty and magnificence, are simply indescribable. All where growth is possible is beautifully clad in green; tall pines and sturdy oaks spring up in seemingly impossible places, covering mountain side and rocky ledge; and from the midst of a luxuriant sea of evergreens which covers the level bottom of the gorge, immense walls of rock rise steep and straight, whose enormous dimensions we can only comprehend as we descend further and further beneath them. To our left is El Capitan, the Indian *Tu-toch-ah-nu-lah*, or "Great Chief of the Valley"— a gigantic projecting mass of smooth, bare granite rock rearing itself vertically 3300 feet out of the valley, and presenting a perpendicular front of more than a mile in length. The imposing sight of the stupendous bulk of the monster-rock is unique—at least in our experiences of travel. Opposite El Capitan, on the other side of the gorge, are the Spires and the Cathedral Rock, the former two pinnacles of granite 500 feet high and 300 feet in diameter, connected with the main ridge behind, but reaching to a height of 2400 feet above the valley; the latter a massive pile standing 2660 feet out of the valley, and resembling— when you get the other side of it and look back—a cathedral or church with a large tower. Immediately to the right of the Cathedral Rock, and nearly opposite to us as we descend, is the Bridal Veil Fall. This waterfall gracefully drops in a long white sheet of 940 feet, and when a wind is blowing, it possesses a singular vibratory motion, at the same time that it is made to sway to one side by the pressure brought to bear on it, the effect of which has caused it to be so named. The Indians call it *Pohonó*, the "Spirit of the Evil Wind."[1] Our first view of this fall was one we shall never

---

[1] "Pohonó, from whom the stream and the waterfall receive their musical Indian name, is an evil spirit, whose breath is a blighting and fatal wind, and consequently is to be dreaded and shunned. On this account, whenever from necessity the Indians have to pass it, a feeling of distress steals over them, and they fear it as much as the wandering Arab does the simoons of the African desert: they hurry past it at the height of their speed. To point to the waterfall, as they travel through the valley, is in their minds to induce certain death. No bribe could be offered large enough to tempt them to sleep near it. It is, in truth, their belief that they hear the voices of those who have been drowned in the stream perpetually warning them to shun Pohonó."—J. M. Hutchings's *Scenes of Wonder in California.*

forget. The breeze was waving it to the side; it fluttered and trembled in its descent like an aspen-leaf; it fell in thick ringlets or curls; and, added to all, a lovely iris was spanning its full, narrow sheet, and the spray which was showered around, the effect of the whole, what with the green forest below and the glistening, almost metallic-looking precipice for a background, being magical and magnificent in the extreme.

THE BRIDAL VEIL FALL.

Such are the more imposing features we see on our left as we descend towards the bottom of the valley. On our right, immense heights shut in the view, the valley contracting into a still narrower gorge, and at the bottom there winds a silver streak of white among green oaks, firs, and pines. It is the Merced River, or "River of Mercy," made up of all the waterfalls in the Yosemite Valley, and it flows the whole length of the gorge.

The slashing pace at which we came down the mountain—rounding the corners so suddenly and approaching at times so unpleasantly near the extreme edge of the cliff—was certainly not calculated to further our enjoyment of the scenery. We asked our driver to slacken speed a little; but his answer was, " It's all right, you shall look up when you come down!" This was no doubt very consoling. But we made the best of the situation and took in by fits and starts as much as we could of the landscape whilst we clung on to the sides of the coach and prevented ourselves from being pitched out. All the drivers in this part of the world seemed to have taken leave of their senses.

We reach the bottom of the gorge, and find a smooth road laid through forest and meadow-land, the Merced River flowing beside us on our right; and we follow by the side of the stream up the valley in the direction of our hotel, now three miles distant, our driver remarking to us that it would be the shortest three miles we had ever driven in our life. On our right is the lovely Bridal Veil Fall, now scarcely distinguishable, partly hidden as it is by the trees of the forest which are now at a level with us. Next to it is the stupendous projecting mass of the Cathedral Rock; and next, again, behind it on the same side, are the Spires. On our left, exactly facing the Cathedral Rock, is El Capitan, and, as we have already indicated, we shall have to drive more than a mile before we have passed its huge, vertical precipice. On the very edge of its summit, far up above, we can just see a speck of green—it makes one dizzy to look up at it. This is a tall sugar pine, not a tiny patch of grass or moss as it seems to be from our standpoint at such a depth below. Almost hidden away in a recess on the left side of El Capitan is a thin white streak, looking like a bit of white tape dangling down the cliff. This is the Virgin's Tears Creek, the *Lung-oo-too-koo-ya*—" Long and slender "—of the Indians, though it is also known by the more suggestive name of the Ribbon Fall. It falls from a height of 3300 feet, filling a hollow or groove in the mountain, with El Capitan projecting far into the valley on its right and a long stretch of the main ridge projecting slightly on its left, so that unless one were looking intently in its direction, or it were specially pointed out, it would probably escape notice altogether.

As we proceed up the gorge fresh wonders come into view. We are literally hemmed in on all sides by towering masses of rock, which rise precipitously around. One of the most remarkable characteristics of the Yosemite Valley is its extreme narrowness in comparison with the great heights deep down among which it is sunk. These heights do not incline, but rise in almost vertical masses, leaving behind them little or no *débris*, whilst their summits are beautifully clothed with pine, and their sides, too, where not actually vertical, are green with the foliage of pine and oak likewise.

But we are driving along the base of El Capitan, and the scene before us is grand and beautiful in the extreme. A succession of domes and peaks close in the valley to its furthest limit, presenting a sight that is truly magnificent. Beyond El Capitan, on the same side, is a triple group of rocks called the Three Brothers, rising in steps the one above the other, at right angles to the valley. The loftiest of these mountains has a height of 3820 feet. At first sight the trio remind one of three frogs about to take a spring, and this has probably suggested their Indian name *Pom-pom-pa-sus*, or the "Playing Leap-frog Rocks." Opposite the Brothers, on our right, appears one of the most imposing sights in the valley. It is an obelisk-shaped tower of granite rising vertically for over a thousand feet from the mountain ridge; but the exact height of its summit from the bottom of the valley is 3043 feet. It has been appropriately named the Sentinel Rock, for, springing up by itself, it seems as it were to hang suspended in the air, and to keep watch over all beneath it.

Opposite the Sentinel Rock, beyond El Capitan on our left, comes into view the great sight of the valley. This is the Yosemite or "Great Grizzly Bear" Fall, perhaps one of the most beautiful and glorious sights in the world. Even Norway's great waterfalls pale before this wonderful fall, not forgetting the Mörke-fos, Vöring-fos, Skjæggedal-fos, and Rjukan-fos in the comparison. You look at it with wonder and delight; you feel that you have before you one of the sights—not only of the Yosemite Valley, but of the world. It cannot be compared to Niagara, which is justly world-renowned for its immense and powerful cataracts, its gigantic bulk of waters, its never-ceasing roar. But

THE YOSEMITE FALL.
(*See Frontispiece.*)

here we have a fall matchless for grace, form, height, impressiveness, beauty, and grandeur ; for its noble surroundings, for its grand accessories. We look in its direction and see a long line of sheer precipice, and over a ledge crowning a recess in the smooth face of an immense wall of rock, far away as it seems, high up above, there pours a beautiful white sheet which gently lets itself descend in one graceful drop the height of 1600 feet clear. It descends in this one long leap into a tremendous trough it has hollowed out of the mountain, gradually spreading itself in its descent like a fan. Dashing up great clouds of spray, it bounds further on, making a second leap of 434 feet, when it is checked by a projecting ridge. Momentarily arrested, it then plunges still further, and makes a third and final descent of 600 feet, till it becomes hidden from view among the green oaks, willows and poplars that are thickly spread over the space intervening between us and the mountain, and which seem to receive its waters and hide them away. Thus the Yosemite Fall consists in reality of three grand leaps, making up a visible descent of 2634 feet.

But it is upon the first of these falls that one's attention is irresistibly concentrated. To say that it "leaps" or "plunges" is to use terms harsh and out of place when applied to the gentleness and grace with which it seems to descend. It neatly and gently lets itself top the scarce-visible ledge, and then, descending a few hundred feet in a sort of twisted stream, it gracefully spreads out like a fan, shooting into a thousand rockets, till in time it becomes lost in the thick white cloud of spray which it showers up around. The two lower falls are both of them superb sights, and in Switzerland would be as much run after as the Reichenbach, or the Staubbach in Lauterbrunnen. But what Professor Whitney has observed is quite true. He says, "Either the domes or the waterfalls of the Yosemite, or any single one of them, even, would be sufficient in any European country to attract travellers from far and wide in all directions. Waterfalls in the vicinity of the Yosemite, surpassing in beauty many of those best known and most visited in Europe, are actually left entirely unnoticed by travellers, because there are so many objects of interest to be visited that it is impossible to find time for them all."

Turning from the Yosemite Fall and looking up the valley the sight presented is one that can never be forgotten. An awful barrier of domes and peaks of gigantic proportions tower up towards heaven, the valley dividing into three deep gorges, with precipices enclosing each rising steep and straight from their bases. It is impossible adequately to describe the sublime grandeur of this sight. You look on one side and see the stupendous half-rounded bulk of the North Dome—the Indian *To-coy-æ*, or "Shade to Baby Cradle-basket"—towering 3568 feet above the gorge; you look on the other side and see, facing it, the great South Dome, the most remarkable precipice of all, which the Indians call *Tis-sa-ack* or the "Goddess of the Vale"—a gigantic mass of granite of 4737 feet, with 2000 feet of its upper part as smooth and vertical as it is possible for it to be. The South Dome is, and rightly, also named the "Half" Dome, for rising a colossal wall of rock, its side away from the valley appears curved and rounded, till, at the top of the curve, it suddenly breaks off short (as we have just seen) a clear drop of 2000 feet, as straight as arrow ever shot from bow, as smooth as the blade of a knife, and then it slopes off at an angle of about seventy degrees until it reaches the bottom of the gorge. It resembles a huge round bee-hive cut in twain. It is said that *Tis-sa-ack* "never has been" and probably "never will be" ascended. Professor Whitney remarks that it is a mountain "seeming perfectly inaccessible, and being probably the only one of all the prominent points about the Yosemite which never has been, and never will be, trodden by human foot." It will soon be seen that the South Dome is not quite so inaccessible as it has been made out to be.

Besides these two striking objects in the imposing view now before us, there are other prominent features which are scarcely less remarkable. Thus there is the Washington Column,—the Indian *Hunto* or "Watching Eye,"—a rounded mass of smooth rock 2200 feet in height, standing as if on guard at the junction of the three cañons at the upper end of the valley. There are also the Royal Arches, to the left of the Washington Column,—great arched recesses in the mountain wall, ninety feet deep, and spanning 2000 feet, formed by the slipping away of large portions of the granite rock; also Mt. Watkins, a mountain named after the photographer who has produced such wonderful views of the valley, and thus brought it into fame; and, far away and above all, Cloud's Rest, rising above the valley a height of 6450 feet, its summit capped with snow. The Yosemite Valley is about 4000 feet above the sea-level, so that Cloud's Rest, its culminating point, is at least 10,000 feet above such level.

We crossed to the other side of the Merced River—it was now on our left—and, with a camp of Indians just visible on our right, pitched among the thick forest which extends to the base of the towering precipices beyond, we were approaching the first of the four inns in the valley, which is known by the name of Black's Hotel. Our driver pulled up suddenly at the door of this inn, and began to advise us, with all the eloquence at his command, to test the comforts of the establishment; while at the same time the proprietor himself came out and stood at the doorway, and, expectorating tobacco-juice, attentively listened to our driver's recommendations. Said the latter, leaning back from his seat and beholding us tenderly:

"Won't ye now jist step in 'ere? Y'll git a gude clain rig, an' they'll treat ye illegant."

We thanked him, of course, but at the same time declined, and told him to drive on to the hotel where he knew all the while we wanted to go—the Yosemite Falls Hotel. He did so, and in a few minutes we reached our destination, a clean comfortable-looking, unpretentious wooden hotel on the bank of the Merced River, with a superb "location" in front and in full view of the three grand descents of the fall which we have attempted to describe, and from which it receives its name.

We will now take a brief glance at one or two matters in connexion with the valley, which may be of interest. And first as to its discovery.

This took place in the year 1850. The Indians had made several raids upon the farms of the white settlers living on the plains—had run off with their horses and cattle, and done other acts to provoke the hostility of the palefaces. It was by following the trail of the redskins and tracing them to their retreat far up among the mountains, where they had hidden away the cattle and where they probably thought no white man would ever find them out, that the Yosemite Valley came to be discovered: it was in fact the Yosemite

THE THREE BROTHERS, YOSEMITE VALLEY.   *Page* 357.

that turned out to be the place of security where all the livestock of the palefaces had been taken. News of the discovery of such a wonderful spot rapidly spread. The following year an expedition was organized to drive out the Indians from their retreat, and make them give up their spoil. This expedition was headed by one Captain Boling, and, without saying more about it, it may be remarked that it was entirely successful.

The attention of Congress assembled at the other end of America now became directed to the valley. Its wonders were represented to the national Legislature. It would become necessary to appropriate the spot and convert it into State property if it were intended to prevent anyone from coming and setting up his shanty there, which someone or other would have been sure to do, and, moreover, would have destroyed the very fine timber, and set up toll-gates at every waterfall and point of observation, to fill his own pockets withal. A word was put in on behalf of the Mammoth Grove of Mariposa at the same time that the representations were made of the wonders of the Yosemite. So Congress then did to the Yosemite Valley and Mariposa Grove what should have been done long ago to Niagara, and what was done in the year 1872 to the famous Yellowstone region—it turned them both into national public parks, and delivered them over to the State of California to hold "inalienable and for all time;" for on June 30, 1864, the then President of the United States (Abraham Lincoln) gave his consent to an Act, the two sections of which we will give *verbatim*:

"*Be it enacted by the Senate and House of Representatives of the United States of America, in Congress assembled,* That there shall be, and is hereby, granted to the State of California, the 'Cleft' or 'Gorge' in the Granite Peak of the Sierra Nevada Mountain, situated in the county of Mariposa, in the State aforesaid, and the head waters of the Merced River, and known as the 'Yosemite Valley,' with its branches and spurs, in estimated length fifteen miles, and in average width one mile back from the main edge of the precipice, on each side of the valley, with the stipulation, nevertheless, that the said State shall accept this grant upon the express conditions that the premises shall be held for public use, resort, and recreation; shall be inalienable for all time; but leases not exceeding ten years may be granted for portions of the said premises. All incomes derived from leases of privileges to be expended in the preservation and improvement of the property, or the roads leading thereto; the boundaries to be established at the cost of the said State by the United States Surveyor-General of California, whose official plat, when affirmed by the Commissioner of the General Land Office, shall constitute the evidence of the locus, extent, and limits of the said Cleft or Gorge; the premises to be managed by the Governor of the State, with eight other Commissioners, to be appointed by the Executive of California, and who shall receive no compensation for their services.

"Sect. 2. And be it further enacted, That there shall likewise be, and there is hereby, granted to the said State of California, the tracts embracing what is known as the 'Mariposa Big Tree Grove,' not to exceed the area of four sections, and to be taken in legal subdivisions of one-quarter section each, with the like stipulations as expressed in the first section of this Act as to the State's acceptance, with like conditions as in the first section of this Act as to inalienability, yet with the same lease privileges; the income to be expended in the preservation, improvement and protection of the property, the premises to be managed by Commissioners as stipulated in the first section of this Act, and to be taken in legal subdivisions as aforesaid; and the official plat of the United States Surveyor-General, when affirmed by the Commissioner of the General Land Office, to be the evidence of the locus of the said Mariposa Big Tree Grove."

The first house built in the valley was in the year 1856, in the autumn of that year. It was our hotel, the Yosemite Falls Hotel, now better known as Bernard's, lately Hutchings's, or in this part of the world it is a common thing for an hotel to have a name of its own besides the name of its proprietor; and it is a still more common thing for the proprietor to paint his name in connexion with his hotel on the rocks and palings by the side of the public way, as Mr. Bernard has done *ad nauseam* along the entire distance between Chinese Camp and the Yosemite Valley, even on the trees in the thick forest, so that there may be no mistaking him. Besides this hotel, there are not more than twenty buildings in the valley; and this is a grand thing to be able to say considering that the Yosemite has been a place of resort for tourists for the space of twenty-four years. No doubt this is owing to the remoteness of the railway, for people do not relish the idea of the two days' staging, and the chance of being half killed by the banging about one gets at the hands of ruthless stage-drivers—though in the opinion of a good many persons it would be worth all this, to be able at last to feast one's eyes upon so glorious a spot as is this wonderful Valley of the Yosemite.

We have had frequent occasion to make use of the word "Yosemite," and it may not be amiss to say something as to its pronunciation. Many persons pronounce it dissyllabically thus—Yose-mite, giving to the last four letters the one-syllable pronunciation of the word "mite;" but this is entirely wrong It is a four-syllable word with the accent on the antepenult thus—Yo-sem'-i-te. This is the only way of pronouncing it correctly. The meaning of the word as translated from the Indian vernacular is, we have already seen, "Great Grizzly Bear." Such, then, is the name by which the valley is known to the civilized world. But the Indians, who had possession of the locality till it was appropriated by white men in the year 1851, have been in the habit of calling it, and still call it, *Ah-wah-nee*.

About three miles above our hotel there is a lake formed by the widening of the Tenaya, a stream flowing down a cañon of the same name, one of the three gorges into which the Yosemite Valley divides at its upper or eastern end. This lake is small and deep, and lies in one of the grandest spots of the valley, at the foot of the fine rounded precipice called the Washington Column. From the reflections in its still waters of this and other great heights in its vicinity, such as the North and South Domes, and particularly Mt. Watkins, it has been called the Mirror Lake. The proper time to see the reflections is early in the morning, when the sun makes its first appearance in the valley over the crest of Mt. Watkins. For this purpose a coach leaves the hotel every morning, and takes those to the lake who wish to have their curiosity gratified.

So the morning after our arrival in the valley (June 26), we got up at six o'clock, and walked the couple of miles up the gorge, discarding the luxury (?) of a ride in the coach, which was meant only for those who were unable to walk that distance.

We had not walked a mile from the hotel before we came upon a camp in the wood, a collection of about a dozen tents all pitched close together, and smoking, as if breakfast was going on this early hour of the morning. Surely these were Indians—some "Diggers," perhaps; and yet the tents looked too clean and respectable to be the wigwams of the redskins. On closer examination we found the camp to consist of a party, or rather several parties of tourists, who instead of putting up at an hotel and indulging in the luxuries of civilized life, preferred this mode of "doing" the Yosemite, and no doubt the most enjoyable way of "doing" it too. But there was not much "roughing it" here, for, with their camp pitched within a few minutes' walk from the hotel, they could not only procure fresh provisions when they found their supplies began to run short, but could—as several of them did—step over to the hotel to get a good meal once in a way, or to have there a comfortable night's rest in comfortable beds when they found they were inconvenienced by the absolute necessity of having their sheets washed.

We reached the lake, which lies imbedded amongst the wildest scenery possible, and found a wooden shed on its bank. We entered, and saw a damsel seated on a stool, looking through a piece of music. Other pieces of music lay upon a form beside the stool. We asked the young lady if she could sing the song she was studying: she "guessed" she could. We further asked her whether she could sing it without having a piano to accompany herself by, and she replied that she could give an idea of what it was like to anyone who wanted to buy it: she also "guessed" she could do the same with the others. As we did not want to buy we did not ask her to sing; but we did ask her when she expected the sun would appear over the cliff, and the reflections be seen in the lake, and she said, "Not till half-past eight." It wanted twenty minutes to that time, so we asked if there was anything interesting to see meanwhile. The musical maid answered,

"Wouldn't you like to see the birds and animals on the mountain?"

We replied we should indeed, but inquired where they were. She explained that she would show us; and said,

"Will you please look at the mountain opposite?"

We looked, and saw a huge precipice almost overhanging the lake before us.

"Now," she said (pointing), "D'ye see that black slit?"

"No, where?" we replied.

"There," she said (still pointing). "Right on the face of that cliff to the right of that large white patch partly surrounded with a dark streak," etc., etc.

We told her we had got it.

"Well, then," she continued, "someways again to the right of it you will see two black patches divided by a patch of gray."

"All right," we exclaimed. "Go on."

"Well, that's our American Eagle—without its head."

"An eagle without its head? Why, how can that be?"

"Oh, the head's not given; but you can see the wings."

We *could* see the wings. They were the two black patches. But as the head was not "given," we had to imagine a good deal to get in a whole eagle.

"Well, now, 'guess I'll show you the British Lion," the maid continued.

"Where's the lion?" we inquired.

"Over there," was the reply. And with up-lifted hand and outstretched finger she directed our gaze to another portion of the cliff, where, after a good deal of explanation, we certainly did see something resembling the figure of the king of beasts. But the more we looked the more we were sure there was something wrong with it.

"That's not a whole lion!" we exclaimed.

"Oh no. It's got no tail!"

"An American eagle without a head and a British lion without a tail? Come, we're getting on," we said. "What next?"

"Now I'll show you a crane," said the young lady.

"A crane with or without legs?" we inquired.

"With everything," she replied. She put up her hand,

pointed and explained. Yes, there was a crane, and a very good representation of one, too. There was no deception. It was a crane.

Amongst other curious formations on the face of the mountain before us, we were shown an elephant without his trunk; a pig without legs; the head of a second elephant on one part of the cliff, and its hinder quarters and tail on another portion of the cliff; an engine and two carriages turned upside down on the mountain, but right side up when seen reflected in the water, with the addition of a station into which the train was on the point of entering; a clothes-line, with three articles of wearing apparel depending from it; a cross; a man's head, with a beard; an angel supposed to be flying, but without wings; a "rooster"—explained by the young lady to mean a hen in a sitting posture; a cow, with half a head; a sheep; and a bottle lying on its side pouring liquid on to George Washington's head, the part of his physiognomy besprinkled being his left cheek. He wore a hat, but it was very badly rent, and looked as if it had been smashed in.

Two lovers were also pointed out to us. They were supposed to be standing and gazing into each other's faces; but with all the stretch of imagination we brought to bear on them—and indeed we brought a good deal—we could see no formation representing such a situation. It was while we were trying to decipher this last-mentioned curious formation that the coach from the hotel arrived, containing those who had got up late, or who found they were unable to endure the fatigue of an early walk of two miles up the splendid forest gorge. All was now stir and confusion, and the echoes of the mountain were aroused. The young lady had to go through a repetition of her performance and show afresh to the new-comers the birds and the beasts the cross and the clothes-line, the railway-train and Washington's head, etc.; and when she had come to the end of her catalogue, time was about up—the sun was on the point of showing itself above the ridge of the opposite cliff. So we all got into a large tub-boat which was alongside, and a few strokes brought us to the middle of the lake, where we were told to keep very still and not move, else we should spoil it all. So we kept very still, neither moved, nor did we like to speak for fear the water would be disturbed, and we should see nothing. We sat therefore in silence and looked into the

THE MIRROR LAKE.

water, where was a clear reflection of Mt. Watkins, the clift over which the sun was fast appearing, the glow of the sun's rays becoming more and more dazzling, when suddenly it burst into sight, and then tenfold more dazzling became the reflected mountain. We could see nothing at all, for the glare was too blinding. By degrees, however, we got accustomed to the light, and the longer we looked into the water the clearer became the objects reflected in it. All the surrounding heights were lit up in a remarkable manner, every tree—I might almost say every branch, every leaf came out in the reflection most marvellously clear. Had it not been for the fact that every object was reversed, it would have been hard to tell which we were looking at, the original or its reflection. After each one had sufficiently admired the scene in the water, we moved ahead, and rowed to the steep wooded bank on the other side of the lake. Here we were shown a singular natural curiosity, namely a laurel growing out of a cedar-tree. The latter was but a small specimen, and the former, which made its appearance out of the cedar a few feet above the ground, was also not more than a few feet—perhaps twelve—in height.

Rowing back to the shed, we were about to take our departure back to the hotel to get breakfast, when the mountain-maid said,

"Stay, and I will show you something else."

She asked us, now that the sun was up, to look into the lake at the reflection of one of the mountains. We all commenced looking.

"Don't you see what I mean?" the maid inquired.

We explained that we did not.

"Don't you see the trees standing right way up instead of on their heads, as they generally do when they are reflected in the water?"

We looked intently, and stretched our imagination to the utmost, but did not succeed in seeing the phenomenon, though she seemed to point out to us the exact spot where it was supposed to be visible. We all gave it up. The reason assigned by the young lady for the phenomenon was a "double reflection" caused by the sun striking against the cliff and reflecting back. But it seemed strange that the sun should have so affected that particular spot, and that the "double reflection" was not visible elsewhere. Indeed this was just the odd thing about it, and required a little explanation.

Returning in a quick walk to the hotel, we had breakfast, and an agile waiter served us. He was an Englishman and a cricketer. He told us much of his prowess in the noble game, and, during the meal, went through a little performance on his own account, for he gave a twist with his wrists and put one leg forward, making an imitation of a forward drive, posing himself in an attitude which evidently showed he was a cricketer.

CHAPTER XIX.

THE YOSEMITE VALLEY (*continued*).

To Glacier Point—The Yosemite Fall—A glorious sight—Mounting the gorge—Union Point—At Glacier Point—The view therefrom—A dangerous leap—A dizzy depth—The great South Dome—Returning to the hotel—A trip up the Merced Cañon—The glories of this trip—The Vernal Fall—Its great beauty—View from above the fall—The Cap of Liberty—The Nevada Fall—Peculiar features of this fall—An eagle's nest—Dropping stones into it—A timely rebuke—The "Grand Register" —A few selections from the volume—High charges in the Yosemite— Herr Sinning's curiosity-shop—A house built round the stump of a tree —An ascent of the South Dome—The formation of the Yosemite.

IN such a spot as the Yosemite Valley there are, of course, a number of excursions to be made, whether on foot or horseback by following the trail up the mountain side to some prominent point of elevation, or by keeping to the bottom of the gorge and visiting at leisure its various waterfalls and precipices. Or if it is the daring climber who requires to be gratified, there is a splendid field open for him here where he can attempt to do the impossible, and risk the chance of breaking his neck by the performance of some foolish, hazardous exploit, one perhaps which no one in his senses would dream of accomplishing except when he happens to be attacked by that strange, irresistible mountain fever, which we have so many of us experienced when breathing the atmosphere of a higher level—that nervous sort of feeling that makes one long to be in action, to be up and doing something adventurous, to be scaling this or that precipice which has hitherto proved insurmountable; and *cui bono?* Simply to be able to say that we have "done it," and having done so, to provoke the keen competition of a host of others, who, the lead once given, will follow as a matter of course, and risk life in the attempt to perform the same exploit.

But we determined to do nothing rash. We were too much fatigued with the two days' jolting we had endured, over the rough, half-made roads, to enter upon an exciting climb. We therefore resigned ourselves to an excursion on horseback to Glacier Point, the summit of one of the heights immediately overlooking the valley.

After breakfast the next morning (June 27th), we started forth on horseback *en route* for Glacier Point. What a glorious morning it was! Not a cloud was in the sky, not a breath was in the air, not a sound but the distant murmur of the three grand plunges of the Yosemite Fall across the valley. A more glorious sight than that fall can scarcely be imagined. A long gigantic barrier of smooth precipice towering vertically 3030 feet above the valley, with a fall pouring over it broken into three visible descents of 2634 feet—this is but a tiny portion of what can be taken in at one glance. The whole cannot be given in words. It is not that first white fan-sheet of 1600 feet which gives rise to expressions of admiration, though even this plunge is itself probably the highest in the world, leaving out of the question the two lower descents which are but part and parcel of the same fall. It is the scene as a whole which renders it so striking, with its freshness and beauty; with the colours so rich and rare, so picturesquely blended, and yet so exquisitely diversified. A bit of bright meadow-land lies at our feet; the stream of the Merced, flowing as clear as crystal among alders and willows, borders it beyond; immense precipitous heights of gray granite tower up before and behind—so steeply do the mountains rise that they seem suspended in the air, and yet they are dotted in places with evergreen pines and firs, so that one cannot help wondering where the soil can be from which they take root, springing as they seem to do out of solid masses of rock. A thick forest is behind us, stretching not a quarter of a mile to the cliffs we are about to ascend. Bright-plumaged birds flit about in all directions—by listening attentively we can hear the voices of many tiny humming-birds, though they are too small to be seen, without going out of the way and cautiously peering about for them. And then, added to all, there is the glorious deep-blue of the sky, its azure colour contrasting with the tops of the precipices, which stand out with marvellous clearness as they appear, clear-cut, against it.

THE YOSEMITE FALL.

We rode for about a mile along the road by which we had entered the valley, and then turned off to the left up the mountain, when almost within sight of Black's Hotel. Following a steep zigzag path, we mounted through the forest till we came to Union Point, a ledge 2400 feet sheer above the valley; and here we got off our horses to approach the edge of the precipice and look over. At this place there is fixed into the rock, a flag-staff or "liberty-pole," which one can catch hold of while gazing straight down into the gorge beneath.

Continuing the ascent, the trail having now become so steep that it was with difficulty our little mustangs could keep on their legs, which they only managed to do by straining every effort and resolutely planting the tips of their hoofs hard into the ground, we wound round the cliff to the left, the path laid on its very edge, and with a dizzy depth to look down into it we had only chosen to do so; but we reserved this for another occasion, when there would be no troublesome horses to manage and we could look over the cliff unconcernedly, for, as is generally the case, our animals delighted in keeping to the brink of the precipice throughout the ascent, edging persistently to the left in spite of our exertions to rein them tightly to the right, thereby causing us to feel very uncomfortable at times and to wish we had only room enough on the trail to belabour them for such unwarrantable pertinacity. We found the sun overpoweringly hot, even in our flannel costume; but we were made still hotter by the uneasiness of mind we were subjected to by the unfortunate, though, one might say, considerate disposition of our horses to select, as we have said, the very edge of the trail, only so long as they might afford us the full benefit of a bird's-eye view of the valley over the uninviting-looking precipice.

At length, after a toilsome climb, we reached Glacier Point. The view we obtained from this eminence, with the Yosemite Valley sunk sheer below us on one side, and a sweeping panorama of the Sierra Nevada to the east and north-east of us on the other side, was one whose memory will cling to us as long as we live. To the north-east there stretched a magnificent sweep of snow-peaks rising out of oceans of forest, while at our feet opened the deep gully of the Merced Cañon, one of the branches from the main valley, with the two fine plunges of the Merced River—the Vernal and Nevada Falls—glistening in the sunshine 3000 feet below us. Some of the highest peaks of the Sierra rose before us in the far distance. There were Mount Dana and Mount Lyell, 13,227 feet and 13,217 feet respectively, surrounded by lesser mountains more or less snow-clad, with forest vegetation extending to the snow-line, and clothing the sides of the precipitous heights.[1] A distinctive feature between the Sierra Nevada and the Swiss Alps could here be noticed at a glance. In the former the forests are magnificent even at an elevation of 7000 to 8000 feet, being as fine near the limit of eternal snow as they are down in the valleys below. But in Switzerland they are not to be found at anything like so high a level.

Turning from this glorious and comprehensive view of the Sierra Nevada to the more awful and overwhelming one of the gorge of the Yosemite, which opened out beneath us on the left it was only a few steps from the one to the other, for by creeping to the edge of the precipice and peeping over we could gaze down into the chasm, and see a sight which was almost bewildering and dazzling. There was a portion of the granite rock here jutting out in mid-air, projecting by itself from the main body of the precipice. It had an even surface, but it was only a few feet square. An irresistible longing came over my friend and myself to get upon it. If we could only manage this we should have the valley at our feet. But how to get upon it was the question—how could we make sure of landing on it safely? We were separated from it by an awkward-looking cavern, over which we should have to leap, and then, when we had once leapt, could we make sure of landing on the projecting piece of rock *without slipping ?* One little slip, one little slide, and we should be hurled into Eternity—we should fall a clear drop of 2000 feet into the valley below! It is the fate of everyone, perhaps, to do something rash during the course of a lifetime. If it is not what will bring retribution in the future, it will, perchance, be something which the doer would not perform again if he could help it. Neither my friend nor I will be found to do again what we did once, and only once, at Glacier Point, for we both of us,

---

[1] Mount Dana is the highest eminence to be seen in the view from Glacier Point. It is not, however, the culminating elevation of the Sierra Nevada Mountains, for this is Mount Whitney, which has an altitude of 14,887 feet above the sea-level.

one at a time, jumped on to that piece of projecting rock, and dropped stones, which we carried in our pockets, into the abyss beneath. Our exact height above the bottom of the gorge was 3700 feet. But a stone would drop 2000 feet before it hit against anything.

We were at such a height above the valley that it was difficult to discern the objects at the bottom of it. Without

VIEW FROM GLACIER POINT.

looking intently and fixedly, we could not distinguish a house from a rock or a group of trees from a field of grass. We did, it is true, see a black speck moving slowly along a thin streak of gray. The latter was the road by which we had entered the valley; but the former we could not decipher, do what we would. The stream of the Merced River seemed like a piece of twisted tape; but as for the boat-house on the Mirror Lake, or even, indeed, the lake itself, though we looked straight down on them, they seemed to have both disappeared altogether.

The view from Glacier Point of the peaks and domes of the Yosemite baffles description. As well might one try to delineate the glories of an Arctic sunset as to attempt to convey an idea of the majesty of their groupings. There is one feature in the landscape that particularly arrests the attention, and that is the precipice of the South Dome. This mountain, as has already been noticed, takes the form of a huge round beehive divided in twain—slit down the middle. How it received its own peculiar formation has been a moot question among geologists. But of this mountain more anon.

There is a "lunch house" set up at Glacier Point, facing the panorama of the Sierra, and of course we treated ourselves and took care of the inner man. We had first-rate appetites, for the air was in our favour, and it was a good number of hours since we had had our breakfast. We had ordered the meal as soon as we reached the Point, so that it was ready by the time we had finished our contemplation of the view. It was a frugal repast—but about the most expensive, comparatively speaking, we had ever sat down to.

A trail leads off from Glacier Point to the top of the Sentinel Dome—not the Sentinel Rock, that obelisk-formed peak we noticed as we entered the valley, which rises to the height of 3043 feet almost sheer above the bottom of the gorge. But the Dome lies almost immediately behind the Rock, and though it has an elevation of 4150 feet above the valley, it can be easily ascended. The view from it is said to be magnificent, extending even to San Francisco and the Golden Gate.

We returned into the valley very much quicker than we had come up from it. Our little nags did not seem at all the worse for the journey. Once on level ground again we had a race to the hotel, and the clatter that we made as we drew up at the door brought out several people to see what it was all about. After supper we took the gun and went in search of small birds, and were successful in obtaining some of the gayest-coloured specimens.

The trip to Glacier Point is one of the best that can be taken

THE VERNAL FALL, YOSEMITE VALLEY.

for surveying the Valley from an elevated position, for contemplating from above the mighty depths to which it is sunk, and for enabling the geologist, more especially, to observe the remarkable verticalness of its precipices and the peculiar rotundity of its domes, whereby he can study its formation and arrive at his own theory concerning it. But the trip to the Vernal and Nevada Falls along the bottom of the gorge is the one to be recommended if one wants to actually feel, to realize to the full the grandeur of its depth, or to contemplate closely the vast proportions of the mountain walls that encompass it, and the dizzy heights to which they soar. This trip, therefore, we set out to do,—on the morning following our visit to Glacier Point,—after we had first partaken of a very early breakfast.

The two falls we have just mentioned are made by the Merced River during the course of its descent from the level of the Sierra into the Yosemite Valley proper, through a deep, still narrower gorge, which is called after the name of the river, the Merced Cañon. The main valley, it will be remembered, branches off into three distinct cañons, about three miles above the Yosemite Falls Hotel. The most northern of these, the one called the Tenaya Cañon, is a distinct continuation of the main valley, having a due north-east direction, and containing such prominent features as the North and South (Half) Domes, the Washington Column, Mt. Watkins, the Mirror Lake, etc. South of this is the Merced Cañon, extending due east; and directly below this is the Illilouette or South Cañon, extending due south. All three gorges branch off together, at about one and the same spot. We will now follow along the Merced Cañon and note some of its salient features.

The excursion along this gorge is about the most charming that can possibly be taken, whether it be accomplished on foot or horseback. The Merced is ever beside you, first gently flowing as you leave the main valley, then madly foaming in wild, headlong career as you penetrate further the ravine and mount higher and higher over immense boulders, till you reach that beautiful fall, the Vernal,—the *Pi-wy-ack* or "Sparkling Water" of the Indians,—which is worth all the trouble of the mounting to see. It is worth the journey across

America, worth the journey from England even to California to look upon free from care and undisturbed ; and this is admitting a very great deal. But there is the wild forest, too, around you all the while, with its splendid variety of stately trees, and with ferns and wild flowers growing profusely at your feet. Cascades trickle down the mountain side, some having sufficient volume to visibly reach the bottom, others becoming gradually lost to view before they have descended half-way. One is awe-struck at the huge proportions of the precipices running down as they do so steep and so straight, with heights of three or four thousand feet, seldom less than a thousand. That piece of projecting rock posed in mid-air at Glacier Point, which we so recklessly jumped upon, we could see by straining our eyes intently, 3700 feet above us. And, close beside it, there poured over the cliff a lovely little fall—a flaky streak of gray which descended for a couple of thousand feet till it became scattered into fragments, diffused into a feathery mist, when at last it melted entirely out of sight into invisible vapour.

It was a climb of some miles to the foot of the Vernal Fall. We were on horseback again, for there were several streams to ford, which crossed the path as they flowed from the mountains on our left to join the Merced River which flowed close beside us on our right. The trail was laid over huge masses of rock, keeping close to the river, where it leaped down the gorge. At length we reached the famous spot where the Vernal Fall first comes into sight. It is a romantic dell in a deep-sunk gully, one of the most fairy-like spots in the whole of the Yosemite. Over a smooth wall of square-cut granite stretching across the ravine, there pours a sheet of glistening white, 400 feet in depth—as near as can be measured—and seventy-five feet in width, perfectly unbroken in its descent, the elegance of whose proportions strikes one immediately as sublime. The peculiar charm of this fall when viewed from below is seen in the striking manner in which it is discharged over the precipice. It does not merely drop into the chasm below, but owing to the steady, gradual slope of its smooth granite channel above, and at the same time to the great speed with which the full volume of water comes rushing on and is propelled over the precipice, it shoots out like an

THE NEVADA FALL, YOSEMITE VALLEY. *Page* 375.

arrow far into mid-air before it commences to bend, and then it seems to part itself and descend in four long, distinctly-defined curls—not in one uniform sheet, but like inverted flutings in a column, like folds of muslin in a dress; and the purity, the bluish transparency of the water is most remarkable. By enduring a thorough soaking from the blinding spray showered around, you can get off your horse and ascend on foot to the top of the fall, by a staircase fixed into the perpendicular wall to the side of it, the guide leading your horse up the mountain trail to meet you above when you have succeeded in climbing the steps. The greatest care, however, has to be exercised in approaching these steps, for everything is made as slippery as ice from the perpetual wetting of the spray. A remarkable naturally-formed parapet of granite runs along the extreme edge of the precipice, which is just high enough to enable you to rest your arms upon it and look down comfortably into the chasm out of which you have ascended, or even directly over the crest of the huge falling wave itself; for, as with the American Fall of the Niagara River, you can stand close enough to catch hold of the swift wave as it smoothly leaps into the abyss to its destruction. And more.—You can lean against that parapet and, secure from danger, yet with the cataract but a few inches from you, contemplate the wondrous view to be here obtained of the whole cañon. It is impossible to represent in words to those who have never seen it the impressiveness of this scene, the awful majesty of that huge background of mountain that bounds the far end of the gorge, the exquisite beauty and richness of the foliage which clothes the whole length of it. And then there is that deadening thud of the cataract as it comes crashing against the rocks 400 feet beneath you, that "eternal sound of many waters," which language cannot express—that overwhelming roar which, like the roar of Niagara, is so stupefying at first, but which becomes in time such an aid to meditation that you stand there and gaze upon the scene till you become unconscious of all around you, regardless even of the presence of the fall so close at hand. And so you will remain till you are roused from your reverie.

But there is that other great plunge of the Merced to be visited—the Nevada Fall, which is just visible from our elevated position a mile further up the cañon. At the same time we can see a huge mass of granite towering close beside it on the left, one of the most remarkable dome-mountains of the region. This is Mt. Broderick; or the "Cap of Liberty," as it is usually called. It is a rounded, smooth-faced, almost vertical precipice rising 2000 feet above the crest of the fall. The effect of the sight of this stupendous, conical-shaped mountain, is exceptionally fine and imposing. So close upon the fall does the base of the mountain lie that it seems to be part and parcel of the wall of rock over which the cataract springs. Its sides are almost vertical, and appear quite smoothed and polished, lying as it were in slices, as if the rock had been carefully pared with a workman's chisel; and this peculiarity of the granite formation is noticeable not only in this instance, but in the case of all the rocks in the Yosemite. At the base of the "Cap" grow many tall pines. Even out of its smooth sides there grow a few, and on its summit can be traced a few more.

Between its two falls the Merced dashes down the gorge at a fearful pace, descending 300 feet in a deep granite channel over huge boulders in a series of little cataracts. It is rough climbing from one fall to the other, and especially will the traveller find it so if he forsake the trail—as we did—and try to pick his way over the rocks by the side of the torrent. Indeed he will probably follow our example and give up the attempt in despair, and, returning to the trail, which keeps to higher ground, adhere to it till he finds himself close underneath and in full view of that glorious plunge, which an authority has described as "one of the grandest waterfalls in the world."

The Nevada Fall fully merits all the eulogy which has been heaped upon it by its admirers, for it is indeed a glorious leap, and one possessing some very remarkable and lovely features. It plunges 700 feet. Yet this plunge is not perpendicular, for not many feet below where it has topped the precipice it strikes with its full force against a projecting ledge of rock, and this causes it to shoot out anew into a still wider sheet, for, expanding now to a width of 200 feet, it descends the remainder of the distance in a net-work of fleecy curls, with an effect which is exquisitely beautiful, and which lends to the fall a peculiarly distinctive charm. The curled, crisped appearance of this fall constitutes one of the most striking sights in the Yosemite. One might liken it to the arrangement or disposition of the sea-waves as they gently break upon a flat, sandy shore. But to this must be added the active force with which each wave is thrown out; and then, if it is also borne in mind that there are hundreds of such wave-jets in this one grand sheet,—hundreds shot out at the same time followed by hundreds more while these are dying out of sight,—some idea, incomplete though it will be, may be obtained of the remarkable form of this most beautiful fall.

There is a "lunch house" set up at the Nevada Fall, as at Glacier Point, and a Mr. Snow keeps it. It is situated near the foot of the cataract. Mr. Snow has a few spare beds, which are occupied at times by hunters and adventurous mountain-climbers, such as those who come in quest of "big game" on the higher Sierra and those who come to try and scale the South Dome, for "Snow's" is a capital starting-point for doing either the one or the other. Here we found some of our friends from the hotel, and we sat down to luncheon a party of nine. A lady and gentleman from Utica, New York State, had come up on horseback from the hotel, having started earlier than we had done in the morning. They had travelled with us all the way from Salt Lake City to Stockton, where they left us to see the Yosemite before proceeding to the Golden City. Meanwhile we had seen the Golden City and had come on to the Yosemite. Two other Americans and three Englishmen, besides my fellow-traveller and myself, constituted the remainder of the party.

The Indians have given poetical names to the prominent objects of the Yosemite Valley: there is poetry in all their terms. The Vernal Fall, we have seen, they call *Pi-wy-ack*, the "Sparkling Water" according to the translation of some, while others have rendered the term to mean the "Shower of Crystals"—or the "Diamond Fall," which is far more expressive. There is no poetry whatever in the American name "Vernal;" indeed it is simply meaningless. The Indians, again, call the Nevada Fall *Yo-wi-ye*, the "Great Twisted" or

"Great Meandering" Fall, which is about the most appropriate name by which it could be designated. The Cap of Liberty they call *Mahtah*, or the "Martyr" mountain.

The white, glistening sheet of the Nevada Fall is thrown into splendid relief by the blackness of the smooth wall of rock over which it plunges, as well as by the fresh greenness of the trees which clothe the sides of its basin. We ascended to the top of the fall by a steep path at the side, and, as we mounted, the roar of the cataract became simply appalling. Once above the fall, however, and gazing down the abyss into that thick cloud of foam, the roar so loud and terrible became changed into a hollow, deadening rumble, somewhat like continual cannonading several miles away.—But it is impossible to write a description of the sound, so that the rest must be left to the reader's imagination.

In a hollow behind a slightly projecting shelf in the wall of the precipice, close by the side of the fall, an eagle had made her nest. We could see two of her young in it tearing away at a squirrel, which the mother had brought them, though she had fortunately since taken her departure. An American gentleman with us stood at the top of the cliff and commenced dropping stones upon the heads of the little creatures, who were about fifty feet below, just to surprise them a little, not to injure them in any way. But a friend of his—another American gentleman—caused him to desist from his occupation by a well-timed rebuke, and to make him feel rather ashamed of himself, for he said to him, "What do you think these Britishers must think of you, throwing stones like that at our American Eagle? *D'you think they'd do it to their Lion?*"

There is a house close beside the Yosemite Falls Hotel which, with all its rooms on the ground floor, is devoted to billiards and hot and cold baths. It is also used as a general laundry. The billiard-room, with one table in it, is commodious, and is resorted to by many persons during the course of an evening. Just inside the doorway, to the left as one enters, there is a high desk supporting a large book bound in morocco, having silver clasps and borders, the worth of the whole volume amounting to 160*l*. This book is the "Grand Register," or the visitors' book of the Yosemite, in which every person who visits the valley is supposed to write his or her name, and to express an opinion as to the valley's beauties, grandeur, sublimity—or otherwise. A set of pages is apportioned to every State and Territory in the country, and to almost every other country in the world. It may not be out of place to give a few extracts from the volume. Thus—a Massachusetts gentleman writes as follows: "Plymouth Rock to the Rocks of the Yosemite, which in their grandeur illustrate the sublime events and principles of which it is itself a symbol, greeting." A lady from Baltimore writes, "Let me embrace thee, beautiful valley—a kiss to thee!" One signing herself "Little Rhody," puts after her name "Hail, Colombia!" An Australian gives his opinion that "America is the dertiest country in the world." Another writes, "This day Freddy strong, 6 years old, rode 38 miles on horseback." But perhaps the redeeming feature of the collection is a verse composed on the name of the valley, showing four of the several ways people are in the habit of pronouncing it. This verse runs as follows:

> "At half-past nine o'clock at night
> Our party reached the Yo-se-*mite*,
> Glad ere the evening lamps were lit,
> To see the valley Yo-se-*mite*.
> Who that has seen it can condemn it,
> The wondrous beauty of Yo-*sem*-ite?
> This ode I dedicate to the,
> O world-renowned Yo-sem-i-*te!*"

The author of these lines, however, has not managed to bring into his composition the only proper and accepted pronunciation, which, as already mentioned, is a four-syllable word with the accent on the second syllable, or antepenult, the other syllables being pronounced equally, thus Yo-*sem*-i-te. This added to the other methods would make a fifth way of pronouncing the word.

A bath in this house costs 3s., though the river flows past the window, where it can be obtained for nothing. With regard to other charges in the Yosemite Valley, 3s. is charged for a small bottle of Bass's Ale; 2s. for a bottle of the ordinary lager-beer; 6s. for a pint-bottle of indifferent St. Julien; and 3s. for having a flannel shirt, a handkerchief, and a pair of socks washed! At one place we stopped at on our way to the valley we had to pay 2s. for having our boots blacked.

There was a little building not far from our hotel, presided over by a German, Herr Adolph Sinning, who (to quote from his card) is "Maker of Small Yosemite Curiosities, Cabinet and Fancy Articles, Walking Canes, Pin Cushions, Ladies' Workboxes, and Manzinita Rulers, inlaid with twelve different woods; all neatly inlaid in various woods of the Yosemite and its vicinity, such as Indian Arrow, Mountain Mahogany, Laurel, Spicewood, Live Oak, Manzinita, Buckthorn, Lilac, Ceanothus, Silver Fir, Douglas Spruce, Juniper, Cedar, Sugar Pine, etc., etc." We made an interesting inspection of Mr. Sinning's curiosity-shop, for here we found tables, chairs, walking-sticks, parasols, cabinets, etc., all fashioned out of the various woods of the valley and vicinity, as well as a fine assortment of seeds; also a collection of fossils and minerals. I have to thank this gentleman for presenting me with several packets of seeds of the Giant Tree, Manzinita, Tamarack fir, etc., which he kindly asked me to take away with me when I left the valley.

Opposite our hotel there was a house built round the stump of a tree. This tree was a red fir, or Douglas spruce; and the stump, which had large proportions,—but which we unfortunately forgot to measure,—formed a conspicuous though rather bulky ornament in the centre of the drawing-room. We found this to be Mr. Bernard's family dwelling-house, though sometimes, when his hotel over the way was overcrowded, he very considerately turned out and gave up to his guests the use of his mansion. Miss Bernard, his daughter, had acquired a reputation as a daring climber of mountains, for she had been to the top of the South Dome, and had safely come to the bottom again. This mountain, it seems, was first ascended in the year 1875. Of course (as we have seen) it is accessible from one side only, namely the side away from the valley, where the mountain is rounded like a ball, the upper portion of the rock facing the valley being a perfectly smooth, clear drop of 2000 vertical feet. To one George Anderson, a Scotchman from Montrose, is due the honour of being the first to "climb off" the mountain; and this he managed to do by drilling holes into the hard granite, into which he drove iron pins, till they stood about six inches out of the rock, and then he extended and fastened to the pins nearly 1000 feet of rope, and hand over hand pulled himself up, and then let himself down in the same sort of fashion.

It may, perhaps, be interesting to describe an ascent of this mountain, which my fellow-traveller accomplished, un-

THE SOUTH DOME.

accompanied, on the third day of our stay in the valley, namely on June 29th.

The day was drawing to a close, and a party of our hotel friends were sitting outside "Bernard's," at 8 p.m., listening to the distant murmur of the Yosemite Fall across the valley—which filled the air like, one might say, the rasping, gentle sound of sea-waves breaking continuously and evenly upon a pebbly beach. Little did I imagine where my friend had betaken himself since I parted with him in the morning. He had started away without telling any of us whither he was bent, with only a few biscuits in his pocket and a little sherry in his flask, trusting simply to the use of his legs and to a stick which he carried in his hand—all which looked very suspicious, so that we wondered where he could possibly be going to. It was getting late, so that I had begun to be anxious. Suddenly he burst in upon our party assembled outside the hotel. He looked wild and scared; his skin was peeled—it was evident he had not been idle since we had lost sight of him in the morning. He told us he had been up the South Dome. "What, up to the top?" we all exclaimed in one breath. "Yes," was the reply.—But no, we could none of us believe it, not even Miss Bernard herself, who, already the vanquisher of that bold, inaccessible-looking mountain, would never believe that it had been scaled in one day, and that, too, by an Englishman, and all by himself! Without more ado my friend produced indisputable evidence that he had actually accomplished the ascent, for he took out from his pocket a certain curious trophy which he had brought away with him from the summit, and this was nothing less than a piece of one of Miss Bernard's stockings, the young lady in question having left behind her, when she was last up the mountain, a sample of this portion of her wearing apparel, which she had fastened on to a low stunted pine that grew out of the hard rock at the very top of the precipice. So my friend had cut off part of the stocking—six square inches of which he found clinging to the tree—and brought it down to show the young lady herself, as the best proof he could give, that he was indeed no gay deceiver.

The following is the description my friend has written of his ascent of the South Dome:

"Leaving Bernard's on foot at 10 a.m., I reached Snow's at 12.10 p.m., had luncheon there, and remained till 1.30. Then, mounting to the top of the Nevada Fall, I struck off by a trail to the left, which led me over a shoulder of the great South Dome till I came to the foot of a conical-shaped rock, called the Little Dome, which I found I was obliged to climb. The latter required great care in the ascent, as it consisted of a 'ball,' as it were, of smooth, polished, round precipice of about 800 feet in height. This successfully scaled, I had to descend again about as many feet as I had just come up, in climbing the Little Dome, this time into a real 'mickledore' or dip between the two Domes, the huge granite mass of the South Dome now looming majestically above me. The rope of the Scotchman now appeared to view, running down straight for 960 feet from the top of the curve, close to the vertical face of the mountain. After resting a while in the dip, I began the ascent in earnest. Great precaution had now to be used. First I made sure of the soundness of the rope by testing its lower portion with my full weight, as I afterwards did with each portion in succession. The sections of this rope are not all equal, some being not more than twenty feet in length, while one or two sections near the top of the curve are nearly 100 feet in length, and, being quite loose, thus oblige one to describe a considerable arc. Where the sections are short you go up like a monkey, hand over hand, close to the rock. The lower portion of the precipice was very steep, having an angle of 10° from the vertical, and this part had to be ascended without any rest. From this point the grand curve of the Dome began, the granite lying here and there in immense overlapping, concentric slabs—like gigantic armour-plates, the 'plates' in this case being three to five feet thick, difficult to climb over, even with the aid of the rope. Over these I had to scramble as best I could; but there were a few cracks in the granite which enabled me to obtain an occasional foothold, and, leaning with my back against the almost vertical wall of rock, rest awhile and contemplate the view. Some people accustomed to mountain-climbing have attempted to scale this precipice, but have not succeeded in getting more than half-way before they have become dizzy and have had to come down again; and this it is easy to understand. In going up a sheer, even a vertical precipice by rope, you have something near at hand to fix your eyes upon; but in going up the South Dome you seem to be climbing over a vast ball of stone, and in one portion of the ascent you can neither see above nor below. You seem to be suspended in the air, and separated from earth altogether, as if you were in a huge balloon. Far away loom the snow-peaks of the Sierra, but many of the objects nearer at hand, such as those down in the valley, which is sunk sheer beneath, are absolutely indistinguishable.

"The gymnastic performance now began to get easier as to the grade; but the fatigue caused by the rarity of the air, and the heat of a blazing Californian sun, glaring as it did directly in my face, caused me to inwardly rejoice when I reached the summit. That this is a much less difficult—though not the less dangerous—climb than it looks, is certain, and provided the soundness of the rope be guaranteed, a lady can without difficulty make the ascent. But her chief embarrassment would be the 'monkey' performance, if she went up in ordinary attire.

"Having rested for a few moments on the top of a stony couch,—which during those few moments vied with the most luxurious feather-bed in pleasurable sensation and comfort,—the next thing to do was to quench thirst, which had become simply unendurable. To this end I made my way to a small snow-field lying about 200 yards off. Then I devoted an hour to the view, sitting down on the edge of the precipice and dangling my legs over, having first lit my pipe that I might enjoy the view the better. Beneath me, dwarfed and in miniature, lay this remarkable Yosemite. Its domes looked like bosses of stone, its mighty waterfalls appeared as threads of gleaming silver streaking the mountain sides; while almost directly under me was the Mirror Lake, now dwindled to the size of a veritable reflector. The platform of the boat-house was indistinguishable, while the house itself seemed a mere dog-kennel, and human beings and animals could not be discerned. Perhaps the finer view lay, at this height, rather in the splendid snow-peaks around than in the Yosemite Valley, though from this eminence one obtained a better idea of the formation of this extraordinary chasm than would be possible from any other. It appeared to me, clearly, to be a drop of 4000 feet in the general base-line of the Sierra, from which the peaks may be said to rise from 10,000 to 14,000 feet above the sea-level. From this vantage-ground one could realize, in a measure, the gigantic action and wondrous effects of the Great Ice Age, or Glacial

Epoch. One can imagine an immense glacier-field, with its icy feelers,—say some thousands of feet thick,—covering the whole of this region, and denuding, eroding, moulding, scoring, polishing the domes and spires of granite; and then, under altered climatic conditions, gradually melting away and evacuating the mighty gorge or chasm which it had previously occupied.

"The descent I found considerably easier than the ascent, for the rope had now been fully tested, and all that it was necessary to do was to cling firmly to it, and let myself down hand over hand. At Snow's I received an ovation. Mr. Snow offered me claret and cigars (both which I accepted), and Mrs. Snow wanted me to stop the evening and write an account of the ascent in her "Book of Wonders;" but this was out of the question. I was given a tallow candle, to light if it should get too dark during my descent into the valley. But it was not brought into requisition, for I reached Bernard's at 8.18 p.m., having been away from the hotel just ten hours and eighteen minutes."

It will be interesting for us to consider, briefly, what were the geological agencies that helped to bring about this unusual form of chasm, gorge, or valley, with such mighty precipices, such perpendicular waterfalls, such a glorious combination, too, of all that is grand and lovely in Nature. The Yosemite Valley, however, presents so many peculiar features that it will be found no easy matter to arrive at a satisfactory conclusion concerning them. These are: the smooth, polished, nearly vertical walls of granite; the almost absolutely level bottom, with a slight dip towards the east; the general absence of *débris* and talus, except such as have recently fallen; the absence of moraine; the abrupt, perpendicular waterfalls; the fact that the sides of the valley do not correspond, but present curious, abrupt angles, at various points of which the corresponding recesses are totally wanting; the fantastic, rounded "domes" and "spires;" and last, but by no means least, the precipice of the South Dome.

Professor Le Conte and Professor Whitney, the two eminent American geologists, entertain distinct theories respecting the formation of this valley. The former regards the whole formation as being due to a gradual and regular operation of erosive agents "assisted by antecedent igneous agencies producing fissures which have been enlarged and deepened by water and by ice, and that during the present or recent geological times." Professor Whitney, on the other hand, attributes the formation to a sudden disturbance of the strata occurring during the upheaval of the Sierra. The latter authority rejects, as a primary cause, (1) ice action and water action, because (Professor Whitney says) cañons or gorges formed by these agents have never vertical cliffs, nor the strange, angular appearance of the Yosemite Valley; also (2) fissures, because the opposite sides of the valley show no correspondence. He rejects, moreover, the idea of (3) folding, or flexures of the strata, because the valley, instead of being parallel with the mountain-range, is transverse to it. The Professor, therefore, admits that he is reduced to a theory of subsidence, or a "drop," and this owing to the withdrawal of support during the great convulsion which occurred when the Sierra was elevated, during the Jurassic Period. He further supposes that all the immense mass of granite blocks and *débris* went to fill up this chasm of unknown depth, thus formed, to nearly its present level.

Without appearing presumptuous, I may here introduce the theory of my fellow-traveller, Mr. A. N. Clarke, who offers, as an opinion, that the valley received its formation by the long duration of ordinary erosive agencies acting on a vein of softer or disintegrated granite; that the Ice Age continued this, during its irresistible progress, by scooping out the chasm, leaving the hard walls nearly vertical on account of the perpendicular cleavage; that the Epoch of Floods completed it—as Professor Le Conte says—by carrying away and re-depositing the glacial *débris*, the lake afterwards formed depositing various other sediments, and leaving the bottom level.

There remains, however, the difficulty of the South Dome precipice of 2000 vertical feet, for clearly the "drop" or subsidence must have taken place prior to the Glacial Epoch, since the sides of the valley show evidences of ice action, and Professor Whitney allows that the valley was certainly once filled by a lake. How then does it happen that this mountain of almost 5000 feet above the valley has its upper portion of 2000 feet as smooth and sharp-edged as though the rock had been hewn in twain by an axe? Surely the glaciers ploughing over the region must have toned down the sharp-cut edges, as they clearly have done in the case of the Captain Rock and the Cap of Liberty, and other great rocks. It may be that the long-continued action of frosts on the perpendicular cleavage separated a portion of the precipice, which in post-glacial times fell, forming the *débris* of the slope, thus leaving the face of the Dome abrupt and clear-cut at the edges. Professor Whitney states that large masses of rock frequently fall from this cause, which will in time alter the appearance of the valley.

We will try to conceive the history of this chasm during the Glacial and subsequent epochs. When the Glacial Epoch was fully established, the greater part of California was doubtless covered with an immense ice-sheet, and the valleys with its icy feelers, or by separate glaciers, which, ever advancing, continued the work already begun by scoring and polishing the walls of this chasm. We can conceive that during the Champlain Epoch, or Epoch of Great Floods, which naturally followed the melting of the ice through successive changes of climate, the Yosemite Valley was filled by a large lake,—of which there are evidences now, as also of the glacier,—and that this completed the sculpture of the chasm by re-polishing the precipices and depositing the gravel and sand which it brought from the higher regions. Picture then for one moment this weird, primæval lake, seven miles long and nearly a mile broad, partially occupied by bergs of ice, with sheer perpendicular cliffs, over which for the first time poured with awful roar tremendous cataracts, whose remains are seen to-day in the several magnificent waterfalls of the valley, as are their sources the dwarfed glaciers hidden away among the deep recesses of the peaks of the Sierra.[1] Little

---

[1] The Skjæggedalvand in Norway is a similar instance of a glacier lake. This is a lake 3000 feet above the sea, five miles in length, scooped out by a glacier which has left plain traces of its course down to the fjord, and is surrounded by nearly vertical walls of rock, with a splendid waterfall—one of the finest in the country—leaping over a lofty precipice into it.

by little the ice-fields and glaciers dwindled away among the loftier peaks. The lake gradually sank, leaving bare the smooth sandy bottom, upon which soil speedily formed as the River Merced drained the valley. Abundant vegetation sprang up; and the chasm became transformed at last from a cold, desolate-looking lake into the lovely *Ah-wah-nee* or Yosemite Valley, teeming with life and peopled with denizens of air and forest.

CHAPTER XX.

AWAY EAST.

Leaving the Yosemite Valley—Eastward to New York—To Chinese Camp—A Jehu madly drives—Copperopolis—To Milton—A bone-shaking ride to catch a train—Back again to Stockton—Left behind—Return to Salt Lake City—791 miles to Ogden—The Fourth of July—Celebrating "the Fourth" at Ogden—On the road to "Zion"—An accident by the way—A serious scrape—Again in the Mormon metropolis—A concert in the Tabernacle—Programme of the concert—Amusements at Lake Point—Brigham Young's Fun Hall—A theatrical performance—Leaving Salt Lake City—Over the Rocky Mountains—A peep into Colorado—A run down to Denver—Cattle in the way—A sample of Coloradan railway-travelling—The chief attractions of Colorado—A glorious country—Denver—Its sudden rise—Its free schools—The American free school system—Denver's fine situation—Clearness of the atmosphere—Prosperity of the State—Its business record of 1879—The mining, live-stock, and agricultural industries—Invigorating climate—Camping out under canvas—Mining cities of Colorado—The trips to Georgetown and Leadville—A railway 10,139 feet above the sea—The "Great Carbonate Camp"—A mining wonder—The mines of Leadville—Their yield in 1879—A mine 14,200 feet above the sea—Leaving Denver—Eastward to the Missourian capital—The fatal heat of St. Louis—A death-stricken city—A hasty retreat—Back again in New York—Conclusion.

LEAVING the Yosemite Valley at six o'clock on the morning of June 30th, we set out upon a long, continuous journey of 950 miles to Salt Lake City, the first halt we intended to make during a rapid journey to New York.

We first took the coach as far as Chinese Camp, a distance of sixty-one miles, reaching the hospitable roof of the Polish Count at 7.30 p.m. The dreadful jolting and banging about we had to endure during the "staging" of this day will be something to remember as long as we live. We were driven with a five-in-hand a good part of the distance. Marvellously directed, the horses spun round the corners at random speed, the reins being handled, we must confess, in a style we have never seen equalled ; so that we could not but admire the dexterity of our driver, although we were unfortunately the victims who were being so ruthlessly experimented upon. We were kept in an intense heat of excitement throughout the drive—what with holding on to the sides of the coach (an open one) when suddenly rounding a corner—keeping an eye at the same time on our packages to see they were not pitched out, and ourselves with them, especially when we darted after one on the point of disappearing, and then had to recover our equilibrium as best we could during the manifold jerks we received as we were bumped and twisted along. And we were indeed in a sorry plight, when we came to our journey's end, for not even the attractions of the Count's two daughters—who waited upon us at supper and talked to us while we ate—could prevent us from going straight to bed directly supper was over, for we felt as if there was hardly a sound spot left in our poor aching limbs.

The next morning (July 1st) we got up at four o'clock, had breakfast in company with our driver of the day before and the one who would take charge of us for the next portion of our drive (to Milton), and started away at five. In returning to Milton to catch the train to Stockton, we took a different route to the one we had come by when approaching the Yosemite Valley, for we coached in the first place to the mining settlement of Copperopolis, thirteen miles distant from Chinese Camp, which we reached at eight o'clock ; and here we proceeded to have a second breakfast. There is no need to explain that copper forms the chief attraction of the little colony of Copperopolis. But though extensive copper workings are to be found here, they are mostly surface-workings, the metal not lying deep in any considerable vein. Therefore it is not improbable that in a few years, Copperopolis will be simply non-existent. At this place, we caught the coach from Sonora, and were driven the remaining twenty miles to Milton. The coach during this part of the journey was a closed one, not the customary open "concord" break. There was room for six people inside, and two on the top of the vehicle by the side of the driver, the roof being reserved for the passengers' luggage. We were, however, overcrowded, most exceptionally so, for there were twenty-four candidates for a ride into Milton, and ten of our party were ladies. Eight of the latter were crowded inside; the two remaining ladies were allotted seats beside the driver; while the rest of us, total fourteen, had to hang about as best we could amongst the luggage at the top, and cling on to whatever was nearest us in the shape of a loose family-trunk or hamper as we were banged along what was nothing better than a cow-track; and the positions we were forced into were at times rather extraordinary. It was the most bone-shaking ride we had ever experienced, and may we never live to experience such an one again!

We were within an ace of missing the train at Milton, for we drove up to the station a quarter of an hour late, and found it just on the point of leaving without us. The hurry, bustle and confusion in getting into the train—in bundling ourselves and paraphernalia from the coach into the railway-carriage—occupied us barely a minute. It was a regular scramble. As it was, we went off, leaving one item behind, namely a box containing two large cones of the pitch pines of the Calaveras Grove. On our arrival at Salt Lake City we wrote to the Milton station-master about it, asking him to forward it on to the Brevoort House, New York, where we would pay for the carriage as soon as it arrived. When we reached New York nine days after writing from Salt Lake City, we found the box waiting there for us, though it had travelled over five companies' lines and a distance of 3200 miles.

On reaching Stockton, after twenty-eight miles' run, we found we had only twenty minutes to get to the Yosemite House—a mile and a half distant from the station—and bring away the heavier luggage we had deposited there, before the train which would take us East was due to arrive from San Francisco. So we jumped into a conveyance (with two horses, told the man to drive to the hotel with all speed, promising him an extra fee for his trouble if he succeeded in bringing us back to the station in time, and off we set at full speed along the streets, racing as if we were firemen on an engine hurrying to a distant conflagration—flying past everybody, raising blinding clouds of dust as we proceeded; and, the hotel reached, we found all our belongings,—which occupied us some minutes, for the chief cashier had mislaid the key of the room where he had deposited them,—bundled them into the carriage, and tore back to the station the same pace we had come. Seeing two trains drawn up alongside of each other, we jumped into the one nearest to us, being told it was "the overland;" and while I looked after the luggage to see that it was properly "checked" to Salt Lake City, my friend set out on an excursion through the train in search of a sleeping-car. The engine bell now began to ring and the train to move out of the station, and at the same time the other train drawn up alongside commenced moving in a contrary direction. I happened to ask a passenger sitting beside me whether I was all right for Ogden—"Not a bit of it," said he, "you're going to San Francisco!" I had, then, in my hurry, jumped into the wrong train. I was returning to the Golden City in the "western overland," and the other train was the "eastern overland" which I ought to have been in! It was too late for me now to shift my position, for the "eastern overland" was puffing away merrily ahead, quite beyond catching distance. But I thought that I would ascertain whether my friend had also been left behind, so I set out on an expedition through the train to look for him. I searched right and left, first in one car then in another, all through the train—but no: he was nowhere to be found. He had jumped on to the "eastern overland" in time, when he had discovered his mistake, and was now well away on his 828-mile journey to Salt Lake City, whereas I happened to be going in the very opposite direction! So I consoled myself with the reflection that he would probably go straight to Salt Lake City, and remain there till I had put in an appearance. Fortunately we pulled up at Lathrop, the next station to Stockton, ten miles from it—and one that possessed a capital *buffet*. Having learnt, when I reached that place, that the next Ogden train would be due the next afternoon, I took the first opportunity and returned to Stockton (by a ballast train) for the night, and waited there patiently for the next "eastern overland."

Stockton, or the "City of Windmills,"[1] has a population of 13,000; has existed for thirty-two years; contains some well-built streets; has fourteen churches; four banks; supports two daily and two weekly newspapers; is the centre of an immense grain trade; is about the hottest place in Cali-

THE PULPIT ROCK, PACIFIC RAILROAD.
(*See page* 143.)

fornia; and, as we have already mentioned, abounds with mosquitos. There is nothing further to say about the place that would be likely to interest the reader—except, perhaps, that it is supplied with water from an artesian well 1002 feet deep, which discharges 300,000 gallons of pure water daily.

[1] See page 283.

On the afternoon following my arrival at Stockton I caught the overland train, and set out for Salt Lake City. Nothing need be said here of my return journey to the Mormon capital, or at least of that portion of it as far as Ogden Junction, for a sufficient description of the route has already been given. After travelling for nearly two days—passing again over the Sierra Nevada and crossing the Nevada and American Deserts; exchanging the Golden State of California for the Desert State of Nevada, and that again for the territory of Utah—I reached Ogden at eight o'clock on the morning of Thursday, July 4th, and found the station gaily decorated with moss and pretty flowers, and a profusion of evergreens intermingled with streamers of the red, white and blue stars and stripes depending from little pieces of stick, the platform crowded with men and women dressed in their very best attire, every man with a little flower-garden in his button-hole and every woman clothed in a garb of purest white calico—all looking very happy and pleased, as if the day were a *dies non*, and it were the duty of everyone to lay aside care and trouble for a little while, and to enjoy the occasion with the best means at disposal. And why such a scene—the station so gaily decked, the people so smartly dressed, everybody looking so happy and contented? It was the Fourth of July, the "great and glorious Fourth," the natal day of the great American Republic, the one hundred and second anniversary of the Declaration of Independence, on which national holiday every city, town, and village in the Union puts on its gayest appearance, and, wherever it is possible, processions are formed and speeches are made, dancing parties and social gatherings of every description are organized, fêtes and amusements are provided for every variety of taste, eatables and drinkables in profusion for all that can buy; in short, the whole nation goes zealously to work and annually celebrates in downright good earnest the birthday of its Freedom, and such a fact says much for the patriotism of the American people. On the morning in question the people of Ogden had turned out *en masse* to spend the festal day in the Mormon capital, to visit their saintly brethren there, to see "Zion's glories," or perhaps to take a trip in the steamer on the Great Salt Lake. On the other hand the people of "Zion" had turned out to spend their day in Ogden, to take a free ride in a street-car through the city, or to loiter about the machine-shops of the Union Pacific Railroad; or perhaps they would take a turn up the mountain overlooking the city, so that they might gaze down in rapture upon the Valley of the Salt Lake—the "Land of Promise," according to the foretelling of their deceased prophet, Brigham Young. But there was more than this to do in Ogden on this festive occasion, judging by the following announcement of the *Salt Lake Daily Tribune:* "Hurrah! Band Excursion for the Fourth! The Tenth Ward Band has completed arrangements to celebrate the Fourth in Ogden. The finest Grove is engaged for the Day. Swings, Croquet, Quoits, Rotary Swing, Horizontal Bar, Fishing, Greasy Pole, Dancing, etc. Immense Hall capable of accommodating 1000 persons in event of a storm. Tickets to Ogden and return One Dollar, including Dancing and Sports in the Grove. The Band will appear in their elegant new Uniform;" and in another portion of the same paper, "Dancing will commence at 4 p.m., and continue until all are satisfied." No wonder, then, that the Ogden station was so crowded this morning, for the train had just come in from Salt Lake City: yet a good number of the people were from Ogden bound for Salt Lake City by the next returning train. This started an hour after my arrival from Stockton, so that I had time to take breakfast leisurely beforehand. When I came to the Salt Lake train I found that there was hardly room even to get upon it, so densely packed were its five cars with the people of Ogden bound for "Zion." These were mostly girls —silly, giddy, frivolous, light-hearted Mormon girls, who with their rigidly-starched, white-cotton dresses showily trimmed with red and blue ribbon, wore on their heads little chaplets of flowers, and all seemed to be provided with small flags of the Stars and Stripes. But so overloaded was the train, that I had to ride all the way—thirty-seven miles—standing on the steps of my car, and had to put up with the full vigour of the strong sulphurous odour that proceeded from some hot springs lying near the railway, as we rode close beside them. However, I was enabled to be an eye-witness of an accident which might have been attended with the most alarming results had it not been for the gentle pace at which we were proceeding at the time, for we calmly and deliberately rode into the midst of a herd of about fifty or sixty oxen, who had chosen to locate themselves on the rails in the very path of the approaching train. As it was we carried one unfortunate victim—a poor luckless cow—for a considerable distance in front of the "scraper" of our engine, before we could pull up so as to enable her to get out of the way. Then indeed the poor creature was found to be so sadly lacerated, that the most humane thing would have been to pack it off at once to the butcher to be turned into beef-steak for a few hungry Mormons, instead of allowing it to remain by the side of the line, there to probably die of its wounds.

Arriving at the Salt Lake City station at 11.30 a.m., I was told that there was a concert taking place in the Tabernacle. So I jumped into a street-car, was driven to the Walker House, and finding there that my friend had safely arrived and that he was in the Tabernacle, listening to the music, I too set out for the Mormon House of Worship, to hear what Mormon singing was like. The concert was got up on behalf of the Tabernacle building fund, and was arranged to be given on the Fourth of July, as there would be a likelihood of a considerable addition to the funds through the presence of so many visitors in the metropolis on that day. When I reached the building I found the concert half over, and the performers about to commence the second part of the programme. About 200 (I should say) people, mostly women, constituted the choir, which was ranged on either side of the large organ. The great building was completely filled, the audience being chiefly composed of the gentler sex. On the rostrum, in front of the organ, was conspicuous the figure of President John Taylor. I was sorry that I did not happen to arrive a little earlier, for, as I learnt from my friend afterwards, President Taylor offered up a remarkable prayer at the commencement of the concert, towards the close of which some babies in the body of the building began screaming, which caused him to ejaculate, by way of conclusion of his prayer, " If those babies squawl, put 'em out.—Amen ! " The following is the programme of this concert, and it will be seen what a mixture there is of the secular and religious in its composition:

PART I.
1. Grand Selection, "Girofle Girofla" . . . . *Riviere.*
    Full Orchestra and Great Organ.
2. Chorus, "Happy and Light" (from Bohemian Girl) . *Balfe.*
    Choir.
3. Duet, "Hard Times" (by request)
    Mr. Wm. W. Willes and Mr. G. Goddard.
4. Organ Solo,
    Mr. J. J. Daynes.
5. Solo, Duet and Chorus, "I waited for the Lord" . . *Mendelssohn.*
    Mrs. L. Careless, Miss S. E. Olsen and Choir.
6. Song, "Once again" . . . . . . *Sullivan.*
    Mr. M. H. McAllister.
7. Duet, "See the Pale Moon" . . . . . *Campana.*
    Miss L. Nebeker and Miss L. E. Olsen.
8. Song, "Ah! Che la Morte" (from Trovatore) . . *Verdi.*
    Mr. W. H. Foster.
9. Solo and Chorus, "Land of the Trumpet" . . . *Donizetti.*

Interval of Ten Minutes.

PART II.
1. Overture, "Semiramide" . . . . . *Rossini.*
    Orchestra and Organ.
2. Duet, "He shall feed his Flock" (Messiah). . . *Handel.*
    Mrs. L. Careless and Miss S. E. Olsen.
3. Chorus, "Behold the Lamb" (Messiah) . . . *Handel.*
    Choir.
4. "Pastoral Symphony" (Messiah) . . . . *Handel.*
    Orchestra and Organ.
5. Solo, "I know that my Redeemer liveth" (Messiah) . *Handel.*
    Mrs. L. Careless.
6. Song, "Tempest of the Heart" (Trovatore) . . *Verdi.*
    Mr. B. B. Young.
7. Four Part Song, "When Evening's Twilight" . . *Hatton.*
    Male members of the Choir.
8. Song, "Bonnie Sweet Bessie" . . . . . *Gilbert.*
    Mrs. L. Careless.
9. Chorus, "We all like Sheep (!)" (Messiah) . , . *Handel.*
    Full Company.

When the women of the chorus were not vocally employed they occupied their time advantageously in another way altogether, for I noticed that a large tankard was passed round for everyone to drink out of; and nearly everyone did. What it contained, I am not in a position to say. It may have been water, or it may have been beer. At any rate, whatever it contained, I cannot say that the singing was improved by the repeated imbibing, for a lamer performance I never heard in my life. Everything was wretchedly executed, even the performance on the organ by Mr. J. J. Daynes. Mr. George Careless was the conductor, and, judging of his powers by the performances of his pupils, he appeared to be very well named.

There were other entertainments, besides the concert in the Tabernacle, provided for the Saints and Gentiles of Salt Lake City on this the great national holiday. There was, for instance, a grand "bathing fête"—whatever that might have meant—in " Utah's briny sea." Perhaps it was in connexion with this "fête" that there had appeared in the *Salt Lake Daily Tribune*, in the morning, the following announcement: " Bathing Suits to order in six hours. We have a large stock of the latest styles of samples to select from, and we will make you a bathing suit to order, any style you wish, guarantee a perfect fit and deliver it in six hours.—Sipman and Davis." Again, another similar notice appeared in the columns of the same paper, as follows : " Goldberg and Co. have a large lot of sample bathing suits. They are the nobbiest yet offered to the public." Then there was an excursion on the lake, in the steamer "General Garfield," starting from Lake Point at 10 a.m., under the auspices of one Captain Douris; but at Lake Point itself there were all sorts of entertainments provided, including, for instance, a regatta, with a yacht race for a silver cup ; a rifle match, open to members of the Utah Rifle Association ; a ladies' rifle match, for 1st, 2nd, and 3rd prizes ; and a free ball, the dancing to be kept up—I suppose in this case also—" until all were satisfied."

But the *pièce de résistance* in the programme of the day's diversions was reserved for the evening in the city, and this was a theatrical performance at the Salt Lake Theatre. Now the building of this theatre was erected by Brigham Young, who, at its completion, consecrated (*sic*) it with prayer, and named it " Fun Hall," explaining himself, in a sermon he once delivered on the subject—from the text " Amusements "—

after the following strange fashion : " It is to be a place," he said, " where the Saints can meet together and have all the fun they desire. No Gentiles shall ever desecrate its sacred stage with their tragedies. It is built exclusively for the use of ourselves and our own holy fun." Again, on the occasion of the dedication of the building, Brigham said, " I will not have a Gentile on this stage, neither will I have tragedies played. I've said that before, and I mean it. I won't have our women and children coming here to be frightened so that they can't sleep at night. I'll have a Saints' theatre, for the Saints, and we'll see what we can do ourselves." But Brigham was not true to his word, for within three months after the theatre was opened, " Gentiles " were " playing tragedies " upon the stage, and now nearly every theatrical troupe going across-continent to California drops in and gives performances at " Brigham's Theatre,"—as it came afterwards to be called,— and among prominent names of those of our English theatrical profession who have acted at this theatre is that of Miss Lydia Thompson. But to return. The performance in the evening consisted of " A drama in three acts, from Tennyson's *Dora*, entitled ' Driven from Home ' or ' The Farmer's Iron Will ; ' " after which came " The rattling farce of ' Taraxicum Twitters ! ' " Then there was a " Grand National Tableau," etc. Of course we went to the performance. We, a party of five, were put into a box by ourselves. The " drama " was not very creditably put on the stage. The old man in the plot was not only " driven from home " himself, but he drove *us* all away with his exceptionally bad acting, and that long before the play was concluded. Plenty of " Utah's best crop " (babies) were there, and did not fail to make themselves heard. The audience was for the most part feminine, and everyone seemed to be provided with a banana or an orange. All ate vigorously during the performance, and scattered the floor with the peelings of the fruit.

Leaving Salt Lake City early on the following morning (July 5th), we set out for Denver, the metropolis of Colorado, 550 miles from Salt Lake City, this being the next place where we intended breaking our long journey to New York.

The route between the Mormon metropolis and Cheyenne—the junction on the Pacific Railroad for Denver—having been sufficiently described, it will be unnecessary to add more to what has already been said on the subject. After penetrating (beyond Ogden) the Weber and Echo Cañons, and traversing vast and monotonous table-lands; after surmounting the Rocky Mountains at Sherman and descending from thence into the Great Plains, we reached Cheyenne at noon on July 6th, after a journey of thirty hours from Salt Lake City, and changed into the Denver train of the Colorado Central Railroad. Cheyenne is distant 138 miles from the Coloradan capital by this railway, and the "Switzerland of America" is entered about ten miles after leaving the station of the Magic City. The line runs direct south, and parallel to the front range of the "Rockies," the view of these mountains throughout the entire distance to Denver being exceedingly fine. They rise abruptly out of the vast open plains to heights of 12,000 and 13,000 feet—a wild, colossal barrier of a hundred peaks or more; and even after an acquaintance with the impressive scenery of California we could not look upon this glorious range without feelings of wonder and awe. Perhaps, however, we saw it, during this ride to Denver, under unusual advantages, for we were the witnesses of a magnificent sunset behind the range; and the effects of light and shade, of the bold relief into which the mountains were thrown, of the brilliant, glowing redness which the declining sun cast upon the tops of the snow-capped peaks, and of the contrast which these afforded with the rich greenness of the forests clothing the mountain sides, constituted indeed a glorious sight.

Our journey from Cheyenne to Denver was much impeded by the number of cows we frequently found located on the road-bed of the railway. Altogether we had to pull up six times, to prevent cattle from being run over. At Golden, sixteen miles from Denver, our train was tacked on to the end of twenty-six freight cars, and from this place it took us two hours before we reached the Coloradan metropolis. Arriving at Denver at 11 p.m., we repaired to the Grand Central Hotel.

A month spent in 1879 in travelling through Colorado was

sufficient to impress me with the fact that this State, so rich in natural resources, and inhabited by a people so energetic and enterprising, has a brilliant future before it such as no other State in the Union can look forward to. For four classes of people, at least, it possesses greater attractions than any other section of the continent. With an area of 104,500

GOLDEN.

square miles,—that is, more than thirteen times the area of Massachussets, or 15,719 square miles larger than that of Great Britain,—the greater portion of this immense tract being occupied by the main range of the Rocky Mountains, which run down the middle of the State, Colorado offers to the lover of the beautiful and the grand in Nature very powerful attractions; to the sportsman it is a hunting-ground

D d

not to be eclipsed in the New World; to the health-seeker it is a resort unsurpassed for climatic and medicinal advantages; whereas to the fortune-hunter it is more especially an elysium, for this State—that is to say, the mountainous portion of it—is simply one vast repository of mineral wealth, the very tops of some of its loftiest mountain-peaks being ribbed with metalliferous veins as richly as the valleys and "gulches" lying several thousand feet beneath them.

Denver, the capital of the State, is the objective-point for all who visit Colorado. Though it has (December, 1880) a population of 35,630, this prosperous city has been but twenty-two years in existence, its first house having been erected towards the close of 1858. Since 1870 its population has increased by 31,000.[2] Its streets are broad—unusually so, like those of Salt Lake City; and it further resembles the Mormon metropolis in the abundance of its shade-trees and ornamental gardens, and in having irrigating streams flowing down the sides of its streets, from which the private gardens are watered. But Denver, unlike Salt Lake City, is solidly built (of red brick); and unlike, again, the Rocky Mountain "Zion," it has a splendid system of free public schools, five of its educational establishments being *graded* free schools. If there is one thing that Colorado has reason to be proud of—indeed the same remark may apply to the whole of the United States—it is the opportunities afforded its people for intellectual culture. Even the rough, rude mining-towns have their free graded schools, besides the ordinary free district school. This system of education prevails everywhere in America. The poorest man can send his son (or daughter) to the free school, and give him as thorough an education as that which the son of his rich neighbour receives. A boy is first sent to the district school (free), until he is qualified to pass into the High or Graded School. Here he stays till he graduates and receives a diploma (not a degree) of efficiency. Then he enters a commercial college, a law college, or—in the case of Colorado—a College of Mines; and there is an ex-

---

[2] In 1870 Denver had 4759 inhabitants; in 1875, 17,000.

cellent institution of this description at Golden, sixteen miles from Denver. These district schools, as well as the High School, are always free, and are to be found in almost every town—certainly in every town in the New England States. In Hartford, Connecticut,—where I spent a fortnight in the summer of 1879,—I found seventeen free schools, with 7680 registered scholars, and an aggregate number of 183 teachers. (Hartford has a population of 42,550.) In the High School a girl receives such an excellent education that she is fully qualified to undertake the responsibilities of a teacher.

There is, however, another view of the matter, for the poor man's son may, as he very often does, become so educated that in course of time he begins to look upon labour as decidedly repugnant to him.

But to return to Denver. The Coloradan capital occupies a glorious position facing the Rocky Mountain range, which rises precipitously out of the Plains—as it were one single immense wall of rock—only twelve miles from the city. The splendid view of the range as viewed from Denver is worth a trip to Colorado to see. The distance embraced is said to be 250 miles. A more magnificent panorama could not be desired. The air is wonderfully transparent in this part of the country, for the mountains rising twelve miles out of Denver seem to be within only half an hour's walking distance. Many persons have been known to make a start for them under the impression that they were not more than two or three miles away, though at the same time fully aware of their actual distance. A carriage-road, lined with trees, has been made between the metropolis and the mountains, and this forms a fashionable and popular promenade of the people of the Queen City.[3]

The visitor to Denver sees, on all sides of him, signs of commercial activity and business prosperity; and the "mountain metropolis" has reason indeed to be congratulated for the increase of its trade and commerce during the past year. The year 1879 was one of general prosperity to Denver, as indeed

[3] Denver is popularly called the "Queen City of the Plains;" also the "Metropolis of the Rocky Mountains;" the "Golden City of the West," etc.

it was throughout the whole of the State. During the last six months of that year there were not more than twenty-four business failures in Colorado, with liabilities of only 29,000*l.*, thirty-one failures occurring during the same period in 1878, with liabilities of 43,183*l.* Denver's total of business done in 1879 may be represented by the sum of 7,510,318*l.* First and foremost amongst the interests that have contributed to the prosperity of this city, is the mining industry. Last year the mines of Colorado yielded a total amount of 3,822,176*l.*, which is an increase of 1,858,023*l.* over the yield of 1878, and 2,378,919*l.* over that of 1877. Next amongst the sources of wealth is the live-stock industry. There were, a year ago, 855,000 head of cattle in Colorado, and 2,000,000 sheep, the latter valued at 4*s.* to 7*s.* per head. The cattle shipments from the State in 1879 reached 107,824 head, rendering a net return of 500,000*l.* Seven million pounds of wool were produced in that year. Next in point of importance comes the agricultural interest. Here, however, Colorado labours under a disadvantage, owing to the uncertainty and insufficiency of the rainfall, which necessitates the employment of artificial irrigation. Canals are therefore opened out on the plains, and filled with water conveyed in "flumes" from the streams flowing down the mountain cañons, and in this way the land is reclaimed and prepared for cultivation. These canals are generally from ten to fifteen feet in width, and run, in some cases, for twenty or thirty miles continuously—or even further. Of all the land in the State available for agriculture, only one-fifth has at present been reclaimed. In 1879, Colorado produced 2,250,000 bushels of wheat, or 940,000 bushels in excess of the yield of 1878. Other industries that might be mentioned are not, either individually or collectively, a source of any considerable revenue to the State; such as fruit culture, for instance. Colorado is a bad country for fruit. Its altitude—a mile above the sea—is not favourable for the successful cultivation of this industry. A few apple and peach-trees are seen here and there; but this is about all.

The stranger on his arrival in Denver cannot fail to be struck with the elasticity that characterizes the movements of the people. Everybody seems on the move, as if everybody had something to do. And no wonder, for the tonic air infuses new life into the veins, being dry, bracing, and exhilarating; and the mean temperature is about 60° all the

LARIMER-STREET, DENVER.

year round. This invigorating effect of the climate is experienced by the stranger himself, for he finds that he is hurrying to and fro, without becoming fatigued, and he eats his meals with a heartiness that would do credit to a "luncher" at the New York Astor House restaurant. One result of the mildness and dryness of the climate is the custom which has grown up of camping out—sometimes for weeks at a time—under canvas. One notices this, more especially, at such health-resorts as Manitou Springs, Idaho Springs, and other places that might be mentioned.

The traveller from the Old World who is anxious to see the busy hum of Western mining life—the eager rush for wealth characterizing the daily life of all around him—will find it to his heart's content in Colorado, if he will visit any one of the little "magic cities" which have sprung up within the last few years among the wilds of the Rocky Mountains; and for this purpose he cannot do better than make an excursion to the settlements of Georgetown, Central City, Black Hawk, or more paticularly to that wonderful place, the new Eldorado of the West—that is, Leadville. These bustling little "cities" he will find to be veritable hives of mining industry, the sides of the mountains in their immediate vicinity being literally honeycombed with prospect holes, shafts, and tunnels; in short with every indication of extensive workings underground. He can put himself into the train at Denver, and be conveyed, amid glorious and impressive scenery, to either one of these busy mining centres—to Georgetown, Central City, or Black Hawk, for instance, by the Colorado Central Railroad, when he will ascend by train to the height of 8520 feet (at Georgetown) above the sea-level, passing through, on his way, the Clear Creek Cañon, which is one of the grandest, at the same time that it is one of the narrowest ravines even in Colorado. Through this ravine a railway has been conducted, the railway in this instance, having a gauge of only three feet in width, being in some places necessarily blasted out of the steep, precipitous walls of rock which tower right above the road-bed to heights of 1000 and 1500 feet. Again, if the traveller please, he can be conveyed from Denver by train to Leadville, by the Denver and South Park Railroad, when he will ascend to the height of 10,139 feet,—this being the highest point attained by any railway in the United States,—and enjoy a ride to the "Great Carbonate Camp" (as Leadville has been called) through the glorious Platte Cañon, the impressions of which trip he will never forget. Those who hurry across the continent and frame their opinions of Rocky Mountain scenery from what can be viewed from the windows of the Pullman palace-car of the Pacific Railroad, have no conception of the glories of Coloradan mountain scenery, such as is seen on trips like those which have just been indicated. Indeed Colorado is a world of scenic wonders in itself. To describe a month's tour among the Rocky Mountains in this State, such as that, for instance, which I took in 1879, would require a considerable-sized volume.

But far away up among the Rocky Mountains, situated amid majestic scenery, over 10,000 feet above the sea, 170 miles (by train) from Denver, a mountain mining-metropolis has suddenly started into life which may fairly be considered the mining wonder of the continent. This is Leadville, which prior to June, 1877, was not in existence, whereas now it contains a population of over 30,000! Until the date mentioned, when the first building was erected, the site of this city was a deserted mining gulch. Since then, however, fortune-hunters of all nationalities have streamed into the place, and still continue to do so, just as they streamed into California upon the first discoveries of gold years ago. To take a trip to Leadville now is to perform a comfortable journey in a luxuriously-fitted drawing-room car; to approach Leadville before the railway brought it into connection with the outer world,[4]—slowly dragged in a canvas-covered waggon, by a team of several oxen along ill-made roads covered with dust lying two-feet deep,—was to endure discomfort indeed. Space does not permit me to do more than allude to this remarkable place. I may mention, however, that when I visited Leadville in 1879, I found it could boast of four daily newspapers; 110 gambling saloons; a branch of the Young Men's Christian Association; five churches; three schools; and a population, mostly German, averaging about five men to every woman. It is said that there are 100 paying mines around this place and about 1000 altogether, the working mines producing 700 tons of ore (chiefly silver and lead) per day. In 1879 the Leadville mines yielded the enormous amount of 122,483 tons of ore, that is an average of $335\frac{1}{2}$ tons

[4] Railway connection was effected between Leadville and Denver in July, 1880.

for every one of the 365 days in the year, representing a total value of 2,295,409*l*.

There are mines in Colorado situated at a greater altitude above the level of the sea than those even at Leadville. Thus there are rich, *paying* mines on Mt. Lincoln—the Present Help mine, for instance, having an altitude of 14,200 feet, being only ninety-seven feet from the summit of the mountain. This is the loftiest mine in the United States. Many, indeed, of the most famous mines in the State are found at heights of 11,000 or 12,000 feet, and the entrances to some of them are perched on the face of perpendicular cliffs, in seemingly inaccessible places, so that they can only be approached by means of rope and aerial tramway.

Continuing our journey to New York, on the evening of July 8th, we took the Kansas Pacific Railroad (now the Kansas division of the Union Pacific Railroad) across the Great Plains to Kansas City, the second city of the State of Missouri, which we reached on the morning of July 10th, after a journey of 638 miles from Denver. At this place we found the heat most intense and oppressive. Surrounded by damp, marshy lowlands, the sun blazed down upon us, producing perspiration in the body and laxity in the limbs. Here, at Kansas City, we were well-nigh melted away. We waited only an hour, and then "changed cars" for St. Louis, 277 miles distant, taking the Missouri Pacific Railroad. The line for the first few miles, after leaving Kansas City, lay through a forest which was sunk in a 2-ft.-deep swamp, or morass,—formed from an overflowing of the Missouri River,—and it was with considerable difficulty we made any progress at all. However, we soon got out of this, and sped away to St. Louis, which we reached at six o'clock the same evening, and put up at the Planter's House.

It chanced that we arrived at St. Louis at the commencement of an intense heat which, for the space of one week, fell upon this city and the neighbouring towns with exceptional severity. On the morning, therefore, after our arrival (July 11th) we found all business suspended, most of the shops closed—everybody and everything in a state of prostration and stagnation. The first piece of news with which we were greeted, came from our negro waiter while we were having our breakfast : it was that a person who had sat at our table the previous evening had died during the night from the effects of a sunstroke! It seemed almost madness to venture out into the street, to encounter there the full force of the sun; yet we did so on the morning in question, to see a little of the city, but were soon compelled to beat a retreat back to the hotel, where we sat for the remainder of the day with coat and waistcoat off, drinking iced cups with a straw. In addition to this we got a nigger to fan us. With a wicker-fan in each hand, darkie fanned himself and us as well. Every waiter in the hotel was provided with a fan— generally with two, one for himself and one for any guest who was unprovided with one. Boys in the street sold fans by the score, at the price of two cents apiece. The thermometer registered $105°$ in the shade.

The following account of this heat appeared in the columns of a New York weekly (*Frank Leslie's Illustrated Newspaper*), of August 3rd : "The first death from sunstroke occurred on July 10th. On the 11th there were five deaths; 12th, three; 13th, fourteen; 14th, thirty-one; and during these five days there were ninety cases that did not prove fatal. On Monday 15th, the heat-wave struck the city with full force, and coroners, undertakers, physicians, and policemen were thoroughly occupied. Forty-nine fatal and one hundred not fatal cases were reported during the day. Twenty-three patients were admitted to the hospital, while many were cared for in the police-stations and at residences. By noon the main thoroughfares were almost deserted. Men and women were prostrated at their work, children fell on the streets, in the yards, and even on the nursery floor. Business seemed suddenly paralyzed. . . . . Great excitement prevailed at the Morgue throughout the sweltering days. The bodies were laid out for identification, and as it was known that the city would bury all that were not claimed within a few hours, people who had missed their friends for half a day flocked thither, prepared to see and learn the worst. Crowds of men, women, and children gathered to look through the heavy glass windows and gaze at the stiff, stark corpses that lay on the marble slabs before them. . . . ."

As might be expected, we thought that the sooner we quitted this place the better it would be for us, unless we wished to be fashionable and get a touch of sunstroke. So we left as soon as possible without seeing the city. We took a "through sleeper" to New York by the Vandalia Line (St. Louis, Vandalia, and Terre Haute Railroad), a distance of 1065 miles, leaving St. Louis the same evening (July 11th) at 7 p.m. After journeying for forty hours, we arrived in the Empire City, glad indeed to be once more among friends, to enjoy whose society we had made this rapid trip, back from California, before returning to England.

ADDITIONS AND CORRECTIONS.

APRIL, 1882.

Page 5.—The Brooklyn Bridge is still uncompleted.

Page 32.—The idea of holding the great "world's fair" at New York in 1883, has been abandoned.

Page 170.—The walls of the new Mormon Temple have now reached the height of sixty-eight feet. "At the last semi-annual Conference (held October, 1881), in the midst of the financial reports handed in, there was no mention whatever made of the Salt Lake Temple Fund. President Taylor dismissed the matter in his easy, off-hand way by saying, 'Brothers, we don't exactly know how the Temple Fund stands. There is no need of keeping any account. There is the building going up right before your eyes, and you can all see for yourselves. We will now sing the 336th hymn.'"—*Salt Lake Tribune.*

Page 229.—European (Mormon) emigration to Utah during the year 1881 reached a total of 2233. During the last four months of that year there were 1500 converts to Mormonism made in England alone.

Page 231.—Christian missionary work in Utah has continued steadily to advance during the last two years. There are now twenty-six church organizations in the Territory, with forty-one ministers, the total membership among the Protestant churches amounting to 958, the Roman Catholics numbering about 3000. There are also forty-six mission schools (both high or graded schools, and primary schools), with 134 teachers and 3820 pupils; and fifty-two Sunday schools, with 180 teachers and 2250 attendants. The Presbyterian Church has increased its staff from eight ministers to seventeen, and it can now boast of forty-one school teachers instead of eighteen. This denomination, moreover, supports ten churches, one high school, and twenty-seven primary schools, with an attendance of 1600 pupils. The Episcopalian Church, on the contrary, has not increased its staff of clergy, and it has established regular Sunday services in but three towns in the Territory, namely in Salt Lake, Ogden, and Corinne. Five mission schools (three high and two primary) are now supported by this church, and there are twenty-four teachers and an attendance of 640 pupils. The Congregational Church has 195 members, and supports four pastors, fifteen school teachers, one high and two primary schools, these having an attendance of 614 pupils. The Methodists have nine pastors, fourteen school teachers, one high and four primary schools, with 466 pupils. Lastly, the Roman Catholics in Utah have five priests (whose salaries are entirely dependent on voluntary contributions); five churches; three high and two primary schools, with 500 pupils—the teachers in these schools being sisters of charity, forty in number, who give their services gratuitously. This last denomination, moreover, supports two hospitals, which treat about 400 patients yearly.

Perhaps there is no stronger evidence of the need of earnest Christian missionary work in Utah than that of the coarse and vulgar style of writing which pervades the Mormon newspaper publications of the Territory. The low indecency and coarse profanity which so frequently characterise the columns of these miserable prints, cannot be too severely reprehended. Indeed, even the "Gentile" newspapers are not altogether free from this taint.

It is still a lamentable fact that there are no free schools in Utah. The common school system is entirely under the control of the Mormons; the schools, moreover, which they have established are not free, since each pupil's education has to be paid for. The teachers at these schools are every one of them Mormons, and the religious education provided is grounded strictly on the dogmas of the pernicious faith of the Mormon Church. The "Gentiles" or non-Mormons cannot, as a matter of course, send their children to these schools to be educated, so that they have necessarily to fall back upon the mission schools of the various Christian denominations of the Territory. It need scarcely be added that the "Gentiles" are taxed to support the Mormon schools.

Page 236.—After many years of procrastination, Congress has at last taken an important step towards the suppression of polygamy by passing (March 15, 1882) the "Edmunds' Bill," which, among its other provisions, disfranchises all polygamists, rendering them ineligible to vote at elections, or to hold office, the control of elections being given to a Commission to be appointed by the President of the United States. Under the Bill, too, all children born before 1883 will be considered legitimate.

Looking at the composition of the Utah Legislature as it existed at the passing of this Act, it will be seen that it was high time for some such sweeping measure as this to be adopted, for of the thirty-six members composing the General Assembly of the Territory twenty-seven were polygamists, besides holding high positions in the Mormon Church!

Of these twenty-seven polygamists, one, namely Erastus Snow, possessed, at the beginning of this year, six wives; three other members of the same Assembly, namely Lorenzo Snow, D. H. Wells, and Lorin Farr, had five wives apiece; two others, namely Joseph F. Smith and Abraham O. Smoot, had four wives each; and the remainder possessed either two or three wives apiece. Erastus Snow, it may be stated, is one of the Twelve Apostles of the Mormon Church; Lorenzo Snow, the same; D. H. Wells holds the position of Second Counsellor to the Twelve Apostles; Lorin Farr is an elder; Joseph F. Smith is also one of the Twelve Apostles; and Abraham Smoot is President of the Utah "Stake," and was previously Mayor of Salt Lake City. The remaining twenty-one polygamists hold positions in the Church either as presidents of stakes, bishops, elders, &c.

But the Edmunds' Bill does not strike at the root of the Mormon evil. It is all very well as far as it goes, but it does not go far enough. Instead of merely disfranchising those living in a state of polygamy, it should have disfranchised *all Mormons*, for the principles of Mormonism are avowedly anti-republican, and antagonistic to the existence of the national Government. Polygamy is but an "indecent detail" of Mormonism. Disloyalty and treason are other incidental evils which, in legislating against Mormonism, should scarcely have been overlooked. However, Congress has no doubt thought it prudent to adopt a milder measure first.

PRESS OPINIONS.

"We have read the book through with unabated and, indeed, increasing interest and entertainment; but we must renounce at the outset any intention or ability to write an adequate review of it. We began by marking passages for quotation; but after having in this manner selected upwards of forty, with the great bulk of the volume yet to hear from, we relinquished the enterprise as useless.... We have an idea that if any one (with adequate raw material at command) were desirous of manufacturing a continent in all respects a fac-simile of the United States, he would find every instruction necessary to his purpose in Mr. Marshall's volume. And yet, as the title-page informs us, the whole is the result of no more than nine months' experience. One thing, at all events, is clear—that the book does not belong to that pallid and ambiguous class of perpetrations which were 'written with no thought of publication.' Mr. Marshall not only went to America resolved to write a book about it, but—what is even less common—he fully and conscientiously qualified himself to put that resolve into execution. In fact, the ordinary indolent mind shrinks from contemplating the amount of material, in the way of notes, journals, mementoes, newspaper-cuttings, photographs, anecdotes, menu-cards, and memorabilia generally, which the indefatigable author must have had by him when he sat down to his task. He has got them all in, and, nevertheless, has contrived to inspire his vast mass of impedimenta with movement and vitality, a feat which does him no small credit. We never forget that we are proceeding towards a goal, and we never lose our belief that we shall arrive there. Under the weight of the statistics of a hemisphere, Mr. Marshall jogs along as lightly and cheerfully as if he were encumbered with nothing more bulky than an ordinary traveller's satchel. If his capacity is the capacity of Pantagruel, his eyes are the eyes of Argus, and his legs the legs of Geryon.... Once more we heartily commend his book to our readers.... In the present volume he has done a great deal towards creating a better understanding of the American Republic on the part of Englishmen, and, consequently, a sounder basis of good feeling between the two countries."
Spectator.

"Nobody will feel inclined to quarrel with Mr. Marshall for having given his power of description full sway, more especially with regard to Mormonism. To this monstrous social scandal, as Mr. Marshall truly calls it, one-fourth of his book is devoted; and after reading it, one is forced to the conclusion that Mormonism, instead of dying out, as is generally thought to be the case, is actually on the increase. A completer *exposé* of humbug than Mr. Marshall gives, cannot be."
Whitehall Review.

"We know no book on America fuller of interest than Mr. Marshall's."—*Graphic.*

"Carefully written, and abounding with interesting information."—*Literary World.*

"Clever, fresh, and spirited writing."—*Daily Telegraph.*

"A very readable book."—*Morning Advertiser.*

"Really uncommonly thorough and readable."—*Truth.*

"Mr. Marshall has done very well indeed."—*Pall Mall Gazette.*

"Mr. Marshall's bulky volume is well worth reading.... The chapter entitled 'A Serious Aspect of Mormonism' is deserving of the careful attention of the legislators of the United States."
St. James's Gazette.

"Mr. Marshall has devoted several chapters to a discussion of Mormonism; and this is decidedly interesting. He has evidently acquired an intimate knowledge of the internal economy, social and political, of the believers in Brigham Young. The conclusions to be drawn from his account are not pleasant."—*Guardian.*

"The author of this work appears not only to have travelled far, but to have enjoyed the privilege of being able to depict scenery with more than ordinary skill. There are many good bits in this volume, and we scarcely know whether the author should be most praised for his work as a traveller, as a topographer, or as an anthropologist.... When we read the author's description of life in New York, we are struck with the accuracy of every petty detail. His arrangement is scientific. He does not expect his readers to be dining and drinking all day, and he never draws on his imagination, nor ekes out his narrative by 'padding' from the advertisement sheets of Transatlantic newspapers. In this respect the work is a contrast to some of its predecessors. He sees Niagara Falls, and, whilst admitting the dampness of the locality, does not fall into any artificial raptures. He gives a description of daily life in California that brings us face to face with the Golden City. One thing we must admire—and there is much to admire in this book—that although sympathizing with the natives, he never seems to lose sight of the fact that he is an Englishman, and never introduces any out-of-the-way Americanisms in his remarkably pure, descriptive English.... There is a certain charm about this work that will enable those persons who have been in America to recognize the spots where they have spent many happy hours, and to provide those who are afraid of a fortnight's steam with a faithful picture of life as it really is in a country that must always have its charms for the European tourist. Mr. Marshall has certainly succeeded in producing one of the most interesting works of the present publishing season."—*Public Opinion.*

"This is a most delightful volume.... There is so much that is new and interesting, that we devour the whole together with equal relish. The description of the hurried life led by people all over the Union is most amusing.... The account given of the Mormons is complete and interesting. Many an individual, who might be doubtful concerning the purity of the doctrine taught at Salt Lake, would be sorely tempted to join the community after reading Mr. Marshall's glowing description of the physical comfort which prevails. The moral influence, however, is painted by the author in its true light, and we must rely upon the odium thrown upon it to counteract the effect produced by the golden promise of liberation from want and pecuniary anxiety experienced by the poorer populations of Europe."—*Court Journal.*

"'Through America,' taken as a whole, is a capital book. It has, for instance, the merit of familiarizing you with what the author has seen, and yet it is never wearisome. Padding has been carefully avoided. It is brightly, and for the most part carefully, written. It also breaks new ground, and it has the additional advantage of being embellished with nearly a hundred admirable woodcuts. . . . Albeit Mr. Marshall evidently attaches most importance to his five chapters about Mormonism and the Mormons, we believe the general reader will be quite as pleased with the rest of the book. Thus his very first chapter, in which he describes New York—he wisely refrains from wasting space in telling us how he got there—is extremely good. The characteristics of 'the Empire City,' from the elevated railways to the white-paint advertisement nuisance, are portrayed to the life. A spirit of impartiality will, in fact, be observed to pervade the work, and this, in the eyes of not a few, will help to constitute its value. If justice is done both to the virtues and to the vices of the American people, there is no disposition to over-praise or to run down the 'lions' of the country. Niagara is fully appreciated, and Chicago excites a just measure of wonder and admiration. But the drawbacks of San Francisco are not overlooked, and while the beauties of the Yosemite Valley are duly set forth, the author does not convey the impression that he has never seen anything like them before. Whatever else he may be accused of, it cannot be averred that he lost much time during the nine months he spent in the States. But he not only went from place to place and saw, with his eyes, everything that was to be seen; he took care to carry away with him correct impressions. We have the benefit of these in 'Through America,' and though we shall not spoil the interest of any one by quoting copiously from the book, we have no hesitation in declaring that it deserves, for several reasons, to be popular both on this, and on the other, side of the Atlantic. It may remove some prejudices here; it may modify some self-conceit there."—*Figaro.*

"This bulky volume has a good deal of value, on account of the very varied nature of its contents. Mr. Marshall evidently addressed himself to the work with all possible earnestness, or he could not have contrived to pick up such a mass of information in so short a time."—*Globe.*

"Mr. Marshall is a painstaking writer. . . . He is careful as to his facts."—*World.*

"We notice with pleasure the extremely well-executed engravings adorning this volume. . . . They are far above any ordinary book illustrations on our side of the Atlantic. Some of the Yosemite views are indeed gems."—*Field.*

"Mr. Marshall has done his work well, but he is especially to be congratulated upon having secured such high artistic aid as should be quite sufficient to secure the popularity of a volume of far less literary merit."—*Echo.*

"We fancy many a stay-at-home traveller will enjoy the perusal of this most attractive volume."
City Press.

"We have more than ordinary pleasure in commending the volume. . . . The truthfully delineated views, illustrated from photographs, convey to the reader's mind actual natural scenery as it is, and not as fancy paints it."—*Rock.*

"Mr. Marshall has certainly contrived to write a readable book, which will give those who have not crossed the Atlantic a very accurate idea as to what is to be found on the other side."
Illustrated Sporting and Dramatic News.

"We cannot have too many books on America, provided they are written as intelligently and as truthfully as the one now before us. . . . Mr. Marshall has produced such a really charming work, that we trust that the success which is sure to attend this book will encourage him to go on and produce others of equal interest. The work is thoroughly well illustrated by many excellent engravings, and the thoughtful remarks which the author makes on what he saw and experienced give an additional value to his descriptions."—*Pictorial World.*

"We have much in this volume which will be found in no other, and at least one or two sections of the route traversed are dwelt upon at greater length, and with more minuteness, than has hitherto been given by the English traveller. . . . If it has not the discursive brilliance of Sala, the historical richness of Dixon, or the political solidity of Dilke, it is characterized by smoothness of diction, considerable descriptive power, and a certain sober charm of detail, without any attempt at fine writing or philosophical theorizing, which enables the reader to see, through a pair of very keen and observant eyes, the form, colour, grandeur, and peculiarities of the objects and incidents which came under the author's notice. . . We are led on, from chapter to chapter, without feeling our interest flag, and on rising from a perusal of the volume had a vivid and clear idea of all that the author saw."
Oxford and Cambridge Undergraduates' Journal.

"A very valuable book of travel, and quite as instructive as entertaining. . . . Mr. Marshall is a sharp observer, and is well able to 'find his way about.'"—*Liverpool Daily Courier.*

"The chief question that occurs to one in looking at such a work as this is as to the extent to which the author has made use of his opportunities and faculties, and his success in presenting something really readable and instructive to the public. We are bound to admit that he has quite succeeded in his task. The book is well worthy of a place on one's table or in one's library."—*Yorkshire Post.*

"Mr. Marshall appears to be a careful and industrious observer. . . . With the faculty to gather material for publication, he has, judging from 'Through America,' the less common faculty of mental digestion and assimilation. His book is admirably arranged."—*Leeds Mercury.*

"Any one wishing to get a good matter-of-fact view of America, its towns, institutions, physical features, and peculiarities, cannot do better than peruse the work of Mr. Marshall."
Edinburgh Courant.

"An interesting and valuable contribution to that class of literature by which our knowledge of America may be extended. The author, indeed, makes no attempt at fine writing, everything is sketched and dashed down naturally as it presents itself. The book, therefore, possesses a raciness, freshness, force, and interest which do not always attach to more artistic and ambitious writings.... Mr. Marshall's work is fitted to convey to the reader's mind a vivid idea of the state of things in America, of the cities and scenes traversed, and it contains much substantial, useful, and curious information."—*Glasgow Herald*.

"A trenchant *exposé* of Mormonism will be found here.... We thank Mr. Marshall for drawing attention to the foulness of Mormonism, and hope that its doom is nearer than it seems to be. Fain would we linger over these admirably written and excellently illustrated chapters. We advise our readers to beg, borrow, or—buy the book and read it."—*Western Morning News*.

"Mr. Marshall has opened a view of Mormonism that is worthy of attention."—*New York Herald*.

"Our author has combined a surprising store of information of a statistical kind, which makes his volume one of the most complete handbooks for tourists ever put together."—*New York Tribune*.

"Mr. Marshall would be unworthy of the name of Englishman if he did not find much that is grotesque and worthy of criticism in American manners and customs. But he finds quite as much to praise.... There is a good deal of confidence in his manner of narrating his experiences, but there is nowhere any of that offensive dogmatism which has been so marked a characteristic of English books about America.... Five of the most interesting chapters are devoted to the Mormons and Mormonism. Concerning the latter, he is very much in earnest, and he closes his demand, in the interests of religion and morality, for a restraint of the Mormon Churches, with the suggestion that 'it does not redound to the credit of Old England that she should allow such a scandalous institution to be fostered and strengthened by the proselytism of so many of her sons.'"—*Detroit Free Press*.

"A most amusing record of nine months' travel in the United States.... It is especially rich in its illustrations of society and manners. Mr. Marshall is an acute observer, with his ears and eyes always open to characteristic sayings and sights. He has so many good things in his store that it is not very easy to make a selection.... His book is indeed a fund of useful and amusing information on the United States."—*Melbourne Argus*.

In reviewing this work, the *New York Herald* makes the following observations respecting the Mormon question:—"The immunity granted to the degrading system has long been a disgrace to the United States. Public opinion has always been unanimously hostile to it; but so many other questions were pressing for a settlement that it has been suffered to exist up to the present without serious hindrance. Mr. Marshall, however, has opened a view of Mormonism that is worthy of attention—namely, that the Mormons are not Americans who differ from other Americans only in religion, but a gathering of foreigners whose beliefs and polity are inimical to our institutions. In the face of our Republic without a trace of State Church they have set up a priestly despotism. Offensive as polygamy is, the theocratic system that upholds polygamy against the laws is more offensive still. The ignorant foreigners who are brought out in shoals to Utah are taught from the moment they arrive that they are the enemies of the United States Government, and that the Government would sweep them off the face of the earth, only it is afraid. After five, ten, or fifteen years' residence these immigrants, though they may have been put through the form of becoming citizens, are foreigners still at heart, and hostile to the United States. These are matters that must be understood when the question comes up, as it soon must, for decisive settlement. The Government has a right to protect itself from such foes, as well as to strike down mercilessly the repulsive practices their religion sanctions. We have a great deal to answer for as a people in permitting Mormonism to gather strength, but it is equally true that foreign Governments are remiss in permitting the Mormon missionaries to promulgate uncontradicted the mass of lies with which they entice people from their homes to build up the fortunes of a crafty priesthood in the heart of an American desert. Mr. Marshall says:—

"'It is a mistake for people to suppose, as many do suppose, that Mormonism is not increasing. On the contrary, Mormonism was never so prosperous, in a quiet way, as it is at the present moment. Recruits from Great Britain and other European countries continue to pour into Utah by hundreds every two or three months, not, as might be supposed, from various quarters of the United States and Canada, for but a very few converts to the religion are obtained in the New World; but it is in England, Wales, Scotland, Denmark, Sweden, and Norway—among the poor and uneducated masses of these countries, in remote districts where the truth of the pernicious "faith" is unknown—that the Mormons win their greatest triumphs; and it may be as well to note the fact that their chief recruiting ground is Wales.'

"The almost complete absence of Irish converts—only two out of a total of 1459 during 1879 is noted—is a curious and creditable fact. Probably the two Irish converts of 1879 were males, for we recall having heard in Utah of but one Mormon Irish woman, and she had grown into a tradition of terror. The scene of domestic destruction consequent on an attempt of her lord to bring home a second wife always baffled the descriptive powers of eye-witnesses. She left her husband in a state of jelly, and the territory soon after. The appearance of her streaming red hair upon the hills around Salt Lake City would to this day, we are persuaded, strike the twelve apostles with panic.

"Mr. Marshall proceeds to point out how, should Utah be erected into a State, the evil would be past all remedy. He fears that in some time of a closely balanced Congress this may be done for the sake of a couple of votes in the Senate on one side or the other. No party at present existing would, we believe, risk such a step. If we have been remiss in dealing with polygamy and the Mormon theocracy, we are nevertheless unlikely to permit a course which would stamp the worst form of government and the utmost social degradation upon any portion of our territory."

A Catalogue of American and Foreign Books Published or Imported by MESSRS. SAMPSON LOW & CO. *can be had on application.*

Crown Buildings, 188, *Fleet Street, London, December,* 1881.

A Selection from the List of Books

PUBLISHED BY

SAMPSON LOW, MARSTON, SEARLE, & RIVINGTON.

ALPHABETICAL LIST.

A CLASSIFIED *Educational Catalogue of Works* published in Great Britain. Demy 8vo, cloth extra. Second Edition, revised and corrected, 5*s*.

About Some Fellows. By an ETON BOY, Author of "A Day of my Life." Cloth limp, square 16mo, 2*s*. 6*d*.

Adventures of a Young Naturalist. By LUCIEN BIART, with 117 beautiful Illustrations on Wood. Edited and adapted by PARKER GILLMORE. Post 8vo, cloth extra, gilt edges, New Edition, 7*s*. 6*d*.

Afghan Knife (The). A Novel. By ROBERT ARMITAGE STERNDALE, Author of "Seonee." Small post 8vo, cloth extra, 6*s*.

Alcott (Louisa M.) Jimmy's Cruise in the "Pinafore." With 9 Illustrations. Second Edition. Small post 8vo, cloth gilt, 3*s*. 6*d*.

——— *Aunt Jo's Scrap-Bag.* Square 16mo, 2*s*. 6*d*. (Rose Library, 1*s*.)

——— *Little Men: Life at Plumfield with Jo's Boys.* Small post 8vo, cloth, gilt edges, 3*s*. 6*d*. (Rose Library, Double vol. 2*s*.)

——— *Little Women.* 1 vol., cloth, gilt edges, 3*s*. 6*d*. (Rose Library, 2 vols., 1*s*. each.)

——— *Old-Fashioned Girl.* Best Edition, small post 8vo, cloth extra, gilt edges, 3*s*. 6*d*. (Rose Library, 2*s*.)

——— *Work and Beginning Again.* 'A Story of Experience. (Rose Library, 2 vols., 1*s*. each.)

——— *Shawl Straps.* Small post 8vo, cloth extra, gilt, 3*s*. 6*d*.

——— *Eight Cousins; or, the Aunt Hill.* Small post 8vo, with Illustrations, 3*s*. 6*d*.

——— *The Rose in Bloom.* Small post 8vo, cloth extra, 3*s*. 6*d*.

——— *Under the Lilacs.* Small post 8vo, cloth extra, 5*s*.

A

Alcott (*Louisa M.*) *Jack and Jill.* Small post 8vo, cloth extra, 5s.
"Miss Alcott's stories are thoroughly healthy, full of racy fun and humour . . . exceedingly entertaining . . . . We can recommend the 'Eight Cousins.'"—*Athenæum.*

Aldrich (*T. B.*) *Friar Jerome's Beautiful Book,* &c. Selected from "Cloth of Gold," and "Flower and Thorn." 18mo, very choicely printed on hand-made paper, parchment cover, 3s. 6d.

Alpine Ascents and Adventures; or, Rock and Snow Sketches. By H. SCHÜTZ WILSON, of the Alpine Club. With Illustrations by WHYMPER and MARCUS STONE. Crown 8vo, 10s. 6d. 2nd Edition.

Andersen (*Hans Christian*) *Fairy Tales.* With Illustrations in Colours by E. V. B. Cheap Edition, in the press.

Angling Literature in England; and Descriptions of Fishing by the Ancients. By O. LAMBERT. With a Notice of some Books on other Piscatorial Subjects. Fcap. 8vo, vellum, top gilt limp, 3s. 6d.

Architecture (*The Twenty Styles of*). By Dr. W. WOOD, Editor of "The Hundred Greatest Men." Imperial 8vo, with 52 Plates.

Art Education. See "Illustrated Text Books," "Illustrated Dictionary," "Biographies of Great Artists."

Autobiography of Sir G. Gilbert Scott, R.A., F.S.A., &c. Edited by his Son, G. GILBERT SCOTT. With an Introduction by the DEAN OF CHICHESTER, and a Funeral Sermon, preached in Westminster Abbey, by the DEAN OF WESTMINSTER. Also, Portrait on steel from the portrait of the Author by G. RICHMOND, R.A. 1 vol., demy 8vo, cloth extra, 18s.

Autumnal Leaves. By F. G. HEATH. Illustrated by 12 Plates, comprising 252 figures of Autumn Leaves and Leaflets, exquisitely coloured after Nature; 4 Page and 14 Vignette Drawings, by FRED. G. SHORT, of New Forest Scenery, and 12 Initial-letter Leaf Designs by the Author. Cloth, imperial 16mo, gilt edges, with special Cover showing Autumn Leaves printed in colours, price 14s.

THE BAYARD SERIES.
Edited by the late J. HAIN FRISWELL.
Comprising Pleasure Books of Literature produced in the Choicest Style as Companionable Volumes at Home and Abroad.

"We can hardly imagine better books for boys to read or for men to ponder over."—*Times.*
Price 2s. 6d. each Volume, complete in itself, flexible cloth extra, gilt edges, with silk Headbands and Registers.

The Story of the Chevalier Bayard. By M. De Berville.

De Joinville's St. Louis, King of France.

The Essays of Abraham Cowley, including all his Prose Works.

Abdallah; or, The Four Leaves. By Edouard Laboullaye.

The Bayard Series (continued):—

Table-Talk and Opinions of Napoleon Buonaparte.
Vathek: An Oriental Romance. By William Beckford.
The King and the Commons. A Selection of Cavalier and Puritan Songs. Edited by Professor Morley.
Words of Wellington: Maxims and Opinions of the Great Duke.
Dr. Johnson's Rasselas, Prince of Abyssinia. With Notes.
Hazlitt's Round Table. With Biographical Introduction.
The Religio Medici, Hydriotaphia, and the Letter to a Friend. By Sir Thomas Browne, Knt.
Ballad Poetry of the Affections. By Robert Buchanan.
Coleridge's Christabel, and other Imaginative Poems. With Preface by Algernon C. Swinburne.
Lord Chesterfield's Letters, Sentences, and Maxims. With Introduction by the Editor, and Essay on Chesterfield by M. de Ste.-Beuve, of the French Academy.
Essays in Mosaic. By Thos. Ballantyne.
My Uncle Toby; his Story and his Friends. Edited by P. Fitzgerald.
Reflections; or, Moral Sentences and Maxims of the Duke de la Rochefoucald.
Socrates: Memoirs for English Readers from Xenophon's Memorabilia. By Edw. Levien.
Prince Albert's Golden Precepts.

A Case containing 12 Volumes, price 31s. 6d.; or the Case separately, price 3s. 6d.

Beauty and the Beast. An Old Tale retold, with Pictures by E. V. B. 4to, cloth extra. 10 Illustrations in Colours. 12s. 6d.

Begum's Fortune (The): A New Story. By JULES VERNE. Translated by W. H. G. KINGSTON. Numerous Illustrations. Crown 8vo, cloth, gilt edges, 7s. 6d.; plainer binding, plain edges, 5s.

Ben Hur: A Tale of the Christ. By L. WALLACE. Crown 8vo, 6s.

Beumers' German Copybooks. In six gradations at 4d. each.

Bickersteth's Hymnal Companion to Book of Common Prayer may be had in various styles and bindings from 1d. to 21s. Price List and Prospectus will be forwarded on application.

Bickersteth (Rev. E. H., M.A.) The Reef, and other Parables. 1 vol., square 8vo, with numerous very beautiful Engravings, 2s. 6d.

—— *The Clergyman in his Home.* Small post 8vo, 1s.

—— *The Master's Home-Call; or, Brief Memorials of* Alice Frances Bickersteth. 20th Thousand. 32mo, cloth gilt, 1s.

—— *The Master's Will.* A Funeral Sermon preached on the Death of Mrs. S. Gurney Buxton. Sewn, 6d.; cloth gilt, 1s.

—— *The Shadow of the Rock.* A Selection of Religious Poetry. 18mo, cloth extra, 2s. 6d.

—— *The Shadowed Home and the Light Beyond.* 7th Edition, crown 8vo, cloth extra, 5s.

Biographies of the Great Artists (Illustrated). Each of the following Volumes is illustrated with from twelve to twenty full-page Engravings, printed in the best manner, and bound in ornamental cloth cover, 3s. 6d. Library Edition, bound in a superior style, and handsomely ornamented, with gilt top; six Volumes, enclosed in a cloth case, with lid, £1 11s. 6d. each case.

Hogarth.	Giotto.	Figure Painters of
Turner.	Raphael.	Holland.
Rubens.	Van Dyck and Hals.	Michel Angelo.
Holbein.	Titian.	Delaroche and Vernet.
Tintoretto.	Rembrandt.	Landseer.
Little Masters of Germany.	Leonardo da Vinci.	Reynolds.
	Gainsborough and Constable.	Velasquez.
Fra Angelico and Masaccio.	Sir David Wilkie.	Mantegna and Francia.
Fra Bartolommeo.	Van Eyck.	Albert Durer.

Price 2s. 6d. each.

Claude Lorraine.	Sir Thos. Lawrence.	Murillo.
Correggio.	Rousseau & Millet.	Early Italian Sculptors.
Watteau, Lannet, and Boucher.	Meissonier.	
	Overbeck.	

" Few things in the way of small books upon great subjects, avowedly cheap and necessarily brief, have been hitherto so well done as these biographies of the Great Masters in painting."—*Times.*
" A deserving series."—*Edinburgh Review.*
" Most thoroughly and tastefully edited."—*Spectator.*

Birthday Book. Extracts from the Writings of Theodore Emerson. Square 16mo, cloth extra, numerous Illustrations, very choice binding, 3s. 6d.

Birthday Book. Extracts from the Poems of Whittier. Square 16mo, with numerous Illustrations and handsome binding, 3s. 6d.

Black (Wm.) Three Feathers. Small post 8vo, cloth extra, 6s.

―――― *Lady Silverdale's Sweetheart, and other Stories.* 1 vol., small post 8vo, 6s.

―――― *Kilmeny: a Novel.* Small post 8vo, cloth, 6s.

―――― *In Silk Attire.* 3rd Edition, small post 8vo, 6s.

―――― *A Daughter of Heth.* 11th Edition, small post 8vo, 6s.

―――― *Sunrise.* Small post 8vo, 6s.

Blackmore (R. D.) Lorna Doone. 10th Edition, cr. 8vo, 6s.

―――― *Alice Lorraine.* 1 vol., small post 8vo, 6th Edition, 6s.

―――― *Clara Vaughan.* Revised Edition, 6s.

―――― *Cradock Nowell.* New Edition, 6s.

―――― *Cripps the Carrier.* 3rd Edition, small post 8vo, 6s.

―――― *Mary Anerley.* New Edition, 6s.

―――― *Erema; or, My Father's Sin.* With 12 Illustrations, small post 8vo, 6s.

Blossoms from the King's Garden: Sermons for Children. By the Rev. C. BOSANQUET. 2nd Edition, small post 8vo, cloth extra, 6s.

Blue Banner (The); or, The Adventures of a Mussulman, a Christian, and a Pagan, in the time of the Crusades and Mongol Conquest. Translated from the French of LEON CAHUN. With Seventy-six Wood Engravings. Imperial 16mo, cloth, gilt edges, 7s. 6d.; plainer binding, 5s.

Bock (Carl). The Head Hunters of Borneo: Up the Mahak- kam, and Down the Barita; also Journeyings in Sumatra. 1 vol., super-royal 8vo. 32 Coloured Plates, cloth extra, 36s.

Book of the Play. By DUTTON COOK. New and Revised Edition. 1 vol., cloth extra, 7s. 6d.

Boy's Froissart (The). 7s. 6d. See "Froissart."

Boy's King Arthur (The). With very fine Illustrations. Square crown 8vo, cloth extra, gilt edges, 7s. 6d. Edited by SIDNEY LANIER, Editor of "The Boy's Froissart."

Boy's Mabinogion (The): being the Original Welsh Legends of King Arthur. Edited for Boys, with an Introduction by SIDNEY LANIER. With numerous very graphic Illustrations. Crown 8vo, cloth, gilt edges, 7s. 6d.

Breton Folk: An Artistic Tour in Brittany. By HENRY BLACKBURN, Author of "Artists and Arabs," "Normandy Picturesque," &c. With 171 Illustrations by RANDOLPH CALDECOTT. Imperial 8vo, cloth extra, gilt edges, 21s.

British Goblins: Welsh Folk-Lore, Fairy Mythology, Legends, and Traditions. By WIRT SIKES, United States Consul for Wales, Author of "Rambles and Studies in Old South Wales." Second Edition. 8vo, 18s.

Burnaby (Capt.). See "On Horseback."

Burnham Beeches (Heath, F. G.). With numerous Illustrations and a Map. Crown 8vo, cloth, gilt edges, 3s. 6d. Second Edition.
"A pretty description of the Beeches."—*Daily News.*
"A charming little volume."—*Globe.*

Burroughs (John). Pepacton: A Summer Voyage, and other Essays. Small post 8vo, cloth, 7s. 6d.

Butler (W. F.) The Great Lone Land; an Account of the Red River Expedition, 1869-70. With Illustrations and Map. Fifth and Cheaper Edition, crown 8vo, cloth extra, 7s. 6d.

—— *The Wild North Land; the Story of a Winter Journey* with Dogs across Northern North America. Demy 8vo, cloth, with numerous Woodcuts and a Map, 4th Edition, 18s. Cr. 8vo, 7s. 6d.

—— *Akim-foo: the History of a Failure.* Demy 8vo, cloth, 2nd Edition, 16s. Also, in crown 8vo, 7s. 6d.

—— *Red Cloud.* Crown 8vo, gilt edges, 7s. 6d. [*In the press.*

CADOGAN (Lady A.) Illustrated Games of Patience. Twenty-four Diagrams in Colours, with Descriptive Text. Foolscap 4to, cloth extra, gilt edges, 3rd Edition, 12s. 6d.

Cambridge Trifles; or, Splutterings from an Undergraduate Pen. By the Author of "A Day of my Life at Eton," &c. 16mo, cloth extra, 2s. 6d.

Changed Cross (The), and other Religious Poems. 16mo, 2s. 6d.

Child of the Cavern (The); or, Strange Doings Underground. By JULES VERNE. Translated by W. H. G. KINGSTON. Numerous Illustrations. Sq. cr. 8vo, gilt edges, 7s. 6d.; cl., plain edges, 5s.

Child's Play, with 16 Coloured Drawings by E. V. B. Printed on thick paper, with tints, 7s. 6d.

—— *New.* By E. V. B. Similar to the above. *See* New.

—— A New and Cheap Edition of the two above, containing 48 Illustrations by E. V. B., printed in tint, handsomely bound, 3s. 6d.

Choice Editions of Choice Books. 2s. 6d. each, Illustrated by C. W. COPE, R.A., T. CRESWICK, R.A., E. DUNCAN, BIRKET FOSTER, J. C. HORSLEY, A.R.A., G. HICKS, R. REDGRAVE, R.A., C. STONEHOUSE, F. TAYLER, G. THOMAS, H. J. TOWNSHEND, E. H. WEHNERT, HARRISON WEIR, &c.

Bloomfield's Farmer's Boy.	Milton's L'Allegro.
Campbell's Pleasures of Hope.	Poetry of Nature. Harrison Weir.
Coleridge's Ancient Mariner.	Rogers' (Sam.) Pleasures of Memory.
Goldsmith's Deserted Village.	Shakespeare's Songs and Sonnets.
Goldsmith's Vicar of Wakefield.	Tennyson's May Queen.
Gray's Elegy in a Churchyard.	Elizabethan Poets.
Keat's Eve of St. Agnes.	Wordsworth's Pastoral Poems.

"Such works are a glorious beatification for a poet."—*Athenæum.*

Christ in Song. By Dr. PHILIP SCHAFF. A New Edition, Revised, cloth, gilt edges, 6s.

Confessions of a Frivolous Girl (The): A Novel of Fashionable Life. Edited by ROBERT GRANT. Crown 8vo, 6s.

Cornet of Horse (The): A Story for Boys. By G. A. HENTY. Crown 8vo, cloth extra, gilt edges, numerous graphic Illustrations, 5s.

Cripps the Carrier. 3rd Edition, 6s. *See* BLACKMORE.

Cruise of H.M.S. "Challenger" (The). By W. J. J. SPRY, R.N. With Route Map and many Illustrations. 6th Edition, demy 8vo, cloth, 18s. Cheap Edition, crown 8vo, some of the Illustrations, 7s. 6d.

Cruise of the Walnut Shell (The). An instructive and amusing Story, told in Rhyme, for Children. With 32 Coloured Plates. Square fancy boards, 5s.

Curious Adventures of a Field Cricket. By Dr. ERNEST CANDÈZE. Translated by N. D'ANVERS. With numerous fine Illustrations. Crown 8vo, gilt, 7s. 6d.; plain binding and edges, 5s.

*D*ANA *(R. H.) Two Years before the Mast and Twenty-Four years After.* Revised Edition, with Notes, 12mo, 6s.

Daughter (A) of Heth. By W. BLACK. Crown 8vo, 6s.

Day of My Life (*A*) ; *or, Every Day Experiences at Eton.* By an ETON BOY, Author of "About Some Fellows." 16mo, cloth extra, 2s. 6d. 6th Thousand.

Diane. By Mrs. MACQUOID. Crown 8vo, 6s.

Dick Cheveley: his Fortunes and Misfortunes. By W. H. G. KINGSTON. 350 pp., square 16mo, and 22 full-page Illustrations. Cloth, gilt edges, 7s. 6d.; plainer binding, plain edges, 5s.

Dick Sands, the Boy Captain. By JULES VERNE. With nearly 100 Illustrations, cloth, gilt, 10s. 6d.; plain binding and plain edges, 5s.

EIGHT Cousins. See ALCOTT.

Elementary History (*An*) *of Art.* Comprising Architecture, Sculpture, Painting, and the Applied Arts. By N. D'ANVERS, Author of "Science Ladders." With a Preface by Professor ROGER SMITH. New Edition, illustrated with upwards of 200 Wood Engravings. Crown 8vo, strongly bound in cloth, price 8s. 6d.

Elementary History (*An*) *of Music.* Edited by OWEN J. DULLEA. Including Music among the Ancient Nations; Music in the Middle Ages; Music in Italy in the Sixteenth, Seventeenth, and Eighteenth Centuries; Music in Germany, France, and England. Illustrated with Portraits of the most eminent Composers, and Engravings of the Musical Instruments of many Nations. Crown 8vo, handsomely bound in cloth, price 3s. 6d.

Elinor Dryden. By Mrs. MACQUOID. Crown 8vo, 6s.

Embroidery (*Handbook of*). By L. HIGGIN. Edited by LADY MARIAN ALFORD, and published by authority of the Royal School of Art Needlework. With 16 page Illustrations, Designs for Borders, &c. Crown 8vo, 5s.

Enchiridion of Epictetus; and the Golden Verses of Pythagoras. Translated into English, Prose and Verse; with Notes and Scriptural References, together with some original Poems. By the Hon. THOS. TALBOT. Crown 8vo, cloth, 5s.

English Philosophers. Edited by IWAN MULLER, M.A., New College, Oxon. A Series of Volumes containing short biographies of the most celebrated English Philosophers, to each of whom is assigned a separate volume, giving as comprehensive and detailed a statement of his views and contributions to Philosophy as possible, explanatory ratherthan critical, opening with a brief biographical sketch, and concluding with a short general summary, and a bibliographical appendix. Each Volume contains about 200 pp. Sq. 16mo, 3s. 6d. each.
Bacon. Professor FOWLER, Professor of Logic in Oxford.
Berkeley. Prof. T. H. GREEN, Professor of Moral Philosophy, Oxford.
Hamilton. Professor MONK, Professor of Moral Philosophy, Dublin.
J. S. Mill. HELEN TAYLOR, Editor of "The Works of Buckle," &c.
Mansel. Rev. J. H. HUCKIN, D.D., Head Master of Repton.
Adam Smith. J. A. FARRER, M.A., Author of "Primitive Manners and Customs."

English Philosophers (continued) :—
  Hobbes. A. H. GOSSET, B.A., Fellow of New College, Oxford.
  Bentham. G. E. BUCKLE, M.A., Fellow of All Souls', Oxford.
  Austin. HARRY JOHNSON, B.A., late Scholar of Queen's College, Oxford.
  Hartley. } E. S. BOWEN, B.A., late Scholar of New College,
  James Mill. } Oxford.
  Shaftesbury. } Professor FOWLER.
  Hutcheson. }
  Arrangements are in progress for volumes on LOCKE, HUME, PALEY, REID, &c.

Episodes of French History. Edited, with Notes, Genealogical, Historical, and other Tables, by GUSTAVE MASSON, B.A.
  1. **Charlemagne and the Carlovingians.**
  2. **Louis XI. and the Crusades.**
  3. Part I. **Francis I. and Charles V.**
     ,, II. **Francis I. and the Renaissance.**
  4. **Henry IV. and the End of the Wars of Religion.**
  The above Series is based upon M. Guizot's "History of France." Each volume choicely Illustrated, with Maps, 2s. 6d.

Erema ; or, My Father's Sin. See BLACKMORE.

Etcher (The). Containing 36 Examples of the Original Etched-work of Celebrated Artists, amongst others: BIRKET FOSTER, J. E. HODGSON, R.A., COLIN HUNTER, J. P. HESELTINE, ROBERT W. MACBETH, R. S. CHATTOCK, &c. Vol. for 1881, imperial 4to, cloth extra, gilt edges, 2l. 12s. 6d. Monthly, 3s. 6d.

Eton. See "Day of my Life," "Out of School," "About Some Fellows."

FARM Ballads. By WILL CARLETON. Boards, 1s.; cloth, gilt edges, 1s. 6d.

Farm Festivals. By the same Author. Uniform with above.

Farm Legends. By the same Author. See above.

Felkin (R. W.) and Wilson (Rev. C. T.) Uganda and the Egyptian Soudan. An Account of Travel in Eastern and Equatorial Africa ; including a Residence of Two Years at the Court of King Mtesa, and a Description of the Slave Districts of Bahr-el-Ghazel and Darfour. With a New Map of 1200 miles in these Provinces ; numerous Illustrations, and Anthropological, Meteorological, and Geographical Notes. By R. W. FELKIN, F.R.G.S., Member of the Anthropological Institute, &c., &c. ; and the Rev. C. T. WILSON, M.A. Oxon., F.R.G.S., Member of the Society of Arts, Hon. Fellow of the Cairo Geographical Society. 2 vols., crown 8vo, cloth, 28s.

Fern Paradise (The) : A Plea for the Culture of Ferns. By F. G. HEATH. New Edition, entirely Rewritten, Illustrated by Eighteen full-page, and numerous other Woodcuts, including 8 Plates of Ferns and Four Photographs, large post 8vo, cloth, gilt edges, 12s. 6d. Sixth Edition.
  "All lovers of ferns will be delighted with the illustrated edition of Mr. Heath's ' Fern Paradise.'"—*Saturday Review.*

Fern World (The). By F. G. HEATH. Illustrated by Twelve Coloured Plates, giving complete Figures (Sixty-four in all) of every Species of British Fern, printed from Nature; by several full-page and other Engravings. Cloth, gilt edges, 6th Edition, 12s. 6d.

Few (A) Hints on Proving Wills. Enlarged Edition, 1s.

First Steps in Conversational French Grammar. By F. JULIEN. Being an Introduction to "Petites Leçons de Conversation et de Grammaire," by the same Author. Fcap. 8vo, 128 pp., 1s.

Four Lectures on Electric Induction. Delivered at the Royal Institution, 1878-9. By J. E. H. GORDON, B.A. Cantab. With numerous Illustrations. Cloth limp, square 16mo, 3s.

Foreign Countries and the British Colonies. Edited by F. S. PULLING, M.A., Lecturer at Queen's College, Oxford, and formerly Professor at the Yorkshire College, Leeds. A Series of small Volumes descriptive of the principal Countries of the World by well-known Authors, each Country being treated of by a Writer who from Personal Knowledge is qualified to speak with authority on the Subject. The Volumes average 180 crown 8vo pages each, contain 2 Maps and Illustrations, crown 8vo, 3s. 6d.

The following is a List of the Volumes:—

Denmark and Iceland. By E. C. OTTÉ, Author of "Scandinavian History," &c.
Greece. By L. SERGEANT, B.A., Knight of the Hellenic Order of the Saviour, Author of "New Greece."
Switzerland. By W. A. P. COOLIDGE, M.A., Fellow of Magdalen College, Editor of *The Alpine Journal.*
Austria. By D. KAY, F.R.G.S.
Russia. By W. R. MORFILL, M.A., Oriel College, Oxford, Lecturer on the Ilchester Foundation, &c.
Persia. By Major-Gen. Sir F. J. GOLDSMID, K.C.S.I., Author of "Telegraph and Travel," &c.
Japan. By S. MOSSMAN, Author of "New Japan," &c.
Peru. By CLEMENTS H. MARKHAM, M.A., C.B.
Canada. By W. FRASER RAE, Author of "Westward by Rail," "From Newfoundland to Manitoba," &c.
Sweden and Norway. By the Rev. F. H. WOODS, M.A., Fellow of St. John's College, Oxford.
The West Indies. By C. H. EDEN, F.R.G.S., Author of "Frozen Asia," &c.
New Zealand.
France. By M. ROBERTS, Author of "The Atelier du Lys,"&c.
Egypt. By S. LANE POOLE, B.A., Author of "Life of E. Lane," &c.
Spain. By the Rev. WENTWORTH WEBSTER, M.A.
Turkey-in-Asia. By J. C. MCCOAN, M.P.
Australia. By J. F. VESEY FITZGERALD, late Premier of New South Wales.
Holland. By R. L. POOLE.

Franc (Maude Jeane). The following form one Series, small post 8vo, in uniform cloth bindings, with gilt edges:—

Emily's Choice. 5s.	Silken Cords and Iron Fetters. 4s.
Hall's Vineyard. 4s.	Vermont Vale. 5s.
John's Wife: A Story of Life in South Australia. 4s.	Minnie's Mission. 4s.
	Little Mercy. 5s.
Marian; or, The Light of Some One's Home. 5s.	Beatrice Melton's Discipline. 4s.

Francis (F.) War, Waves, and Wanderings, including a Cruise in the "Lancashire Witch." 2 vols., crown 8vo, cloth extra, 24s.

French Revolution (The Great). Letters written from Paris during the Progress of the Great French Revolution, by Madame J—— to her Husband and Son. Edited by her Great-grandson, M. EDOUARD LOCKROY. From the French. Crown 8vo, cloth, 10s. 6d.

Froissart (The Boy's). Selected from the Chronicles of England, France, Spain, &c. By SIDNEY LANIER. The Volume is fully Illustrated, and uniform with "The Boy's King Arthur." Crown 8vo, cloth, 7s. 6d.

From Newfoundland to Manitoba; a Guide through Canada's Maritime, Mining, and Prairie Provinces. By W. FRASER RAE. Crown 8vo, with several Maps, 6s.

GAMES of Patience. See CADOGAN.

Gentle Life (Queen Edition). 2 vols. in 1, small 4to, 10s. 6d.

THE GENTLE LIFE SERIES.

Price 6s. each; or in calf extra, price 10s. 6d.; Smaller Edition, cloth extra, 2s. 6d.

The Gentle Life. Essays in aid of the Formation of Character of Gentlemen and Gentlewomen. 21st Edition.

About in the World. Essays by Author of "The Gentle Life."

Like unto Christ. A New Translation of Thomas à Kempis "De Imitatione Christi." 2nd Edition.

Familiar Words. An Index Verborum, or Quotation Handbook. Affording an immediate Reference to Phrases and Sentences that have become embedded in the English language. 6s.

Essays by Montaigne. Edited and Annotated by the Author of "The Gentle Life." With Portrait. 2nd Edition.

The Countess of Pembroke's Arcadia. Written by Sir PHILIP SIDNEY. Edited with Notes by Author of "The Gentle Life." 7s. 6d.

The Gentle Life. 2nd Series, 8th Edition.

The Gentle Life Series (continued) :—

The Silent Hour: Essays, Original and Selected. By the Author of "The Gentle Life." 3rd Edition.

Half-Length Portraits. Short Studies of Notable Persons. By J. HAIN FRISWELL.

Essays on English Writers, for the Self-improvement of Students in English Literature.

Other People's Windows. By J. HAIN FRISWELL. 3rd Edition.

A Man's Thoughts. By J. HAIN FRISWELL.

German Primer. Being an Introduction to First Steps in German. By M. T. PREU. 2s. 6d.

Getting On in the World; or, Hints on Success in Life. By W. MATHEWS, LL.D. Small post 8vo, cloth, 2s. 6d.; gilt edges, 3s. 6d.

Gilpin's Forest Scenery. Edited by F. G. HEATH. Large post 8vo, with numerous Illustrations. Uniform with "The Fern World," 12s. 6d.

"Deserves to be a favourite in the boudoir as well as in the library."—*Saturday Review.*

"One of the most delightful works ever written."—*Globe.*

Gordon (J. E. H.). See "Four Lectures on Electric Induction," "Physical Treatise on Electricity," &c.

Gouffé. The Royal Cookery Book. By JULES GOUFFÉ; translated and adapted for English use by ALPHONSE GOUFFÉ, Head Pastrycook to her Majesty the Queen. Illustrated with large plates printed in colours. 161 Woodcuts, 8vo, cloth extra, gilt edges, 2l. 2s.

—— Domestic Edition, half-bound, 10s. 6d.

"By far the ablest and most complete work on cookery that has ever been submitted to the gastronomical world."—*Pall Mall Gazette.*

Great Artists. See "Biographies."

Great Historic Galleries of England (The). Edited by LORD RONALD GOWER, F.S.A., Trustee of the National Portrait Gallery. Illustrated by 24 large and carefully-executed *permanent* Photographs of some of the most celebrated Pictures by the Great Masters. Vol. I., imperial 4to, cloth extra, gilt edges, 36s. Vol. II., with 36 large permanent photographs, £2 12s. 6d.

Great Musicians (The). A Series of Biographies of the Great Musicians. Edited by F. HUEFFER.

1. **Wagner.** By the EDITOR.
2. **Weber.** By Sir JULIUS BENEDICT.
3. **Mendelssohn.** By JOSEPH BENNETT.
4. **Schubert.** By H. F. FROST.
5. **Rossini,** and the Modern Italian School. By H. SUTHERLAND EDWARDS.
6. **Marcello.** By ARRIGO BOITO.
7. **Purcell.** By H. W. CUMMINGS.
8. **English Church Composers.**

⁎⁎ Dr. Hiller and other distinguished writers, both English and Foreign, have promised contributions. Each Volume is complete in itself. Small post 8vo, cloth extra, 3s.

Guizot's History of France. Translated by ROBERT BLACK. Super-royal 8vo, very numerous Full-page and other Illustrations. In 8 vols., cloth extra, gilt, each 24*s.* This work is re-issued in cheaper Monthly Volumes, at 10*s.* 6*d.* each, commencing Nov. 1, 1881. Subscription to the set, £4 4*s.*
> "It supplies a want which has long been felt, and ought to be in the hands of all students of history."—*Times.*

——————————— *Masson's School Edition.* The History of France from the Earliest Times to the Outbreak of the Revolution; abridged from the Translation by Robert Black, M.A., with Chronological Index, Historical and Genealogical Tables, &c. By Professor GUSTAVE MASSON, B.A., Assistant Master at Harrow School. With 24 full-page Portraits, and many other Illustrations. 1 vol., demy 8vo, 600 pp., cloth extra, 10*s.* 6*d.*

Guizot's History of England. In 3 vols. of about 500 pp. each, containing 60 to 70 Full-page and other Illustrations, cloth extra, gilt, 24*s.* each.
> "For luxury of typography, plainness of print, and beauty of illustration, these volumes, of which but one has as yet appeared in English, will hold their own against any production of an age so luxurious as our own in everything, typography not excepted."—*Times.*

Guyon (Mde.) Life. By UPHAM. 6th Edition, crown 8vo, 6*s*

*H*ANDBOOK *to the Charities of London.* See Low's.

——— *of Embroidery; which see.*

Hall (W. W.) How to Live Long; or, 1408 *Health Maxims,* Physical, Mental, and Moral. By W. W. HALL, A.M., M.D. Small post 8vo, cloth, 2*s.* 2nd Edition.

Harper's Monthly Magazine. Published Monthly. 160 pages, fully Illustrated. 1*s.* With two Serial Novels by celebrated Authors.
  Vol. I. December, 1880, to May, 1881.
  ,, II. May, 1881, to November, 1881.
Each cloth extra, with 400 magnificent illustrations, 8*s.* 6*d.*
> "'Harper's Magazine' is so thickly sown with excellent illustrations that to count them would be a work of time; not that it is a picture magazine, for the engravings illustrate the text after the manner seen in some of our choicest *editions de luxe.*"—*St. James's Gazette.*
> "It is so pretty, so big, and so cheap. . . . An extraordinary shillingsworth—160 large octavo pages, with over a score of articles, and more than three times as many illustrations."—*Edinburgh Daily Review.*
> "An amazing shillingsworth . . . combining choice literature of both nations."—*Nonconformist.*

Heart of Africa. Three Years' Travels and Adventures in the Unexplored Regions of Central Africa, from 1868 to 1871. By Dr. GEORG SCHWEINFURTH. Numerous Illustrations, and large Map. 2 vols., crown 8vo, cloth, 15*s.*

Heath (Francis George). *See* "Autumnal Leaves," "Burnham Beeches," "Fern Paradise," "Fern World," "Gilpin's Forest Scenery," "Our Woodland Trees," "Peasant Life," "Sylvan Spring," "Trees and Ferns," "Where to Find Ferns."

Heber's (Bishop) Illustrated Edition of Hymns. With upwards of 100 beautiful Engravings. Small 4to, handsomely bound, 7s. 6d. Morocco, 18s. 6d. and 21s. New and Cheaper Edition, cloth, 3s. 6d.

Heir of Kilfinnan (The). New Story by W. H. G. KINGSTON, Author of "Snow Shoes and Canoes," &c. With Illustrations. Cloth, gilt edges, 7s. 6d.; plainer binding, plain edges, 5s.

History of a Crime (The); Deposition of an Eye-witness. The Story of the Coup d'État. By VICTOR HUGO. Crown 8vo, 6s.

—— *Ancient Art.* Translated from the German of JOHN WINCKELMANN, by JOHN LODGE, M.D. With very numerous Plates and Illustrations. 2 vols., 8vo, 36s.

—— *England. See* GUIZOT.

—— *France. See* GUIZOT.

—— *of Russia. See* RAMBAUD.

—— *Merchant Shipping. See* LINDSAY.

—— *United States. See* BRYANT.

History and Principles of Weaving by Hand and by Power. With several hundred Illustrations. By ALFRED BARLOW. Royal 8vo, cloth extra, 1l. 5s. Second Edition.

Holmes (O. W.) The Poetical Works of Oliver Wendell Holmes. In 2 vols., 18mo, exquisitely printed, and chastely bound in limp cloth, gilt tops, 10s. 6d.

How I Crossed Africa: from the Atlantic to the Indian Ocean, Through Unknown Countries; Discovery of the Great Zambesi Affluents, &c.—Vol. I., The King's Rifle. Vol. II., The Coillard Family. By Major SERPA PINTO. With 24 full-page and 118 half-page and smaller Illustrations, 13 small Maps, and 1 large one. 2 vols., demy 8vo, cloth extra, 42s.

How to Live Long. See HALL.

How to get Strong and how to Stay so. By WILLIAM BLAIKIE. A Manual of Rational, Physical, Gymnastic, and other Exercises. With Illustrations, small post 8vo, 5s.

Hugo (Victor) "Ninety-Three." Illustrated. Crown 8vo, 6s.

—— *Toilers of the Sea.* Crown 8vo. Illustrated, 6s.; fancy boards, 2s.; cloth, 2s. 6d.; On large paper with all the original Illustrations, 10s. 6d.

—— *and his Times.* Translated from the French of A. BARBOU by ELLEN E. FREWER. 120 Illustrations, many of them from designs by Victor Hugo himself. Super-royal 8vo, cloth extra, 24s.

——. *See* "History of a Crime," "Victor Hugo and his Times."

Hundred Greatest Men (The). 8 portfolios, 21s. each, or 4 vols., half morocco, gilt edges, 12 guineas, containing 15 to 20 Portraits each. See below.

"Messrs. SAMPSON LOW & Co. are about to issue an important 'International' work, entitled, 'THE HUNDRED GREATEST MEN;' being the Lives and Portraits of the 100 Greatest Men of History, divided into Eight Classes, each Class to form a Monthly Quarto Volume. The Introductions to the volumes are to be written by recognized authorities on the different subjects, the English contributors being DEAN STANLEY, Mr. MATTHEW ARNOLD, Mr. FROUDE, and Professor MAX MÜLLER: in Germany, Professor HELMHOLTZ; in France, MM. TAINE and RENAN; and in America, Mr. EMERSON. The Portraits are to be Reproductions from fine and rare Steel Engravings."—*Academy.*

Hygiene and Public Health (A Treatise on). Edited by A. H. BUCK, M.D. Illustrated by numerous Wood Engravings. In 2 royal 8vo vols., cloth, one guinea each.

Hymnal Companion to Book of Common Prayer. See BICKERSTETH.

ILLUSTRATED Text-Books of Art-Education. Edited by EDWARD J. POYNTER, R.A. Each Volume contains numerous Illustrations, and is strongly bound for the use of Students, price 5s. The Volumes now ready are:—

PAINTING.

Classic and Italian. By PERCY R. HEAD. With 50 Illustrations, 5s.	German, Flemish, and Dutch. French and Spanish. English and American.

ARCHITECTURE.

Classic and Early Christian.
Gothic and Renaissance. By T. ROGER SMITH. With 50 Illustrations, 5s.

SCULPTURE.

Antique: Egyptian and Greek.	Renaissance and Modern.

Italian Sculptors of the 14th and 15th Centuries.

ORNAMENT.

Decoration in Colour.	Architectural Ornament.

Illustrations of China and its People. By J. THOMPSON, F.R.G.S. Four Volumes, imperial 4to, each 3l. 3s.

Illustrated Dictionary (An) of Words used in Art and Archæology. Explaining Terms frequently used in Works on Architecture, Arms, Bronzes, Christian Art, Colour, Costume, Decoration, Devices, Emblems, Heraldry, Lace, Personal Ornaments, Pottery, Painting, Sculpture, &c., with their Derivations. By J. W. MOLLETT, B.A., Officier de l'Instruction Publique (France); Author of "Life of Rembrandt," &c. Illustrated with 600 Wood Engravings. Small 4to, strongly bound in cloth, 12s. 6d.

In my Indian Garden. By PHIL ROBINSON, Author of "Under the Punkah." With a Preface by EDWIN ARNOLD, M.A., C.S.I., &c. Crown 8vo, limp cloth, 3s. 6d.

Involuntary Voyage (An). Showing how a Frenchman who abhorred the Sea was most unwillingly and by a series of accidents driven round the World. Numerous Illustrations. Square crown 8vo, cloth extra, 7s. 6d.; plainer binding, plain edges, 5s.

Irving (Washington). Complete Library Edition of his Works in 27 Vols., Copyright, Unabridged, and with the Author's Latest Revisions, called the "Geoffrey Crayon" Edition, handsomely printed in large square 8vo, on superfine laid paper, and each volume, of about 500 pages, will be fully Illustrated. 12s. 6d. per vol. *See also* "Little Britain."

JACK and Jill. By Miss ALCOTT. Small post 8vo, cloth, gilt edges, 5s. With numerous Illustrations.

John Holdsworth, Chief Mate. By W. CLARKE RUSSELL, Author of "Wreck of the Grosvenor." Crown 8vo, 6s.

KINGSTON (W. H. G.). See "Snow-Shoes," "Child of the Cavern," "Two Supercargoes," "With Axe and Rifle," "Begum's Fortune," "Heir of Kilfinnan," "Dick Cheveley." Each vol., with very numerous Illustrations, square crown 16mo, gilt edges, 7s. 6d.; plainer binding, plain edges, 5s.

LADY Silverdale's Sweetheart. 6s. *See* BLACK.

Lectures on Architecture. By E. VIOLLET-LE-DUC. Translated by BENJAMIN BUCKNALL, Architect. With 33 Steel Plates and 200 Wood Engravings. Super-royal 8vo, leather back, gilt top, with complete Index, 2 vols., 3l. 3s.

Lenten Meditations. In Two Series, each complete in itself. By the Rev. CLAUDE BOSANQUET, Author of "Blossoms from the King's Garden." 16mo, cloth, First Series, 1s. 6d.; Second Series, 2s.

Library of Religious Poetry. A Collection of the Best Poems of all Ages and Tongues. With Biographical and Literary Notes. Edited by PHILIP SCHAFF, D.D., LL.D., and ARTHUR GILMAN, M.A. Royal 8vo, pp. 1036, cloth extra, gilt edges, 21s.

Lindsay (W. S.) History of Merchant Shipping and Ancient Commerce. Over 150 Illustrations, Maps, and Charts. In 4 vols., demy 8vo, cloth extra. Vols. 1 and 2, 21s.; vols. 3 and 4, 24s. each.

Little Britain; together with *The Spectre Bridegroom,* and *A Legend of Sleepy Hollow.* By WASHINGTON IRVING. An entirely New *Edition de luxe,* specially suitable for Presentation. Illustrated by 120 very fine Engravings on Wood, by Mr. J. D. COOPER. Designed by Mr. CHARLES O. MURRAY. Square crown 8vo, cloth extra, gilt edges, 10s. 6d.

Low's Select Novelets. Small post 8vo, cloth extra, 3s. 6d. each.

Friends: a Duet. By E. S. PHELPS, Author of "The Gates Ajar."
"'Friends' is a graceful story ... it loses nothing in the telling."—*Athenæum.*

Daby Rue: Her Adventures and Misadventures, her Friends and her Enemies. By CHARLES M. CLAY.

The Story of Helen Troy.
"A pleasant book."—*Truth.*

The Clients of Dr. Bernagius. From the French of LUCIEN BIART, by Mrs. CASHEL HOEY.

The Undiscovered Country. By W. D. HOWELLS.

A Gentleman of Leisure. By EDGAR FAWCETT.
"An amazingly clever book."—*Boston Transcript.*

Low's Standard Library of Travel and Adventure. Crown 8vo, bound uniformly in cloth extra, price 7s. 6d.

1. **The Great Lone Land.** By Major W. F. BUTLER, C.B.
2. **The Wild North Land.** By Major W. F. BUTLER, C.B.
3. **How I found Livingstone.** By H. M. STANLEY.
4. **The Threshold of the Unknown Region.** By C. R. MARKHAM. (4th Edition, with Additional Chapters, 10s. 6d.)
5. **A Whaling Cruise to Baffin's Bay and the Gulf of Boothia.** By A. H. MARKHAM.
6. **Campaigning on the Oxus.** By J. A. MACGAHAN.
7. **Akim-foo: the History of a Failure.** By MAJOR W. F. BUTLER, C.B.
8. **Ocean to Ocean.** By the Rev. GEORGE M. GRANT. With Illustrations.
9. **Cruise of the Challenger.** By W. J. J. SPRY, R.N.
10. **Schweinfurth's Heart of Africa.** 2 vols., 15s.
11. **Through the Dark Continent.** By H. M. STANLEY. 1 vol., 12s. 6d.

Low's Standard Novels. Crown 8vo, 6s. each, cloth extra.

My Lady Greensleeves. By HELEN MATHERS, Authoress of "Comin' through the Rye," "Cherry Ripe," &c.

Three Feathers. By WILLIAM BLACK.

A Daughter of Heth. 13th Edition. By W. BLACK. With Frontispiece by F. WALKER, A.R.A.

Kilmeny. A Novel. By W. BLACK.

In Silk Attire. By W. BLACK.

Lady Silverdale's Sweetheart. By W. BLACK.

Sunrise. By W. BLACK.

The Trumpet Major. By THOMAS HARDY.

An English Squire. By Miss COLERIDGE.

Low's Standard Novels (continued):—

    Mary Marston. By GEORGE MACDONALD.
    Guild Court. By GEORGE MACDONALD.
    The Vicar's Daughter. By GEORGE MACDONALD.
    Adela Cathcart. By GEORGE MACDONALD.
    Out of Court. By Mrs. CASHEL HOEY.
    History of a Crime: The Story of the Coup d'État. VICTOR HUGO.
    Alice Lorraine. By R. D. BLACKMORE.
    Lorna Doone. By R. D. BLACKMORE. 18th Edition.
    Cradock Nowell. By R. D. BLACKMORE.
    Clara Vaughan. By R. D. BLACKMORE.
    Cripps the Carrier. By R. D. BLACKMORE.
    Erema; or, My Father's Sin. By R. D. BLACKMORE.
    Mary Anerley. By R. D. BLACKMORE.
    Christowell, a Dartmoor Tale. By R. D. BLACKMORE.
    Innocent. By Mrs. OLIPHANT. Eight Illustrations.
    Work. A Story of Experience. By LOUISA M. ALCOTT.
    The Afghan Knife. By R. A. STERNDALE, Author of "Seonee."
    A French Heiress in her own Chateau. By the Author of "One Only," "Constantia," &c. Six Illustrations.
    Ninety-Three. By VICTOR HUGO. Numerous Illustrations.
    My Wife and I. By Mrs. BEECHER STOWE.
    Wreck of the Grosvenor. By W. CLARK RUSSELL.
    John Holdsworth (Chief Mate). By W. CLARK RUSSELL.
    A Sailor's Sweetheart. By W. CLARK RUSSELL.
    Far from the Madding Crowd. By THOMAS HARDY.
    Elinor Dryden. By Mrs. MACQUOID.
    Diane. By Mrs. MACQUOID.
    Poganuc People, Their Loves and Lives. By Mrs. B. STOWE.
    A Golden Sorrow. By Mrs. CASHEL HOEY.
    Out of Court. By Mrs. CASHEL HOEY.
    A Story of the Dragonnades. By the Rev. E. GILLIAT, M.A.

Low's Handbook to the Charities of London. Edited and revised to date by C. MACKESON, F.S.S., Editor of "A Guide to the Churches of London and its Suburbs," &c. Paper, 1s.; cloth, 1s. 6d.

*M*ACGREGOR (*John*) "*Rob Roy*" *on the Baltic.* 3rd Edition, small post 8vo, 2s. 6d.; cloth, gilt edges, 3s. 6d.

—— *A Thousand Miles in the "Rob Roy" Canoe.* 11th Edition, small post 8vo, 2s. 6d.; cloth, gilt edges, 3s. 6d.

Macgregor (John) Description of the "Rob Roy" Canoe, with Plans, &c, 1s.

—— *The Voyage Alone in the Yawl "Rob Roy."* New Edition, thoroughly revised, with additions, small post 8vo, 5s.; boards, 2s. 6d.

Macquoid (Mrs.) Elinor Dryden. Crown 8vo, cloth, 6s.

—— *Diane.* Crown 8vo, 6s.

Magazine. See HARPER, UNION JACK, THE ETCHER, MEN OF MARK.

Magyarland. A Narrative of Travels through the Snowy Carpathians, and Great Alföld of the Magyar. By a Fellow of the Carpathian Society (Diploma of 1881), and Author of "The Indian Alps." 2 vols., 8vo, cloth extra, with about 120 Woodcuts from the Author's own sketches and drawings, 42s.

Manitoba: its History, Growth, and Present Position. By the Rev. Professor BRYCE, Principal of Manitoba College, Winnipeg. Crown 8vo, with Illustrations and Maps, 7s. 6d.

Markham (C. R.) The Threshold of the Unknown Region. Crown 8vo, with Four Maps, 4th Edition. Cloth extra, 10s. 6d.

Maury (Commander) Physical Geography of the Sea, and its Meteorology. Being a Reconstruction and Enlargement of his former Work, with Charts and Diagrams. New Edition, crown 8vo, 6s.

Memoirs of Count Miot de Melito, Minister, Ambassador, Councillor of State, and Member of the Institute of France, between the years 1788 and 1815. Edited by General FLEISCHMANN. From the French by Mrs. CASHEL HOEY and Mr. JOHN LILLIE. 2 vols., demy 8vo, cloth extra, 36s.

Memoirs of Madame de Rémusat, 1802—1808. By her Grandson, M. PAUL DE RÉMUSAT, Senator. Translated by Mrs. CASHEL HOEY and Mr. JOHN LILLIE. 4th Edition, cloth extra. This work was written by Madame de Rémusat during the time she was living on the most intimate terms with the Empress Josephine, and is full of revelations respecting the private life of Bonaparte, and of men and politics of the first years of the century. Revelations which have already created a great sensation in Paris. 8vo, 2 vols., 32s.

—— *See also* " Selection."

Menus (366, one for each day of the year). Translated from the French of COUNT BRISSE, by Mrs. MATTHEW CLARKE. Crown 8vo, 10s. 6d.

Men of Mark: a Gallery of Contemporary Portraits of the most Eminent Men of the Day taken from Life, especially for this publication, price 1s. 6d. monthly. Vols. I. to VI., handsomely bound, cloth, gilt edges, 25s. each.

Mendelssohn Family (The), 1729—1847. From Letters and Journals. Translated from the German of SEBASTIAN HENSEL. 2 vols., demy 8vo, 30s.

Michael Strogoff. 10s. 6d. and 5s. See VERNE.

Mitford (Miss). See " Our Village."

Music. See "Great Musicians."

My Lady Greensleeves. By HELEN MATHERS, Authoress of "Comin' through the Rye," "Cherry Ripe," &c. 1 vol. edition, crown 8vo, cloth, 6s.

Mysterious Island. By JULES VERNE. 3 vols., imperial 16mo. 150 Illustrations, cloth gilt, 3s. 6d. each; elaborately bound, gilt edges, 7s. 6d. each. Cheap Edition, with some of the Illustrations, cloth, gilt, 2s.; paper, 1s. each.

NARRATIVES of State Trials in the Nineteenth Century. First Period: From the Union with Ireland to the Death of George IV., 1801—1830. By G. LATHOM BROWNE, of the Middle Temple, Barrister-at-Law. 2 vols., crown 8vo, cloth, 24s.

Nature and Functions of Art (The); and more especially of Architecture. By LEOPOLD EIDLITZ. Medium 8vo, cloth, 21s.

Naval Brigade in South Africa (The). By HENRY F. NORBURY, C.B., R.N. Crown 8vo, cloth extra, 10s. 6d.

New Child's Play (A). Sixteen Drawings by E. V. B. Beautifully printed in colours, 4to, cloth extra, 12s. 6d.

New Guinea: What I did and what I saw. By L. M. D'ALBERTIS, Officer of the Order of the Crown of Italy, Honorary Member and Gold Medallist of the I.R.G.S., C.M.Z.S., &c., &c. In 2 vols., demy 8vo, cloth extra, with Maps, Coloured Plates, and numerous very fine Woodcut Illustrations, 42s.

New Ireland. By A. M. SULLIVAN, M.P. for Louth. 2 vols., demy 8vo, 30s. Cheaper Edition, 1 vol., crown 8vo, 8s. 6d.

New Novels Crown 8vo, cloth, 10s. 6d. per vol. :—
    Christowell: a Dartmoor Tale. By R. D. BLACKMORE. 3 vols.
    The Braes of Yarrow. By CHAS. GIBBON. 3 vols.
    A Laodicean. By THOMAS HARDY, Author of "Far from the Madding Crowd," "Trumpet Major," &c., &c. 3 vols.
    Waiting. By Miss A. M. HOPKINSON. 3 vols.
    Don John. By Miss JEAN INGELOW. 3 vols.
    Warlock of Warlock. By GEORGE MACDONALD. 3 vols.
    Riverside Papers. By J. D. HOPPUS. 2 vols., small post 8vo, 12s.
    Cecily's Debt. By Mrs. A. B. CHURCH. 3 vols.

Nice and Her Neighbours. By the Rev. CANON HOLE, Author of "A Book about Roses," "A Little Tour in Ireland," &c. Small 4to, with numerous choice Illustrations, 12s. 6d.

Noah's Ark. A Contribution to the Study of Unnatural History.
By PHIL ROBINSON, Author of "In my Indian Garden," "Under the Punkah," &c., &c. 2 vols. Small post 8vo, 12s. 6d.

Noble Words and Noble Deeds. From the French of E. MULLER. Containing many Full-page Illustrations by PHILIPPOTEAUX. Square imperial 16mo, cloth extra, 7s. 6d.; plainer binding, plain edges, 5s.

Nordenskiöld's Voyage around Asia and Europe. A Popular Account of the North-East Passage of the "Vega." By Lieut. A. HOVGAARD, of the Royal Danish Navy, and member of the "Vega" Expedition. Demy 8vo, cloth, with about 50 Illustrations and 3 Maps, 21s.

North American Review (The). Monthly, price 2s. 6d.

Nothing to Wear; and Two Millions. By W. A. BUTLER. New Edition. Small post 8vo, in stiff coloured wrapper, 1s.

Nursery Playmates (Prince of). 217 Coloured Pictures for Children by eminent Artists. Folio, in coloured boards, 6s.

OFF to the Wilds: A Story for Boys. By G. MANVILLE FENN. Most richly and profusely Illustrated. Crown 8vo, cloth extra, 7s. 6d.

Old-Fashioned Girl. See ALCOTT.

On Horseback through Asia Minor. By Capt. FRED BURNABY, Royal Horse Guards, Author of "A Ride to Khiva." 2 vols., 8vo, with three Maps and Portrait of Author, 6th Edition, 38s.; Cheaper Edition, crown 8vo, 10s. 6d.

Our Little Ones in Heaven. Edited by the Rev. H. ROBBINS. With Frontispiece after Sir JOSHUA REYNOLDS. Fcap., cloth extra, New Edition—the 3rd, with Illustrations, 5s.

Our Village. By MARY RUSSELL MITFORD. Illustrated with Frontispiece Steel Engraving, and 12 full-page and 157 smaller Cuts. Crown 4to, cloth, gilt edges, 21s.; cheaper binding, 10s. 6d.

Our Woodland Trees. By F. G. HEATH. Large post 8vo, cloth, gilt edges, uniform with "Fern World" and "Fern Paradise," by the same Author. 8 Coloured Plates (showing leaves of every British Tree) and 20 Woodcuts, cloth, gilt edges, 12s. 6d. Third Edition. About 600 pages.

Outlines of Ornament in all Styles. A Work of Reference for the Architect, Art Manufacturer, Decorative Artist, and Practical Painter. By W. and G. A. AUDSLEY, Fellows of the Royal Institute of British Architects. Only a limited number have been printed and the stones destroyed. Small folio, 60 plates, with introductory text, cloth gilt, 31s. 6d.

*P*AINTERS *of All Schools.* By Louis Viardot, and other Writers. 500 pp., super-royal 8vo, 20 Full-page and 70 smaller Engravings, cloth extra, 25s. A New Edition is issued in Half-crown parts, with fifty additional portraits, cloth, gilt edges, 31s. 6d.

Painting (A Short History of the British School of). By Geo. H. Shepherd. Post 8vo, cloth, 3s. 6d.

Palliser (Mrs.) A History of Lace, from the Earliest Period. A New and Revised Edition, with additional cuts and text, upwards of 100 Illustrations and coloured Designs. 1 vol., 8vo, 1l. 1s.

―――― *Historic Devices, Badges, and War Cries.* 8vo, 1l. 1s.

―――― *The China Collector's Pocket Companion.* With upwards of 1000 Illustrations of Marks and Monograms. 2nd Edition, with Additions. Small post 8vo, limp cloth, 5s.

Parliamentary History of the Irish Land Question (The). From 1829 to 1869, and the Origin and Results of the Ulster Custom. By R. Barry O'Brien, Barrister-at-Law, Author of "The Irish Land Question and English Public Opinion." 3rd Edition, corrected and revised, with additional matter. Post 8vo, cloth extra, 6s.

Pathways of Palestine : a Descriptive Tour through the Holy Land. By the Rev. Canon Tristram. Illustrated with 44 permanent Photographs. (The Photographs are large, and most perfect Specimens of the Art.) Published in 22 Monthly Parts, 4to, in Wrapper, 2s. 6d. each. Vol. I., containing 12 parts, 24 Illustrations, cloth, gilt edges, 31s. 6d.

Peasant Life in the West of England. By Francis George Heath, Author of "Sylvan Spring," "The Fern World." Crown 8vo, 400 pp. (with Autograph Letter of seven pages from Lord Beaconsfield to the Author, written December 28, 1880), 10s. 6d.

Petites Leçons de Conversation et de Grammaire: Oral and Conversational Method ; being Lessons introducing the most Useful Topics of Conversation, upon an entirely new principle, &c. By F. Julien, French Master at King Edward the Sixth's School, Birmingham. Author of "The Student's French Examiner," "First Steps in Conversational French Grammar," which see.

Photography (History and Handbook of). See Tissandier.

Physical Treatise on Electricity and Magnetism. By J. E. H. Gordon, B.A. With about 200 coloured, full-page, and other Illustrations. In respect to the number and beauty of the Illustrations, the work is quite unique. 2 vols., 8vo, 36s.

Poems of the Inner Life. A New Edition, Revised, with many additional Poems. Small post 8vo, cloth, 5s.

Poganuc People: their Loves and Lives. By Mrs. BEECHER STOWE. Crown 8vo, cloth, 6s.

Polar Expeditions. See KOLDEWEY, MARKHAM, MACGAHAN, NARES, and NORDENSKIÖLD.

Poynter (Edward J., R.A.). See "Illustrated Text-books."

Publishers' Circular (The), and General Record of British and Foreign Literature. Published on the 1st and 15th of every Month, 3d.

Pyrenees (The). By HENRY BLACKBURN. With 100 Illustrations by GUSTAVE DORÉ, a New Map of Routes, and Information for Travellers, corrected to 1881. With a description of Lourdes in 1880. Crown 8vo, cloth extra, 7s. 6d.

RAMBAUD (Alfred). History of Russia, from its Origin to the Year 1877. With Six Maps. Translated by Mrs. L. B. LANE. 2 vols., demy 8vo, cloth extra, 38s.

Recollections of Writers. By CHARLES and MARY COWDEN CLARKE. Authors of "The Concordance to Shakespeare," &c.; with Letters of CHARLES LAMB, LEIGH HUNT, DOUGLAS JERROLD, and CHARLES DICKENS; and a Preface by MARY COWDEN CLARKE. Crown 8vo, cloth, 10s. 6d.

Rémusat (Madame de). See "Memoirs of," "Selection."

Richter (Jean Paul). The Literary Works of Leonardo da Vinci. Containing his Writings on Painting, Sculpture, and Architecture, his Philosophical Maxims, Humorous Writings, and Miscellaneous Notes on Personal Events, on his Contemporaries, on Literature, &c.; for the first time published from Autograph Manuscripts. By J. P. RICHTER, Ph.Dr., Hon. Member of the Royal and Imperial Academy of Rome, &c. 2 vols., imperial 8vo, containing about 200 Drawings in Autotype Reproductions, and numerous other Illustrations. Price Eight Guineas to Subscribers. After publication the price will be Ten Guineas.

Robinson (Phil). See "In my Indian Garden," "Under the Punkah," "Noah's Ark."

Rochefoucauld's Reflections. Bayard Series, 2s. 6d.

Rogers (S.) Pleasures of Memory. See "Choice Editions of Choice Books." 2s. 6d.

Rose in Bloom. See ALCOTT.

Rose Library (The). Popular Literature of all Countries. Each volume, 1s.; cloth, 2s. 6d. Many of the Volumes are Illustrated—

1. Sea-Gull Rock. By JULES SANDEAU. Illustrated.
2. Little Women. By LOUISA M. ALCOTT.
3. Little Women Wedded. Forming a Sequel to "Little Women."
4. The House on Wheels. By MADAME DE STOLZ. Illustrated.
5. Little Men. By LOUISA M. ALCOTT. Dble. vol., 2s.; cloth, 3s. 6d.
6. The Old-Fashioned Girl. By LOUISA M. ALCOTT. Double vol., 2s.; cloth, 3s. 6d.
7. The Mistress of the Manse. By J. G. HOLLAND.
8. Timothy Titcomb's Letters to Young People, Single and Married.
9. Undine, and the Two Captains. By Baron DE LA MOTTE FOUQUÉ. A New Translation by F. E. BUNNETT. Illustrated.
10. Draxy Miller's Dowry, and the Elder's Wife. SAXE HOLM.
11. The Four Gold Pieces. By Madame GOURAUD. Illustrated.
12. Work. A Story of Experience. First Portion. By L. M. ALCOTT.
13. Beginning Again. Sequel to above. By L. M. ALCOTT.
14. Picciola; or, the Prison Flower. X. B. SAINTINE. Illustrated.
15. Robert's Holidays. Illustrated.
16. The Two Children of St. Domingo. Numerous Illustrations.
17. Aunt Jo's Scrap Bag.
18. Stowe (Mrs. H. B.) The Pearl of Orr's Island.
19. ——— The Minister's Wooing.
20. ——— Betty's Bright Idea.
21. ——— The Ghost in the Mill.
22. ——— Captain Kidd's Money.
23. ——— We and our Neighbours. Double vol., 2s.
24. ——— My Wife and I. Double vol., 2s.; cloth, gilt, 3s. 6d.
25. Hans Brinker; or, the Silver Skates.
26. Lowell's My Study Window.
27. Holmes (O. W.) The Guardian Angel.
28. Warner (C. D.) My Summer in a Garden.
29. Hitherto. By the Author of "The Gayworthys." 2 vols., 1s. each.
30. Helen's Babies. By their Latest Victim.
31. The Barton Experiment. By the Author of "Helen's Babies."
32. Dred. Mrs. BEECHER STOWE. Dble. vol., 2s.; cloth gilt, 3s. 6d.
33. Warner (C. D.) In the Wilderness.
34. Six to One. A Seaside Story.
35. Nothing to Wear, and Two Millions.
36. Farm Ballads. By WILL CARLETON.
37. Farm Festivals. By WILL CARLETON.
38. Farm Legends. By WILL CARLETON.
39 and 40. The Clients of Dr. Bernagius. BIART. Parts I. & II.
41. Baby Rue; her Adventures and Misadventures. C. M. CLAY.
42. The Undiscovered Country. By W. D. HOWELLS.
43. Friends: a Duet. By ELIZABETH STUART PHELPS.
44. A Gentleman of Leisure. A Novel. By EDGAR FAWCETT.
45. The Story of Helen Troy.

Round the Yule Log: Norwegian Folk and Fairy Tales.
Translated from the Norwegian of P. CHR. ASBJÖRNSEN. With 100 Illustrations. Imperial 16mo, cloth extra, gilt edges, 7s. 6d.

Russell (W. Clarke). See "A Sailor's Sweetheart," 3 vols., 31s. 6d.; "Wreck of the Grosvenor," 6s.; "John Holdsworth (Chief Mate)," 6s.

Russell (W. H., LL.D.) Hesperothen: Notes from the Western World. A Record of a Ramble through part of the United States, Canada, and the Far West, in the Spring and Summer of 1881. By W. H. RUSSELL, LL.D. 2 vols., crown 8vo, cloth, 24s.

—— *The Tour of the Prince of Wales in India.* By W. H. RUSSELL, LL.D. Fully Illustrated by SYDNEY P. HALL, M.A. Super-royal 8vo, cloth extra, gilt edges, 52s. 6d.; Large Paper Edition, 84s.

SAINTS and their Symbols: A Companion in the Churches and Picture Galleries of Europe. With Illustrations. Royal 16mo, cloth extra, 3s. 6d.

Science Ladders. Fcap. 8vo, stiff covers, 6d. each.

SERIES I.
No. I. **Forms of Land and Water.** With 15 Illustrations.
„ II. **The Story of Early Exploration.**

SERIES II.
„ I. **Vegetable Life.** With 35 Illustrations.
„ II. **Flowerless Plants.**

SERIES III.
„ I. **Lowest Forms of Water Animals.** With 22 Illustrations.
„ II. **Lowly Mantle and Armour-Wearers.**

Schuyler (Eugène). The Life of Peter the Great. By EUGÈNE SCHUYLER, Author of "Turkestan." 2 vols., demy 8vo, cloth extra.

Selection from the Letters of Madame de Rémusat to her Husband and Son, from 1804 to 1813. From the French, by Mrs. CASHEL HOEY and Mr. JOHN LILLIE. In 1 vol., demy 8vo (uniform with the "Memoirs of Madame de Rémusat," 2 vols.), cloth extra, 16s.

Seonee: Sporting in the Satpura Range of Central India, and in the Valley of the Nerbudda. By R. A. STERNDALE, F.R.G.S. 8vo, with numerous Illustrations, 21s.

Seven Years in South Africa: Travels, Researches, and Hunting Adventures between the Diamond-Fields and the Zambesi (1872—1879). By Dr. EMIL HOLUB. With over 100 Original Illustrations and 4 Maps. In 2 vols., demy 8vo, cloth extra, 42s.

Serpent Charmer (The): a Tale of the Indian Mutiny. From the French of LOUIS ROUSSELET. Numerous Illustrations. Crown 8vo, cloth extra, gilt edges, 7s. 6d.; plainer binding, 5s.

Shadbolt (S.) The Afghan Campaigns of 1878—1880. By SYDNEY SHADBOLT, Joint Author of "The South African Campaign of 1879." Dedicated by permission to Major-General Sir Frederick Roberts, G.C.B., V.C., &c. 2 vols., royal quarto, cloth extra; to subscribers before publication, 2l. 10s.; to non-subscribers, 3l.

Shooting: its Appliances, Practice, and Purpose. By JAMES DALZIEL DOUGALL, F.S.A., F.Z.A., Author of "Scottish Field Sports," &c. New Edition, revised with additions. Crown 8vo, cloth extra, 7s. 6d.

"The book is admirable in every way. .... We wish it every success."—*Globe.*
"A very complete treatise. .... Likely to take high rank as an authority on shooting."—*Daily News.*

Sikes (Wirt). Rambles and Studies in Old South Wales. With numerous Illustrations. Demy 8vo, cloth extra, 18s. By WIRT SIKES, Author of "British Goblins," which see.

Silent Hour (The). See "Gentle Life Series."

Silver Sockets (The); and other Shadows of Redemption. Eighteen Sermons preached in Christ Church, Hampstead, by the Rev. C. H. WALLER. Small post 8vo, cloth, 6s.

Smith (G.) Assyrian Explorations and Discoveries. By the late GEORGE SMITH. Illustrated by Photographs and Woodcuts. Demy 8vo, 6th Edition, 18s.

—— *The Chaldean Account of Genesis.* By the late G. SMITH, of the Department of Oriental Antiquities, British Museum. With many Illustrations. Demy 8vo, cloth extra, 6th Edition, 16s. An entirely New Edition, completely revised and re-written by the Rev. PROFESSOR SAYCE, Queen's College, Oxford. Demy 8vo, 18s.

Snow-Shoes and Canoes; or, the Adventures of a Fur-Hunter in the Hudson's Bay Territory. By W. H. G. KINGSTON. 2nd Edition. With numerous Illustrations. Square crown 8vo, cloth extra, gilt edges, 7s. 6d.; plainer binding, 5s.

South African Campaign, 1879 *(The).* Compiled by J. P. MACKINNON (formerly 72nd Highlanders), and S. H. SHADBOLT; and dedicated, by permission, to Field-Marshal H.R.H. The Duke of Cambridge. 4to, handsomely bound in cloth extra, 2l. 10s.

Stanley (H. M.) How I Found Livingstone. Crown 8vo, cloth extra, 7s. 6d.; large Paper Edition, 10s. 6d.

Stanley (H. M.) "My Kalulu," Prince, King, and Slave. A Story from Central Africa. Crown 8vo, about 430 pp., with numerous graphic Illustrations, after Original Designs by the Author. Cloth, 7s. 6d.

—— *Coomassie and Magdala.* A Story of Two British Campaigns in Africa. Demy 8vo, with Maps and Illustrations, 16s.

—— *Through the Dark Continent*, which see.

Story without an End. From the German of Carové, by the late Mrs. SARAH T. AUSTIN. Crown 4to, with 15 Exquisite Drawings by E. V. B., printed in Colours in Fac-simile of the original Water Colours; and numerous other Illustrations. New Edition, 7s. 6d.

—— square 4to, with Illustrations by HARVEY. 2s. 6d.

Stowe (Mrs. Beecher) Dred. Cheap Edition, boards, 2s. Cloth, gilt edges, 3s. 6d.

—— *Footsteps of the Master.* With Illustrations and red borders. Small post 8vo, cloth extra, 6s.

—— *Geography*, with 60 Illustrations. Square cloth, 4s. 6d.

—— *Little Foxes.* Cheap Edition, 1s.; Library Edition, 4s. 6d.

—— *Betty's Bright Idea.* 1s.

—— *My Wife and I; or, Harry Henderson's History.* Small post 8vo, cloth extra, 6s.*

—— *Minister's Wooing.* 5s.; Copyright Series, 1s. 6d.; cl., 2s.*

—— *Old Town Folk.* 6s.; Cheap Edition, 2s. 6d.

—— *Old Town Fireside Stories.* Cloth extra, 3s. 6d.

—— *Our Folks at Poganuc.* 6s.

—— *We and our Neighbours.* 1 vol., small post 8vo, 6s. Sequel to "My Wife and I."*

—— *Pink and White Tyranny.* Small post 8vo, 3s. 6d. Cheap Edition, 1s. 6d. and 2s.

* *See also* Rose Library.

Stowe (Mrs. Beecher) Queer Little People. 1s.; cloth, 2s.

—— *Chimney Corner.* 1s.; cloth, 1s. 6d.

—— *The Pearl of Orr's Island.* Crown 8vo, 5s.*

—— *Woman in Sacred History.* Illustrated with 15 Chromo-lithographs and about 200 pages of Letterpress. Demy 4to, cloth extra, gilt edges, 25s.

Student's French Examiner. By F. JULIEN, Author of "Petites Leçons de Conversation et de Grammaire." Square cr. 8vo, cloth, 2s.

Studies in the Theory of Descent. By Dr. AUG. WEISMANN, Professor in the University of Freiburg. Translated and edited by RAPHAEL MELDOLA, F.C.S., Secretary of the Entomological Society of London. Part I.—"On the Seasonal Dimorphism of Butterflies," containing Original Communications by Mr. W. H. EDWARDS, of Coalburgh. With two Coloured Plates. Price of Part. I. (to Subscribers for the whole work only), 8s; Part II. (6 coloured plates), 16s.; Part III., 6s.

Sunrise: A Story of These Times. By WILLIAM BLACK, Author of "A Daughter of Heth," &c. Crown 8vo, cloth, 6s.

Surgeon's Handbook on the Treatment of Wounded in War. By Dr. FRIEDRICH ESMARCH, Surgeon-General to the Prussian Army. Numerous Coloured Plates and Illustrations, 8vo, strongly bound, 1l. 8s.

Sylvan Spring. By FRANCIS GEORGE HEATH. Illustrated by 12 Coloured Plates, drawn by F. E. HULME, F.L.S., Artist and Author of "Familiar Wild Flowers;" by 16 full-page, and more than 100 other Wood Engravings. Large post 8vo, cloth, gilt edges, 12s. 6d.

TAINE (H. A.) "Les Origines de la France Contemporaine." Translated by JOHN DURAND.
    Vol. 1. **The Ancient Regime.** Demy 8vo, cloth, 16s.
    Vol. 2. **The French Revolution.** Vol. 1. do.
    Vol. 3. **Do.**   do.   Vol. 2. do.

Tauchnitz's English Editions of German Authors. Each volume, cloth flexible, 2s.; or sewed, 1s. 6d. (Catalogues post free on application.)

—— *(B.) German and English Dictionary.* Cloth, 1s. 6d.; roan, 2s.

* *See also* Rose Library.

Tauchnitz's French and English Dictionary. Paper, 1s. 6d.; cloth, 2s.; roan, 2s. 6d.

────── *Italian and English Dictionary.* Paper, 1s. 6d.; cloth, 2s.; roan, 2s. 6d.

────── *Spanish and English.* Paper, 1s. 6d.; cloth, 2s.; roan, 2s. 6d.

Through America ; or, Nine Months in the United States. By W. G. MARSHALL, M.A. With nearly 100 Woodcuts of Views of Utah country and the famous Yosemite Valley; The Giant Trees, New York, Niagara, San Francisco, &c.; containing a full account of Mormon Life, as noted by the Author during his visits to Salt Lake City in 1878 and 1879. Demy 8vo, 21s.; cheap edition, crown 8vo, 7s. 6d.

Through the Dark Continent: The Sources of the Nile; Around the Great Lakes, and down the Congo. By H. M. STANLEY. Cheap Edition, crown 8vo, with some of the Illustrations and Maps, 12s. 6d.

Through Siberia. By the Rev. HENRY LANSDELL. Illustrated with about 30 Engravings, 2 Route Maps, and Photograph of the Author, in Fish-skin Costume of the Gilyaks on the Lower Amur. 2 vols., demy 8vo, 30s.

Tour of the Prince of Wales in India. See RUSSELL.

Trees and Ferns. By F. G. HEATH. Crown 8vo, cloth, gilt edges, with numerous Illustrations, 3s. 6d.
  "A charming little volume."—*Land and Water.*

Tristram (Rev. Canon) Pathways of Palestine: A Descriptive Tour through the Holy Land. First Series. Illustrated by 22 Permanent Photographs. Folio, cloth extra, gilt edges, 31s. 6d.

Two Friends. By LUCIEN BIART, Author of "Adventures of a Young Naturalist,". "My Rambles in the New World," &c. Small post 8vo, numerous Illustrations, gilt edges, 7s. 6d.; plainer binding, 5s.

Two Supercargoes (The); or, Adventures in Savage Africa. By W. H. G. KINGSTON. Numerous Full-page Illustrations. Square imperial 16mo, cloth extra, gilt edges, 7s. 6d.; plainer binding, 5s.

UNDER the Punkah. By PHIL ROBINSON, Author of "In my Indian Garden." Crown 8vo, limp cloth, 3s. 6d.

***Union Jack** (The).   Every Boy's Paper.*   Edited by G. A.
HENTY.   One Penny Weekly, Monthly 6*d.*   Vol. III. commences
with the Part for November, 1881, and contains the first Chapters
of Three Serial Stories by G. MANVILLE FENN, LOUIS ROUSSELET,
and W. H. G. KINGSTON, from the French of "Landelle." Illustrated
by the Best Artists. With the first Part is presented a Photograph of
Jules Verne, and a Coloured Plate, "Rounding the Lightship," a
Yachting Incident; and this Volume will also contain New Stories by
Col. BUTLER, Author of "The Great Lone Land," JULES VERNE, an
Historical Story by the Editor, &c., &c.   Volume II. for 1881, beautifully bound in red cloth (royal 4to), 7*s.* 6*d.*, gilt edges, 8*s.* Beautifully
Illustrated with over 400 Illustrations, including 52 full-page Engra-
vings, 8 Steel ditto, 7 Coloured Plates, and Photograph of the Editor.

The Contents comprise:

The Cornet of Horse: a Tale of Marlborough's Wars. By the
EDITOR.
The Young Franc-Tireurs: a Tale of the Franco-German War.
By the EDITOR.
The Ensign and Middy: a Tale of the Malay Peninsula. By G.
MANVILLE FENN.
The Steam House: THE DEMON OF CAWNPORE. A Tale of India.
By JULES VERNE.
Rawdon School: a Tale of Schoolboy Life. By BERNARD
HELDMANN.
Dorrincourt: a Story of a Term there. By BERNARD HELDMANN.
Peyton Phelps; or, Adventures among the Italian Carbonari. By
G. STEBBING.
Gerald Rattlin: a Tale of Sea Life. By GEO. ELFORD.
A Fight in Freedom's Cause.
An Eventful Ride.
The Ghost of Leytonstone Manor.
An Editor's Yarns.
True Tales of Brave Actions.
 And numerous other Articles of Interest and Instruction.
 A few copies of Volume I., for 1880, still remain, price 6*s.*

Upolu; or, A Paradise of the Gods; being a Description of
the Antiquities of the chief Island of the Samoan Group, with Remarks
on the Topography, Ethnology, and History of the Polynesian Islands
in general.   By the late HANDLEY BATHURST STERNDALE. Edited
and annotated by his brother, Author of "Seonee," "The Afghan
Knife," &c.   2 vols., demy 8vo.

***VICTOR** Hugo and his Times.*   Translated from the French
of A. BARBOU by ELLEN E. FREWER. 120 Illustrations, many of
them from designs by Victor Hugo himself. Super-royal 8vo, cloth
extra.

***Vincent** (F.) Norsk, Lapp, and Finn.*   By FRANK VINCENT,
Jun., Author of "The Land of the White Elephant," "Through
and Through the Tropics," &c. 8vo, cloth, with Frontispiece and
Map, 12*s.*

BOOKS BY JULES VERNE.

WORKS.	LARGE CROWN 8vo. Containing 350 to 600 pp. and from 50 to 100 full-page illustrations.		Containing the whole of the text with some illustrations.	
	In very handsome cloth binding, gilt edges.	In plainer binding, plain edges.	In cloth binding, gilt edges, smaller type.	Coloured Boards.
	s. d.	s. d.	s. d.	
Twenty Thousand Leagues under the Sea. Part I. Ditto Part II.	10 6	5 0	3 6	2 vols., 1s. each.
Hector Servadac	10 6	5 0	3 6	2 vols., 1s. each.
The Fur Country	10 6	5 0	3 6	2 vols., 1s. each.
From the Earth to the Moon and a Trip round it	10 6	5 0	2 vols., 2s. each.	2 vols., 1s. each.
Michael Strogoff, the Courier of the Czar	10 6	5 0	3 6	2 vols., 1s. each.
Dick Sands, the Boy Captain	10 6	5 0	3 6	2 vols., 1s. each.
Five Weeks in a Balloon	7 6	3 6	2 0	1s. 0d.
Adventures of Three Englishmen and Three Russians	7 6	3 6	2 0	1 0
Around the World in Eighty Days	7 6	3 6	2 0	1 0
A Floating City	7 6	3 6	2 0	1 0
The Blockade Runners			2 0	1 0
Dr. Ox's Experiment			2 0	1 0
Master Zacharius	7 6	3 6		
A Drama in the Air				
A Winter amid the Ice			2 0	1 0
The Survivors of the "Chancellor"	7 6	3 6	2 0	2 vols. 1s. each.
Martin Paz			2 0	1 0
THE MYSTERIOUS ISLAND, 3 vols.:—	22 6	10 6	6 0	3 0
Vol. I. Dropped from the Clouds	7 6	3 6	2 0	1 0
Vol. II. Abandoned	7 6	3 6	2 0	1 0
Vol. III. Secret of the Island	7 6	3 6	2 0	1 0
The Child of the Cavern	7 6	3 6	2 0	1 0
The Begum's Fortune	7 6	3 6		
The Tribulations of a Chinaman	7 6			
THE STEAM HOUSE, 2 vols.:—				
Vol. I. Demon of Cawnpore	7 6			
Vol. II. Tigers and Traitors	7 6			
THE GIANT RAFT, 2 vols.:—				
Vol. I. Eight Hundred Leagues on the Amazon	7 6			
Vol. II. The Cryptogram	7 6			

CELEBRATED TRAVELS AND TRAVELLERS. 3 vols. Demy 8vo, 600 pp., upwards of 100 full-page illustrations, 12s. 6d.; gilt edges, 14s. each:—
(1) THE EXPLORATION OF THE WORLD.
(2) THE GREAT NAVIGATORS OF THE EIGHTEENTH CENTURY.
(3) THE GREAT EXPLORERS OF THE NINETEENTH CENTURY.

Waitaruna: A Story of New Zealand Life. By ALEXANDER BATHGATE, Author of "Colonial Experiences." Crown 8vo, cloth, 5s.

Waller (Rev. C. H.) The Names on the Gates of Pearl, and other Studies. By the Rev. C. H. WALLER, M.A. Second Edition. Crown 8vo, cloth extra, 6s.

—— *A Grammar and Analytical Vocabulary of the Words in* the Greek Testament. Compiled from Brüder's Concordance. For the use of Divinity Students and Greek Testament Classes. By the Rev. C. H. WALLER, M.A. Part I. The Grammar. Small post 8vo, cloth, 2s. 6d. Part II. The Vocabulary, 2s. 6d.

—— *Adoption and the Covenant.* Some Thoughts on Confirmation. Super-royal 16mo, cloth limp, 2s. 6d.

—— *See also* "Silver Sockets."

Wanderings South by East: a Descriptive Record of Four Years of Travel in the less known Countries and Islands of the Southern and Eastern Hemispheres. By WALTER COOTE. 8vo, with very numerous Illustrations and a Map, 21s.

Warner (C. D.) My Summer in a Garden. Rose Library, 1s.

—— *Back-log Studies.* Boards, 1s. 6d.; cloth, 2s.

—— *In the Wilderness.* Rose Library, 1s.

—— *Mummies and Moslems.* 8vo, cloth, 12s.

Weaving. See "History and Principles."

Where to Find Ferns. By F. G. HEATH, Author of "The Fern World," &c.; with a Special Chapter on the Ferns round London; Lists of Fern Stations, and Descriptions of Ferns and Fern Habitats throughout the British Isles. Crown 8vo, cloth, price 3s.

White (Rhoda E.) From Infancy to Womanhood. A Book of Instruction for Young Mothers. Crown 8vo, cloth, 10s. 6d.

Whittier (J. G.) The King's Missive, and later Poems. 18mo, choice parchment cover, 3s. 6d. This book contains all the Poems written by Mr. Whittier since the publication of "Hazel Blossoms."

—— *The Whittier Birthday Book.* Extracts from the Author's writings, with Portrait and numerous Illustrations. Uniform with the "Emerson Birthday Book." Square 16mo, very choice binding, 3s. 6d.

Wills, A Few Hints on Proving, without Professional Assistance.
By a PROBATE COURT OFFICIAL. 5th Edition, revised with Forms of Wills, Residuary Accounts, &c. Fcap. 8vo, cloth limp, 1s.

With Axe and Rifle on the Western Prairies. By W. H. G. KINGSTON. With numerous Illustrations, square crown 8vo, cloth extra, gilt edges, 7s. 6d.; plainer binding, 5s.

Woolsey (C. D., LL.D.) Introduction to the Study of International Law; designed as an Aid in Teaching and in Historical Studies. 5th Edition, demy 8vo, 18s.

Words of Wellington: Maxims and Opinions, Sentences and Reflections of the Great Duke, gathered from his Despatches, Letters, and Speeches (Bayard Series). 2s. 6d.

Wreck of the Grosvenor. By W. CLARK RUSSELL, Author of "John Holdsworth, Chief Mate," "A Sailor's Sweetheart," &c. 6s. Third and Cheaper Edition.

Wright (the late Rev. Henry) Sermons. Crown 8vo, with Biographical Preface, Portrait, &c. [*In the press.*

www.ingramcontent.com/pod-product-compliance
Lightning Source LLC
Chambersburg PA
CBHW021420300426
44114CB00010B/577